PREPARED FOR

THE HORACE MANN-
LINCOLN INSTITUTE OF
SCHOOL EXPERIMENTATION
TEACHERS COLLEGE, COLUMBIA UNIVERSITY

Understanding

Group Behavior of Boys and Girls

By RUTH CUNNINGHAM AND ASSOCIATES

ANNA ELZI · JAMES A. HALL · MARIE FARRELL · MADELINE ROBERTS

ALL PHOTOGRAPHS COURTESY OF DENVER PUBLIC SCHOOLS

Bureau of Publications

TEACHERS COLLEGE · COLUMBIA UNIVERSITY · NEW YORK

1951

Foreword

One of the principal emphases of the Horace Mann–Lincoln Institute program during its first six years has been cooperative action research. The assumption has been that methods of working as well as results will have greater validity if teachers, pupils, and parents participate in the research process. Hence, there has been a continuous attempt to include in the research undertaken to improve a particular educational activity all who are directly concerned. This study of group behavior is a report of cooperative action research.

An interesting characteristic of this investigation is that the teachers involved participated fully in reporting how they worked and what they discovered. The present book is not the work of experts in the field of child development or of group behavior. Rather, it is the picture of how teachers without special background or training, in cooperation with the research associates of the Institute staff, approached the problem of becoming more expert. Many of their insights and tentative findings should be suggestive to other teachers, as well as to research workers in this area.

Our personal association with the teachers during the course of their work convinced us that not only were they enthusiastic about the project but they found it to result in significant improvement in their ways of working with boys and girls. It seemed to us that if these individuals could derive so much benefit from their study of group behavior, many other teachers could undertake similar studies for their own personal satisfaction and for the contribution these studies would make to their professional thinking and activity.

Understanding Group Behavior of Boys and Girls should be helpful to all elementary and secondary school teachers who are interested in working more effectively with boys and girls in group situations. Because the attention of the authors is focused on the problems arising when a teacher and his pupils undertake tasks together, the research findings have interesting and valuable implications for the grouping of pupils, classroom teaching, group dynamics, and learning.

GORDON N. MACKENZIE
STEPHEN M. COREY
Horace Mann–Lincoln Institute of
School Experimentation, Teachers
College, Columbia University.

October, 1949

Preface

We feel as though we have a comet by the tail. The more we investigate the forces of human relations and of group dynamics, the more we recognize their power and the more we know that there is need for further study of these areas by groups of boys and girls, teachers, parents, and other youth leaders.

We know that in these times it is not necessary to point out to teachers the importance of giving consideration to a study of human relations—the way people get along together, the way people operate when they are in groups. The urgency of the problem is brought to our attention by the psychologist, the sociologist, the anthropologist, the statesman. The need for a better understanding of human relations is manifest in problems ranging from those of personal adjustment, classroom living, family relations, and vocational efficiency to those of intergroup tensions and international relations.

Nor is it necessary to point out to teachers concerned with curriculum development—with providing better experiences for boys and girls—the relevance of a study of human relations to curriculum improvement. We realize that the major objective of curriculum experience is to modify behavior—to help individuals and groups learn to act in such a way that there is maximum growth for each and social development for all. The more we realize this, the more certain we become that it is behavior rather than rote memorizing or the content of knowledge that is the substance of education.

It is agreed that the understanding of problems in human relations is urgent, and that educators are willing to give their best energies to the solution of these problems. Beyond this point, however, there are difficulties. It is hard to discover the means for attacking problems of such magnitude.

THE AREA OF INVESTIGATION

In this study we have attempted to learn how pupils and teachers, working with parents, may study the group behavior of boys and girls, and what the findings may mean for the experiences provided for pupils in elementary and secondary schools. Our objectives were to explore the area, discover the problems involved, test means of studying these problems, and examine what they mean for curriculum development. With such a wide area of investigation, it is not surprising that on the following pages there are more questions raised than answers given. The very fact that this report points to inadequacy of evidence in many areas may lead other teachers to undertake studies which will contribute to the understanding of group behavior.

Though our primary purpose is to report the results of our investigation, we have not hesitated to look beyond our objective data. We hope it may be helpful if we report our analysis and the questions that we have raised, even in those areas where we do not have any supporting evidence.

PATTERN OF THIS STUDY

Members of the staff of the Horace Mann–Lincoln Institute of School Experimentation have felt, from the early days of their field studies, that a study of human relations could be of major significance. Representatives of the Associated Schools agreed. All urged that such a study be undertaken, but the area was so broad that it was difficult to know where to begin.

Getting Started

In the summer of 1946 a group of members of the Institute Workshop at Teachers College met to discuss the problem. These people drew up the following proposals:

1. That a point of departure be the study of acceptance and rejection of individuals and groups by individuals and groups.
2. That a pioneer group of a few teachers explore the area, discover the questions involved, test means of studying these questions, and

examine their implications for the selection of school experiences of boys and girls.

3. That from the beginning boys and girls and parents be asked to work with teachers as co-researchers, to help define the problem, to suggest procedures, and to evaluate progress.

Three teachers, one with a first grade group, one with a fourth and fifth grade group, and one with an eighth grade group, undertook the pioneering job, with a representative of their city central office and a member of the Institute staff as consultants.

The Problem Evolves

The pioneer teachers started their work with the opening of school in the fall of 1946. As they talked with boys and girls, parents, and one another, problem definition shifted, but continued to broaden and clarify as the study progressed. The researcher operating in the traditional pattern might regret this shift in problem definition, but we felt that the defining of a problem was of itself an important aspect of the research, and thus the shift was desirable. The cooperation of boys and girls and parents in the problem definition was, of course, a factor in developing greater insight into the nature of the problem. They brought to it concepts unforeseen by the original planners.

The best definition of the problem as it has evolved is now used as the title of this report—*understanding group behavior of boys and girls.*

Methods Emerge

As the definition of the problem evolved, the need for various methods of study emerged. As each new aspect of the problem was identified, an attempt was made to find or invent techniques for studying it.

In the study of some aspects of the problem, we pushed through in a systematic manner to marshal data and interpret and evaluate our findings. In the study of many aspects, however, we found opening up such broad vistas for research that we merely put down a marker to indicate an area in need of further study and pushed on to survey other areas. Thus in many places in this report we raise questions, and sometimes suggest approaches to their solution that we think might be helpful; but we do not carry the investigation through to a conclusion.

In a number of important areas we have attempted to formulate working hypotheses, even though we have insufficient data to substantiate the postulated statements. As one of our objectives was to explore the area and discover the problems involved, we believe this procedure is legitimate. Moreover, we have used a range of methods—from the use of relatively precise instruments of measurement to broad analyses of problem areas. This range, too, we believe necessary in an exploratory study such as this.

Structure of the Study

There was no neat preconceived structure other than that indicated in the broad objective of exploration. Nor was there clear structure in the chronology of the investigation as it progressed. At the end of a year's work, however, we can look back and see that a pattern has emerged.

In general the pattern of the investigation was as follows:

1. Starting with a study of behavior of boys and girls, we became conscious of the significance of goals as behavior determinants. This led to:

2. An investigation of goals of individuals and groups, their nature and sources. An attempt to analyze and evaluate the sources of goals made us conscious of the roles of the teacher and the group in determining interaction patterns. This suggested:

3. A study of patterns of group interaction employed by teachers and groups. Once we felt we had identified a range of patterns, we attempted to discover clues to:

4. The means for judging the appropriateness of patterns. Judging this appropriateness proved to involve the study of some complex aspects of group interaction. In other words, we came to realize that teachers and groups who are to judge such appropriateness need to know many things about the group concerned.

5. In an attempt to discover what might be helpful in making these judgments, we tested a range of techniques and devices for studying groups.

6. Throughout we attempted to discover implications for the selection of experiences for boys and girls, and

7. Throughout we also attempted to discover experiences which could help teachers and parents as well as boys and girls develop insight and understanding, and find satisfactions.

Interaction

We cannot overestimate the significance of the interaction which took place among the various people concerned—boys and girls, parents, teachers, consultants, resource people. Each brought a particular competence to the study which contributed to its soundness and balance. Without this teamwork, we are confident we should have had a much narrower view of the problem studied.

There was differentiation of function, however. The three teachers and the two consultants operated as coordinators, and set the stage for the interaction of the wider group. It was this core group who took leadership in organizing the processes involved, and it was they who took responsibility for the preparation of the report, though drawing on the experiences of all.

Our own group processes as we studied the problem were so much a part of the investigation that it is difficult to see one without recognizing its relationship to the other. Thus in this report, we attempt to tell how we operated as well as what we discovered, believing these two elements to be so intimately related as to be meaningful only if both are included.

Reporting

The backbone of this report is the experimentation of the three teachers and the pupils and parents of the three groups. However, we have included, also, certain experiments undertaken by other Institute schools, when they have seemed pertinent to the study.

The thumbnail case reports of individuals and groups used as illustrations were derived from many sources. We drew on our own past and present experience and on that of many other teachers. Thus these cases should be regarded as they are intended—as illustrations rather than as reports of research.

As is indicated above, the core research group composed of the three teachers and the two consultants took responsibility for the preparation of the report. The process involved the preparation of a series of outlines of increasing length and detail, a first rough draft, and a final report. Each outline and each draft was discussed by the core group, and subsequent revisions were made in terms of the suggestions of the group.

THE PEOPLE WHO HELPED

The report is primarily the result of the thinking and investigation of five people: Marie Farrell, first grade teacher, Emerson School; Madeline Roberts, fourth and fifth grade teacher, Swansea School; Anna Elzi, eighth grade teacher, Grant Junior High School; James A. Hall, director, department of instruction (all of the Denver, Colorado, Public Schools), and Ruth Cunningham, Horace Mann–Lincoln Institute of School Experimentation, Teachers College, Columbia University. We have spent many hours together, observing one another's classrooms, determining areas of study, devising means to study, and discussing our ideas and findings. We all decided what was to be reported and how, working cooperatively at all stages of the production of the final report. There was some division of labor, however. The three teachers were primarily responsible for the classroom experimentation and the relations with parents; James A. Hall was coordinator of the project in Denver and took major responsibility for analyzing and interpreting our objective findings; and Ruth Cunningham acted as consultant, coordinator, and writer.

Many other teachers have contributed to the study. Our special gratitude is due the following individuals, groups, and faculties: Gretchen Collins, eighth grade teacher, Glencoe, Ill.; Ruth Pente, high school counselor, Battle Creek, Mich.; Nelson Scull, teacher of inter-age group, Horace Mann–Lincoln School; Frank Vaughn, counselor, Emily Griffith Opportunity School, and Paul Rhodes, examining physician, Denver Public Schools; workshop groups in child development in Springfield, Mo. (1946) and in a workshop of the Horace Mann–Lincoln Institute, Teachers College, Columbia University (1946); the group studying "Ways of Studying Children," Horace Mann–Lincoln Institute Conference, St. Mary's Lake, Mich. (1947); the faculties of Junior High School 44, Bronx, and Public School 94, Bronx, New York City; and the faculties of the Dora Moore, University Park, Twenty-fourth Street, and Emerson Schools of Denver, Colo.

Special thanks for help throughout the development of the project are due Gordon N. Mackenzie, executive officer (1945–48) and Stephen M. Corey, executive officer (1948—), both of Horace Mann–Lincoln Institute of School Experimentation, Teachers College, Columbia University; Maurice Ahrens, then director of instruction, Denver Public Schools, and coordinator of all Horace Mann–Lincoln Institute projects for Denver; and the principals of the schools where the three teachers carried on intensive studies: Norris Bush, Emerson School; Alvin Yordy, Swansea School, and Clark Stone, Grant Junior High School, all of the Denver Public Schools.

The entire staff of the Horace Mann–Lincoln Institute of School Experimentation has reviewed the project at several stages of its development and has contributed valuable criticisms and suggestions.

Special consultants to the project on various occasions included: Fritz Redl, School of Social Work, Wayne University; Chester Harris, School of Education, University of Wisconsin; Willard Olson, School of Education, University of Michigan; Guy Fox, director of pupil personnel, Denver Public Schools; Amos L. Beaghler, director of health service, Denver Public Schools; Kenneth Benne, School of Education, University of Illinois; Arthur T. Jersild, Percival M. Symonds, L. Thomas Hopkins, and Gertrude P. Driscoll, Teachers College, Columbia University.

We wish to express our thanks to teachers throughout the country who cooperated in the tryout of special instruments, such as the "Classroom Social Distance Scale," the "Check Sheet of Opportunities in Human Relations," and "Reaction to Pictures."

Our greatest debt of gratitude is due the boys and girls and their parents and teachers who have worked cooperatively with us throughout this study. You will meet many of them in the following pages. Although pupils, parents, and teachers who speak to you through the text are real people, very much alive, all names used, except those identified by footnotes, are fictitious.

EVALUATION

As we said earlier, the more we investigate the force of group dynamics, the more we realize its power and the more we know that boys and girls need the help of teachers who understand the importance of the problems in this area and are willing to investigate them.

We have attempted to evaluate our work in terms of the reactions of teachers, pupils, and parents, and in terms of the effectiveness of changed practices in achieving goals determined by the people involved. These evaluations are incorporated in the body of the report.

The broader evaluation of this study cannot be made until we discover the usefulness of our investigations to others. If our work encourages others to undertake similar studies or to follow through in the investigation of some of the many questions we raise, we shall feel that it has achieved a major purpose.

THE AUTHORS

October, 1949

Contents

CONTENTS

CONTENTS

Understanding
GROUP BEHAVIOR OF BOYS AND GIRLS

1

The Significance of Groups

HAVE you ever wondered why things go well with one group, but less well with another although there may be fewer individual "problem" children in the group which has the most trouble?

Have you ever found that certain classroom procedures are successful with one group but not with another, or at some times but not at others even within the same group?

Do you sometimes feel baffled and wonder what to do next when a group seems to go "wild" for no apparent reason? Or when the group fails to respond to what you thought was a "sure-fire" suggestion? Or when the group laughs at Tom's clowning but says it's "silly" if David does the same thing?

Are you curious about why certain boys and girls are more popular in the group, even though others seem to you equally attractive? Or why certain youngsters are chosen as captains of teams, or chairmen of committees, although you think others are obviously better qualified?

Hasn't it amazed you to find the group showing great tenderness and sympathy toward unfortunate group members, interspersed with outbursts of equally great cruelty of group members to one another?

Have you ever wished you could do more to help Betty make friends and become better accepted by the group?

Why is it that on occasion the group is capable of unusual depth of insight and is willing to give time and energy to the solution of a problem, and then, soon after, reverts to immature, superficial behavior?

Haven't you often thought that if you knew how to find answers to these questions, you might be able to provide better learning and living for pupils in your group?

[1]

THE TEACHER IS A GROUP LEADER.

It is with matters such as these that this book is concerned. Other teachers have asked similar questions, and on the following pages are reported their attempts to find leads to the answers. The results of their thinking and investigation do not provide final answers; rather they raise more questions. But in raising these questions they may point directions and suggest procedures which will be of help to you and other teachers who want a better understanding of group living of boys and girls, and of how such understanding will contribute to meeting their needs and the demands of society.

YOU ARE A GROUP LEADER

Whether or not you have ever thought of yourself as such, you are a group leader. Our schools today are organized on the basis of groups, each with a teacher-leader.

The idea of thinking of boys and girls in school in terms of groups is not a new one. The typical school today is organized on the basis of groups called grades, classes, Miss Thompson's room, Room 4, freshman mathematics, seven-year-olds, the Team, Boy Scouts, Blue Birds, Safety Patrol, and a host of other names. But whatever they are called, pupils are brought together in groups, and teachers are the adult leaders.

[2]

As we have moved from a concept of education bounded by subject matter to be taught, to a concept of education as the guidance of the behavior of people in a democracy, we have become conscious of an increased responsibility for developing the potentialities of the individual. And as we, in our teaching of democracy, have come to realize this increased responsibility to the individual, we have become more and more aware of our responsibility for creating better group living.

SIGNIFICANCE OF GROUP LIVING

Teachers have always known that boys and girls in a classroom form something more than an aggregation of individuals. Here is a clear case of the whole being more than the sum of the parts, or, at any rate, the whole being something different from a mere sum. We hear teachers speak of "difficult" groups and "good" groups, even though the individuals seem equally well placed in the two groups, or there are no more "problem" pupils in one group than in the other. There is probably no teacher with a few years of experience who cannot recall some group in which the general "tone" was unusually fine, or some group with which everything seemed to go wrong and in which everyone seemed to get on the nerves of everyone else. This is the sort of thing we are talking about —or part of it. We believe, however, that the matter transcends mere "niceness" or mere annoyingness. In fact, we feel that the concept of group living is one of the most important, exciting, pervasive ideas in modern education. The quality of group living is, we believe, the factor having the most significant effect on the quality of education in our schools.

Classroom Management

Group interaction is a powerful force. There is plenty of evidence that this force may be used for either good or ill. If you are using it intelligently and well, you have mastered the techniques of "method" and "discipline." Many successful teachers are using the force of group dynamics wisely, but some are doing so without quite knowing why what they do works as it does. Other teachers cannot understand why their groups are so troublesome, why their pupils are not learning as they should, why they have so many problems in discipline. An understanding of group dynamics can do much to provide insight into these problems of group management.

Methods of Teaching

No matter what the approach to curriculum development, a greater understanding of group living has much to offer. If curriculum development is conceived as the process of selecting significant experiences for learners in terms of their needs, interests, and capacities, with the learners having a part in the selection, then the group process—the way the group members interact and learn through this interaction—must be an integral part of the method of teaching and learning. However, even if the curriculum is conceived as a predetermined body of knowledge, skills, and understandings to be transmitted to young learners, there is still the problem of how it is to be transmitted and how learners may be made receptive to such learning. A study of group dynamics can do much to explain how this transmission may take place effectively in a group situation. For example, we find that the types of group guidance and control are important factors in determining motivation of the group; that there are situations in which we may employ the force of the group for the accomplishment of even the most routine or unpleasant task. Moreover, it is known that there are factors in group interaction which provide group-linked gains—gains for everyone beyond that which they would achieve individually—and that these factors may be in operation even

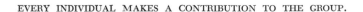

EVERY INDIVIDUAL MAKES A CONTRIBUTION TO THE GROUP.

in the classroom when the teaching process is of a so-called traditional type.

Selecting Experiences

To the extent that we see learning linked to problem-solving, and to the extent that we see the problems to be solved as within the experience of learners—the problems arising from the group becoming the areas of the curriculum—to the same extent we see how group processes contribute to and are a part of teaching and learning. We might state this even more strongly. If our groups are to identify problems in their experiences and learn how to solve these problems, they *must* be able to apply group techniques to these ends. Group problem identification and solution are not automatic, nor easily achieved, as many well-intentioned but unskilled and uninformed teachers have learned to their discomfort. A number of complex group skills are involved, and these skills are to be taught and learned, just as the skills in other areas are taught and learned. And in this teaching and learning we find an area of curriculum content.

Moreover, as every teacher who is sensitive to group reaction well knows, learning is closely related to the climate of the group—the morale, the happiness or unhappiness, the adjustment or tension of the group. No doubt you have noticed in your group how much more is accomplished when everyone is relaxed and happy. A teacher who understands group dynamics can do much to determine this climate and thus influence the amount of achievement as well as the emotional adjustment of pupils.

The Needs of the Individual

We have had so much to say about the group that we may have given the impression that we have no interest in the individual. Quite the contrary. It is known that favorable group living contributes to the development of individual pupils. Teachers who have become aware of the personal needs of children and young people know that many of these needs are related to group living. The need to "belong" and the need to feel important are examples.

An understanding of group dynamics gives the teacher an increased control of group situations. He thus has a greater opportunity to provide for meeting the needs of individual pupils.

—learning

Some teachers think of learning as the acquiring of predetermined bodies of knowledge and of certain skills. Others think of learning as the identifying and solving of problems. Still others see learning as a means to adjustment and to better living. Whatever the concept held, the group processes employed and the group climate achieved will be factors in determining the degree to which goals are reached.

Moreover, a deepened understanding of how groups react may be a means to clarifying concepts of how learning takes place.

—social skills

Teachers are becoming increasingly aware of their responsibility to help every pupil acquire the immediate social skills of getting along with others and becoming an adjusted and effective group member. We are told that in business and industry many more lose their jobs because they do not get along with people than because they lack technical competence to perform the required tasks. Those interested in the increasing divorce rate in this country have much to say about the need for skills of inter-personal adjustment. Many other examples could be cited.

If we have a responsibility for the adjustment of our pupils—and most of us think we have—we dare not overlook our responsibility for developing these social skills. But social skills cannot be learned in isolation. We know they are gained through guided experience in a social setting. Through group experience, the group contributes toward the guidance, and provides the setting. When teachers and groups are aware of the processes necessary for developing social skills, they can provide for effective teaching and learning.

—creativity

Even creativity, often thought to be a purely individual matter, is frequently group-linked. The creative person is one who is able to see wide implications in his experience, and is able to express them. Some experience is, of course, individual and isolated. But in any society, and especially in a modern democratic society, much experience is in terms of the interaction of people. Group dynamics may provide the skills in plumbing this experience, as well the experience itself. Moreover, we are growing in our awareness that there is such a thing as group creativity—creative action by the group. Group art, as in planning and executing murals, group creation of music, poetry, dramatics, rhythms, dance, and other creative activity not only are important expressions of the group process but may be important forms of art. The attainment of favorable group living may itself be creative expression.

Thus, rather than submerging the individual, group interaction may be a major factor in developing the individual, meeting his needs, and providing the setting in which he may develop and find adjusted selfhood, as well as helping him to be a worthy group member.

Developing Concepts of Democracy

Democracy is not merely an idea; it is a way of behaving. If we are to teach both the idea and the way of behaving in ever broadening areas of concern, the school experiences of children and youth must include those which provide opportunities for learning respect for other individuals and for developing a sense of responsibility of the individual to the group and the group to the individual.

—skills

Democracy demands skills as well as attitudes and understandings— skills of leadership and group membership, skills in delegating responsibility, skills in evaluating individual and group contribution to democratic life. As with other skills, these skills are *learned*. As with other learning, learning of these skills takes place when there is meaningful experience. Boys and girls, as well as teachers, see new meanings and importance in democratic action as they learn to put into practice the skills necessary to its attainment. And, as they see through experience how skills contribute to such action, they learn to respect the skills. Circular thinking? No—spiral experience, in which democratic skills and democratic action each reinforce the other toward a growing democracy.

—practice

Practice of democratic skills and development of democratic concepts within the classroom are of paramount importance. They provide the bases of understanding of the wider group dynamics of the community, of democratic society, of world cooperation. It is with the equipment of such skills and concepts that individuals and groups are able to operate as forces in community betterment, whether the term "community" means "my school friends," "my neighbors and I," "Centerville," "my country," or "one world."

—definition of democracy

Democracy, unlike other forms of human control (of which government is but one aspect), is constantly being re-created, and must have a means by which this re-creation can be achieved. Group interaction, group dynamics, and creative group living provide this means.

When political democracy was first formulated and put into operation in this country, it was defined by a Bill of Rights, and was stated as the virtues to be achieved, such as "liberty," "equality," and "freedom." These terms meant something very specific to our founding fathers. We respect the meaning they gave them and we still hold to the ideals they imply, and we still use the machinery they employed to achieve them. But the terms themselves are vague and unreal today. What is "equality" within our economy, within our knowledge of individual differences, within our complex social pattern? There is a great need for a definition of what democratic living means today. Democracy itself denies the validity of a process by which some individual or minority group hands out "answers" about how we shall live. The process by which such definitions are achieved must be a democratic process. In other words, if we are to keep democracy alive and appropriate to modern society, we must have means to group thinking and action in order to achieve it. The charge to the schools should be clear.

Toward World Cooperation

In a modern world, we must learn to think beyond national boundaries and forms of government. Today we are committed, through the United Nations, to group action toward world cooperation. If we are to play our part in world cooperation, we must learn to cooperate through groups with the power of group action. This is no longer a matter for starry-eyed idealism. The reality has been forced upon us by the impact of atomic energy, by the fact of people starving in a world of plenty, by wars and rumblings of wars while we are still recovering from a world war. It may well be that our culture, our civilization, our hopes and aspirations will depend on our achieving effective group thinking and action.

WHAT IS OUR JOB?

The more we broaden our vision and see our responsibilities to the community, to democracy, to the world, the more we see the need to concentrate on learnings really important to the children and young people with whom we live; the more we realize our tremendous responsibilities to them; and the more we recognize the need to understand the power of group dynamics.

Do you agree with us that the values mentioned above are important —the values of knowing how to guide a group, of providing meaningful experience (curriculum development), of creating favorable climate, of developing the individual in the group, of developing concepts of democracy and means for achieving its perpetual re-creation, of re-thinking means to world cooperation? If you do, you will agree that schools have a job to do; teachers have a very important job to do. We must be aware of the power and potential values of group action and be fully prepared (be willing and able) to provide means to the attainment of favorable group action.

The school is the agency in society through which a youngster is first introduced to intensive group living outside the family. Though we may wish that group living were consciously developed in all group situations, for most children it may be that the school is the only institution, or, at least, the dominant institution, for teaching an understanding of group dynamics.

What Are We Teaching?

We are teaching concepts of group living in our classrooms every day, whether we know it or not. The question is, what principles are we *really* teaching? What are boys and girls *actually* learning? How many youngsters are we teaching that it is smart to acquiesce without question to superior authority; that might makes right; that ends are all-important and any means are justified? How many youngsters are learning that the way to get along in the world is to say "Yes," and then "get by" with as little as possible; that caste and class are inevitable; that "good" is determined by I.Q. or color of skin or ability to do or say what authority (the teacher) happens to like?

Good intentions are not enough. We need to learn to look at ourselves critically and realistically. A conviction of the importance of group living is not enough. We need to learn the skills, the means to attainment, the means to learning and teaching. There is still much we do not know, not only as individuals but as a profession. We do not know enough about group reactions to various types of group management. We have much to learn about the relation of a classroom group to the school; of the school to the community. We have much to learn, but we have a means to learn. It is up to us.

Group Processes Are Not a Cure-all

Perhaps a word of caution is in order. We do not intend to imply that we believe that group study and action is a panacea. Group study is not a substitute for individual child study—the two supplement each other. Moreover, pupil needs, whether individual or group, are but one basis for determining criteria for experiences of boys and girls. The needs of society and the values held by teachers and parents must carry great weight. However, group dynamics is an area which has been so neglected in education that particular emphasis, such as we give in this report, is in order.

WHY EVERY TEACHER SHOULD STUDY HIS OWN GROUP

What we have been saying is this: Group living is important in many aspects of living and learning, for individuals and for groups, and the implications range from those applicable to classroom discipline to those significant to world understanding.

At this point you may be tempted to say: "If this problem is so big and important, why doesn't someone tell me what to do with and for my group?" It would be comforting if there were a set of rules, something like Robert's *Rules of Order,* to tell us exactly what to do under every circumstance. Several things get in the way of relying on a book of rules. First, we don't know enough; nobody does. Educators are just beginning to grasp the significance of the ideas and to try out some means of achieving objectives for group living. Second, nobody will ever know enough to give you the answers for *your* group. We know just enough to be able to say with conviction that the needs and reactions of boys and girls are, in large part, not absolutes (true of *all* boys and girls) but are functions of a particular setting.

Thus, the boys and girls in your group must be studied in relation to the kind of lives they have lived, are living, and want to live. Another way of saying this is to state that behavior is caused. Boys and girls, and adults too, for that matter, act the way they do because of something that has happened or is happening to them. What it is that causes them to act as they do differs from individual to individual, from group to group, and from situation to situation. There are no over-all "master an-

EACH GROUP DIFFERS, AS DOES EACH INDIVIDUAL.

swers." There are some general principles of cause and effect in behavior which seem to hold for most individuals and groups; but the specific causes leading to particular effects in behavior must be studied for each person, group, and situation.

Why Doesn't the Expert Do It?

Another question you might raise is this: "If this matter is so important, and if each group is to be studied in its setting, why doesn't the school system provide specialists, people skilled in sociology, psychology, or psychiatry, who might visit my group, analyze the situation, diagnose, and prescribe action?" That sounds reasonable. The only difficulty with such a plan is that it doesn't work.

We put emphasis on *your* study, because you, as the teacher, are in daily contact with your group, and therefore have the best opportunity to study it. You, as the teacher, are in a position to develop programs with your group; thus you, as the teacher, are *the only person* who can

[11]

carry out investigations in program development, to see the problem as a whole, to study cause and effect. Moreover, you, as the teacher, are the only one who can help pupils study themselves, study their own group processes, develop their skills and understandings, and evaluate their own progress—all a means to favorable group living. If you don't do it, it won't get done; it can't get done.

Teachers Can Help One Another

This does not mean that what one teacher learns has no value for other teachers. What one teacher learns about *his* group may be a guide for study by other teachers. Findings for one group may indicate areas for investigation with another group. Procedures for study developed with one group may be useful with other groups. But, as far as we can see, the best way for you to find meaningful answers to *your* questions about *your* group is for *you* to study your group and experiment with procedures.

HOW DOES A TEACHER STUDY HIS GROUP?

In the following chapters you will find descriptions of how various teachers have worked with their groups, their findings for their groups, and the questions they raise. As was suggested above, their work may give you ideas concerning what to look for in your group and how to study your group, but it cannot provide all the answers for the problems of group living of your group.

How a teacher may go about studying his group and creating better group living is the major thesis of this book. We try to look at this problem from many angles. As a preview of coming chapters, we might say that we feel that to develop good group living, a teacher must be able to recognize the factors involved in group living; know how the goals of a group are derived; understand how interaction operates, how a group responds to various situations, people, ideas; devise means of studying structure and interaction; and, above all, gain sufficient mastery to be able to guide group dynamics, goal-setting, goal-seeking behavior, and group adjustment. Providing appropriate experiences for boys and girls, and helping a group to study itself, in order to develop understanding of its own group processes, are, we believe, major aspects of curriculum development.

II

Group Interaction

"Old Suzanna, don't you cry for me, I'll come from weezy Anna with a band-aid on my knee." Thus a six-year-old interpreted in terms of his own experience what he thought he heard. Perhaps much of the group living of boys and girls is also without meaning and understanding—an attempt to comply but with no real insight into the basic principles of group life.

Learning the effective use of group processes requires the learning of skills and techniques. However, as in any learning—learning to read, for example—techniques without understanding can be hollow, meaningless, and practically useless. The task of the teacher is thus clearly defined—to provide experiences which develop good group living, and to help boys and girls to understand the meaning of such experiences. As pupils grow in this understanding, they may assume increasing responsibility for planning group experiences for themselves.

A lack of understanding of group processes may be true of adults, too. Those of us who worked in this study discovered that there were many concepts we had to struggle to perceive. But once being understood, they became so simple and clear that we asked ourselves, "Why didn't we think of that before?"

There was a time when the individual was considered the only unit of human energy. There is a growing realization, however, that there may be other units of human energy, designated as groups. There is nothing mystic in the concept of the group as a unit of human energy. The idea is no more difficult to come by than the transfer of one's conception of world space from miles to air-travel time, and is no less important in any consideration of today's living.

CHILDREN STUDY THEMSELVES

We believe we have ample evidence from this study that even young pupils in school can become aware of their interaction patterns and can consciously work to improve them. For example, in reporting a playground incident, a ten-year-old says: "We started arguing, so we planned how we were going to quit arguing." The planning took the form of stopping to analyze what they were doing, and why. In other words, these children were aware of the processes they were using and knew some techniques for examining and improving their own interaction patterns.

True, this was not easily achieved. When we began to talk with youngsters about their group interaction, many of the responses reflected preaching of adults or memorized codes and rules which had been taught in a moralistic context. It was evident that these youngsters had not done much thinking in this direction, but had learned a list of platitudes concerning taking turns and loving one's neighbor, which they would produce verbally when called upon. We began to hit bedrock when we got responses such as: "Don't punch a guy unless you gotta." This had a ring of reality, and lent itself to a discussion of the "gotta" situations— the working codes of interaction by which youngsters operate in their group living.

And, probably to a greater extent than we realized, we, as teachers, had to free ourselves of preconceived theories and learn to listen objectively to the real ideas of boys and girls in order to study the group processes of youngsters. No doubt, we have still a long way to go in this respect. We are convinced, however, that both we and the youngsters grew and learned as they analyzed their own processes.

Learning That Behavior Is Caused

When, as adults, we undertake a study of children, one of the major concepts we must grasp is that behavior is *caused;* that there are reasons for what children do. Behavior is not the result of innate meanness or of inborn goodness, but is caused by what a person has experienced or is experiencing. True, an individual may differ from his neighbor in the type of equipment with which he was born—his present and potential physique or mental power—but his experiences determine how he uses this equipment. A major task in working with children, then, is to provide experiences which will cause the maximum development of and satisfaction for the individual.

Since this concept of behavior, as being caused, is of such importance in understanding and guiding behavior, it follows that we should help children grasp this idea, and learn to plan in terms of it.

In a classroom discussion to try to analyze why they didn't get along together so well one day, one child (a ten-year-old) contributed the comment, "Some days we just feel mean." This led to a discussion of why people feel mean. Comments were: "I was sleepy." "When I got up my brother and sister started socking me and I got mad and came to school grouchy." Such an awareness that physical state or prior events may influence current behavior involves quite mature concepts.

Another youngster, more poetic than literal, said: "Some days we're out of tune like a violin." Even in this vague statement, the idea of the "tune" or harmony of a group is a sign of considerable insight.

The problem, then, is to suggest solutions for getting "in tune." These same ten- and eleven-year-olds made these suggestions, which they headed, "What We Can Do to Plan Together Well."

DORIS: Choose a good planning leader. Don't just choose the person you like best.

SUSAN: Give your attention to the ones that's talking.

MARGARET: Don't be afraid to speak up. The idea you are thinking of may be the one the class will want to use.

BOB: Be sure to take everyone's ideas.

NAN: Watch what's going on or a change might be made that you don't know about. It would make you not to know what to do next.

DAVID: Don't be afraid to suggest changes if you don't like the plans we have.

GERALD: Don't have the planning period too long.

MARIE: Yes, but before you stop be sure everyone knows how to get started on what you've planned to do.

(Some adult groups might well profit from similar mature consideration of their own processes.)

On another occasion, in a discussion of how to get in and out of the room without disturbing groups in neighboring rooms, these comments were made: "Some people think that if they do the right thing around the teacher, they can do the wrong thing away from her. That's wrong." "People cannot think independently. They cannot think for themselves."

The dawning of social consciousness and personal responsibility is a wonderful and awesome thing to see.

Learning to Evaluate Behavior

This same group took considerable time at the end of the year to evaluate its progress in group interaction in terms of goals it had set earlier.
Some of their comments follow.

RUDDY: We never used to play together. Now we do. (Indicating that
"groupness" has moved from the classroom to out-of-school relations.)

KATHERINE: We don't argue so much. (Either there is less conflict or there
is an awareness of other techniques for resolving conflicts.)

BOB: I've learned many things in working this year. I've learned to work
alone sometimes. I've learned to work better with other people.

GORDON: I've got more friends than I had at the first of the year. I've
learned to like other people.

TIMOTHY: I've learned not to fight unless it is to protect myself. I've learned
not to quarrel because it will turn into a fight. I've learned not to be sassy
because it starts a fight, too.

BARNARD: Now I don't want everything somebody's got.

RAY: I think I have improved in listening to other people's ideas.

GLORIA: We don't butt in very much anymore.

MANDEL: I used to not listen to people, but now I do.

TOM: We were still rude to Gerald when he read the other day, but we
have improved most of the time.

PEARL: We're not all truthful all the time, about candy for instance, but we
usually are.

ROBIN: We are grown up now. We don't act smart. We don't act stuck up.
But sometimes we show off a little.

ELIZABETH: We don't try to show people how smart we are. We act our
normal selves. It looks dumb to act smart.

JOHN: We don't hurt people's feelings very often.

DENBY: We don't call people "fatso," "cooties," and things like that so much.

BETTY: We try to be serious at serious times and silly at silly times.

SUSAN: We usually try to think for ourselves. We don't do the wrong thing
when we should do something else that is the right thing. We usually can
decide between right and wrong.

GORDON: (By this time feeling quite self-righteous.) We are nice people.

POLLY: (Furnishing a neat summary and conclusion.) It seems to me we're
doing a lot better now than we did the first of the year.

There was evidence of negative realism, too.

FOSTER: I didn't improve in liking each other, but I have more friends now.

BILL: I've not improved in fighting. (In not fighting.)

SUE: We have not improved in arguing as much as we could.

BETTIE: We still argue a little.

TIM: I still can improve in listening to people.

LARRY: I still want the biggest piece.

The range of items considered in this evaluation is revealing. Even the negative items indicate an acceptance of a group ideal, though it was not attained. Many of the items are individual and self-evaluative, but most of these are in terms of what are obviously accepted as group goals. On the other hand, it is interesting to note the number of items which imply identification and group consciousness: "*We* have improved; *we* still argue a little; *we* usually try."

Perhaps we should say again that this type of evaluation was not achieved easily. It is the result of a year's work with a group, of constantly examining goals and processes, planning for programs of improvement, and evaluating results.

Learning to Analyze Attitudes

An eighth grade group, trying to analyze its own interaction, decided that the group reaction pivoted on ideas concerning qualities of people liked by the group. In order to get at these qualities, each person wrote a description of his best friend. Some examples follow:

JOANN: My best friend is very nice and practically everyone likes her. She is tall and nice looking. She dresses well too. She has ideas of her own and does what other people want to. She likes the same things I do and we get along very well together. She is a different religion than I am, but we don't let that bother our friendship.

DONALD: My best friend. It's a girl. I like the way she dresses. Her clothes are the prettiest clothes we ever saw and she's just as sweet as she can be. She's a good sport and seems to always be happy. She has real white teeth that shine and sparkle like the sun. I like the way she rolls her hair. She's always happy but she always teases me only it's just in fun. But usually somebody's always picking on her or breaking her heart.

IRIS: My best friend is very sweet and cute. She rates above all in popularity and is easily liked by everyone and she dresses nice and is always neat and her big brown eyes set her off perfectly. She's really wonderful.

DONNA: My best friend has a personality and always is clean. She can get along with any type of person. She uses the best language and speaks well of any person. When you first meet her she looks like a person you would like to have a good friend. She speaks when she sees you on the street. She does not use language any one would be ashamed to be introduced to.

PETER: My best friend is a boy. He has a nice personality and when we can't think of anything to play he usually has some ideas. When he loses his temper he always makes up. He can play baseball pretty good. Almost everybody likes him but they sometimes think he's a poor sport.

BOB: My best friend has a nice personality. He never tries to boss anyone. He dresses very nicely. He likes sports and he's not a killjoy. He's always game in doing things. He likes to go places. He's always clean and his hair is always combed. He never gets into serious trouble. The trouble he gets into don't amount to much. He minds his mother and we get along just fine.

These statements are poignantly but unconsciously revealing of self-goals: Donna, who has difficulty mastering English, says her best friend "uses the best language" and "speaks well." Bob, who probably never owned a suit (he wears sweaters and dungarees or overalls), says of his best friend, "He dresses very nicely." Joann, who is not well accepted by her group, claims for her best friend that "practically everyone likes her." Donald, a mature boy in comparison with other eighth graders, makes his description of his best friend a poetic paean of love: "She has real white teeth that shine and sparkle like the sun."

These self-revelations may seem to be intimately personal matters, yet they have a relevance to group living. They reveal the degree to which the individual adheres to group goals, the strength of group goals, and the relation of the individual to the group.

Analyzing descriptions of best friends such as these made by the class, a committee of pupils prepared this list of twenty items which they headed "Qualities of Our Best Friends":

1. Athlete	11. Good-looking
2. "Little mean"	*12. Does what other people want
3. Likes to read	13. Dresses well
4. Smart	*14. Good sport
5. Likes to go to bed early	15. Very popular
* 6. Nice personality	*16. Easily liked
* 7. Always neat	17. Always considerate
8. Never in trouble	*18. Comes from a nice home
* 9. Have fun with him or her	*19. Not conceited
*10. Has other friends	*20. Never loses his temper

The committee presented the list to the group, who discussed each item, and then decided that ten (the ones starred) were of major importance. On further consideration, however, it was decided that item 6, "Nice personality," was too inclusive and should not be on the list. By vote of the group the other nine statements were used as a check list on which every pupil rated every other pupil on nine points. As the teacher reports:

"The children listed the names and after each put the strong points, by number of item on the revised list. At their request I tabulated them. If half or more of the thirty-five pupils rated a person strong in any one respect, this was to be considered an indication of an outstanding quality. I returned to each child a slip showing his two or three strongest points and weakest points. They seemed to consider this valuable and a definite starting point for improving their personalities and their group interaction."

Situations Cause Behavior

Six- and seven-year-olds tried very hard to analyze their own group processes. When asked to list desirable behavior they came up with items such as "Keep your hands to yourself," "Leave sand on the playground (don't throw it)," "Take your turn," and "Don't push." Although we have deep respect for the sincerity of their statements, we suspect they are repetitions of things adults have said to them rather than their own analysis of factors in group interaction. Their teacher came to the conclusion that the dominant factor in creating good group interaction for children of this age is not a rational analysis by the children, but provision by the teacher of appropriate experiences for the group in terms of her understanding of the needs of the group. This does not imply that six-year-olds are incapable of planning. Far from it. We cite examples later of their ability to plan. It does suggest, however, that the younger the child, the more difficult it is for him to generalize, and the less we should expect him to indulge in abstract thinking. Moreover, the younger he is, the less control he has over his environment, which implies that the responsibility of the teacher to regulate the environment is proportionally increased.

This teacher gave emphasis in her study to identifying points of tension in group life, and to analyzing the causal factors related to these tensions. She had not gone far, however, before she realized that she needed the help of parents both in identifying points of tension and in analyzing causes. She therefore held conferences in school with parents of her pupils and visited them in their homes. We quote from her reports comments which are particularly revealing.

Before giving these quotations, however, may we inject a thought which we believe to be important? If we are to achieve good group living with boys and girls, it is necessary to provide time for *all* teachers to meet with parents; but the younger the children in the group, the more important such conferences become. This first grade teacher spent uncounted hours holding conferences with parents both at school and in their homes. Most of these conferences were held after school hours.

A certain amount of after-school time may be legitimate, but the time found necessary to do the thorough job this teacher felt important if she was to contribute to good group living, is, we believe, beyond the bounds of legitimate expectation. It follows, then, that if administrators, parents, and teachers expect teachers to deal adequately with group living, time must be provided for all teachers to confer with parents.

The following are excerpts from conference reports:

"Tommy lives in a duplex. The house was sparingly furnished but neat and clean and comfortable looking. Tommy's mother was pleasant and nice. She said that Tommy had had low blood pressure, but was normal now. She said he had had a very bad ear infection last year when he was in kindergarten. Tommy brought out that he did not get to play with other children as much as he would like, so we decided to have him play several nights a week with other boys his age. . . ."

"I met Mrs. Brown on the street on the way to the dry cleaners. I went with her to the shop, then we went to her house. They live in a roomy downstairs apartment in an old house. Mr. Brown and the boys were bringing wood for the fireplace. When they had left I mentioned to Mrs. Brown I felt that Don seemed tired. She told me that, of late, he had been very disagreeable. He whined and cried a good deal, which was a very unusual way for him to act. We decided to try to find the cause. She said she was sure it was not lack of rest, for Don goes to bed at 6:30 or 7:00 winter and summer. . . . Mrs. Brown called me by telephone and told me about Don getting his new glasses and that he wasn't too pleased about wearing them. I told her I was glad she called because I could plan my comments accordingly. Then I told her about Don's efforts to make himself accepted by the boys and improvement in his relations on the playground. We talked about an hour."

"Marie's mother came to school and I showed her some samples of Marie's work. We discussed her nervousness and some trouble she was having getting along in the group. She told me that when the children were small they lived in a neighborhood where there were droves of children and there were many bad influences, but where they were living now, there were few children. Sometimes Marie's older sister brought home friends from school and Marie would play with them. . . . We decided to try a one-half hour rest before the evening meal, more outdoor play, and to try inviting Marie's girl friends for after-school play."

"After visiting in the room, Mrs. Briston came to me and said, 'Is that the way John acts all the time? He didn't pay any attention to you at all!' We discussed possible reasons for this inattentiveness. Mrs. Briston told me she thinks it may be due to their living conditions and to her yelling at the children so much. She explained that they were living with their grand-parents and in-laws, which had a tendency to make them all more or less tense. She said she would try hard to be more calm with John."

Even in these few examples there may be seen the cooperative efforts of the parents and the teacher to identify points of tension and to analyze causes. Over and over, parents identified fatigue, overexcitement, and lack of skills in getting along with others. They recognized causes of tension in their handling of their children, their living situation, and the experiences they provided for their young sons and daughters. Parents and the teacher together were able to suggest remedies for tension in both the home and school programs of boys and girls.

As a result of her observation of the group and her conferences with parents, this teacher did many things to improve group living, but she considers most important five aspects of the program:

Finding that many children were nervous and fatigued, she provided a rest period after lunch for every child, at least one half hour, longer for those who seemed to need it.

Deciding that pushing children beyond their readiness was contributing to nervousness and fatigue, she relaxed the reading program, providing wider experiences and a wider range of reading materials to promote readiness and to meet the range of individual differences.

Convinced that report cards can contribute to tensions and that parent conferences are very helpful, she held conferences with parents to replace the usual report cards of her school.

Finding that many children in the group had little opportunity to play with other children after school, and that, although after-school supervised play was provided by the school, first graders need added help in learning to play together, she planned with the mothers for a special period once a week when she would be on hand to help the group.

Knowing more about each child, she could better interpret not only his individual behavior, but also the influence of his behavior on the group, and the response of the group members to him. This greater clarity of interpretation made it possible for her to provide more meaningful guidance in group living.

Co-researchers

From the beginning, we asked boys and girls and parents to work with us as co-researchers. The few examples cited above may serve to indicate how they worked in helping to define problems, marshal evidence, and evaluate progress. In giving these examples we are not implying that the activity described was the total program of each group and teacher.

We were impressed by the ability of boys, girls, and parents, when given opportunity and encouragement, to apply problem-solving techniques to matters of group living. In fact, when the problems were real —and group-living problems are always real to the group, whether consciously identified or not—the skills of intelligent problem solution seemed to be more readily mastered than when they were applied to what we tend to consider the more "simple" situations, like those posed by arithmetic problems.

TEACHERS EXAMINE THEMSELVES

Not to be put to shame by the youngsters' thoughtful analysis, we, as teachers, attempted to analyze our own actions and the reaction of groups to our actions.

Anyone who goes from one classroom to another is aware of the differences in groups. (Incidentally, we recommend that teachers find more opportunity to do this for wide observation and study of many groups, as it can give increased insight into factors in group processes.) As we started our study, we were aware of these differences in groups, but it was only after many months of observation and analysis that we were able to state some of the dimensions of group interaction. Finally, we were sufficiently clear in our thinking to devise the "Guide for Group Observation" (Appendix, page 413) which helped us objectify our observations.

We found that we could identify various types of interaction, such as extreme "order," with little inter-personal reaction; rowdy, uncontrolled, patternless behavior; informal, "comfortable," but not active participation; or active participation and inter-personal reaction, yet with goal-centered control—a control exerted by the group to achieve a goal the group had determined.

We could see variations in reactions of groups to the teacher: active negativism, open hostility, fear, apathetic indifference, or warm, friendly, personalized give-and-take.

There were observable differences in forms of inter-personal relations, from keen individual competition to willingness of each to play his part toward meeting group goals and to help others play their parts.

We could measure patterns of interaction. For example, in one situation the pattern of discussion may be teacher—child 1—teacher—child 2—teacher—child 3—etc., and in another, child 1—teacher—child 2—child 1—child 4—child 5—child 2—teacher, etc. (See page 23)

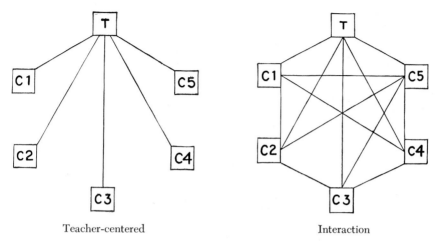

Teacher-centered

Interaction

PATTERNS OF DISCUSSION.

We began to identify patterns of control and specific control devices used by teachers, and we studied the relation of the way a group operates to the results it achieves.

SPECIFIC CONTROL DEVICES

As we studied, we became increasingly aware of the role of the teacher in setting the stage for group interaction through his own actions. We began by identifying some of the devices that we and other teachers use in directing the group. No doubt additions could be made to this list.

1. Imposing own authority (I won't have that!).
2. Pointing to consequences (If you do that you'll get hurt).
3. Giving affection (I like boys and girls who are quiet).
4. Withholding affection (I won't like you if you do that).
5. Giving personal praise (I think that is good).
6. Using threats, or appeals, to:

   Morals (Good boys, nice boys, don't do that).

   Age status (Big boys don't do that).

   Sex status (Don't be a "sissy" or "tomboy").

   Parental control (I'll tell your father).

   Higher authority (I'll send you to the principal).

   Group status (Other boys and girls won't like you).
7. Ridiculing, using sarcasm (Now, isn't that silly!).

8. Offering bribes, threatening action (I'll give you a good grade; I'll fail you).
9. Ignoring (Teacher acts as though the individual were not present).
10. Taking direct action (Isolates individual from group; administers physical punishment).
11. Asking for individual or group evaluation (What do *you* think of that?).
12. Showing enthusiasm (Let's do this. I think it would be fun).
13. Offering suggestions (Why not try it this way?).
14. Providing "busy work" (To center attention).
15. Varying routine (To avoid boredom or to distract attention).
16. Posing a problem (What should we do?).
17. Pointing out alternatives (Couldn't we do this, or this, instead?).
18. Asking group to look at self to see process and progress (How are we doing?).
19. Suggesting resources (Maybe Miss Thompson would know. See the map).
20. Giving opportunity for releasing tension (Getting it off my chest).
21. Helping group to participate in formulation of guides to action and evaluation.

Probably most teachers know these devices, but it was interesting to use even a part of this list as a check list while visiting classrooms. In one teacher's classroom in a junior high school, for example, it was possible to find during three periods use of only two of these devices: No. 8, Bribes and threats having to do with grades or academic success or failure, and No. 10, Isolating the individual from the group, physically ("Go stand in the hall") or psychologically ("You're not to say anything more this period"). Moreover, it seemed likely that the youngsters did not give a hoot whether they passed or failed or received good grades or bad, and that they rather welcomed the opportunity to be isolated from the group, all of which points out that although *range* of patterns and devices may be interesting, much more significant is the *appropriateness* of the teacher's action to the group and the situation.

FIVE PATTERNS OF INTERACTION

As we continued our study of groups, we began to realize that the specific control devices were but small aspects of something much bigger —the general pattern of interaction as set by the teacher or the group.

We were aware of the study of Lewin, Lippitt, and White,[1] describing reactions of groups to "autocratic," "laissez-faire," and "democratic" situations. The report of this investigation helped us in our study.

We identified five types of group interaction and found that we could reach complete agreement in designating them to groups observed.

1. Adult rule, pupil obedience.
2. Planless catch-as-catch-can control.
3. Teacher planning with individuals.
4. Adult-directed group planning.
5. Group self-management through group planning.

The identification of these types of interaction came after much study of groups in our own and other classrooms. Having hypothesized the types, we tested them in further observations, and although we found numerous subtle variations, we decided that these five could stand as workable, recognizable classifications.

Our methods of study included observation and reports of classroom situations, which were then discussed and analyzed, and supplemented by the use of the "Guide for Group Observation" (Appendix, page 413). We have not attempted a statistical analysis of our data, but we found that almost without exception we could reach consensus concerning identification of the interaction pattern used, and that the close relation of pattern to group reaction was so prevalent as to give emphasis to the rare exception. Thus we present with considerable confidence the following statements of relationship, though we recognize the need for further testing and the use of more refined measures.

1. Adult Rule, Child Obedience

The teacher employing this pattern assumes that he holds absolute authority and that pupils should respond unquestioningly with the demanded behavior. He acts accordingly.

Miss Armstrong was, to the best of our knowledge, a sincere teacher attempting to carry out her functions as she deemed necessary. In one observed period of sixty minutes she issued forty orders, from "Class, come to attention" to "John, put your pencil away." Approximately 50 per cent of her verbal interaction with the class, as classified by the observer, took the form of directives, such as "David, take question four,"

[1] K. Lewin, R. Lippitt, and R. White, "Patterns of Aggressive Behavior in Experimentally Created 'Social Climates,'" *Journal of Social Psychology*, Vol. 10, pp. 271–99, 1939.

"Mary, read the next paragraph," or of the type exemplified by the earlier statements. An additional 30 per cent might be classified as directives, though in question form, such as "Why did you do that?" or "Where is Boston?" Another 10 per cent was classified by the observer as dictums, such as "That's right," or "Correct!" The remaining 10 per cent of her verbal comment was put into a miscellaneous grouping and included such statements as "John, are you listening?" and "Do you understand?"

Miss Armstrong held the reins with a strong hand. This is our most extreme example. Many other teachers employing patterns that we classified under this heading were more subtle, in words at least, substituting for the direct approach of Miss Armstrong more tactful verbal forms, such as "David, wouldn't you like to put your pencil away?" or "Now let's turn to page 67, shall we?" But both the teacher and her pupils knew such statements were teacher commands.

The variations we have just cited indicate the difficulty of objective classification of patterns. Yet the more we observed, the more we felt competent to classify the pattern that the teacher was employing, whatever the variations in subtlety.

As we attempted to analyze the effect on the group of this pattern of adult rule, child obedience, we found it necessary to indicate two divergent types of reaction: *docile obedience* and *open hostility*. At first this had us baffled, but we finally agreed that the variation in response depended on the experience or expectation of the group. Pupils accustomed, through long experience, to such obedience patterns as part of the total school pattern react with docile acceptance. There are always, of course, deviates who do not conform because of home training or other factors, and who are therefore classified by the teacher as "discipline problems." On the whole, however, the group used to obedience patterns seems to comply with unquestioning docility.

On the other hand, we found situations in which teachers attempted to employ an obedience pattern, and the group reaction was obvious hostility. We were at a loss for an explanation until we began to dig into the past history of groups and into the total school patterns. If the group has known a pattern which involves self-direction, or if there are other types of patterns in the school of which the children are aware, the reaction may be violent aggression. This type of aggression seems to be particularly marked in certain secondary schools and in certain types of communities. Again we wish to emphasize that our evidence is limited, but from our observation we would conclude that the farther advanced in school, the greater the probability that the group has known patterns other than strict teacher rule, and therefore the greater the possibility of resistance to such a pattern. The difficulty encountered by a third grade teacher in enforcing such a pattern after the group had had experience with a second grade teacher who had employed other patterns substantiates this view. The same could be said for a fifth grade, after wider experience in the fourth, or of a seventh grade after the sixth, and so on.

In general, it seems to us, on examination of our records, that compliance to teacher rule is most likely to be manifested by children of middle-class communities, while hostility to such a pattern is demonstrated by children of lower or upper socio-economic groups. Our tentative conclusion is that home patterns of adult rule are strongest in the middle class and less strongly enforced in the lower and upper-class homes. Thus, if we are correct in our earlier interpretation, experience with other than adult rule patterns at home makes imposing such patterns at school more difficult.

We should not leave this discussion without pointing out that the designation by the teacher of student chairmen, or permission given to the group by the teacher to elect such chairmen, does not necessarily negate the adult rule pattern. Sometimes a teacher merely delegates power to a pupil, who may employ a rigid rule-obedience pattern.

2. Planless Catch-As-Catch-Can Pattern

When this pattern is employed, there is no attempt by the teacher to control or organize the group. We did not find many instances of the use of this pattern. It was most frequently encountered when teachers employing pattern 1—Adult rule, child obedience—loosened the reins for brief intervals. For example, we found it in some schools on the playgrounds, in lunchrooms, in halls, and in extracurricular activities. Our general impression is that it occurred most frequently in schools where pattern 1 was most prevalent in the school as a whole. The reaction of the group seemed inevitably to be confusion, insecurity, and keen competition for power among group members, among subgroups, or between the group and the teacher.

Miss Towsen, principal of Summerset school, prided herself on the "discipline" of "her" school. She tended to rate teachers on their ability to impose a teacher-rule, child-obedience pattern. She claimed she expected "pin-drop" silence during reading periods. It would require a long search to find a school where there was more confusion and rivalry on the play-

THE GROUP PATTERN MAY BE "CATCH-AS-CATCH-CAN."

ground, or where there were more personally insecure individuals. Released from the control of teachers and required to direct themselves in free periods, youngsters seemed to have meager skills in interaction.

In one situation we found a teacher, trying sincerely, we believe, to practice democracy as she interpreted it, who employed the catch-as-catch-can pattern in the classroom. The results were devastating to her and disastrous to group interaction.

3. Teacher Planning with Individuals

There are teachers, we found, who interpret planning as a process of individual pupil-teacher interaction. Each individual in turn has an opportunity to plan a course of action with the teacher. Sometimes this was found coupled with rigid enforcement of the teacher-rule pattern and employed only for those who completed work ahead of the group. Without exception, in our experience, teachers who employ this pattern believe they are using liberal planning techniques and fail to see that they are circumscribing group interaction.

Mr. Bishop saw himself as a "democratic" teacher. He gave careful consideration to individual differences. The first part of each period was devoted to what he termed a planning period, during which he tried to discuss individually with at least a fifth of the pupils of his class their special difficulties in mathematics. In this way, he managed a conference with each pupil at least once a week. While such conferences were in progress, and during the remainder of the period, he enforced rigid rules of individual work. No pupil was allowed to speak to any other, or to look at another's work. As is indicated above, Mr. Bishop believed that he was providing for group planning.

Some groups, we found, reacted rather well to such procedure during the class period. We concluded that if the degree of rapport with the teacher was high, the members of the group appreciated the individual attention given them. On the other hand, we could find no evidence of favorable group interaction in these situations. The teacher employing such a pattern is doing no more than allowing some play of individual initiative while curtailing group interactions.

4. Adult-directed Group Planning

Teachers using this pattern allow for group interaction and planning within boundaries set by themselves.

Miss Borsney was eager to teach her second grade group how to plan cooperatively. She had done some experimenting with planning, so she told us, and had discovered that in some areas the group could plan quite effectively, but in others they floundered pitifully. For example, her group could do a good job of planning how they would conduct themselves during a walk around the block, but were unable to plan a whole day's program.

We met many Miss Borsneys. They had discovered that, although "all-out" group planning was their goal, it is necessary for them to designate the scope of the area of planning, particularly for younger children and for groups not yet skilled in the techniques of group action.

Miss Symonds, for example, suggested to her first grade group members that they plan first how they might put on their outdoor clothes, then how they would play together during a fifteen-minute recess, then how they would plan a program for their mothers. Miss Peters suggested to her home economics class members that they plan how they might arrange the equipment, then how they might divide responsibility for a class luncheon, then how they might carry out plans for a dinner for

sixty people. The difficult job is for the teacher to know how to determine progressive degrees of difficulty in planning.

Group reaction will depend on the insight of the teacher in keeping
pace with the skills and maturity of the group. The teacher who provides
opportunities far beyond the capabilities of the group will find he is
creating insecurities, such as those of the catch-as-catch-can pattern; the
teacher who provides less than the class can handle is tending toward
adult rule. The teacher who can successfully "pace" the group in terms of
its interaction skills may expect maximum cooperation and learning.

5. Group Self-management Through Group Planning

As we observed groups, we found that this pattern might be considered,
pragmatically, the ideal. A group that was able to develop goals, plan
attainment of goals, cooperate in achieving them, and evaluate progress
was the group that learned, grew, and developed. Moreover, we believe
this to be the ideal for development of the individual and the group in
terms of learning efficiency and attainment of democratic goals. We recognize, however, as we note under pattern 4, that it is unrealistic to attempt complete and unlimited self-management with immature children
and with groups that lack skills. It may actually be damaging to the
group to attempt to use complete self-control until it has learned some
skills in group interaction by practicing them in limited areas. Only as
the group learns to find security in its own skills and in group goals, is it
possible to shift from adult-given security to group-given security. However, we have ample evidence, we believe, that these skills and this
security can be achieved; that groups can learn, with wise teacher leadership, to manage themselves in ever-widening areas of experience.

Range of Pattern

It might be assumed that in a democratic society good teachers would
use only patterns of interaction 4 or 5, but this does not seem to be the
case. Teachers whom observers agreed were most effective used the
widest range of patterns, according to the appropriateness of the pattern
to the situation. Emergency situations (and what teacher hasn't known
emergencies on occasion!) may demand pattern 1. Pattern 2 may provide
a valuable learning situation; and pattern 3 may be necessary for certain
individuals who are not so skilled as others in the use of group processes.
Thus seemingly less desirable patterns may provide important experiences
(if used appropriately), even though patterns 4 and 5 are the ideal.

JUDGING APPROPRIATENESS OF PATTERN

It would seem that the wise teacher employs a range of interaction patterns. Judging what pattern is appropriate is no easy task. We have tried to analyze the factors involved, using our own experiences as group leaders, our analysis of situations observed, and the statements of teachers who explained to us, when asked, why they had operated as they did.

Evaluation of Pattern in Terms of Goals

—of the group

"Good" group interaction in terms of group goals is that pattern which contributes to the attainment of the aims of the group. For example, a group was interested in learning a song that they planned to sing for their mothers at a program a few days later. The group as a whole had decided that this was their goal, but seemed to lack the skills for organizing themselves to attain their goal. One seven-year-old said, "Miss Browning, won't you tell us how and make us do it?" The group responded with a chorus of yeses. In other words, the group requested a pattern of adult rule to achieve its goal.

The teacher complied, in terms of this particular goal-directed activity, but she knew that for learning social skills—skills of participation and interaction—other patterns are desirable. Hence she employed this one pattern for only a brief period.

Aims of the group vary with the situation, so it is impossible to provide a "prescription" for a type of group interaction. Perhaps it should be noted, too, that having designated a major goal, subgoals may determine a variety of patterns within a larger pattern for reaching a larger goal.

—of the teacher

When the goals of the teacher deviate from group goals, there is often trouble ahead. The teacher may impose his own goals and his own pattern regardless of the hostility of the group—in other words, there is adult rule; or he may assume the group goal is all-important, which tends to lead to harmony but at a price. No teacher dares consent to socially undesirable group goals unless he feels secure that the experience will lead to a realization of more socially acceptable goals. Thus, there may be certain extreme cases when there seems to be no way out but through the use of what the teacher may feel to be a less desirable pattern.

—of the community

When the community goals are not those of the broader society, the teacher is in a difficult position. A community may dump its sewage in the river, knowing it contributes to ill-health in a down-river community, or it may allow itself to be dominated by the interests of a small percentage of its citizenry. In such a situation the teacher may be confronted with the problem of attempting to use one pattern in the school while the pupils learn another pattern, by precept, in their community. This dilemma is not unusual. Teachers indicate that the best solution is to lead children toward as favorable a pattern as possible in school, with the hope that when they are sufficiently mature they may be able to analyze the community pattern in terms of basic principles learned in school. This is not so simple as it sounds, of course, and needs further investigation concerning the effect on children of divergent social forces.

—of society

In general, it is recognized that the professed aim of our society is to develop the skills and attitudes which contribute to democracy and to individual and group welfare. It is expected that the pattern of interaction in the classroom will contribute to attaining this objective. However, the gap between ideals, stated goals of society, and operational goals of society poses a difficult problem for teachers. How should the teacher handle this difference between stated aims and behaviors of society? Much study needs to be given to the nature of this conflict between words and deeds in our culture. We need to locate and identify the areas of difference as seen by children as well as those recognized by adults. We need to know much more about how we may strive for mutual understanding of adults and children. (This is discussed further in Chapter III, "Group Goals.")

Evaluation of Pattern in Terms of Security Needs

—of the group

Freedom may be frustrating to an individual or group if no security is provided. It is evident that certain skills are needed if an advanced pattern of self-management is to be attained. If the freedom is provided before the appropriate skills have been learned, there is little likelihood that other than a chaotic situation will result. Frustration due to lack of security will lead, almost without exception, to aggression or withdrawal.

GROUP PARTICIPATION CAN GIVE SECURITY.

Many are the teachers who have said, "But I tried it and it didn't work" ("it" being the provision of freedom for self-management). Of course, "it" does not work if lack of guidance and skills lead to thwarting and frustration. If aggression results, it is likely to be unpredictable and inexplicable in form, a turning against the teacher, against an "outside" group, or against the group itself in subgroup conflict or in hostility toward a scapegoat. If withdrawal results, the teacher may say: "But they *want* me to tell them what to do." This is usually an indication that the group lacks skills in group interaction sufficient to give security, so chooses domination in preference to insecurity. During the learning of these skills of interaction, it may be necessary for an adult to direct the learning and to choose the areas in which the skills are to be practiced.

—of the teacher

Just as it is unrealistic to think in terms of complete and unlimited self-management until the group attains security in skills, so it is unrealistic

[33]

to think in these terms unless the teacher himself has skills. Again, the means to learning is in experience, and a teacher may provide for himself ever-widening areas of experience as he finds security in his skills. These teacher-skills include not only immediate self-skills for directing group interaction but the skills implicit in determining areas for self-management in terms of the maturity and skills of the group. There are teachers who find it difficult to wait until a group works out its own problems, and other teachers who find it difficult to step in and help when help is needed. A teacher who learns the reactions of groups to various patterns and can judge the appropriateness of such patterns has a control of the situation which gives a basis for personal and professional security.

Evaluation of Pattern in Terms of Other Adjustment Needs

In addition to security, other adjustment needs, particularly those of "belonging" and "selfhood," must be considered in judging a pattern for group interaction.

—need to "belong"

It is normal, it seems, for a young child to find security in adult approval, but usually this shifts during the early school years to a need to belong to a peer group. An adult-rule pattern fosters reliance on adults which may obstruct this normal shift to peer relations. It is not unusual for a teacher to feel flattered by the need of an individual or a group to find security in him as an adult, or for him to fail to see that as he caters to this dependency he is hindering the healthy growth of the individual and the group. It is difficult to foster a shift from adult-given security to group-given security unless there is ample opportunity for group interaction. If belonging is not found in the total group, there may be splits into gangs, cliques, and pal-patterns. If belonging is not found in a school group, it may be sought in out-of-school gangs, free of adult supervision.

—need for sense of "selfhood"

It seems a normal aspect of maturing to test one's self as a means of attaining a sense of selfhood. There is no doubt that competition has been misused in the classroom, being employed to provide motivation for substitute goals rather than real goals growing out of needs and interests of boys and girls. As so used, it is rightly frowned upon. However, if there is genuine need for individuals to engage in self-testing, there may be a place for competition in certain areas of the school program. The key to understanding, to judging the appropriate pattern, would seem to be found in the types of self-testing employed. There is no clear evidence concerning where the need for self-testing is most urgent, but it would seem to be in both physical and intellectual strength and skill. Reaction to pictures of children fighting (Appendix, page 423) indicates that mere testing of physical strength may be seen by children as a motive for physical combat. As the intellect matures, it is possible that this wish to test strength is transferred from physical to intellectual activities. Our observations of children in groups give us great sympathy for this desire. On the other hand, we feel this drive may be *group*-directed. Intellectual combat in the form of debates is, we know, popular with young adolescents. If this same urge were group-directed, through group discussion, we feel that it might be of greater value to group living, yet maintain the self-testing quality evidently valued by young people.

Evaluation of Pattern in Terms of Situation
—"emergency" situations

As realists, we are aware that occasionally the immediate demands of a situation rather than the ideal may dominate the choice of pattern of interaction. We know that there are times when the situation dictates a less desirable pattern.

Miss Garson, a third grade teacher, had planned with her group, prior to the trip to the zoo, how they should act, but when the group was on the streetcar they began to "cut up." She knew that, even with the best planning, the insecurity of a new situation may cause a group to revert to less mature patterns of behavior. Although she believed in and practiced a pattern leading toward group self-management, Miss Garson realized that adult action was called for.

En route in a streetcar was no time or place for a planning period. She exerted adult rule, demanding pupil obedience as the situation demanded. But, and this is important, the next day the group spent considerable time analyzing *why* they had acted as they did and discussing what they would need to do on another trip. Thus, she used the unfavorable situation as an opportunity for learning.

Teachers in Lincoln High had done a great deal of work with their group in planning for the forthcoming basketball game with Washington High. In spite of this, there was considerable hissing, booing, and other unsportsmanlike behavior on the night of the game. The Lincoln High coach found it necessary to stop the game and demand order. The next day the student council sent its representative to each room to discuss the situation and to plan what they should do at the next game.

Every teacher recognizes in these illustrations familiar emergency situations in which he has found it necessary to use less desirable patterns of control. The important factor, we believe, is that the group should evaluate the situation which made these stringent measures necessary, and plan how they should act when they are again in such situations. It is interesting that if it is clear that the situation demands autocratic measures, a group accustomed to self-management will recognize the need for emergency measures and will readily plan to make their further use unnecessary. If, however, the group is accustomed to autocratic patterns, there seems to be no realization of the emergency nature of the situation, and attempts to discuss it merely result in aggression against the one who imposes authority. He is a "kill-joy," a "sourpuss," if not something worse. Experiences of teachers in discussions of this nature when autocratic patterns have been employed often lead them to believe that democratic methods won't work. True, frank discussions won't work in emergencies unless the group has become accustomed to free group interchange of ideas in non-emergency situations.

—deviates

Deviates in the group often pose a difficult problem. When the teacher is trying to develop group self-management, what shall he do with the little fellow who is so immature that he does not know any security other than that achieved through identification with the teacher? What does one do with the "tough guy" who, unused to group action, feels that aggression against the teacher is the way to fame and glory? Obviously, such individuals demand special teacher attention, but the problem is to provide the special action they require without damage to the *group*. Once again we are in an area for which we have insufficient evidence, but our experience leads us to believe that if the group is accustomed to self-management it will accept variation in the teacher's reaction to individuals. A teacher may rely heavily on this general acceptance, but when special action toward individuals is continuous or unduly conspicuous, the teacher may need to take the group into his confidence.

Susan, a thirteen-year-old, was pathetically in need of affection and adult-given security. Deserted by her parents, she lived with an unsympathetic grandmother. The group paid little attention to her. It wasn't hard to discover why she was rejected by the group. She was "different" by many standards of group culture, in clothing, in speech, and in ways of spending leisure time. Knowing this, the teacher went out of her way to show Susan that she was loved and wanted. This could easily have led to accusations of "teacher's pet" by the group, but the teacher took aside several key people in the class and explained that Susan needed "extra help" and that she hoped they would help her make Susan feel at home. Such action is not without its dangers. Unless there is a high degree of rapport between teacher and group, special attention to an individual may serve merely to intensify group rejection, which in turn requires more teacher-given security. This teacher, however, knew what she was doing and was able to use one interaction pattern with the group while employing another with Susan until such time as she felt Susan was sufficiently adjusted to be treated like the rest of the group.

Evaluation of Pattern in Terms of Growth and Learning

Our studies were not sufficiently precise to report accurate results, but our general observation substantiates findings of other experimenters who report group-linked gains and social increments of learning. We feel reasonably confident that there was greater learning, even in the areas of the 3 R's, because of good group morale and a high level of group interaction. To the extent that standardized tests measure growth in learning, results for the groups with which we worked indicate that the time taken from formal learning in the usual academic areas for group discussion of the means of developing good group living (and it *did* take time) did not hinder normal growth in academic areas.

Having made this cautious statement, we should like to report that we believe the gains we observed are greater and more important than those indicated by the results of standardized tests in academic areas. We are confident that there have been immeasurable gains in social learnings. That the pupils themselves were aware of these gains is evidenced by the statements of evaluation of the year's work by the group members (page 16).

Many teachers hesitate to take time away from academic work because they fear the disfavor of parents. But it has been our experience that parents, too, recognize and appreciate the value for their children of growth, both social and academic, in a good group atmosphere. This is evidenced by these statements of the parents of a first grade group at the end of a year during which the teacher worked for good group living as well as for academic growth:

"We are happy to know that Elinor is doing so well. We appreciate all the extra time and effort on your part that is necessary for this type of program." ("This type of program" meant a program of social growth in which children learned to get along together and enjoy group living.)

"We are proud of the progress Susan has made in school and want to express our thanks to you for helping her so much." (Susan was a very shy child who had found her place in the group.)

"I can truly say that Tommy has improved more than I ever thought possible." ("Improved" here meant development from an unsocial youngster to one who was happy in social relationships.)

"Thank you for the time and personal interest you have taken." (This mother realized that her child did not overcome his aggressive behavior toward others in the group without a great deal of teacher help.)

Evaluation of Pattern in Terms of Expectation

A group comes to a teacher with the expectation that certain interaction patterns will be used. There is likely to be difficulty when the teacher and the group have divergent expectancies. Recognizing this factor, we attempted to determine through role-playing what children expect in a situation. A child, a ten-year-old, played the part of the teacher while others played the part of pupils. This incident occurred after several months of group living with an understanding teacher. This is an account of what happened:

MARIE (playing role of teacher): The class must come to order. (Her teacher never used this phrase.) Now we'll do arithmetic. Anyone who doesn't get this right will be paddled!
CHILD 1: I don't want to do arithmetic.
MARIE: That doesn't matter. You've got to do it anyway. Now get busy.
CHILD 2: Teacher, Tom passed a note to Billy.
MARIE: Bring me that note right away! Tom, come here. I'm going to paddle you. (Administers paddling to glee of all children.) Etc.

We are at a loss to interpret this demonstration. It is possible that it indicates the real expectancy of the group, but knowing the teacher and the group, we doubt it. We are inclined to believe that cultural patterns are strong and that "playing school" is governed by such rigid rules that the real feeling of the group is not evident. In other words, although role-playing would seem to be a logical means of determining expectancy, in this situation the cultural factors colored the acting to such an extent that this means was unfruitful. It is possible that, with different teacher-pupil planned preparation, role-playing might be more revealing.

—as others see us

Some indications of children's expectations, or at least their hopes, may be found in their statements headed "If I Were a Teacher" and "My Favorite Teacher." The statements are colored by the experiences of the pupils, of course. These fourth and fifth grade boys and girls were in a situation where considerable attention was being given to group interaction. If their sights had not been lifted by this experience, we might have found quite a different list of factors mentioned.[1]

If I Were a Teacher

"If I were a teacher I would try to understand my children's problems. I would also try not to fly off the handle but I probably would. I would not drown my children in arithmetic and reading and I would give them a few privileges. And when they got into trouble we'd discuss it in class to find out what to do."

"If I were a teacher I would let my class work for awhile then they could have something that they would enjoy. I would teach them as best as I could."

"I would let people choose their own leaders. When they were stuck on a problem I would help them. If I told them something and it was hard to understand I would tell them again. I would give them things so they could get out of seats and wouldn't get tired."

"I would discuss things with them often. I would let them have Group Work.[2] I'd let them make friezes and big books, like our Manners Book. I wouldn't have monitors. Because it makes "tattle tales" of people. I would let them choose their morning. Then I would plan their afternoon. I would like to be well liked."

My Favorite Teacher

"I like the way my teacher talks and the way she lets us talk. I like the nice things we do in Group work. We have a manners book. We had a Juvenile Jury and we have health charts."

"I liked her because she had parties for the mothers at her house."

"She was nice to the children. She would let them help before or after school."

"I had a favorite teacher once. She was very nice. I liked her very much.

[1] This matter of expectation of teacher action is discussed further in Chapter IV, under the heading "The Teacher As Group Member."
[2] Class organization in interest groups, committees, clubs, etc.

She did not like to talk like some teachers do. She did not like teachers that talk all the time."

"She gave me just the right time to do everything. She did not tell us to do this and this in so much time or else. This teacher told me if I was slow in anything try to catch up if I can. This teacher gave us a chance to do everything at least once. The teacher I'm talking about gives me enough time, and just enough work. She gives us activities and responsibility."

"She let me help my friend when he needed help. She would let us work together in groups. She would let us knit things and let us sing, work and play and do arithmetic and she took us places and did things with us. She would let us tell jokes to each other and play games."

"I liked the way she lets us get into clubs, and in committees, and the way we get to plan, and go different places. I liked the way she was so patient and kind. And she was very good. I liked the way she made the children do their work and stick with them until they got it."

—adult control

Another aspect of expectation may be examined in terms of responses of boys and girls concerning the degree of adult control exerted. We asked pupils how they felt about adult control.

Perhaps we should not have been surprised, in terms of what we know about expectancy—but we must admit that we were—to learn the reactions of boys and girls to questions concerning adult control of them. (Check Sheet of Opportunities in Human Relations, Appendix, page 407.) Responses to the question, "How do you feel about the amount of adult control of you by your family?" were distributed as follows:

Family Control	4th and 5th Grade (group of 30) %	8th Grade (group of 32) %
Too much	13.3	9.4
About right	76.7	68.7
Too little	10.0	21.9

To the question "How do you feel about the amount of control of you by your school?" responses were as follows:

School Control	4th and 5th Grade (group of 29) %	8th Grade (group of 34) %
Too much	6.9	11.8
About right	93.1	50.0
Too little	0	38.2

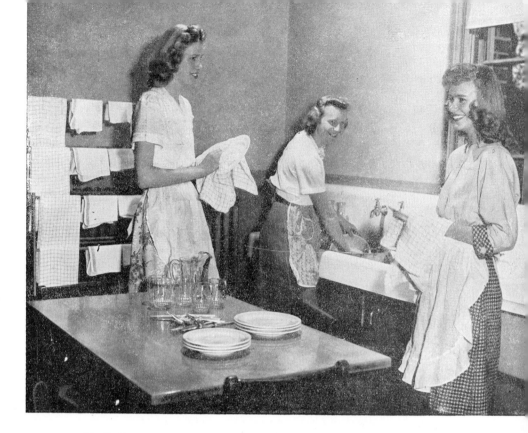

EVERYONE WANTS THE OPPORTUNITY TO CONTRIBUTE.

The eighth grade teacher makes this comment: "Many of these children (those designating school control as too little) are unwilling to assume the responsibility expected by school life."

Fourth and fifth graders, asked to be more explicit about their feeling of amount of adult control over them, gave these responses:

I think our teacher makes you work too much.
I feel that you need adult control so you will not get hurt.
We need adult control at school.
I think we need some control.
I think that we should have control by parents and school when ever we need it because if we didn't we would always be getting hurt.
I think adults boss me about right.
We need some adult control or we'd be bad.
We should have control to help us out of trouble and to tell our troubles to.
I think my family controls me just right. They let me do things I like to do but do not let me do some things.
I think we need control because we get confused.

Knowing something of the types of control to which these young people are subjected, we wonder that they submit so readily to them. We know, for example, that some of the fourth and fifth graders are subject to rigid control at home, yet only four admit to too much control. We suspect, too, that some eighth graders are subjected to rather rigid control in some of their classes, yet few claim that there is too much. The number of youngsters who complain of too little control is the biggest surprise. We might expect that adolescents, trying to establish independence, would complain of too much adult control, yet it is they who tend to claim there is too little. The implication may be that in the unsettled state of transition from childhood to adulthood, adolescents seek the security of adult control.

—is youth too docile?

Whatever the interpretation, we are more alarmed than pleased by the docility of youth. We might feel that a degree of resistance is a healthy sign of self-assertion. The fact that certain types of adult control, which, because we know the form, we feel to be unfortunate for children, are accepted because they are expected, or because they are needed for security, is, we believe, a danger signal. We should like to check this interpretation against responses of other groups and reactions of other teachers. Moreover, we feel that here is an area for cooperative study by adults—teachers and parents—in an attempt to understand the wide significance of the patterns of control they use with children, a significance which moves beyond immediate reaction to color the expectancy of boys and girls. This pattern of expectation of control should be of grave concern to adults responsible for the education of young people in a democracy.

—adjustment within a day

One interesting study involved following a junior high school class throughout the day, analyzing the teacher-control patterns to which the group was subjected and the reaction of the group.[1] In this particular situation, the group was subjected during the course of a day to patterns ranging from complete adult domination to relatively free self-management. The amazing aspects of this situation is the degree to which pupils adjusted to the expected pattern. Knowing that Miss Beagler expected extreme order, obedience, and no interaction, the class filed silently into

---

[1] This study was undertaken with the full knowledge and cooperation of all the teachers involved. Without such cooperation, a study of this type might be dangerous to teacher group morale.

the room and took their places one behind another. There was no informal conversation beyond the door of the room, even though formal class procedure had not yet begun. After this class period, the group moved to Mr. Reynolds' room. Here there was definite hostility against the teacher and his control patterns (adult-dominated in every detail). The group was noisy as it entered the room, continued to be a "nuisance" by shooting rubber bands, passing notes, and carrying on other such activities, even after the teacher had called for order. This same group then went to Miss Smith's room. They chatted comfortably as they came into the room, took their places, and began small-group committee work before the teacher entered. Remember that this is the same group in all three situations. Evidently the pattern of expectation was functioning even beyond immediate teacher control.

One alarming aspect of this observation is the realization of how easily a group adjusts to teacher expectation. This indication of teacher power, even *in absentia,* gives us pause. It underlines the need for teachers to be clear in regard to their own expectations of control and to realize the power they wield.

We feel that there is a place for further investigation in this area of group expectation. As we have indicated, we tried role-playing in a very limited way and found it unsatisfactory as a means of determining expectation, probably because of cultural influences. We attempted some cautious discussion with pupils, but felt that this approach was dangerous as it might tend to alienate pupils from their teachers. There is need to find other means of studying this problem.

—trouble for teachers

We do know that variations in pattern, and consequent variation in expectancy of pupils, may lead to friction among teachers. As we have indicated, the rigid-control pattern based on authority results in docile compliance if the expectation is autocracy, but may lead to hostility against the teacher if the group has ideas of its own about self-management. Thus, in a school where all teachers exert rigid adult rule, where pupils have no opportunity to learn the possibilities of self-management, the docility of the group is more easily maintained. If docility is our objective, it is clear how it can be achieved.

We find that there are teachers who complain because other teachers "put ideas into pupils' heads." It is true some freedom of self-management makes the authoritarian pattern more difficult to impose. The situation is reciprocal, however, though less obvious in reverse. The teacher who allows self-management to the group finds it more difficult to use such a pattern if pupils have come from an authoritarian situation. There seems to be a certain amount of pent-up energy, frequently unspent in the classroom where adult authority is imposed, which must find release. Unless acceptable means for release are found, even the most democratic teacher is in for difficulty.

—release of tension

A psychologist once remarked that he could tell the type of school (the type of interaction pattern employed) by watching the children come from the building at the end of the day. If pupils marched out in lines, and then burst forth with wild energy in yells and running, he knew, he said, that there had not been opportunity for release of energy during the school day. If, on the other hand, pupils tumbled out with normal exuberance but no wild outburst, he felt that normal release had been offered

TENSIONS MUST BE RELEASED.

during the day. To some extent, this same criterion might be applied as pupils move from classroom to classroom. The democratic teacher has a more difficult time if the pupils come from an obedience-pattern room where no normal release is offered. As we have said, this points to the need for every teacher to understand what he is doing to his group, and what has happened to his group during previous periods; but further, it points to the need for teachers to meet, as groups, to discuss the patterns of interaction they are using and the way the patterns may be modified in terms of goals for group living.

—transition

As the heading of this section implies, the expectation of the group may influence the appropriateness of the pattern to be used. A sudden shift of pattern, without a shift in expectation, may lead to confusion. Many a teacher, with good intentions, has tried to swing from the one point on the pendulum's arc to the other. When the group reacts, in expectation, to a prior pattern while the teacher tries to employ another pattern, trouble is ahead. We need to know more about transitions and how we may shift group expectation as the pattern is changed.

GROUP CLIMATE

As was indicated in the previous section, we believe the interaction pattern employed by teachers is a dominant factor in determining group reaction. Yet, as we studied, we were made aware that other factors were in operation. Such factors as teacher attitudes, common goals, common experiences, realism of goals, and general arrangements of the school could be important in determining the group reaction.

Such factors as these may determine the general group climate, that is, the emotional tone of group interaction. This climate is a part of the group reaction to the situation. The term "group morale" is frequently applied to the reaction of a group to its climate.

We recognize that patterns of interaction and climate are interdepend-ent. An appropriate pattern may create a favorable climate. We believe we have evidence that a high type of interaction is usually accompanied by favorable climate; yet, seemingly inexplicably, a poor pattern may be accompanied by favorable climate too. We tried to analyze this reaction and found such interesting suggestions as that a kind teacher can "get by" with use of a rigid adult-rule pattern, the pupils being more responsive to kindness than to pattern; that a failure experience of a group may negate a favorable pattern, killing motivation for self-management, the failure being more dominant than the pattern.

Obviously, then, factors other than the pattern are in operation. Unless these are recognized, a teacher may be thwarted in attempting to shift the interaction pattern he employs.

Teacher Attitude

Of all factors other than those inherent in the pattern itself, the general attitude of the teacher seems to hold greatest importance. As suggested above, a kind teacher may employ a rigid adult-control pattern and yet retain the affection and respect of pupils. Probably each of us can recall such a teacher, who dominated the classroom but through force of personality gave us to understand he was "with" us. When we ask adults, or children too for that matter, to describe their favorite teacher, they frequently describe such a teacher. The implication, erroneously drawn we believe, is that the interaction pattern was favorable. "My favorite teacher made us mind," "She was strict," "He wouldn't take any monkey business." As we have said, we believe that this is not a sanction of the interaction pattern but an indication that general attitude may transcend pattern. The master teacher not only uses a favorable pattern but is able to transmit to his pupils his faith in them (I believe in you. I like you. I want to help you). How this faith is transmitted needs further investigation, but of this we are convinced: it cannot be simulated. Children and young people seem to be amazingly sensitive to this quality, quickly sensing hypocrisy or sincerity.

Through our observations we are led to believe that the means of showing affection used by the sincere teacher vary with the maturity of the children. (The insincere teacher may use all the "tricks" and still not convince the group.) The teacher of young children seems to make use of tone of voice and physical contact to express affection (hug, pat on back, soothing tone in expressing appreciation), while the secondary school teacher uses more subtle methods, ranging from non-verbal expression of pleasure in the company of an individual to verbalization of respect for behavior or work product. Again, this is an area which requires further investigation. By whatever means affection or approval is transmitted, however, the teacher who can let a group know that he is "with" it, who will "stick by" even if mistakes are made, has control beyond that of the teacher who gives the impression of being on the lookout for mistakes which call for reprimand. The implication for certain types of "discipline" are clear.

Common Ground

It has been our observation that a group which starts with a realization of common ground in common interests and goals has achieved a more favorable climate than a disintegrated group. It is interesting to note that there may be favorable climate in a group united in its hostility—against the teacher, against the school, or against society itself. In the classroom such a situation may be very uncomfortable for the teacher, but pleasant for the group. We quickly add, however, that this teacher has little chance to teach, in the broadest sense, for although the climate may be favorable, there is no teacher leadership. Moreover, there may be climate favored by the group when it is united in aggression against a scapegoat, against an idea, or against a common enemy. It is easy for a teacher to yield to the temptation to exploit such unity, in the hope of leading to good climate. On the other hand, a wise teacher may see the opportunity for developing group goals as a means of creating a favorable climate and contributing to learning.

Common Experience

An interesting aspect of group climate is the influence of common experience. Common success or common failure may make a profound impression on a group, but there are few experiences more interesting than being present when a group discovers it can do more as a group than it can as individuals.

Miss Baxter had been trying all semester to develop a climate of group feeling, by helping the group toward group goals, trying to establish self-management, and similar means, with but nominal success. Then came the election of officers of the student council and the concomitant campaigning. The group, a tenth grade, which had felt rejected because new to the high school, found itself bombarded with campaign propaganda. It discovered it had position, force, and influence in the political structure of the school. Almost spontaneously, or so it seemed, the group achieved unity in order to wield its power effectively. Another tenth grade group, however, with a teacher less interested in group living, found the election just another disintegrating factor. It split into factions and subfactions, warring among themselves. Miss Baxter's seemingly ineffectual attempts to develop group feeling found flower in an experience which was initiated by the group, but to which her earlier efforts had contributed. The line between unity and disunity is thin, yet carefully drawn in terms of previous as well as current experiences of the group.

Realism of Goals

Common goals may provide unity, but if they are beyond attainment, these same goals are disintegrating. A seventh grade group decided it would win the baseball pennant of its school. If they had been realistic, they would have known that seventh graders had little chance to attain this goal in competition with more mature groups; that they might better have aspired to winning the seventh grade championship. Nothing daunted, however, they clung to their goal, feeling considerable unity as a group while the goal was held. Once it was recognized that the goal was beyond attainment (realization coming through the hard fact of defeat) the group disintegrated, breaking into subgroups warring among themselves.

A twelfth grade group aspired to remake the political machine of the community. Strong in their conviction of right, the group had amazing unity, until, confronted with the hard fact that political change comes slowly and is not necessarily swayed by enthusiasts for right, they broke into disunited factions.

A fifth grade group, fired with zeal, decided to write a history of the world for the edification of all future fifth grade groups. The aspiration may have been noble, but it was not long before they realized that its goal was unattainable. The disillusionment led to dissolution of the group.

A teacher interested in developing a unified group may have to assume responsibility for helping a group set its goals within the realm of possibility of accomplishment.

Whole-School Pattern

In a study of group interaction, the relation of any one group to the whole-school pattern cannot be overlooked. Even in an elementary school where a teacher may be the sole adult leader of his group, the patterns of other groups are an influence. Children discuss such matters on the playground. "Miss Smith lets us talk about what we do on Saturdays." "Miss Brown won't let us talk to each other at all. We can talk

A GOOD GROUP APPRECIATES INDIVIDUAL DIFFERENCES.

only when we've held up our hands and are called on." Discussions at home, particularly those involving older or younger brothers or sisters attending the same school, help spread news from room to room. Obviously, the situation is complicated when a youngster is a member of a group which meets several teachers, as is the case in most secondary schools. "What the school stands for" may be a composite of various patterns, or of the dominant patterns of certain teachers.

Certain school-wide practices, such as those involving punishment or reward patterns, are a strong influence, we believe, in setting group climate. Practices which give recognition only to athletics (a means often available to boys only) condone and encourage "spectator" status or the finding of other means to recognition, such as having a reputation for wide sex experience or for being the "meanest" guy in school. Practices of academic recognition, such as reports to parents based on arbitrarily assigned grade accomplishment, or honor rolls, may have similar results. So may assignment to groups based on academic achievement or intelligence quotient.

[49]

Individual teachers in a school which condones or encourages such practices have a much more difficult time than do those in schools dedicated to democratic living. Realizing this added handicap, we want to say, however, that even teachers in such schools can do much to improve the group living within their groups. The degree of prestige given by the teacher to these school-wide control patterns is a powerful determinant of how seriously they are taken by the group. A teacher who makes little of a school-wide honor roll has, we believe, a far better chance to create good group living than does the teacher who makes much of such a device.

On the other hand, the school which through school-wide practices promotes democratic ways of living gives the individual teacher considerable support. When a group can say, "But it's important that we be careful how we behave on the bus, so we won't hurt the school's reputation," there is indicated an all-school awareness extending beyond competition among individuals or school groups.

GROUP CULTURE

A phenomenon of group interaction which cannot be overlooked is that of group culture. We attempted to approach a study of groups as we would that of a foreign culture, or as an anthropologist would study a group, and found much to indicate the presence of a distinctive culture for each group. One thing we discovered early in this study was the need for us, as investigators, to free ourselves of our own cultural limitations, so that we could study youth cultures without applying the label "right" or "wrong." Frequently, we found the cultural manifestations to be neither right nor wrong but merely different, though there were some that we found difficult to condone (and thus found difficult to recognize). As with the "gotta" situations discussed in relation to determining group goals ("Don't fight unless you gotta"), we had to learn to think objectively if we were to study the situation.

Below we report a few results of our observations as examples of what teachers studying group behavior may learn to see as they observe the cultures of their groups.

Language

We found peculiar language patterns in every group. "Coined" words were popular in the early elementary grades. Moreover, with some groups particular words carried a connotation far beyond their usual meaning. For example, in a group of fourth and fifth graders to be said to have "cooties and fleas" was felt to be the ultimate in insults, and evidently had nothing to do with the presence or absence of the insects named. "Secret" languages or written codes seemed to be popular with middle elementary grade children, while knowing the latest "jive talk" was essential to the junior or senior high school pupil. Each group seemed to develop its own pattern of acceptance or rejection of certain "naughty" or "dirty" words. Trying out such words to discover the reactions of adults or peers to them seemed to be a form of self-testing for children of early and middle elementary grades.

Some of the words which youngsters were interested in "trying out" are not printable, but we take as example a mild sample of vocabulary. Mildred was intrigued with the word "puke." Where she had learned it we do not know, but it seemed to hold a fascination for her. According to accounts of her mother and of Mildred she had used it at home and had been reprimanded. Her mother said, in an interview with the teacher, "We don't know where she learns such language, but we just won't tolerate it in our home." Mildred, describing the incident to her teacher, maintained, "All I said was, 'The way Billy acts makes me puke.' All the kids say that when they don't like a person—but you'd think I'd committed some sort of crime."

Learning the delicate amenities of language in social intercourse must be extremely difficult for boys and girls. The teacher who can help guide young people in the matter of language which, however descriptive, is or is not acceptable in polite society has a job on his hands.

Particularly delicate is the job of teachers who want to help youngsters achieve social acceptance beyond that of their parents and their immediate social environment. One teacher reports, "My youngsters can as easily call each other 'bastard' and 'son of a bitch' as you or I would say 'naughty boy' or 'mischievous child.' I know they hear these phrases at home. I know they'll get in trouble when they use this vocabulary outside their immediate circle, yet I hate to seem prudish to them."

It seems evident that there are occasions when a teacher, recognizing the culture of the group, may wish to bring to their consciousness the consequences of their acts in a larger society. To achieve this end without seeming to ridicule the culture of the group and their families requires a high degree of rapport between teacher and group. In general, it would seem that the teacher who finds himself in a group of a different culture must learn to "take it" without being shocked until rapport has been established. Then, and only then, if he feels it desirable for the sake of the group, he may be able to influence shifts in the language, recognizing that the culture pattern may be commendable while the language is unacceptable in the wider society.

One approach may be for the teacher to suggest that just as one behaves differently in different places, so some types of language are not appropriate in school or other public places. Many children understand that it is appropriate to clap at a show but not in church and can apply the analogy to language. If a teacher can convey this idea of appropriateness, then she can help a child develop socially acceptable language habits without seeming to disparage the child's family.

Other Forms of Symbolism

Evidently youth cultures are highly sensitive to symbolism. Particularly significant with young people, as with adults, are symbols dealing with belonging. If bottle-top caps are the vogue, then every boy must have such a cap if he is to feel he belongs. If dirty saddle shoes are a mark of group membership, then every girl will strive to achieve dirty saddle shoes, even if she has to make her new shoes dirty by smearing them with mud. Attaching importance to school songs, school colors, and school cheers is an indication of a dawning group awareness and a desire to express this awareness in symbolism.

Initiation and Other Rituals

Initiation ceremonies, both formal and informal, were popular in the youth cultures we observed. Initiation ceremonies ranged from "trial by fighting" on the playground dominated by a group of sixth grade boys to elaborate ceremonies of fraternities or sororities. These ceremonies have two things in common, however. One, the initiate must prove his power to "take it" in terms of the group's values; and two, the initiate must acquaint himself with the lore of the group. The ability to "take it" may be physical (it often is) or psychological (willingness to take taunting, teasing, etc.). Acceptance of group lore may mean no more than knowing who is "boss," but it may involve performance of elaborate rituals or memorizing names of national officers, etc. Organized youth groups, realizing this aspect of culture, often provide codes or laws which must be learned before the individual is admitted to the group.

Rituals may range from simple "spit on the ball" and "cross my heart" to elaborate affairs involving mastery of a "language" and a secret handshake.

Prestige-giving Factors

We found a wide range of prestige-giving factors, from being able to spit the farthest to receiving the most bids for the senior prom. Whatever the qualifications may be for a particular group, they evidently are extremely powerful. Closely associated are areas of pride, fear, or shame. The group may sanction the pride of one who is brave enough to "sass" the teacher, or it may understand the fear of the high school girl that she may not be asked for a date, or the shame of the youngster who is thought younger than his years.

Codes, Rules, Play Patterns

Most groups that have any degree of unity hold rigid ideas of acceptable conduct for their members. Even young children have strong feelings about play patterns and will exclude from the group the individual who will not "play fair" according to their standards. Older children are no less rigid in enforcement of their "rules." In one group, a girl who did not know that as the most recent member of the group she was supposed to provide a nickel for the juke box was excluded from the corner drugstore "sorority."

Significance of Group Culture

A study of the culture of children and youth is fascinating. That there is such a culture for various age groups and for each individual group is clearly evident. We feel, however, that the study of culture does not serve our purpose unless it is seen as a means to further understanding of a group for the purpose of providing more appropriate experiences for its members. This understanding, we believe, is attainable; and it is also, we believe, the duty of every teacher to acquire it.

We have given considerable attention to group goals and to the need of the individual "to belong." Whether self-determined or determined by home mores, the culture of the group is an important, though often unconscious, aspect of group goals. The individual who is unaware of the form of the group culture may be ostracized by the group.

Thus, we believe, it is of great importance that a teacher be aware of group cultures. Without this awareness he will be less able to help the group bring its goals to the level of consciousness for examination and modification, if this is desired. He will be less able to help the non-accepted child find acceptance in the group. He will be less able to participate with the group in desirable goal-setting. In other words, unless he understands the culture of the group, he will be less able to select experiences wisely for boys and girls, less able to develop a curriculum suited to their needs, interests, and capacities.

We have indicated that we see significance in language and other forms of symbolism, in initiation and other prestige factors, and in group codes, rules, and play patterns. No doubt there are a number of other aspects of group culture which could be identified and described. Recognizing the significance of group culture in influencing group behavior, we believe the understanding of this factor cannot be overemphasized. Other teachers could make a significant contribution to education if they would study group cultures and report their findings to their professional colleagues.

IN SUMMARY

In conclusion, we would like to reaffirm our belief in a series of statements made in this chapter.

1. Techniques of group living must be learned, but technique without understanding is hollow and meaningless. Boys and girls can develop insights into the principles involved in group living.

2. Behavior is caused. We need to realize this if we are to be able to help children as individuals or as groups. Boys and girls, too, need to understand this concept. We are convinced that they can understand it, and use it constructively in their planning.

3. In putting to work the concept of behavior as caused, we need to look to the situations and experiences which cause group behavior.

4. The interaction pattern with which the teacher sets the stage for group living is a major factor in determining the nature of group living. It is possible to identify the types of such patterns and analyze the resultant group reaction to each of them.

5. The appropriateness of each type of interaction pattern is determined by a wide range of factors. In order to employ the appropriate pattern, teachers must be aware of these determinants and judge patterns in terms of them.

6. An aspect of group living is the group climate, which is influenced

by such factors as teacher attitudes, common experiences, and the whole-school pattern.

7. Every group creates its own group culture, which must be studied and understood by teachers if they are to help the individual members and the group as a whole.

8. The need for further study in this area of group interaction is an imperative if we are to learn how to develop good schools and good citizens for our democracy. We hope our initial attempts may serve as a "call to study" for teachers.

III

Group Goals

"My records show that you haven't turned in a single one of your book reviews for English," said Miss Froman.

"Yes, ma'am," answered Marie.

"You know what that means, don't you? You'll fail this course unless those reports are turned in before the end of next week."

"Yes, ma'am," answered Marie.

"Well," thought Miss Froman as Marie went out the door, "at least we're seeing eye-to-eye now."

But were they?

As she closed the door behind her, Marie was thinking of the date she was to have with Bob, the basketball captain. She re-counted lovingly the number of dates she had had—seven in three weeks.

Seeing eye-to-eye? Miss Froman's goal was to help a girl whom she liked and respected to graduate from high school. Marie's goal was, in general, to be popular, and, specifically, to have more dates with Bob. Each was acting in terms of a goal important to her.

Groups as well as individuals operate in terms of goals. The drive to action is furnished by goal-seeking. The appropriateness of behavior is determined by what is judged by the group to be the best way to reach the goal.

If, in trying to reach its goal, a group meets a barrier, it may try battering-ram tactics and attempt to destroy the barrier. Or it may detour, and try to go around the barrier. If neither battering-ram nor detour is successful, the group may react to being thwarted by finding a substitute barrier against which to take out its aggression. Or it may aggress against itself.

[56]

GROUP GOALS DETERMINE BEHAVIOR.

We sometimes speak of a thwarted person as "going to pieces." When a group is thwarted, it may literally go to pieces, lose all semblance of a unit, break into subgroups, gangs, cliques, pal-patterns. When this happens, the teacher has trouble on his hands. Not only has the powerful group drive been lost, but innumerable inter-personal and intra-subgroup difficulties arise. So long as the group was a group, such intra-group difficulties could be handled as a group problem. Now, with no unified group through which to work, each difficulty must be handled separately.

No doubt you have known teachers who seem to spend their whole time unraveling little difficulties which seem to be endless. Most teachers who find themselves in this position revert to "iron-hand" techniques. They take the law unto themselves, thus depriving themselves of the power to direct and use group drive. These are the teachers who are likely to be loud in their claims that democratic methods and group planning won't work. They are right in a sense. They won't work unless the group has developed group goals and the concomitant drive to attain them. Without

[57]

such goals, so-called democratic methods and group planning are hollow forms—mere mechanical techniques.

GOALS IN ACTION

Let's look at an example of how group goals operate.

Longfellow School decided to go all-out for a paper-collecting drive. An elaborate system of inter-class competition was organized. Miss Thompson's room, a fifth grade class that had never come out very well in other types of competition, such as those involving honor roll scholarship or attendance records, saw in the paper-collecting competition an opportunity to show the world (their world being bounded largely by Longfellow School) that they were important people. We have, then, as diagramed in Figure 1, a fifth grade group (A) in its field of operation (F) striving to achieve a definite goal (G), the winning of the paper-collection competition.

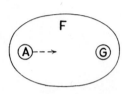

FIGURE 1

F—Field of operation
A—5th grade group
G—Goal (winning paper collection drive)
—→Drive toward goal

—enthusiastic action

The group started to collect paper with vim, vigor, and enthusiasm. In spite of the efforts of the group, however, the big chart in the front hall indicated that the sixth graders were ahead, were collecting more paper. This increased the efforts of group members for a time, but finally they realized that the sixth grade group was a major threat to their success. The sixth graders became a barrier (B) to achievement of their goal (Figure 2). Obviously (to fifth grade members) something must be done about the situation. The solution seemed easy. The fifth graders waylaid the sixth graders one evening after school and told them that if they didn't quit bringing in so much paper they'd "lick the living daylights out of them." There ensued a terrific fight that resulted in a number of black eyes and bloody noses. In other words, the group took direct action against the barrier to achievement of the goal. Unfortunately (from the standpoint of the fifth graders, for they were getting along pretty well in the battle), the principal came on the scene and broke up the fight. He got to the bottom of

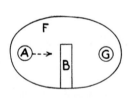

FIGURE 2

F—Field of operation
A—5th grade group
G—Goal
—→Drive toward goal (fight)
B—Barrier to goal (6th grade group)

the matter and warned the fifth graders that they would be eliminated from the competition if they persisted in such methods. This was a terrible thought. Their goal was endangered. Evidently (so far as they could see) direct attainment was impossible because of the barrier created by the sixth graders. It was not possible to remove the barrier, because if they did so, with the means they saw, the goal would be taken out of reach by action of the principal.

—ways around barriers

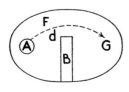

FIGURE 3

F—Field of operation
A—5th grade group
G—Goal
d---→Detour action toward goal (stealing)
B—Barrier to goal (6th grade group)

After a series of playground conferences, the group saw the possibility of another way out. They developed a systematic plan for stealing paper—from newsstands, from smaller children, from whatever source they could find. In Figure 3 we see the stealing campaign as a detour action (d) around the barrier (B) toward the goal (G). All went well until one of the fourth graders, robbed of his papers, made a tearful report to his teacher, who in turn reported it to Miss Thompson, the fifth

grade teacher. Miss Thompson did some investigating, aided by one fifth grader who was not well accepted by the rest of the group and, feeling left out of the excitement, did not share in the group goal. In fact, the isolated youngster had a private goal, to show the group that he had strength of his own, even if rejected by them. He used "telling on the group" as his detour means to attain his private goal. Miss Thompson, now aware of what the group was up to, severely reprimanded it and said that if it did not change its ways immediately, she would report the matter to the principal, who would eliminate the group from the contest. Now the group found that there was a barrier, the teacher (B_2) across the detour path to the goal (Figure 4). The drive toward the goal seemed utterly blocked.

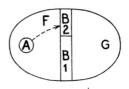

FIGURE 4

F—Field of operation
A—5th grade group
G—Goal
B^1—Barrier (6th grade group)
B^2—Barrier 2 (teacher)
---→Action toward goal (thwarted)

—disintegration

There was some feeble attempt to show aggression toward the teacher by doing those things which the group members knew would annoy her. But the group found that this was about as effective as hitting one's head

against a stone wall. There might be some personal satisfaction in the
hitting, but it didn't get one anywhere. Made unattainable (or so it
seemed to the group), the group goal lost all attraction (lost power
to create drive to action). With no group goal,
there was nothing to create group unity, and the
social cement of the group crumbled (Figure 5).
The group disintegrated into subgroups (A_1, A_2,
A_3, etc.), each with individual goals, often conflicting, which led to intra-group hostilities. Inter-
personal frictions flared within the subgroups, and
finally the subgroups, too, disintegrated, leaving
a collection of frustrated individuals, hostile to
each other and to their teacher. Miss Thompson
found she was dealing with an exceedingly "difficult" class.

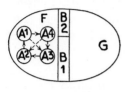

FIGURE 5

F—Field of operation
A_1, A_2, A_3, A_4—Sub-
    groups of original A_1
    (5th grade group)
G—Goal: unattainable
    because of barriers
B_1 and B_2—Barriers
--→Inter-personal friction

What Does It Mean?

What is the meaning of this illustration of group action? Are there implications for examining the means schools use to set goals? For knowing
the need areas of groups which lead them to accept goals? For helping
groups find acceptable detours to action? For providing substitute goals
on occasion?

As the mentor of the group, the teacher may easily become a barrier
and, unknowingly, cause the group to adopt unpredictable and sometimes
antisocial detour action. If, on the other hand, the teacher understands
the goal-seeking behavior of groups, is aware of
how goals are set, how drive operates, how group
unity is created or destroyed, he has the key to
giving direction to group living.

FIGURE 6

F—Field of operation
A—1st grade group
G—Goal (picnic)
--→Action toward goal

A Rained-out Picnic

Miss Brown's first grade group (A) had planned
a picnic (G) (Figure 6). A picnic may be a strong
goal for any first grade group, but it was particularly strong for the children in Miss Brown's room.
They lived in congested areas of a large city, and seldom had an opportunity to see trees or to roll on the grass. The picnic was an important
event in their lives. Miss Brown had tried to warn the group of the
awful contingency of bad weather, but she knew her warnings were

weak compared with the strong drive the children felt toward going on the picnic.

—barriers happen

Her fears were realized. On the day of the picnic the skies were definitely threatening (B) (Figure 7). In her judg-
ment, the group should not be taken to the park.
The risk to the health of group members who
did not have adequate rain equipment was more
than she dared assume. She might have put the
matter up to the group for decision (she would
have done so if the group had been older or
more mature), but she knew the picnic-drive was
stronger than the health-drive, and the group's
judgment was not sufficiently developed to make
a rational decision. She knew, too, she might go

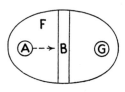

FIGURE 7

F—Field of operation
A—1st grade group
G—Goal (picnic)
B—Barrier (teacher)
--→Action toward goal

through the forms of group planning and manipulate the setting in such
a way that it seemed to be the consensus of the group to stay home. But
Miss Brown knew that such manipulation eventually destroys respect for
group action, and this respect was one of the major objectives she held
for her group. She felt that this was a case in
which it was necessary for her to make the decision for the group rather than leave it to the children themselves.

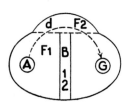

FIGURE 8

F1—Field of operation
F2—Field extended (in
time)
A—1st grade group
G—Goal
B1, 2—Barriers (teacher
and weather)
d---→Detour action (in
time)

—making decisions

Determining which areas are appropriate for
group decision and which for teacher decision is
one of the toughest of a teacher's jobs. Miss Brown
was well aware that it is easy for a teacher to be
overly cautious, thus restricting the learning of the
group. For this reason, she did not decide to make
this decision for her group without giving the mat-
ter careful consideration. She knew it would be inevitable that when she
told the group her decision, there would be some aggression against her
as the barrier (B₂) (Figure 8) to attaining the goal, but she wanted to
indicate that the weather was also a barrier (B₁), and, most important,
she wanted the group to find both acceptable detour action (d) and substitute (G₂) goals (see Figure 9).

—positive action

When Miss Brown told the group it would not be possible to go on the picnic, she immediately asked for suggestions of what might be done instead (d). The first suggestion was: "Can't we go tomorrow?" "Yes," she replied, "if the weather lets us." This established the weather as the barrier, and (Figure 9) the passage of time was an acceptable detour. (See F_2). Other suggestions for substitute action for that day provided substitute goals (G_2), and the group decided on one which had relatively high strength for them, even though its strength was less than the picnic-drive. The group spent a reasonably profitable and happy afternoon, but Miss Brown was not surprised when there were some minor evidences of hostility toward her (B_2) by the group. She understood them, and knowing their cause did not try to place blame on the group, an action which would have elicited further hostility.

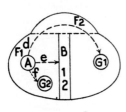

FIGURE 9

F_1—Field of operation
F_2—Field extended (in time)
A—1st grade group
G_1—Original goal (picnic)
G_2—Substitute goal
$B_{1,2}$—Barriers (teacher and weather)
d--→Detour action
e---→Action against barriers (hostility against teacher)
f--→Action toward substitute goal

No Situation Is Simple

The examples above are perhaps oversimplified. Most classroom situations are more complex, for there are likely to be cross currents of conflicting goals and other aspects of the problem. But these examples may serve to indicate the relation, as we see it, of goals to group behavior and to a teacher's responsibility.

The teacher who sees his responsibility in relation to group goals recognizes that he has a fourfold job: *first,* to learn to recognize existing group goals; *second,* to learn to participate with the group in the development of group goals; *third,* to participate with the group in achieving group goals, assuming a special role as facilitator when the situation demands; and *fourth,* to assist in resolving a situation in which group goals are in conflict.

DISCOVERING GROUP GOALS OF BOYS AND GIRLS

It is a simple matter to say that it is important to know the goals of boys and girls, and it may seem just as simple a matter to discover these goals.

Actually, we have found that it is an extremely difficult and complex job. A number of factors operate to make the job a tough one.

We Don't Know Our Goals

First, boys and girls (and adults too, perhaps) are frequently unaware of their goals. True usually of individuals, this is even more often true of groups. They may be able to state what seems to them to be their goal, but may not recognize it as but a means to a larger goal. For example, the group in Miss Thompson's room knew they wanted to win the paper-collection contest but may have been unaware that they were striving for status in their school, desire for which was intensified because of past failures in competitions for honor roll membership and attendance records. Sometimes even immediate goals are not recognized. Young children, restless on a rainy day, may say that their goal is to play outdoors. The teacher knows the goal is physical activity, a need intensified by the restriction of such activity by the weather and by parents who will not let children play outdoors in the rain.

Learned Responses Are Barriers

Second, it is difficult to learn the real goals of boys and girls because adults have taught them a series of responses. Moralistic statements, codes, or laws may be repeated by pupils either because they have learned that this is what is expected, whether they believe them or not, or because they accept them as so many words, even though they see little relation between the words and their everyday living. "Being a good boy," "being a good citizen," "loving everyone" are easy to state as goals, but are seldom if ever real goals of boys and girls. It is easy to verbalize a general ideal without understanding what it means.

Boys and Girls Are Response-Wise

Third, it is difficult to learn the goals of boys and girls because, by the time they are of school age, most of them have acquired extreme skill in concealing their goals. They have found that repeating the statements given them by adults as codes or laws saves a lot of trouble and is the easiest way out. Moreover, concealing goals may be a way of avoiding punishment. If Johnny snatches Jimmy's blocks and is asked why he did it, he is wise enough to say, "They are *my* blocks. They belong to *me*" (he knows adults have strong feelings about property rights), rather than the real goal, "I don't like him. I wanted to annoy him" (although adults

ACTIONS CAN SPEAK LOUDER THAN WORDS.

can be very annoying in action, they seem to have strong feelings against admitting it or allowing anyone else to admit it). On the secondary school level, a boy caught copying the answers to algebra problems worked out by a friend will admit to fear of failure (academic accomplishment seems to be prized by teachers and is considered a legitimate goal, though there may be a difference of opinion concerning legitimate means to this end), but not to the real goal—to play on the football team —a goal which may be thwarted if he fails in algebra (many teachers seem naively unaware of some of life's most important activities, as seen by boys, such as playing on the football team!).

MEANS OF DISCOVERING GROUP GOALS

As a means of discovering goals, we employed a variety of methods, some more fruitful than others but all revealing.

Direct Questioning: Verbal

There are many reasons why, as we noted above, it is difficult to learn the goals of boys and girls. They may not be aware of their goals; they may have learned that certain responses are acceptable; and they may have skill in concealing their real goals. When children are unaware of their goals, direct questions or discussion concerning them is futile, unless in the process of discussion boys and girls are made conscious of their goals. Sometimes it may be helpful to start with a discussion of hopes or fears. Needless to say, it is useless to attempt direct questioning or even discussion unless the degree of rapport of teacher and group is high.

A skillful teacher may help a group to verbalize its goals. We told you earlier of one such teacher who was discussing with a group of ten- and eleven-year-olds the behavior they felt they needed to practice if they were to get along well together. Responses came thick and fast. One boy suggested, "We mustn't fight." The teacher asked, "Never?" Members of the group looked gravely at one another and at the teacher, and finally someone suggested it might be wise to add the phrase, "Unless you gotta." The group then could discuss the "gotta" situations.

This group developed, over a period of a year, thirty goal areas that they hoped to achieve. Each goal was discussed and described by the group. We present these statements of goals to show both the amazing range of insights of boys and girls and to indicate the startling immaturity of concept which might escape the teacher unless he probed deeply for meanings (Not to be a coward means not to be scared of mice!).[1]

Stated Goals of Ten- and Eleven-Year-Olds

Learn to like each other
> Like each other no matter what they look like or what color they are.
> Learn not to call people names.
> Learn not to want everything your way.

Listen to other people's ideas
> If you didn't listen to other people's ideas you'd be dumb.
> Keep your ears open and your mouth closed and you will learn many things.
> Don't laugh at other people's ideas.
> Don't just use your own suggestions if the other one is better.

Be a good sport
> Don't always try to have your own way.
> Don't fight in games.
> It means not to cry when you don't get your way.
> It means when you're playing ball don't be stuck-up if you win.
> If you are a good sport you stick in the game even if it is not the game you want to play.

[1] The complete list is presented in the Appendix, pages 434 to 439, to indicate the type of thinking which can be achieved by boys and girls of this age.

Don't "act smart," "show off," or be "stuck-up"

Don't go around being mad at someone.
It means not to tease and to get along with people.
Help other people to do the right thing.
Don't think you're smart and that you're pretty.
Don't go around with your nose in the air.
Don't make silly noises or faces. Don't blow up if someone does something
you don't like.

Don't be a coward

Means not to be scared of mice.
Don't pick on little kids, then be afraid to start something with your size
and age.
Don't run away from fights.
It means not to start a fight and then run away.

Don't hurt people's feelings

Don't tease people.
Don't call people names or tell them they are awful. They may not be
awful to other people.
Don't call people "cooties" and "fleas"; it is not nice.
Means not to say that they are fat or too skinny.

Know when to be serious and when to be silly

It means if something bad happens you can feel sad.
Don't be silly all the time and don't be serious all the time.
It means to be silly where there is something to be silly about.

Have a good reason for everything you do

It means to know what you are going to do.
Don't just do things to be doing something.
Don't do something because you want to but have a reason for what you do.
Don't just do things to get attention.

Be able to think and decide for yourself

Don't do things just because your best friend does.
Don't do things because someone else told you to.
Think of your own ideas.
Don't let other people decide things for you.

Six-year-olds who were asked to state goals made comments which
led us to think that their verbalizing of goals was associated with their
dependence on adults. They tended to parrot the "do" and "don't" rules
they had heard parents and teachers express. Their statements of goals
included statements such as the following.

Stated Goals of Six-Year-Olds

Keep your hands to yourself.

Be quiet, so we can listen well and hear what people say.

Leave sand on the playground.

Color on your paper and not the tables and chairs and walls and on the buildings.

Take your turn.

Don't push.

Don't take anything that doesn't belong to you without asking.

Mind all the traffic rules.

In one sense, the statements of eighth graders were as difficult to interpret as were those of six-year-olds, for without definition it was difficult to know their meaning.

Stated Goals of Eighth Graders

The need to find out our own interests.

Learn to share equally.

Be well mannered. No showing off.

Be honest.

See both sides of the question.

Be agreeable.

Hunt for wide friendships.

In all three groups, first grade, fourth and fifth grades, and eighth grade, these lists were posted and referred to from time to time for additions and deletions. The statements gained in realism and meaning as time went on, and the boys and girls learned that the teacher would not be shocked to know what they felt to be really important.

Direct Questioning: Written

Of one thing we are confident: the goals of a group are not necessarily the sum of the goals of the individuals in the group. Group discussion, in which consensus of goals may be formulated and stated, is thus of prime importance in determining group goals. We recognized that it might be possible, however, to find clues to group goals through the study of individual responses to check lists and questionnaires. For example, when individual responses indicated that half the group felt it highly important to be a member of a club, we could use this goal as a basis of group discussion to determine the degree to which it was a group goal. For example, responses on the Check Sheet of Opportunities in Human Relations (Appendix, page 407) showed variations in types of experiences felt to be important by the different age groups. The opportunity to talk with adults engaged in various types of work was important to members of the eighth grade group, but was not among the items most frequently listed as valuable by the younger boys and girls.

Experiences felt to be most valuable by a fourth and fifth grade group and an eighth grade group are indicated in Table 1. These responses are presented not as statistical evidence of group goals but as leads to group discussion which might reveal group goals.

TABLE 1

EXPERIENCES FELT TO BE OF VALUE

Experiences (in a list of 40 items)	Number of Pupils Responding
By a Fourth and Fifth Grade Group (34)	
Work or play in a group of thirty to fifty people	21
Be a member of a club	19
Be a leader or representative of a group of people my age	19
Visit communities other than my own	19
Be a member of a group which elects its own leaders	18
Work or play with people much older than I am (5 or more years older), not including teachers or youth leaders	17
Work at home (do chores) without pay	17
By an Eighth Grade Group (32)	
Talk with adults engaged in various types of work	23
Work for pay	22
Work or play in a group of four or five people	21
Be a member of a team for some sport	21
Spend leisure time with friends of my own choice	21
Discuss with others of my age what is going on in the world	21
Observe adults engaged in various types of work	20
Work or play in a group of ten or twelve people	20

It is interesting to note that there is no overlapping of items considered important by these two age groups.

Answers to the question, "What three things would you like to improve about yourself" (Check Sheet of Opportunities in Human Relations, Appendix, page 407) also reveal goals, direct or implied. Table 2 gives the free responses of two groups—eighth graders and fourth and fifth graders.

Table 2

"Things I Want to Improve about Myself" (Free Responses)
Eighth Grade (32)

GIRLS   BOYS

Personal Attributes (56 responses)

Looks (8)*	Personality (4)
Personality (7)	Brains (3)
Temper (4)	Temper (3)
Posture	Looks (2)
Cattiness	Saving money (2)
Shyness	Not argue (2)
Habits	Clothes (2)
Sports	Sports (2)
Complexion	Manners (2)
Brains	Keep my mouth shut
Clothes	Have good ideas
Conversation	Health
	Work habits
	Be a gentleman
	Act right

Inter-personal Relations (15 responses)

Get along with people (3)	Make friends (2)
Make friends (3)	Be popular
Get along	Understand people
with Dad	
with Mother	
with my sister	
Be a leader	
Be in Sam's gang	

Academic Achievement (5 responses)

Studies (2)	English
School work	Studies

General (3 responses)

Everything	Everything
	Myself

* Numbers in parentheses indicate number of pupils making responses.

FOURTH AND FIFTH GRADE* (34)

Personal Attributes (14 responses)

Not to have a feeling to run in the hall
Not want to talk so much
I want to get smarter
I would like to be interested more
Wish I were pretty and weren't so shy
Not be so shy
Not to be so talkative and so silly
Be more considerate
Be polite to people I don't like
Be a better athlete
I would like to be more intelligent
Wish I wasn't so shy
Be just as smart as others
I want not to be so bossy and not to tease people

Inter-personal Relations (23 responses)

Get along with my sister better
Make more friends
Have people like me
I want to be nice to people I don't like
Don't fight so much
Get along with people
Have more friends
Being liked by more people
Could make friends better
Improve the way the kids feel about me
I would like to be well liked
Share more
Like people more
Learning to do more with people
I want people to like me
I want to have more friends
I want to make friends
Be more interested in people
How to make more friends
I want to be understood by more people
I want to be liked
I don't want to be disliked
To learn about other people; to learn how they live

* Sex differentiation was less marked in this group than in the older group, so differentiation was not made in the tabulations.

Skills (9 responses)

Play ball better
Draw better
Improve my practicing (piano)
Improve my ice skating
Improve my sleeping
Improve my classwork
I want to remember things better
Keep neater; keep my hair combed; keep my shirt in
Improve my sports and my schoolwork

—it's important to be liked

Inter-personal relations rank high in both groups. Moreover, we believe it is probable that the items listed as "personal attributes" of eighth graders are largely reflections of desires for more satisfactory interpersonal relations. The girl who wants to improve her conversation and the boy who worries about "looks" are interested in their group status. The same may be true of items mentioned by fourth and fifth graders, such as "Wish I were pretty and weren't so shy," or "Be just as smart as others." Even the item "Keep my shirt in" may be of this category.

To the extent that goals are set by thwarted need, responses to questions such as those of the California Test of Personality[1] may give leads. For example, in one first grade group, twenty-five pupils out of a group of thirty-seven answered "Yes" to the question, "Do you have fewer friends than other children?" Thirteen answered "Yes" to the question, "Do you wish you could live in some other home?" Nine answered "Yes" to the question, "Do you think that some teachers do not like the children?"

In a fourth and fifth grade group of thirty-one pupils, thirteen answered "Yes" to the question, "Do you often think that nobody likes you?" Sixteen answered "Yes" to the question, "Do you often think about such things as failing in your studies, losing money, losing your parents, or dying?" Eleven said "No" when asked, "Do you think that boys and girls like you as well as they should?"

—my three wishes

Indications of goals implied in statements of wishes and interests may be found on forms such as the Springfield Interest Finder (Appendix, page 418). A first grade group indicated the wishes given in Table 3.

[1] California Test of Personality, California Test Bureau, Los Angeles, Calif.

TABLE 3

WISHES OF FIRST GRADE GROUP (FREE RESPONSES)

Wishes	Number Responding (group of 38)
Toys	31
A bicycle	7
A bigger or better house	5
Little sister or brother	4
To be a dancer	4
To do better in school	3
To be a better help to mother	3

Other wishes were for clothing (3), a pony (3), a car (3), a dog (2), a better report card (2), to do better in reading (2), and so on, to "hope my cat has kittens."

A fourth and fifth grade group, more sophisticated in ways of the academic world but no less materialistic than the first graders, expressed these wishes:

TABLE 4

WISHES OF FOURTH AND FIFTH GRADE GROUP (FREE RESPONSES)

Wishes	Number Responding (group of 32)
Better grades	8
A horse	7
Riches	6
A bicycle	5
A well dad	4

Some children wished for change of residence: to a farm (3); to another house (3). Others had wishes for everything from open-heel-and-toe shoes to "to be lucky" and "to be twenty years old." [1]

We found that statements of hopes, fears, and wishes—particularly those based on individual reactions, anonymously reported to the group by the teacher—could be a significant means to revelation of group goals. A teacher using this means for determining goals will want, of course, to make sure that a few of the more vocal individuals are not dominating the group discussion. However, having obtained prior evidence from written responses, he can inject these ideas for discussion if they are not

---

[1] For evidence that these types of wishes are typical of children of these ages, see *Children's Interests*, Arthur T. Jersild, Ruth J. Tasch, *et al.* Horace Mann–Lincoln Institute of School Experimentation. Teachers College, Columbia University, Bureau of Publications, 1949.

mentioned by group members. He can test out with the group individual statements of hopes, fears, wishes, or goals. Often, we found that the verbalization of an idea by the teacher—thus indicating to the group that it was a legitimate goal (while otherwise it might be thought "silly" or "naughty")—led to consensus of the group, although the idea was originally expressed by only a few individuals.

STUDYING SOURCES OF GOALS

Not only is it necessary to know goals if we are to direct group action, but further, if we are to help pupils grow and learn, we must be aware of how goals are developed and how this development is influenced. It may be said that a major purpose in education is to help individuals and groups examine their goals and, when it is desirable, modify them. In the light of goal-seeking behavior, we might well define, as an important aspect of the process of education, the development of evolving goals. Moreover, as we suggested earlier, a responsibility of democratic society today may be to re-examine and re-assess its goals and means to goal development—and thus educate itself to meet its current needs.

It's Not Easy to Determine Sources

Despite the importance attached to the understanding and directing of goals, there seems to have been little conscious effort on the part of schools to examine group goals. The simplest explanation for lack of study in this area may be that little attention has been given to group life. It seems to be assumed that the group goal is the sum of individual goals, which is not necessarily true.

Another explanation may be that it is assumed that goals are absolutes, to be transmitted to boys and girls by purely intellectual means. There seems to be evidence that this is but *one* way in which goals are set.

A third possible explanation is that some teachers may not realize the relation of goals to behavior. Even assuming that goals are absolutes, such as those we attempt to teach directly (goals of democracy, for example) or those we teach indirectly (by extolling the Horatio Alger story or giving prestige to "white collar" jobs, for example), what have we done to indicate the relation of long-term goals to immediate goals, such as learning to spell "cat" or learning to solve an algebraic equation? We have tended to assume that the goals of the group are those we should like the group to have, and to operate from that premise.

Another reason why little study has been given to this area may well be that it is exceedingly difficult to examine. As has been indicated, it is not easy to identify existing goals, and it is even harder to track down their origins. However, using the means described in the preceding section, we have attempted such a study. The results presented here are tentative and not fully substantiated, but they seem to us to be useful as working hypotheses.

As we worked with pupils and examined our records, it seemed that there are three major sources of goals: (a) identification; (b) unsatisfied basic needs and interests; and (c) reason.

Identification

By "identification" is meant a psychological merging of self with another person or with a group. This does not necessarily imply physical membership in the group. One may psychologically identify one's self with a person or group, yet have no direct interaction with that person or group. Moreover, membership in a group is not necessarily accompanied by identification. One may hold group membership in one group, yet be psychologically identified with another.

Identification, the psychological merging of one's self with another person or group, seems to carry with it the acceptance of the goals of the person or group: "I am he; therefore his goals are mine." It is difficult to present evidence to support this hypothesis (that identification is a source of goals) for when an individual (or group) was pushed further, he began to rationalize. When the argument he presented was in defense of the *group* or *person*, we felt that evidence of identification was clear. But when he defended the *ideas* held by the group or person, it was difficult to know whether he was identifying himself with the group or person, or rationally accepting the ideas. Thus, although we find it difficult to produce objective evidence, it seems to us that identification is an extremely important determinant of individual and group goals.

—with peers

The most easily studied area of identification in schools is that of pupils with peer groups. Tom, going from an elementary school to a junior high school, observed that one of the rites of initiation was the smearing of lipstick on the boys' faces. Somehow or other he was overlooked in the play and received no lipstick daubs. But he was determined to be identified with his group. After lunch, Tom appeared with lipstick on his face, self-daubed. This act was utterly meaningless except as a symbol of identification. The study of peer culture and its influence yields many examples. Group experience, such as joint planning or joint creative experience, seems to intensify the identification of the individual with the group. Emotionally tinged experiences, such as group success, group failure, or aspects of the situation which threaten the group, as in intergroup competition, have the same effect.

—with teachers

Identification with the teacher or other adult leader occurs frequently. When the teacher is kind and rapport is good, this identification seems to be easy. It is especially evident among young children transferring identification with mother to teacher, and among adolescents trying to free themselves from family domination.

—with family

As would be expected, identification with parents and family is strong. Young children, particularly, cling to this source of goals. Transition from this identification to identification with others is easy if the goals of the family are similar to those of the school and to those of the wider society. However, there is real trouble ahead for the youngster who finds that there is conflict between the goals of home and school. What should a teacher do when, during a discussion of the evils of over-use of alcoholic beverages, Johnny says: "My Dad says it's all right to drink. He says a good drunkard is better than a wet blanket. He knows, for my Dad gets drunk every Saturday night"?

—with heroes

It seems that all youngsters, but particularly boys of upper elementary school age, find pleasure in identifying themselves with heroes. Superman, Joe Louis, Dillinger—whoever personifies the qualities admired by the youngster or his group—become the idols of the day, and the goals of the heroes become the goals of the group.

—with the wider society

"I'm a Methodist," "I'm a Boy Scout," "I'm a Dead End Kid," "I'm a Republican," "I'm an American," "I'm upperclass"—statements such as these, if accompanied by evidence of psychological identification, indicate a feeling of merging with units of the wider society.

What does this mean for teachers? Children identify themselves with others. That's a good thing, isn't it? It gives them security and a sense of belonging, doesn't it? Moreover, in adult life today we have to be identified with groups or we can never make ourselves felt. "My father has voted the same ticket for fifty years, regardless of the candidates for office." "My country, right or wrong."

How about it? Let's look at what identification means. Have you ever stopped to think that there is no difference *in process* between identification with the Dead End Kids and with the Boy Scouts? There is no difference *in process* between identification with the teacher and with Dillinger. That's a disturbing idea.

Our observations would indicate that much identification is unconscious. Few individuals or groups who find their source of goals in identification recognize the source.

Unless there is active participation by the individual or group in the group with which identified, the identification may be developing a habit of passive acceptance of goals. Such acceptance can be dangerous. It paves the way for Hitlers and lynch-mob leaders.

There are factors which make it difficult to combat such blind identification. A teacher may find it flattering to have an individual or group identify with him. It makes it easy for him to control group behavior. The temptation to exploit such identification is tremendous. It is given further impetus by parents who claim, "Our Mary learned to be honest in Miss Baxter's room because she admired Miss Baxter so much." But what happened to Mary's honesty when she left Miss Baxter's room and joined Miss Bailey's group? Maybe Miss Bailey was not so honest. Or perhaps Mary did not find identification with Miss Bailey. Or what happens when Mary leaves school, and, still relying on identification as a source of goals, finds herself working for an unscrupulous employer? Will she still rely on identification, this time with her employer playing the role of teacher?

If identification has been the only means of deriving goals, there may be grave disruption at periods of change in status. The adolescent, seeking independence from adult control, may be at "loose ends" (without means of determining goals) if there has been no basis for goal determination other than identification. The youngster who discovers that his hero has feet of clay will be in a similar predicament.

Unsatisfied Basic Needs and Interests

There are many ways of describing how people feel if a basic need is not being met or an interest not being satisfied. We say they have a sense of unbalance, hunger (physical or psychological), unrest, annoyance, irritation, anxiety, or disturbance. Any of these feelings may be conscious or unconscious on their part, and the individual may or may not be aware of the cause. However, such feelings may indicate an important source of goals. A hungry person is one who is thwarted in meeting a basic need. The procuring of food becomes a goal for him. When he has eaten, the need satisfied he no longer has this as an immediate goal. This simplified description may serve as an illustration of what seems to be the process involved in much goal-setting by individuals and groups. But, the basic need may be more difficult to identify.

Perhaps you will recall Miss Thompson's fifth grade class in the paper-collection drive. It was suggested that the group had a need to achieve status, to feel important in the school. Such a need is usually designated as a "self-need," but it seems to us as we study boys and girls that it may be a group-need, too; for example, when there is ability grouping, the "slow" group, *as a group,* may have such a need.

—does the child know best?

Some psychiatrists, some psychologists, and the extreme proponents of the child development approach ("the child knows best") seem to assume that unmet needs are the *only* basis of goals. This assumption poses a neat dilemma. To achieve the adjusted personality, so they tell us, we must strive to meet the needs of pupils. But—to follow their own logic— the more we are able to meet needs, the fewer or less strong are the goals. A state of fulfilled needs may be nirvana, but if so, it follows that there is no growth, no education, in that blessed state. Perhaps the answer these people would give us is that we are never able fully to achieve needs, so there are always goals. If this is their logic, however, it would seem undesirable to try to meet all needs (and thus weaken goals) and it might be desirable to set up thwarting situations (as means to goal development). This doesn't make much sense to us, so we have postulated two other dimensions (besides need)—interest and reason.

Interest, we feel, may be the state of unbalance created by the thwarting of the desire to know. Perhaps the proponents of the unmet needs approach will accept as a basic need the desire to know. If so, here is no conflict of opinion. "Curiosity" is the term we usually give to the drive toward the goal to know. Our experience indicates that the desire to know may be a strong determinant in goal-setting. Oddly enough, though, it is the very stuff of which education is made. It is frequently thwarted or misused and so pupils take unpredictable (detour) action to achieve it. The following sample of experience may show what we mean.

—comic books give a clue

Miss Jones was having trouble with her fourth grade class. There was a "rash" of comic-book reading during class time and Miss Jones didn't approve. If you had looked over the shoulders of the pupils (at least of the boys), you would have found that the comics preferred by the group had to do with airplanes, pilots, and other matters associated with aviation. If you had talked to a few of the youngsters, you would have learned that the interest in aviation was keen. If you had talked to Miss Jones she would have told you that aviation was not supposed to be studied until the sixth grade. The course of study said so.

The youngsters in Miss Jones's room had an interest in aviation. Miss Jones was a barrier to this interest because she said they must study "community helpers." (Incidentally, we can't overlook the fact that the

INTEREST IS A CATALYTIC AGENT.

course of study was a barrier to Miss Jones.) Not being able to satisfy their interests directly, the group members used detour reactions by reading comics. When Miss Jones found them reading comic books, she took the books away and scolded the group, who reacted with aggression against the barrier (Miss Jones) to their goal (knowing about airplanes). Miss Jones wondered why she had such a "difficult" class.

Whether goal-seeking springs from need or interest, there is frequently difficulty in analyzing it. It may be unconscious on the part of the group, and the reaction to being thwarted may take the form of detours.

Obviously, it is important that the teacher learn to recognize needs and interests, remove thwarting factors wherever possible, and provide experiences which will satisfy the needs and interests revealed. To do these things is not always as simple as it may sound. Sometimes we may need to redirect goals or find more socially acceptable means to need or interest attainment. For example, when adolescents begin to feel the need for sex experience, society has codes which make it impossible for the teacher to provide means for meeting the need. Thwarting is inevitable. But the teacher may provide means for meeting the concomitant curiosity about the need and the attitudes of society, and may be able to provide substitute goals. When underprivileged youngsters indicate interest in acquiring property which they can't afford (this is usually known as stealing), the teacher may remove the thwarting factor (e.g., provide food, if the drive is hunger and the theft is that of food items) or provide substitute goals. This is no easy job. We'll talk about it further in the next section.

—learning to be interested

Certain needs, such as those of physical well-being, social adjustment, and sense of personal worth, may be basic and hence difficult or impossible to change. Interest, however, may be a by-product of experience and subject to influence. Groups who have had no experience in good group living have no interest (goal) in good group living. The range of experience we provide is an important factor in determining interests, and thus in determining goals. Because this is true, schools have a serious responsibility to provide a range of experience which will lead to socially acceptable goals.

Perhaps before leaving this area, we should point out that we are aware that identification, discussed in the previous section, may be an aspect of thwarted need or interest to the extent that it is a manifestation of thwarted need to "belong." We are not inclined to argue this point. We have given it precedence and the dignity of a separate treatment because we found it to be so prevalent a source of goals.

Rationally Derived Goals

A rational determination of goals implies the application of understanding of cause and effect and the interplay of factors in a situation ("If I do this, this will be the result. This is good because . . ."), or an experimental approach ("I don't know which is better, but I'll try to find out"). Frequently (perhaps always, when a rational approach to goals is employed), reason is the source of subgoals, while long-range goals are set by other means. A group may have a thwarted need to achieve a sense of importance, yet set a rational subgoal, such as to win in a competition.

It appeared to us that reason was frequenty employed as a *means* to goals, though seldom as a *source* of goals. However, on many occasions this distinction could not be clearly made. Moreover, the distinction we have tried to make between subgoals and long-range goals is difficult to defend because we realize that subgoals are in the nature of means to larger goals.

The more we push this investigation, the more we are inclined to believe that major goals of boys and girls are seldom, if ever, set in terms of pure reason. Reason may seem to be the source, on occasion, but if we probe more deeply, what passes for reason turns out to be either identification or thwarted need, or both. True, reason may be used to justify action toward subgoals. In other words, one may attempt to use reason to explain current behavior. This process is usually termed rationalization. But rationalization is after-the-fact thinking, not a source of goals.

DIMENSIONS OF GOALS

It would seem that goals are not absolutes, but are related to the motivation of the individual. Moreover, goals may have varying dimensions, such as dominance, force, or source. Or one may think of dimensions as quantity, scope, or quality. For a starving person to have as a goal the attainment of food is not the same as for a mildly hungry person to have this goal. The goal to achieve status in school may not be the same for a "slow" group as for a group that feels less rejected. In other words, similar goals may have different degrees of strength for different individuals or groups. And further, to use the same illustrations, the starving person may hope to achieve only a crust of bread and a drink of water, while the mildly hungry person hopes to achieve a highly palatable meal. The "slow" group may hope only to achieve more poundage in the paper drive, while another group may hope to achieve not only *more* than any of the others, but *twice* as much, or *ten times* as much; or it may hope to achieve not only more poundage of paper, but a better attendance record as well; or it may scorn all other achievement in order to attain high honors in athletics because it feels this to be most important. In other words, levels of aspiration may differ, the levels being defined by *quantity, scope,* or *quality* as determined by the individuals or groups.

Dominance

It is possible that a hungry man finds hunger so dominant that he has the attainment of food as his only goal, while another man finds that he has difficulty in determining whether the attainment of food or of social acceptance is more powerful. He has difficulty in deciding whether to steal the food in order to attain his goal for appeasement of hunger, or to avoid stealing in order to avoid arrest (avoid the risk of social ostracism implied by being arrested). A group may have difficulty deciding whether winning approval of the teacher (identification) is more to be valued than winning a playground fight (achievement of status with peers). Do you remember Miss Thompson's fifth grade group? Members of this group were so interested in social dominance that they were willing to subordinate other values, such as their values of honesty and their need for status with their teacher and their principal. In other words, an individual or a group may find that one goal is of such importance that it transcends all others, even though the one goal negates goals which may be stated as important under other circumstances.

Multiple Derivation of Goals

As the illustrations above suggest, goals may be either singly derived (e.g., identification) or of multiple derivation (e.g., identification plus reason). It is probable that the multiple source is the more usual.

We think it likely that teachers often recognize but one of a multiple of sources and assume that this is the only one. Having found one which seems to strike fire, they tend to assume that it is the *only* source, even though there may be others of equal importance.

Do you remember Marie? She wanted to "pass" English and graduate from high school, but her popularity with her group and her dates with Bob had appeal, too. Her teacher, dealing with one type of goal only, failed to recognize the multiple sources of Marie's goals—sources derived from urges to "belong," sex interests, and status interests. The teacher who recognizes one source of goals only will contribute little to the harmony of many goals which motivates most individuals.

EVALUATING SOURCES OF GOALS

Whether teachers recognize the fact or not, they are constantly playing upon individuals and groups by creating situations which influence the sources of goals. They encourage or discourage identification; they thwart needs and interests or they provide opportunities for meeting them; they stimulate thought or discourage it, and when thinking is stimulated, they direct or do not direct the reasoning. Some teachers, consciously or unconsciously, attempt to exploit identification of individuals and groups with themselves, so that they may more easily control behavior. Some teachers, consciously or unconsciously, attempt to meet basic needs, so that unpredictable "detour" behavior is less likely to occur. It is improbable that any teacher would consciously misdirect the thinking of pupils if he were aware of the process he was using, but undoubtedly such misdirection does take place on occasion.

Each Has Its Dangers and Its Advantages

That each process of goal determination has its dangers has been pointed out above—the dangers in unfortunate identification, the dangers in undesirable means used to attain thwarted needs, the dangers in a belief that one is rational in goal-setting while merely employing reason as a *means* to goals not rationally derived.

That each process of goal determination has its advantages is clear. It is possible that a degree of identification with the group may be necessary for democratic action. Loyalty, patriotism, and similar concepts probably have their roots in identification, and, within limits, are considered virtues. The basis of religious faith may well be in an identification with a higher power. Goals determined by thwarted needs are the very means to survival; goals determined by thwarted interests may be our chief means to education.

It seemed to us, as we examined teachers' practices, that teachers tend to give highest value to goals derived from reason. In fact, it seemed that some teachers may feel so strongly about this that they indulge in wishful thinking (thus being unreasoning about reason!) and assume that reason is the *only* basis of goals.

Thus it seems that each goal source is both desirable and undesirable, and we are forced to admit that, although we felt we could analyze, however crudely, the sources of goals and could see how teachers were able to use these sources, we had no means of evaluating the sources. We were forced to conclude that we would have to go beyond the processes themselves to find criteria. In other words, we recognized that the only way to evaluate goal-setting was in terms of another set of goals.

This Is What Happened to Us

If, as we began to study boys and girls in groups, it had been suggested that we would get into areas of abstract theory such as this, we would have scorned the idea. We started out to make scientific studies of behavior, substantiated by objective evidence. This is what happened to us:

First, we realized that the material with which we dealt was behavior, that our investigation was focused on behavior, that the experiences we provided for boys and girls were designed to change behavior.

Second, we were convinced through our study that behavior is determined by goals, and so, to understand behavior, we must learn the goals held by boys and girls and attempt to determine their sources.

Third, as we analyzed sources of goals we found that the teacher can be a powerful influence, consciously or unconsciously, through means he employs to use sources of goals.

Fourth, if teachers exert such power, we felt that it was necessary to provide criteria for action.

Fifth, we attempted to find criteria in the processes of goal-setting, but were unable to do so. This brings us to the dilemma under discussion. If criteria are not to be found in the processes, where can we find them?

Our experience has convinced us that we cannot study boys and girls in the abstract. They are people, living as individuals and as groups in our classrooms, where what happens to them day by day changes their behavior. To make a thorough study and sound analysis of the behavior of boys and girls, it is inevitable, we believe, for teachers to face problems of aim and direction as well as those of kind and quantity. In other words, as we study boys and girls, we must examine what we are trying to do as well as what boys and girls are like.

We Examine Our Own Goals

As we launched into our study of criteria for sources of goals, we began by examining our own goals for group living of boys and girls. Below is the listing devised by three teachers working with groups of children in a first grade, a fourth and a fifth grade, and an eighth grade.

GOALS FOR BOYS AND GIRLS STATED BY TEACHERS

Growth in the ability to get along with one another.
Evidence of an intelligent interest in the world in which we live.
Development of habits and skills which will help one live more effectively.
Improvement in social participation.
Increased ability to deal with environmental forces and factors.
Development of an understanding of the responsibilities to be accepted as well as the privileges to be extended to people who live in a democracy.
Interest in maintaining a healthy body.
Development of a responsibility for providing for individual and group safety.
Recognition of one's own value.
Appreciation of the value of others.
Understanding of why people in home, school, and community behave as they do.

Next we went to parents of the boys and girls in these groups, and in group meetings asked them to state the goals they held for their sons and daughters. The statements of the parents of the first grade group follow.

GOALS STATED BY PARENTS OF THE FIRST GRADE GROUP

Good reading and writing.
Kindness and consideration.
Concentration and broadened interests.
Personal appearance.
Self-discipline.
Sense of responsibility, dependability,
Promptness.
Poise.
Intelligent self-direction.
Social skill.

The principal in the school of this first grade stated the following as his goals for children:

GOALS FOR CHILDREN STATED BY THE PRINCIPAL

To develop within each one intelligent self-direction so that each may live happily and effectively with others in the group.

To gradually learn to be considerate and kind to others.
To learn to laugh and have fun—to laugh at oneself.
To develop the ability to achieve with graciousness.
To learn to take the reprimands of one's associates and authority without irritation.
To learn the new 3 R's, respect, responsibility, and human relations.

Parents of the fourth and fifth grade group stated these as their goals for their sons and daughters:

GOALS STATED BY PARENTS OF THE FOURTH AND FIFTH GRADE GROUP

Development of character (tolerance, patience, understanding).
Personal cleanliness.
Spiritual values.
Intercultural relations.
A good healthy curiosity.
A definite liking for reading.
Appreciation for good things of life.
A feeling of humility (less foolish pride).

Eighth grade parents, when asked what they wanted for their sons and daughters, stated these as their goals:

GOALS STATED BY PARENTS OF THE EIGHTH GRADE GROUP

To be able to take constructive criticism as well as to give it.
To establish good human relationships.
To eliminate the personal element in criticism, thus making an objective approach to a subject.
Courtesy, consideration for the feelings of others at all times but particularly in public places such as streetcars, buses, etc.

The goals stated by parents are somewhat difficult to interpret. Evidently each parent wants his son or daughter to achieve not only in the realm of academic learning but also in areas of personality adjustment and human relations. How far these parents would go in the matter of *group* education is difficult to determine, yet goals such as "sense of responsibility" and "intercultural relations" indicate a social interest beyond mere individual achievement.

—further steps

Perhaps we should have gone further—beyond statements of goals of boys and girls, teachers, administrators, and parents. We might have examined goals in terms of the "ideal man," in terms of the "good state," in terms of the "ideal situation" for solving the problems of our current society, in terms of the maximum development of the individual. We might have examined the role of the school in our democratic society, or the nature of the learning process. We might have studied the goals stated by the immediate community, by our nation, by our world society. We might have studied the statements of goals made by the respected leaders of our time, or of the past.

Maybe other groups of teachers going beyond our beginning steps, as many have, will make such studies. We hope, however, that they will see, as we have, an immediate and urgent need for studying goals in order to determine how to proceed, and that they will not approach the problem as an academic exercise in stating objectives as a first step to providing better experiences for boys and girls.

However limited our investigation, it did give us some leads. From the goals stated by boys and girls, by teachers, administrators, and parents, we felt confident that two ideals shone through with clarity. The first seemed to concern the maximum development of the individual. This seemed to be in the ascendancy, yet was accompanied by the second: the development of group action. These goals we interpreted as "respect for the individual" and "respect for group action." These are goals we might have arrived at had we started with an examination of democratic living or of "the American way." The current fashion is to regard as suspect statements which reveal that "the people" believe as it is hoped they will believe. That group goals—of parents, teachers,

A GROUP GOAL HAS MANY ORIGINS.

pupils, administrators—lent themselves to an interpretation which coincided with theoretical goals was a source of satisfaction to the teachers. Whether or not the stated goals of these groups would stand the test of action is beyond the point. The stated goals gave a point of departure, a measure of goals in terms of "respect for the individual" and "respect for group action."

This process and these broad statements of goal may sound elementary. Maybe they are. We do know, however, that they made it possible for us to return to the question of evaluation of sources of goals with a measuring stick.

—using identification

As we saw earlier, we were able to say that it is not possible to identify, out of context, the relative value of sources of goals. With this new measure, however, we were able to say: "If identification with the group in a classroom leads to respect for group action, identification may be a legitimate means for setting goals if the means is compatible with the end, and if it should be used by the teacher." If, on the other hand, identification with the teacher is used by the teacher merely as a means to personal satisfaction, it is not a justifiable means. Moreover, although reason may not be better *per se* as a means to goal-setting, our analysis would indicate that it is less easily exploited than other means.

As has been suggested, a teacher may employ identification for desirable ends, but such identification is not different *in process* from identification with a gang leader or an unscrupulous employer. If we, as teachers, are to influence goal-setting beyond our control area, reason would seem to be the most effective means. Perhaps this is another way of saying that rationally derived goals give the individual (or group) greater control of his own destiny. To this extent, reason, beyond other means of goal-setting, meets the criteria of "respect for individual" and "respect for group action."

—for us, illumination

A philosopher might well smile at the elementary nature of our study, and find wanting a clear formulation of ideas; but for us the process was illuminating. Where once the philosophy of education had been in one compartment and a study of children in another, the two were now beginning to merge and offer us a means of determining what experiences to provide for boys and girls (how to determine the curriculum). Equally important, perhaps, our study made us aware of a need to be conscious of, and to analyze, the consequences of our acts as teachers. Where once there had been general, hazy good will toward boys and girls, there were now the beginnings of some specific values; where once there had been a vague group of ideas about goals in classroom management, there was an emerging analysis of the processes involved.

Perhaps it should be explained that the study did not take the form of a neat logical sequence of operations, as this description might seem to imply. We did not consciously move from a study of boys and girls to a study of goals held by others. We carried on studies in the two areas simultaneously. There was much fumbling and almost random discussion over a period of more than a year before these concepts began to emerge, and they are still emerging and being clarified by further study.

MEANS TO GOAL-SETTING

With a keener awareness of the importance of goals, with a greater understanding of sources of goals, and with some indication of a measure of goals, it was possible for us to examine critically our classroom practices. Incidentally, we recognized that what is usually termed "character education" is essentially an attempt to influence goal-setting.

One thing seems quite clear. There is little hope of making any differences in goal-setting unless the goals are brought to the level of consciousness, examined, and, if desired, changed either through reason or through a shifting of the situation so that interests and needs are met.

If a teacher is to guide such processes, it is evident that his own goals will need to be conscious in order that he may see without prejudice. And, obviously, a teacher must be aware of sources of goals if he is to guide young people in the examination and shift of goals. We believe it to be self-evident that consciousness of goals and their examination and evaluation cannot take place unless there is opportunity for such experience. This means that opportunity must be provided for choice-making, both by individuals and by groups, and for experimentation and discussion of the basis of choice.

Usual Means to Goal-setting

Through discussion and observation, we identified and evaluated the most common practices employed by adults in an attempt to influence goal-setting of boys and girls.

1. *Argument, persuasion.* It would seem that such measures can be effective only if the goal-setting is of rational origin. Some of the most bitter and futile disagreements arise when two people or two groups with different goals of non-rational derivation try to defend their positions through rationalization. The hungry man, with a goal growing out of a thwarted basic need, may grow eloquent about the rights of men for food and the obligation of government to provide it, but he has little chance of changing the goal of the man who, lacking security in "belonging," rationalizes about rugged individualism with equal eloquence. The teacher who assumes that all goals are of rational origin may actually increase tensions among individuals and groups when he relies on argument alone as a means of changing goals. Formal debates on matters which are closely related to goals are often futile for this same reason. The only result is that the non-rational goal of each individual or group is intensified and supported by rationalization.

2. *Preaching, exhorting, other hortatory measures.* Unless the goals of the exhorter are those of the listener, there seems to be little hope that this means can operate to change goals. The ideas expressed are merely rejected. On the other hand, if there is a high degree of identification of the listener with the exhorter, this may be an extremely effective means (though, as we see it, a dangerous one).

3. *Threats, scolding.* As the negative parallel of preaching or exhorting, threats would seem to have little effect unless there is identification, or unless the threats because of their nature are in the area of the rational goal of the individual or group. We found many examples of the use of threats which seemed to have little relation to the goals of the listener. For example, a teacher who threatens a failing grade has no influence with an individual or a group for whom academic failure holds no threat to goal achievement.

4. *Codes, laws, pledges.* Provision of preconceived codes, laws, or pledges may be considered an extension of preaching, with the same degree of effectiveness. (This may not apply to codes developed by groups themselves.) It is interesting to note that such means are often introduced in situations of high emotional tone, such as those involving rituals or ceremonies. There seems to be a general understanding, conscious or unconscious, that such means are non-rational, even when presented as rational.

5. *Precept.* Many adults rely heavily on precept as a means of influencing goal-setting. They do not realize that the only circumstances

under which it is effective is where there is a high degree of identification.

6. *Experience.* Broadened experience may be used consciously by teachers as a means of meeting needs, offering substitute interests and transfer of identification, or providing a basis of rational goal-setting. In a broad sense, this is the foundation of all education, but it may not be used consciously. For example, the teacher who is concentrating on the teaching of long division may be unaware of the relation of this act to the pupils' goal-setting. On the other hand, when a teacher supplies a particular experience in conscious realization of the processes of goal-setting, he may set in motion a powerful influence.

7. *Discussion.* Discussion with individuals or groups seems to assume a rational derivation of goals, but may operate effectively in other source areas as well. Identification with the group may give an added dimension to group discussion, as may a thwarted need to "belong" satisfied through a sense of contribution to the group. The discussion may be a way of bringing to consciousness the goals of individuals and groups, and a means of examining them, as well as an opportunity for redirecting goal-setting. With these possibilities in mind, a teacher can recognize the tremendous potential power of group discussion.

As we said above, although we can find both favorable and unfavorable aspects of each means to goal-setting, the possibilities for exploitation of the non-rational sources is so frightening that the use of non-rational methods should be viewed with caution, and used only when completely understood and under circumstances when such approaches are necessary because the rational is inappropriate.

RECOGNIZING CONFLICT OF GOALS

The more one becomes conscious of the goals of boys and girls, the more one realizes the numerous goal conflicts which any individual or group must face.

Conflict within Self

Goals of boys and girls are constantly shifting and changing as the children grow and learn. It is not surprising, then, that a youngster may hold goals which are mutually incompatible. For example, a boy may have a desire for social life and for high grades, while recognizing there is not time for both. Or he may desire to please his parents, yet want to

NOT EVERYBODY HAS THE SAME GOALS.

be acceptable in a peer group which engages in activities to which his parents object. He may want to save money to go to college, yet want to spend money taking girls on dates. He may want to be considered grown up, yet enjoy children's games.

In similar manner, groups may hold conflicting goals. A group may wish to hold an "exclusive" class activity, yet want to bring dates from "outside." Or it may want to attend a program, yet wish there were more time to finish an interesting activity. It may want to please the teacher, yet want to be acceptable to its peer group.

The fifth graders in Longfellow School were very fond of the librarian. They practically fell over one another trying to please her. Great was the rejoicing on the day she asked the group if they would be willing to help her dust the books and wash the shelves the next day. Would they! They could scarcely wait till the morrow. The next day they pitched in with vim and vigor. All went well until some sixth grade boys, jealous, perhaps, because they hadn't been asked, began taunting the boys about being "sissies" and the whole group for being "suckers." The struggle that went on between the desire of the fifth grade group to please the librarian and their wish to show the older boys they weren't suckers was almost visible. A few of the boys got as far as the door, and no one knew, probably the boys least of anyone, whether they would join the sixth

[91]

graders in the hall, or take punches at their noses. The librarian stepped into this crisis, inviting the sixth graders in to help, or to leave. They left. There was marked tension for about fifteen minutes, but finally, with the older boys out of sight, all was well again.

Conflicts with Peers

With the rapidly shifting goals of boys and girls, it is inevitable that there should be conflicts. The child who has not yet achieved identification with the group and sees the teacher as a mother substitute may find himself in conflict with the child who is striving to assert independence. The boy who, in adolescence, is developing heterosexual interests may be in conflict with the less mature boy who thinks dates are "silly." In like manner, the immature group may find itself in conflict with the more mature group, or the subgroups within the larger group may be in conflict. Maturity, of course, is but one basis for differing goals which lead to conflicts within groups, but it is one which provides dramatic examples.

Conflict Between the Group and the Teacher

The teacher, as the mentor of a class group, may find himself not infrequently in the position of a barrier to group goals. Whether or not this is necessary will depend on the degree of divergence between the goals of the teacher and those of the group. It would seem that it is necessary on occasion for a teacher to become the barrier, as was the case when Miss Brown's first grade wanted to go on the picnic in spite of the rain (page 60). But it is possible that a teacher puts himself in the position of barrier more often than is necessary. This occurs when he mistrusts the group processes and takes authority unto himself, even in situations which a group could handle satisfactorily for itself, or when he unthinkingly assumes *his* goals are "right" and those of the group are "wrong." A middle-class teacher working with a lower-lower or an upper-upper-class group may assume his goals are the "right" goals, and the pupils' goals "wrong," even though the pupils are operating in terms of accepted behavior patterns of their social-class group. This underlines the necessity for a teacher to be very sure that his own goals are based on reason, not merely on a prejudice of social class or experience.

—trying to be popular

At the opposite extreme is the teacher who, realizing that he will achieve status with the group if he identifies himself with the group goals, exploits this identification in order to be popular. With a "tough" group, he purports to be a "tough guy," blaming on higher authority the conformity he enforces.

Mr. Dennis used this technique when his group of white boys wanted to get into a stone-throwing fight with a group of Negro boys. He explained that he had nothing against such fights personally, but he'd get in trouble with the principal if he allowed the fight to take place. Mr. Dennis, having identified himself with group goals, helped the group to identify with him. This identification with him dissuaded the group from immediate action. The kickback came, however, when the boys had the fight after school hours and came to class the next morning boasting of their exploits. Mr. Dennis was then in a dilemma. If he rejoiced with the group, he realized he would be deepening the mistaken goals of the group. If he took issue with the group members, he would lose the control he had gained by identifying with group goals, which, in turn, had caused the group to identify with him. It is probable that seldom if ever are other than immediate gains achieved when a teacher identifies with unacceptable group goals. And even these immediate gains are open to question. Thus a teacher who attempts to gain popularity through such identification is usually, perhaps always, forfeiting the opportunity to teach, to redirect group goals.

—emergencies

This seems to us to be a sound generalization, yet we recognize that there may be "emergency" circumstances in which it does not hold. Who hasn't heard the story of the unruly school boys who threw out teacher after teacher until one schoolmaster gave a thorough thrashing to the leader, and henceforth all was peace and quiet? We see in this situation the possibility that the group recognized no goal but brute force, so it was necessary for the teacher to show that he could achieve in terms of the goals of the group before he could be sufficiently acceptable to the group to begin to redirect goals. Such dire situations may exist, but if so, we believe they are few and far between, and that the story is incomplete until we are told whether, after "emergency" action, the teacher was able to direct the group values into more acceptable channels. After the teacher had established rapport and group acceptance through the use of brute force, was he then able to move the group toward adult-directed group planning? Unless he was able to do so, we feel there is no justification for the means employed.

TABLE 5

PARENTS' RANKING OF VALUE OF EXPERIENCE
(EIGHTH GRADE)

Experiences (in a list of 40 items)	Rank by Parents	Rank by Pupils (group of 32)
Work at home (do chores) without pay	1	9
Work or play with people much younger than I am (five or more years younger)	2	33
Be a leader or representative of a group of people my own age	3	13
Spend leisure time with friends of my own choice	4	6
Discuss with others of my own age what is going on in the world	5	5
Discuss my vocational choice	6	16
Take part in community affairs	7	9
Do useful work for the community without pay	8	16

(Correlation between ranks of items by parents and children: $rho = +.441$)*

TABLE 6

PUPILS' RANKING OF VALUE OF EXPERIENCE
(EIGHTH GRADE)

Experiences (in a list of 40 items)	Rank by Pupils	Rank by Parents
Talk with adults engaged in various types of work	1	9
Work for pay	2	32
Work or play in a group of four or five people	3	21
Be a member of a team for some sport	4	21
Discuss with others of my own age what is going on in the world	5	5
Spend leisure time with friends of my own choice	6	4

* Throughout this study, when correlations are reported, they have been computed by the Spearman rank-difference method, with the formula $rho = 1 - \dfrac{6\Sigma d^2}{N(N^2 - 1)}$. *Rho* is the measure of correlation, d the difference between the two ranks given for each individual, and N the number of individuals.

This formula was used as being most appropriate because the scores obtained through measures employed were very rough and would be more valid if we compared ranked responses rather than attempted to establish the extent of differentiation.

Conflict with Adults

We came upon some evidences of differing values when parents and children were asked to evaluate experiences on the Check Sheet of Opportunities in Human Relations (Appendix, page 407). The parents of the eighth grade group listed, as in Table 5, those experiences they considered the most important for their sons and daughters to have. The ranks given these items by pupils are indicated at the right; those of the parents at the left. In other words, while parents felt that working or playing with younger people is the second most important experience in a list of 40, the eighth grade boys and girls assigned to this item a rank of 33.

In Table 6 is a list of the experiences ranked highest by the pupils in this same group, with the rank indicated on the left, and the rank given the same experience by parents indicated on the right. The most severe difference of opinion is in the value of work for pay, the pupils indicating that the experience is highly important to them, and the parents relegating it to thirty-second rank in a list of forty. Here the possibility for conflict is clearly apparent.

It did not require a check list to discover that Allan wanted to take a paper route and his mother wouldn't let him, or that Mary objected strenuously when her mother wanted to invite to her birthday party two cousins who were two and three years younger than Mary. But the results of the compared ranks made it possible for the group to see their group problems more clearly and to plan what should be done about them.

A similar comparison of values of a fourth and fifth grade group produced the rankings by parents that are shown in Table 7A. The boys and girls of this group listed as most valuable the experiences listed in Table 7B.

The teacher of this fourth and fifth grade, who knew the group well, could have predicted most of these responses, but even she was startled at the relative values given to home chores by parents and by children. The children gave this experience a high rank and the parents ranked it thirtieth in a list of forty! This may serve as warning that we cannot judge the value assigned to an experience by the enthusiasm shown for it or the dislike expressed for it.

As we examined these differences in opinion, we found, as might be expected, that there was greater agreement between the ten- and eleven-

TABLE 7A

PARENTS' RANKING OF VALUE OF EXPERIENCE
(FOURTH AND FIFTH GRADES)

Experiences (in a list of 40 items)	Rank by Parents	Rank by Pupils (group of 34)
Work or play in a group of four or five people	1	8
Work or play with people of differing religious beliefs	2	24
Be a member of a group which makes its own rules	3	19
Be a member of a group which elects its own leaders	4	5
Be a leader or representative of a group of people my own age	5	3
Visit communities other than my own	6	4
Talk with adults engaged in various types of work	7	13
Spend leisure time with friends of my own choice	8	8
Discuss with others my age what is going on in the world	9	8

(Correlation of rank of items by parents and children: $rho = +.518$)

TABLE 7B

PUPILS' RANKING OF VALUE OF EXPERIENCE
(FOURTH AND FIFTH GRADES)

Experiences (in a list of 40 items)	Rank by Pupils	Rank by Parents
Work or play in a group of thirty to fifty people	1	37
Be a member of a club	2	10
Be a leader or representative of a group of people my own age	3	5
Visit communities other than my own	4	6
Be a member of a group that elects its own leaders	5	4
Work or play with people much older than I am (five or more years older), not including teachers or youth leaders	6	30
Work at home (do chores) without pay	7	30

year-old pupils and their parents ($+ .518$) than between the junior high school pupils and their parents ($+ .441$). Moreover, there was greater agreement between these two groups of youngsters ($+ .631$) than between either group and its parents. These figures may not be significant because they were computed for such small numbers, but the trend is of interest.

A Warning

Figures have a way of looking so authoritative and final that their limitations are easily overlooked. The figures we present tell something about the groups with which we are working, but do not necessarily tell anything about *your* group. As we have said before, we feel that *each* group must be studied in its particular setting, and that this study is the job of every teacher. If many teachers find similar results in an area of study, it may be that generalizations can be derived useful to many teachers; but even such generalizations will need testing for a particular group.

We do feel, however, that it can be very useful for teachers to exchange ideas concerning *areas* for investigation and *means* of study. Moreover, we feel very strongly that "study" means much more than mere "digging up data." It involves program planning and testing, including evaluation by pupils, parents, and teachers.

Role of Youth in Society

In addition to making a specific study of the different values held by children and adults in a particular group, we attempted to identify some of the chief areas of conflict between children and youth and adults in our society.

It is evident that there is no clear concept of the appropriate role of youth in our society. The roles assigned to children and young people by their families and the immediate community seem to depend on many factors.

Dominant among the factors operating in assignment of roles to children and youth is the pleasure and personal satisfaction which adults derive from children. The degree of pleasure seems to vary with maturity. There is first the "everyone-loves-a-baby" period. The child then progresses to the "cuddly" stage and then to the "cute" stage. With what must be a rude shock to them, many children find themselves in the unbeautiful "toothless age," when their unbounded energy is considered a nuisance. The "toothless age" gives way to the "awkward age" and then

to adolescence, which is considered either as amusing or as an unfortunate "waiting" period.

—home background

The economic status and mores of the family and the community seem
to be a powerful determinant of status of children. In families and communities of low economic level, particularly those in rural agricultural
areas and also, to some extent, those in industrial areas, children are considered real or potential wage earners, and as such are given favorable
status. In middle and upper class society, however, the child cannot find
status through such means. Rather, status seems to be assigned in terms
of the degree to which the child provides an emotional outlet for the
parent, or is the object for transfer of the parent's personal ambition.

In other words, our observation leads us to the conclusion that, except
among certain lower economic groups, children tend to be assigned the
role of performing toys (amusing, to be owned and demonstrated with
pride) or vessels to hold the otherwise unreleased emotions of adults.
Some of these emotions, such as those of affection and pride, may not
hinder the growth of the child, but some, based on release of adult emotion, such as transfer of intense ambition, must be thwarting to individual growth. We are hard put to find examples of role assignment of
children in society based on real respect for the worth of the individual,
except as it is manifest in love and affection. (There are exceptions in
individual families, of course, but here we are discussing the general role
assigned by society.) We feel that these role assignments are a negation
of democratic concepts.

The job of thinking through the role appropriate for citizens growing
up in a democratic society, and how it may be achieved, is an area of
investigation badly in need of attention, we believe. It seems important
that teachers and other youth leaders become concerned about the place
of young citizens in our society. Until their role is given dignity and is
clarified, it is inevitable that there will be conflicts between youth and
adults.

Fluctuations in Role Assignment

Not only is the role assignment undefined, but, further, it is allowed
to fluctuate widely for any one individual or group in terms of the immediate situation. The seven-year-old is held responsible for care of
personal property (he must not lose his cap, leave his coat on the play-

YOUNG PEOPLE ARE SERIOUS, AND WANT TO BE TAKEN SERIOUSLY.

ground, etc.), but frequently he is not considered old enough to have a voice in the selection of his clothing. The sixteen-year-old is considered old enough to take major responsibility for the complex job of tending younger members of the family, but is not considered old enough to drive the family car. The eighteen-year-old, in time of war, is considered sufficiently mature to fight in the defense of his country, but not old enough to vote. The many inconsistencies of role assignment according to the immediate situation must be extremely confusing for the youngster growing up in our society. It is inevitable that such inconsistencies lead to conflicts, if for no other reason than that the child is unsure of which of the many roles expected of him is appropriate for any one situation. It is amazing that, with the many complex adjustments required of children, there are not more major conflicts between youth and adults!

"Do As I Say, Not As I Do"

Still another area of confusion for children in interpreting goals of grownups is the gap between the stated goals and the operational goals

of adults. This is further confused by the variations of goals among adults
as individuals and groups.

The school does not lessen this confusion between "do as I say" and
"not as I do" when it teaches the evils of nicotine and alcohol to children
who see their parents smoke and drink, or when it teaches that "honesty
is the best policy" to youngsters who know their parents boast of dis-
honesty in areas ranging from cheating at cards to "pulling off a deal" of
a shady nature.

Psychologists and psychiatrists tell us that such conflicts, particularly
if non-rational or of unconscious origin, can be extremely disintegrating.
Unless he is to "go to pieces" between the countertugs of the two value
systems, the child (or the group) must reject one or the other. Many
youngsters find it convenient to reject the teaching of the school, mean-
while keeping out of trouble by pretending a docile acceptance. Certainly this is not the adjustment which is acceptable to teachers. The
alternative would seem to be for the child to reject his home teaching.
The latter may be the case more often than we realize, particularly for
older children. But when this happens, and the parents have no control
over the behavior of their children, the school blames the parents! In
other words, we may be putting a child (or a group) in the unfortunate
position of having to choose between two sets of values, either choice
leading to consequences unacceptable to society. It is not surprising that
he not infrequently finds another way out, rejecting all adult values and
relying on his peers to direct his goal-setting.

What Can We Do?

What is the responsibility of the school? To avoid conflict, should we
extol the operational goals rather than the stated goals of adults in the
community? Or should we insist that the school is "right" and parents
and the community are "wrong"? Obviously neither is a satisfactory
solution, although the second alternative is frequently employed by the
school, consciously or unconsciously.

We believe we are in an area which needs much more careful thought
than we have given it. We have, however, taken several exploratory
steps.

First, it would seem that a most satisfactory solution would be to
achieve a common acceptance of goals by parents and the school. We
asked parents to explore with us their goals for their children (p. 84).
This gave an opportunity for a general discussion of goal-setting and goal

conflict. We make no claims to other than minor success, however. Some of the parents operated solely on the "do as I say" level of discussion. The role of children as release for parental emotion contributes to keeping discussion on this level. "I want Mary to be better than I am" may well indicate that the parent uses Mary as a release for personal guilt feelings. Or if parental pride is personified in Mary, any admission that Mary is confused may be an admission of personal confusion. Such admissions are not likely to be made in parent-teacher meetings. Moreover, although we were able to reach nearly all parents either in meetings or in conferences, some of the situations which indicated the most severe conflicts involved parents whom we did not reach.

Second, we as teachers examined our own goals for children (page 84). This process helped us to weigh our actions in terms of our goals and to see if we were letting personal prejudices contribute to the conflicts we might create.

Third, on the assumption that a conscious approach to goal-setting may give clearer insight into conflict situations, we attempted to help children to examine their own goals (pages 65 and 67).

Finally, and perhaps most important and implied in each of the above steps, we attempted to locate the areas of conflict, to bring them to the consciousness of parents, pupils, and teachers, and to find solution through mutual agreement.

DEALING WITH GOAL CONFLICTS

A conflict implies a problem. A problem offers opportunity to apply problem-solving techniques. Problem-solving is the basis of learning, of the process of education. It follows, then, that the conflicts we have been discussing offer opportunities for educational experience on a high level if we but use them wisely.

Two factors seem to be implicit: One, if goal conflicts are to be used as an opportunity for learning, goals and goal conflicts must be discovered and brought to the level of consciousness where they can be discussed. Two, whether rationally derived or not, goal-setting may be controlled by reason. This second point may need some amplification.

An eleventh grade group of girls had formed a film star "fan club." They identified with the star, but not knowing how their heroine behaved, they acted as they *imagined* she behaved. Movie magazines and "sultry" movies fed their imagination. Their teacher discovered that members of the fan club were earning a reputation for being daring, usually in sex experimentation. She was able to talk to the group and reason with them that, although the identification might be fine, the group should use reason in the means they employed (these are not her words, of course). The group members were willing to examine their behavior and, without diminishing their admiration for the film star, recognized, through use of reason, that what they had been doing was not necessarily what the star would do. Incidentally, in this situation, a second non-rational goal ("belonging") played an important part in shifting the behavior patterns. A rational recognition that they were jeopardizing their status with their peers was a powerful force in changing their behavior. In other words, even if goals are non-rationally derived, reason may operate to shift the means to their attainment.

Less complex, perhaps, was the handling of the situation when the group discovered that their evaluation of experiences on the Check Sheet of Opportunities differed from that of their parents (pages 94–97). In this case, it was possible to bring together parents, pupils, and teachers for a discussion of their problems. The result was far from a complete resolution of conflicts, but the discussion did much to bring to consciousness for both parents and pupils their own as well as one another's goals, which, in turn, made possible the resolution of some of the conflicts.

Isolated Youth

In the area of general conflict of youth and adults in our society the problem is even more complex than the conflict between individual children and adults. We have discussed the problem of role assignment of youth. Closely related to this problem is the fact that children and youth are, to a great extent, isolated from society, as has been previously stated. They are not accepted in many adult group experiences. In contrast with the past, when children were a part of community living, playing a part in production and to some extent in management, children today are relegated to an isolated realm of their own. Small families, apartment house living, the increased specialization of adults, and similar factors contribute to this isolation.

As educators, we recognize experience as a base for learning, but the isolation of youth tends to force learning through secondhand experience. Observation is about as close as children come to the adult world. Where once a ten-year-old might pitch horseshoes with adults, today, at best, his Dad takes him to see a big league baseball game. Even our best intentions may contribute to this isolation. Educators have made such a point of providing experiences appropriate to various maturity levels, of recognizing "the child's world," that, unthinkingly, they may misuse this concept of the dignity of childhood and force isolation.

—"belonging" to society

Finding no active part in adult affairs, it would seem that boys and girls turn to the experiences available to them through radio, movies, and reading. We have made no careful study, but our general observation leads us to believe that the movies, radio programs, and comics most popular with boys and girls, at least with those of certain ages, depict *adults*, not children. "Westerns" on the screens, crime stories on the radio, and "Superman" in the comics are examples. We shrink from recognizing that these media may be the chief, or almost the exclusive, means that boys and girls may find for interpreting the goals of current adult society. What are they learning about adult goals? True, the Western and Superman are usually on the right side of the law, but almost without exception, they achieve the "right" through might. Can we be surprised that youngsters not only believe that "might makes right" but, further, believe that adults hold this belief, too? Yet mere condemnation of these forms is futile unless we provide suitable substitutes.

It is possible that certain maturity factors should be considered as we plan programs for children and youth which will break through the isolation and provide for induction of youth into adult society. There is some evidence that on the whole young children accept without question adult goals for society, for it would seem that the major source of goals (other than those derived from basic needs) is the identification with adults—parents, and then the teacher. The healthy youngster next moves to identification with his peers, and so the power of adult goals is lessened. At adolescence, the young person (or the group) finds himself in a no man's land, where he has strong inclination to identify with adults yet an urge to be freed of adult domination. It is at this point, perhaps, that respect for youth could pay large dividends if we could give them an opportunity for participation without domination.

—unanswered problems

Still unanswered, we believe, are several problems in this area. One has to do with how the individual maintains the security of "belonging" while moving from one culture to another (as from peer culture to adult culture). Our best guess is that security found in reasoned goals is the chief stabilizer, but further investigation in this area is in order.

Another problem has to do with how the individual or group exerts self-domination. Does adult influence fade gradually in all areas as the adolescent matures, or is it transmitted in certain areas and does it become non-existent in others? From what little we know, it would seem that the latter is the case, for a group of adolescents may cling to an adult in an almost infantile fashion for security in one type of situation, while exerting the utmost independence in another.

Does the influence of all adults fade equally, or does influence shift from one adult or one category of adults to others? The indications are that the latter is true. The popularity of fan clubs gives some indication of shift from individual identification with immediate authority (parents and teachers) to group identification with other adults, such as radio and movie stars.

We feel, however, that questions such as these have been incompletely investigated, and that teachers could make a major contribution if they would explore them and suggest means to their further study.

THE ROLE OF THE SCHOOL

The literature of child development is filled with illustrations of the importance of early childhood experiences. In terms of individual behavior, many of these experiences occur prior to school years. However, for many children, perhaps for most children, the school offers the first opportunity for experiences in groups of peers (other than very small groups of five or six, at most). In other words, though the school may lack influence over early, highly important personal experiences, it must take responsibility for the initiation of group experiences and for their development over a period of years.

The school is considered the agency which transmits the culture—which is another way of saying that it is responsible for transmitting the goals of society (with hopes that it may inculcate the stated goals rather than the operational goals!). The more we study groups of boys and girls, the more we are aware that the so-called "content" of the curriculum is but a small factor in transmitting the culture. The three R's may be a means to the culture, but are not its goals, and, as we have indicated in this chapter, we believe the goals are the behavior determinants, the factors that make a difference in boys' and girls' behavior. Thus, if evaluation of the curriculum is in terms of behavior, our major focus in effecting change will be in the area of goal-setting.

—participation is the key

It follows, then, that the school must take the initiative in breaking through the current pattern of isolation of youth, and must provide experience in participation rather than in mere observation. Programs designed to this end would seem to be of importance for children at all levels of maturity, but may be of greatest importance to adolescents who are seeking identification with adult society but are attempting to break away from domination by adults. We have few examples of programs of this type, but the most promising seem to be those which provide for community service; for participation in groups of mixed age, such as community folk-dancing; for representation on adult councils recognized as important to the community; and for work experience. No doubt it would be possible to find other means, and certainly all such means could be employed more extensively and with clearer purpose than at present.

IN SUMMARY

In summary, we might say that we see the search to achieve goals as the major determinant of behavior, and therefore that desirable goal-setting is a major function of education—of groups as well as individuals.

Discovering the current goals of groups is an essential preliminary step in guiding a group toward desirable goals. The process of discovering group goals is not easy, but a number of techniques, including observation of behavior and of group discussion, may furnish valuable clues. Although the goal of the group is not necessarily the sum of the goals of the individual members, discovering individual goals may provide avenues for further exploration toward discovering group goals.

A difficult and most elusive aspect of the study of goals is that having to do with goal sources—the origins of goals of individuals and groups. Our observations lead us to postulate three sources: identification, unsatisfied needs, and reason.

Each of these sources poses certain advantages and disadvantages. Evidently the sources cannot be evaluated of themselves. We went to our own thinking and that of parents for an estimate of the value of sources. Other investigators may wish to go farther afield—to the community, to society and its values—to discover other criteria.

As we analyzed the means of goal-setting as observed in classrooms, we found that each could be weighed in its effectiveness in terms of the sources of goals identified above. Some means to goal-setting on which teachers have tended to rely can be seen to be relatively ineffective when examined in this light.

A study of goals quickly leads to the realization of the many types of goal conflicts experienced by boys and girls—conflict with self, with peers, with adults, with society. The conflict with society is heightened because our culture has tended to isolate youth and has not formulated a clear concept of the role of children and young people in the social group.

Dealing with these goal conflicts poses a difficult but important task for the school as it guides individuals and groups.

*In which we describe how Johnny
helps make the group and the
group helps make Johnny*

IV

The Individual in the Group

Eight-year-old Johnny didn't want to go to school that morning. This
was obvious. He kept finding excuses to put off the moment when he
must open the door and start off—a drink of water, another pencil, a kiss
for his mother. Finally, he could think of no more. He would have to
go, he knew, but the idea of leaving home was not a pleasant one. At
home he was loved, he was secure, he was important. But at school
Johnny felt he was in a hostile world. He felt that the other children
didn't like him, that the teacher thought he was dumb. He hated school.

The way a person thinks about himself, his sense of personal worth,
his emotional security, is in large measure determined by what he thinks
other people think of him. He feels superior or inferior, depending on
what status he thinks the group has given to him. This is true of children
as well as of adults.

—growing in groups

Individuals develop, learn, change as they react to their environment. An important part of that environment is people. These people
are in groups called families, classrooms, communities, social classes,
nations. And, in turn, it is the individual, along with a number of other
individuals, that makes the group. In other words, the individual and
the group are interdependent.

Every teacher knows these things, but it is easy to overlook, or to try
to discount, the tremendous power of the group in the development of
the individual pupil. Many teachers, it would seem, try to operate as
though they, as teachers, plus the course content, materials and equipment, and the four walls of the classroom were the chief factors in the

[107]

school environment which influence pupils. From our experience, we are inclined to believe that the group has more influence on the individual than any of these factors, and often more than all the other factors combined.

Thus we see a study of groups as important for an understanding of *individual* development, as well as a means to achieving both immediate and long-range social values for the group.

NEED TO BELONG

The need to belong in a group is a powerful force. Some psychologists claim that it is an innate, basic human need. Others point out that it is culturally developed. Whatever its origin, all agree that it furnishes strong motivation for behavior. In our society, every individual attempts to find himself belonging in some group. For some boys and girls belonging is chiefly found in the family, for others in a school group, for still others in a club, and so on. Many are able to achieve a sense of belonging in several groups.

It is important for the development of most boys and girls of school age that they find belonging in groups of their peers. We can see this taking place in the shift from belonging in the family only to belonging in a schoolroom group. In most elementary schools this shift is facilitated by placement of an individual in a group in which he remains throughout the school day. In secondary schools, and in the few elementary schools which operate on a departmental, or platoon, basis, belongingness may be more difficult to achieve and it is obviously more difficult for the teacher to influence.

Individual Differences in Need

As we study school groups, it becomes evident that there may be individual differences in the intensity of the need to belong. No doubt many factors are operating. Just as individuals differ in their requirements as to amount and kind of food, so it may be that although all individuals need to belong, they have basic differences in the degree and kind of belonging they require.

We are more inclined to believe, however, that *experiences* of an individual influence the strength of the need. For example, opportunity for expression of a keen interest in a purely individual activity which gives a high degree of satisfaction, such as painting, playing the piano,

THE 3 R'S ARE LEARNED THROUGH EXPERIENCE, AND SO ARE GROUP SKILLS.

or studying nature, may replace in some measure the need to belong (though it does not necessarily do so). A high degree of personal security may operate similarly; or a high degree of insecurity may influence an individual to shun groups and seek other avenues of expression and satisfaction. In general, however, we believe that no pupil is completely happy and adjusted unless he feels he belongs in his school group.

Failure to Belong

If he doesn't feel that he belongs in his school group, a youngster may exhibit unpredictable behavior. (Unable to reach his goal, he uses "detour" behavior, which is difficult to predict. See Chapter III.) Much of the seemingly inexplicable behavior of pupils may have this origin. In general, a teacher is better able to predict reactions when *all* members of a group have achieved belongingness. He is in a better position to set the stage for desired reactions. On the other hand, if many individuals in the group employ unpredictable reactions as detours because they feel a lack of belonging, the teacher is hard put to know how to handle the situation. Thus an important task of the teacher, if he is to be effective as a group leader, is to locate the children who do not "belong" and find means to work with the individual and the group so that "belonging" may take place for all.

Locating Lack of Belonging

Sociometric techniques (discussed in Chapter V) are an important means of identifying those who don't belong. The assumption, when such techniques are used, is that the person rejected by the group realizes that he is rejected (that he doesn't belong). As we shall see, this assumption is not always substantiated. It is sometimes the case, too, that a child who is well accepted may not correctly assess his group status, and so may lack a feeling of belonging. We were interested, therefore, in discovering both the status of the individual as indicated by the group and his feeling about his relation to the group. This latter factor is more subtle and difficult to discover. Probably the best means to use to discover that a child feels he does not belong in the group is to watch him at work and play with his associates, and listen to what he has to say to them, and to his teacher. Clues may be found in conferences with parents, as when Mrs. Thomson reported, "Tom just won't go out to play with other boys after school. He says they don't play fair."

Certainly no one remark or action can be taken as evidence of lack of feeling of belonging. Moreover, it seems that one's feelings may fluctuate widely and rapidly, accordingly to the situation. This is particularly true of young children. A discerning teacher will watch for recurring symptoms such as use of attention-getting mechanisms, withdrawal, overly aggressive behavior, or undue dependence on adult approval or protection.

—supplementary techniques

To supplement such observation, we found clues in reactions reported in various interview or paper-and-pencil techniques. In this study we used a wide range of such techniques in order to test their usefulness as a means to knowing the boys and girls in the groups as well as possible. On examining the responses, we found a number which might indicate lack of feeling of belonging. Such responses pointed to the need for further study through observation and interview. The California Test of Personality[1] gives opportunities for pupils to reveal their feeling about belonging. Answers to questions such as the following may be revealing:

Do you often think that nobody likes you?
Are you proud of your school?
Do you feel that most of your classmates are glad that you are a member of the class?

The Wishing Well [2] devotes a section to identifying the degree of feeling of belonging through statements such as the following.

I wish I felt as though I really belonged to my school group.
I wish my class in school really wanted me there.
I wish some gang or club would want me to join them.
I wish other children wanted me to go more places with them.
I wish I liked the things other children liked.

The Check Sheet of Opportunities in Human Relations (page 407), in a section asking pupils to describe themselves, gives opportunity to express degree of feeling of belonging:

Find it easy to make friends.
Find it difficult to make friends.
Well liked by most.
Liked by few but not many.
Disliked by many.

This Check Sheet also provides an opportunity for each individual to express things he feels he should improve about himself. Statements such as the following ("Things I want to improve about myself") may indicate a lack of sense of belonging:

4th Grade

BERTHA: Have people like me.
DON: Be alone more often.
PETER: Have more friends.
PAM: Wish I was pretty (because I wear glasses and I'm ugly).

8th Grade

BETTY: My cattiness.
BILLY: Be in James' group gang.
RUTH: Get along better.
DOLORES: About everything.

[1] The California Test of Personality, California Test Bureau, Los Angeles, California.
[2] The Wishing Well, Ohio State University, Columbus, Ohio.

CHRISTINE: Make good friends.
JANE: To get over my shyness.
PATSY: How to be popular.

The Springfield Interest Finder (page 418) may reveal feelings of degree of belonging when children express items such as these:

4th Grade

PETER: Wish I were more like other people.
GERTRUDE: Wish I had more friends.

Children who place their names under items such as the following, on the Social Analysis of the Classroom form (page 419) may show symptoms of lack of belonging:

Here is someone whom nobody seems to care much about: people do not notice when he (or she) is around.

Here is someone who doesn't care much to make friends or who is bashful about being friendly, or who doesn't seem to have many friends.

Rating one's self on the Classroom Social Distance Scale (page 401) offers an opportunity for expressing feelings of degree of belonging. Interestingly enough, the children in this study as a rule rated themselves in group 1 of the scale (the high group). In the fourth and fifth grade group, a few rated themselves in group 2, but only one child felt that the class would place her in a low grouping. This girl, who rated herself in group 5, achieved a very high Group Social Distance Score and is very well liked by her group. It may be that she was trying to be modest by rating herself low, but from other evidence we feel she did not assess her group acceptance correctly. This girl is the one who wears glasses and who says: "I wish I was like other children." "I wish I was pretty. (Because I'm ugly and wear glasses)."

Except for rare cases such as this, the Classroom Social Distance Scale, as used with these groups, did not provide a sound basis for determining the extent to which the children did or did not feel that they belonged in their groups. We felt, however, that it is an excellent instrument to measure status given by the group to the individual.

Autobiographies and descriptions of use of leisure time may give some indication of degree of sense of belonging. Statements like the following, made by children in free, undirected situations, may provide such clues:

PETER: In grade school, few of my teachers liked me.
DOROTHY: When I first came to this junior high school I didn't like it very well because the members of the class treated me cold.

Although these responses in somewhat formal situations may provide clues, we feel strongly that they are no more than clues which lead to further study.

We want to emphasize the need for follow-up study. The responses on these paper-and-pencil devices cannot be taken as "answers" to our problems in attempting to know boys and girls. But they may help to point the direction for subsequent observation. No device can be a substitute for an observant and understanding teacher, but it may be of assistance to such a teacher.

BELONGING AND GROUP CULTURE

In most situations, belonging in a group carries with it an adoption of group culture. When the need to belong is high in degree, such adoption of culture may supersede all other values. In other words, a thwarted need (need to belong) develops such close identification by the individual with the group that goals of the group are accepted as individual goals. Arnold, feeling rejected by his school group, found belonging in a gang which required stealing of an item from the five-and-ten-cent store as an initiation. His value pattern rejected such behavior, but his need to belong and the importance of accepting the culture of the group, if he was to belong, were dominant. He stole the item and was satisfied with his group belongingness as a consequence.

However, Arnold was caught. Brought before the principal, he was faced with the dilemma of negating his values of truth and respect for property or his belongingness. The need to belong was dominant. He lied about the situation. It is not infrequent, it seems, that boys and girls of so-called "good families," where truth and respect for property are taught as major values, are caught in such situations. Parents are at a loss to understand. They say, "But we gave him an allowance, and he could have anything he asked for." Yes, he could have anything he asked for other than belonging to the group. Not finding belonging through other means, he was willing to violate all other values to achieve that which he felt to be of major importance.

—making problems

There is probably no teacher who has not met some such experience. Few, however, seem to realize the situation as an indictment of their teaching methods. In the case cited above, it is easy to blame Arnold for stealing, not realizing that Arnold was forced to this action because his teacher and his group had not helped him to find belonging in his group.

We recognize, however, that at times there are requirements of group membership in which difficulties such as Arnold's are not present. Evidently, under certain circumstances an individual's membership is so highly desired by the group on other bases that he is accepted in spite of the culture of the group. Dorothy, an attractive child of fourteen, was sought as a group member by several "secret societies." She accepted the invitation of one of these societies. Her status in the group as a whole was high. Thus when she accepted membership she was able to name her terms. She could resist the group culture. Such ability to resist, however, seems to be accompanied by a strong sense of belonging, and by acceptance in the group as a whole. It is unrealistic to hope for such resistance by a pupil who does not feel accepted by the larger group.

Nor should the fact be overlooked that the culture of the group is developed by the group itself, and thus is subject to change by members of the group. Gertrude, a girl of sixteen, secure in her acceptance by the total group, joined a sorority and, through force of social prestige, was able to change the cultural pattern of the group with which she associated herself.

—belonging in society

Perhaps we should repeat, however, that acceptance of the individual in spite of difference, or change of culture because of dominance of the individual, is only possible when the sense of belonging in a wider society is well established. If there has been no such established belonging, the individual tends to capitulate to the culture of the group, for better or for worse.

In discussing this point, we may have given undue emphasis to the "for worse" situations, as they are the more disturbing and also the more dramatic. We could cite similar examples of youngsters whose need to belong led them to identify themselves with socially acceptable groups and who thus lifted the level of their personal values.

This discussion stresses the responsibility of the teacher to know the degree of sense of belonging of each pupil, and, if that sense of belonging is lacking, or slight, to help him find acceptance in a group which holds socially acceptable values. The most favorable group, we believe, is one directed by the teacher, where the group may participate in leadership and in goal-setting.

HELPING THE ISOLATE

Her teacher was aware of what was happening when Susan came in crying because other children had said she had cooties and fleas. Some teachers might have passed this over with a laugh, but this teacher knew that, in the culture of this group, such name-calling was a drastic measure. She knew that the term "cooties and fleas" was, in the culture of this group, the ultimate in rejection. She knew, too, by the response of the pupil, that she was well aware of the rejection the name-calling implied. Her job, then, was to try to discover why the group rejected Susan, and to try to work both with the group and with Susan to develop belongingness for Susan.

There are several questions a teacher will want to find answers for if he is to know how to help the child who is rejected or who feels he doesn't belong.

—is he rejected?

Children may feel rejected even when they are not. Obviously, the plan of action will depend on whether the rejection is real or imagined. Observation and sociometric techniques (Chapter V) can be helpful in determining the degree of rejection. Perhaps a word of caution is in order. It seems that it is easy for a teacher to fail to assess the group structure correctly, particularly if one of its members has habits which are objectionable to the teacher. Tommy seldom bathed. The meticulous, dainty young woman who was his teacher felt that no one could want to associate with him. She assumed he must be an isolate. Quite the contrary; his classmates found him to be a good sport and "lots of fun"— qualities far more important to them than his bathing habits.

Conversely, the child who is polite, attentive, and bright in his classroom work may be assumed by a teacher to be popular because he wins favor in the teacher's eyes. The assumption may or may not be valid.

—does he know he is rejected?

Some rejected children, particularly those in the lower grades or those who are immature or mentally retarded, show little awareness of their lack of belonging. However, we believe this lack of awareness to be only temporary. Sooner or later, such children will become conscious of their isolation. It is therefore important to help them achieve acceptance, if possible, before a time of rude awakening. It is certainly very difficult to work directly with these children in helping them achieve acceptance. Here is probably a situation calling for work with the group.

—does he care?

Probably no child is totally immune to the feeling a group holds for him, but evidently there is wide variation in response, from deep, troubled concern to relative disinterest. As was noted earlier, this range may be due to individual differences, but we think it more likely that children who seem disinterested have learned to compensate through relationships with other individuals or groups, such as their families, or by developing individual interests in prestige-giving activities. We know that people who have not developed social skills are in for trouble in our society; so even if the child himself does not seem to be interested in belonging to the group, he presents a problem to the teacher.

—what is the group culture?

It has been our observation that all too often a child is rejected by the group because he does not conform to the culture pattern of the group. Often he is unaware of the group culture. On a simple level, we might cite the case of seven-year-old Gerald. The group of which he was a member was in the throes of a shoestring-collecting fad. Number, length, and variety of strings was a major topic of conversation (and, incidentally, the consternation of parents when they went to their shoe closets knew no bounds!). Gerald stood on the side lines, watching and listening to these conversations about the current collectors' items, but he did not participate. His teacher, noticing this, said, "Gerald, why don't you collect shoestrings, too?" After lunch that day, Gerald appeared with a small collection of strings and immediately plunged into the group activity of comparative measurement and comment. He was "in the swing" of the group culture.

Seldom is it as easy as this to introduce a child to the culture of his group, but even this simple case may point to the need for a teacher to be aware of the group culture and to help interpret it to the individual. This example may serve also to indicate the inexplicable nature of the factors which give prestige. For this group, shoestrings had become a symbol of "groupness." Such symbols of group culture or of prestige may be many and varied, and must be recognized as *symbols*. The actual value of the symbol as seen by adults may be nil. A teacher needs to be careful to interpret the prestige-giving value, not the value as *he* sees it.

—to what factors does the group give prestige?

In addition to those aspects of the culture to which all must conform, what are the individual factors to which a group gives prestige? For example, physical attractiveness may or may not be considered an asset, but even if it is, the measure of attractiveness may be group-determined. "Prettiness" or "good looks" are frequently interpreted by children differently from what they are by adults. It is not unusual for a child to mention the prettiness of another child who seems to the adult to be unusually plain or homely.

Other factors we observed to be prestige-giving include: athletic prowess; dress; having a job of one's own; having spending money, owning certain material things, such as a bicycle or a car, physical size, maturity, wit, special talents or skills, dating power, freedom from family control, and membership in exclusive groups, such as athletic teams or clubs which elect members.

May we say again that any one of these might or might not be seen by adults as prestige-giving. The type of wit admired by the group might not be that admired by an adult. A talent for making extra-fine bubbles of gum might not be considered important by an adult, but may hold a strong prestige value for the group.

Moreover, the factors which give prestige fluctuate in value. Ability to "skin the cat" may be admired by six-year-olds but hold no value for twelve-year-olds. Many of these prestige-giving factors have their counterparts in rejection-giving. When dating power is important, the girl without dates tends to be rejected. When special skill in playing marbles is important, the boy who does not know how to play the game tends to be rejected.

It is no easy task, but the teacher who hopes to help an isolate to be accepted must be aware of the factors which *the group* feels give prestige or detract from it.

—who can help him?

It is the teacher who is in the position to set the stage for helping the isolate, but the teacher alone cannot achieve the acceptance of the individual. Sometimes it is possible to elicit, either directly or indirectly, the cooperation of other individuals in the group. If directly, it may involve discussion of the situation with a cooperating individual, with a subgroup, or with the group as a whole. If indirectly, it may mean finding situations in which the isolate may associate with the cooperating individual, in subgroups, committees, or teams.

Sociometric techniques, such as The Classroom Social Distance Scale (page 401), may be helpful in selecting cooperating individuals. The isolate's own choices of those who he feels are his friends or whom he would like to have as friends may give a clue. This doesn't necessarily work, however, for it is not unusual for an isolate to chose as his friends the most popular persons in the room, and the distance between these two extremes may be too wide to bridge. Moreover, it is our experience that to attempt to team two isolates in an attempt to achieve belonging for both can seldom, if ever, be successful. Most helpful, we have found,

EVERY CHILD WANTS TO BELONG IN HIS SCHOOL GROUP.

was to discover in the group the person who least rejected the isolate (we failed to find any isolate who was totally rejected by everyone), and to try to establish rapport through indirect methods, such as providing opportunity for these two to work together within the same committee.

We believe that, in attempting to establish a feeling of belonging, a teacher must work with *the group* as a whole as well as with the individual and with cooperating persons. Much of the literature in child development would imply that the approach to the establishment of belongingness is through work with the individual to help him be acceptable to the group. Equally important, we are convinced, is work with the group to establish acceptance for the individual. In fact, the latter approach may be more important; for the rejection or acceptance is group-centered, and further, work with the group gives an opportunity to discuss with it the importance of careful judgment of the individual, thus furthering the awareness that each individual can make a contribution but the nature of the contributions may vary.

The more clearly we recognize the tremendous influence of the group on the individual, the more we should see the need to help the group feel its responsibilities to its members.

On the other hand, it is possible to lose important educational opportunities unless such occasions are made use of. We feel that teachers have an obligation to help groups see their responsibilities to the individuals in their midst. At what age such maturity of concept is possible we do not know, but we do know it was possible with the ten- and eleven-year-olds who discussed the "cooties and fleas" situation with objectivity and understanding.

ACHIEVING STATUS IN THE GROUP

The group holds within itself a power of great influence—the power to assign status and roles to its members. "Status" implies the high or low rank assigned by the group to the individual. "Role" implies the function the group assigns to the individual. A role may have high or low status by rank of function or by rank within function. For example, Billy was assigned, by the group, to the role of clown. The role of clown in this group was of high rank, topped only by that of leader (one who moves to action). However, Billy was "fifth place" clown, four other clowns taking precedence over him; thus his rank in role was high, but his status within the role was fifth place in role rank.

The status and rank assigned to an individual are closely related to the group goal. Thus, if the group values "pleasing the teacher," then the "teacher's pet" may achieve rank and status. If the group goal is excellence in sports, athletes gain status. If the goal is to make a good school garden, persons with gardening knowledge and skills achieve status.

Since situations may determine goals, status-giving qualities may vary with situations. However, certain types of behavior seem to provide *general* status and role assignments which operate in a wide range of situations. It would seem that such general status and role assignments are based on the continuing, relatively unchanging group values and goals, which transcend the demands of an immediate situation. Common generalized roles of high status value include those of leader, popular person, rejected person, and group pet.

THE LEADER

Leadership, as we use the word, implies the power to move a group to action. It seems that this power derives from four types of strength: physical power (members of the group fear bodily harm); social strength (the individual has power to bestow or withdraw belongingness for the other individuals) or ability to meet emotional needs (the group, consciously or unconsciously, recognizes that the individual helps to meet thwarted needs and interests; he may help people feel that they are important, that they belong); rational power (the group recognizes the worth of the intellectual powers of the person); and skills (the group recognizes that the particular skills of the individual help to move the group toward its goal).

Whatever the area of group acceptance, there seems to be an irrational "halo effect" of leadership. Just as Henry Ford was frequently asked for opinions on matters ranging from education to world affairs, even though his "power to action" was in terms of skills for automobile production, so pupils may assign to their leader omnipotence of judgment beyond the area of his activities.

Peter is an undersized but extremely wiry boy who has "licked" every boy in the classroom on one pretext or another. No one seems to be able to match his quickness, agility, or high degree of muscular coordination. By threats of physical violence he is able to dominate the free-choice situations in the room so that the group is always doing, however unwillingly, what he wants done. Such leadership is greatly deplored by the teacher of the group, and is hardly the type a democratic school system tries to promote; but it must be recognized that until the situation changes and the group is able to devise effective means of coping with Peter's physical domination, he is going to continue to be a dominant factor in this group's life.

Sally, an eleven-year-old, on the other hand, is much more likely to be ridiculed or tormented than she is to be followed. In her case, however, there are several records of occasions when her suggestions, because of their aptness and peculiar applicability to the problems under consideration, have been followed with success. Here we see the power of rational persuasion to move a group to action even though the persuader is not generally accepted socially by the group. In no way should one confuse with the idea of popularity Sally's ability to lead.

Lucy, in the eighth grade, represents the qualities greatly admired by social groups of her class. She is a member of the Girls' Cavalier Corps (a group chosen to render service to school, and membership in which is highly prized). By a few simple words, Lucy is able to heap scorn and ridicule on those who envy her social position and wish to improve theirs by association with her. Lucy decided that she didn't want to be given a physical examination by a man docter. Because of her ability to give or withhold social acceptance, she almost created a major obstacle to the success of the voluntary physical examination program in her room. Here is an example of leadership exerted because of social power, not because of any rational persuasion or the ability to inflict bodily harm.

There are sometimes those who are leaders because of their ability to develop in the group skills which enable it more readily to achieve its goals. In many classrooms the teacher assumes this role—and to do so is probably a legitimate function of the teacher, but certainly not one exclusively his. Our experience with children leads us to believe that this type of leadership is more frequently exerted by children when on the playground or in the "extracurricular activities" than when in the classroom. (We use quotes because we feel the program of clubs and social affairs is very much *curricular*, contributing as it does to the education of boys and girls.) Very often, children who are able to get a playground group to play together happily, or a junior class to work effectively to put on a prom, find themselves in a position of leadership just because they are able to develop these necessary skills. It is, perhaps, an indictment of teacher ability that we found less evidence of this type of leadership among children in classroom situations.

The Group Selects Its Leaders

Except for some uses of physical power, which may be imposed by the individual himself, leadership is *conferred by the group.* Thus, leadership is not a mystic innate quality of the individual, but is status given *by the group* to the individual who demonstrates power respected by the group. This concept gives a new turn to the usual concept of "leadership training." It has been customary for schools to accept as leaders those who are made leaders by the group and to attempt to "develop their leadership." Actually, such leadership is group-given, and we need not look far to find examples of withdrawal by the group of leadership power once adults have decided to "develop" it in an individual. In other words, in a democratic society (or in any society for that matter, but of particular pertinence in a democracy) we might better put more of our energies into training *groups* to choose their leaders, rather than expend it all in developing some mystic force that is called "leadership."

This concept is not easy to come by, for we have so long assumed that persons, as individuals, "had" or "had not" leadership that we find it hard to recognize the group-given nature of leadership. True, some individuals to a greater extent than others tend to have, or to discern and achieve, that which the group requires. To the extent that group goals are permanent, these individuals will tend to maintain their leadership over a period of time. Thus leadership becomes personified. But it is subject to change whenever the group goals shift, which may be quite frequently with groups of immature children.

One factor sometimes stands in the way of recognition of group power. A teacher who is not aware of the subtle influences of group interaction may assume that certain individuals are true leaders when actually they are merely "fronts" for the group. A smart group of tenth graders knew what the teacher expected of a group discussion leader, so they elected Sam to the position though in reality Sam had no influence in the group. Having elected Sam, the group sat back to enjoy its own modes of operation. The group still relied on its own operational leaders, confident that the possibility of interference with this leadership was lessened because the teacher was "appeased" by the election of Sam. The teacher, feeling confident that he had allowed democratic election, could not understand why Sam was unable to exert the leadership (power to action) expected from an elected representative.

Delegation of Leadership

Perhaps it would be well at this point to re-emphasize that the group gives leadership power to its members *in terms of its goals,* and that these goals are derived, we believe, from identification, thwarted needs and interests, or rational power.

As a rule, it is not difficult to spot the leader who achieves this status because goals are derived from identification. When a "muscular" hero is the idol of the group, the member who can display the most such power becomes the leader (the one who can move to action). When a film star is the heroine with whom a group of teen-agers identify, the person in the group who most nearly resembles her, as the girls interpret her, becomes the leader. This sort of assignment of leadership roles serves to underline the importance of the teacher's understanding and knowing means of controlling goal sources.

Except in the situation cited above, in which Sam was elected as a "front," a teacher is usually aware of the leader who attains prominence because the group respects his rational power. It is this type of leader who is most commonly hailed by adults as having qualities of "leadership," yet even a cursory examination of power patterns of a school indicates that this leadership pattern is often assigned less status than other patterns. Again, this emphasizes the need to be concerned with *group* education rather than with so-called "leadership" education based on the theory that leadership is innate.

Perhaps the most subtle and insidious type of leadership, and the one most difficult for the majority of teachers to detect, is that achieved by the individual who is able to contribute status and belongingness to those who have thwarted needs and interests. Such a person plays upon the need of people to belong and to feel important. Much of what some people interpret to be the message of Dale Carnegie's *How to Win Friends and Influence People* is based on this type of leadership power. It is this kind of power, too, which is used by the political leader who promises racial superiority or world domination. It is our opinion that such leadership is most to be feared. Programs fostered by schools which are merely on the level of "how to win friends" or "how to get ahead of the other fellow" without accompanying programs for developing the idea and ideals of group membership are, we believe, dangerous.

ASSESSING LEADERS

In our modern society, the opportunity to make decisions about the group is moving, whether we like it or not, from the individual to representatives of individuals—chairmen, delegates, congressmen, governors, presidents, of clubs, of governments, of the United Nations. The implication for school experience is clear. We are charged to help people learn to assess their leaders, to choose those who meet their standards, and to measure the qualities of those to whom they entrust their individual convictions.

In the light of what we know about how people learn, we know that the best way to teach skills is through direct experience coupled with thoughtful evaluation of the experience. This is as true of social skills as it is of the three R's. To help youngsters learn to delegate leadership, there must be *experiences* for delegation and evaluation.

The group of fourth and fifth graders with whom we worked most intensively had many experiences in delegating leadership, but they felt that the position of gravest responsibility was that held by the planning leader, one of the group chosen by them to chair the group planning of the daily and weekly program. As the person who led them in discussion of group destiny for a week—a long time, to a ten-year-old— these leaders and their procedures were evaluated with grave concern for those aspects felt to be of major importance to good group living. Thus the aspects of leadership they chose to mention in their evaluations became a rough index of the dimensions of group interaction recognized by the group members. We present these statements as examples of what a fourth and fifth grade group may achieve.

Our Leaders Should:

—provide spread of participation

The aspect of leadership having by far the greatest frequency of mention had to do with spread of participation.

"Norma gives everybody a chance."
"She sees that everyone gets to give ideas!"
"Tom took all the hands." (Called on all who volunteered.)
"He got around to everyone."
"I think Jane should be a planning leader again because she called on not only her friends. She calls on others. She calls on everybody."

Sometimes the evaluation was quite personal:

"She was a good planning leader to me. She called on me and other children."

When the leader did not provide for spread of participation, group members were quick to note it:

"He just took his friends' hands." (He called on his friends only.)
"Sue is good in leading but plays favorites sometimes."

—represent the group

Group members were quite conscious of the role of the leader as group representative, leading the *group* toward decision:

"She wrote the plans up the way they came out from us."
"Don wanted what we wanted to do."
"She gave her suggestions but she took ours."
"He asks if we should and if the class says yes, then we do."
"He didn't write down what he wanted. He wrote down what we wanted. He always wanted what we wanted."
"He planned the things like we wanted him to."

Sometimes special techniques helped convey the idea of representation:

"I like the way she asked us if it would be all right to do things."
"He said have you got any suggestions and we give him some suggestions and we have something to plan with."
"After she was done she would ask, 'Is that all right with you?' "
"Gordon didn't argue with us."

The leader who was too dominating was quickly spotted:

"I think Norma is a good leader sometimes but sometimes she is too bossy."
"I liked everything Joan did except the way she told the kids to shut up."

—have skills

A discerning group will recognize and demand skills of leadership:

"She did things right and knew what she was doing."
"Marie was the best leader we ever had. She didn't have to be told what to do."
"She knew how to get started and got things done."
"She made good reasons for what she did."
"He got straight to the point and didn't act silly."
"He did a nice job and he asked questions well."
"She kept the planning going."

"She handled things nicely."

"She kept on the beam and stuck to the subject."

"He never talked all the time like some leaders. He let us talk."

"If some one would say something she would ask why so we'd all know."

"I thought Doris was a good thinker."

"She got down to facts."

"Some were silly but she didn't blow up. She is as good as any leader could be."

"She knew when to stop."

—learn as they lead

We were interested to find that boys and boys could be quite sympathetic if they felt the leader was trying to do better and was achieving improvement:

"He tried very hard."

"Betty is improving."

"I thought she got some good experience out of it and she learned to stand on her own two feet."

"At first she wasn't so good but now she is just about perfect."

"She learned a lot I think."

"I liked the way he improved while he was leader."

"He was good after he got onto it."

—be understood

In these meetings the leader was responsible for writing the plans on the blackboard; so matters of penmanship and spelling, as well as speech, were of importance:

"Sometimes she would write uphill and downhill and she would write so light that you can hardly see the letters."

"I thought Sam was a good planning leader, all but his spelling."

"He could write so we could read it."

"He needed to write straighter and not go downhill."

"She talked so soft nobody could hear her. She never talked loud enough."

"She talks so everyone can hear her and she could talk awfully loud."

—be free of personal mannerisms

Even small matters of personal habit come under the scrutiny of the group:

"She was bashful and couldn't stand still."

"Nan is polite in everything."

"She didn't act silly."

"She didn't show off and was very good in front of the room."

—create a friendly atmosphere

General liking and personal warmth are important in a leader:

"She was nice to us and she never fought with us and we all liked her."
"I have enjoyed him very much and I think the other kids liked him very much."
"Mabel was nice to us so we had to be nice to her."

Sometimes personal feelings color the evaluation of the leader:

"I liked Martha as a planning leader because she is my girl."

—overcome obstacles

The group is tolerant of difficulties and makes allowances when they are felt to be due:

"She's good for only a 4A." (Younger than most group members.)
"Gary is a good leader, even if he is a boy."
"Mostly she talks soft so when she was leader she didn't talk loud enuf but we understand."
"She can't write good so she had a scecktary but all but that she was good."

—achieve results

Young pragmatists evaluated their leaders in terms of results achieved:

"She got things done."
"We done what we wanted and learned what we wanted when Gary was leader."
"When she was leader things went right."

—meet general standards

Sometimes group members found it difficult to point to specifics, but felt strongly about general impressions.

"I thought Marilyn was the worst planning leader we ever had and will ever have and I hope we never have one like her."
"Norma handled planning as good as any child could."
"Patsy was a very good leader, and I don't think we will ever have a better one."

Personification of Leadership

It is our belief that as a group gains skill in using the powers of individuals, accompanied by skill in evaluating the powers of individuals, there is less personification of leadership. This is another way of saying, perhaps, that as the group matures in group skills, it gives less credence to the "halo" effect of certain types of power and attains skill in evaluating the contribution of each member. As the latter skill is acquired, there is less tendency to point to one individual as "*the* leader," and more to point to each person and say, "He is good in helping us do so and so," and "He is skilled in helping us achieve so and so."

There is need, we believe, to increase and spread the leadership opportunities offered in the classroom. This can be achieved by giving boys and girls many more chances to make group choices and group decisions, and to operate as a group in working toward their objectives. The organization of the classroom into subgroups and committees for certain purposes offers wider opportunity for leadership, as does the provision of a wide variety of experiences in various situations, such as opportunity to work and play with people of varying ages, in out-of-classroom activities, in community participation.

OTHER STATUS ROLES

The leader, the individual with power to move the group to action, is demonstrating but one status role. Others may be classified as popular person, special enemy, or pet.

Popular Person

Not to be confused with leadership (though often so confused) is popularity, or the recognition of ability to contribute to group goals or satisfactions, not necessarily accompanied by power to move the group to action.

Earl, who dares to mimic an unpopular teacher, may achieve high status in this fashion, yet identical behavior in the case of another pupil mimicking another teacher may be cause for rejection. Billy, who is considered "cute" because he is little and agile in a group of awkward adolescents, may find himself ostracized a year or two later because the latter are shaving and he doesn't even have any fuzz on his upper lip. Marie, who can outrun the boys, may find herself left out at a dance but in great demand at a picnic. Gerald, a good student, may be popular in his fraternity but would be quite out of place in one where "gentlemen's grades" (nothing above a C) are the accepted thing.

It is important for the teacher to be aware of the type of behavior to which the group ascribes popularity. He may use this knowledge to help him become acceptable to the group, and to assist him in helping the non-accepted children find their places in the group.

Special Enemy

"It is better to be hated than ignored." At least this seems to be the feeling of some of the children in a group. Unable to achieve status in any other way, some attempt to do so by becoming more and more aggressive in their unacceptable behavior. Many of the so-called "teacher's pets" belong in this category. Alice C. was one of these. For some time she had tried to find a means of being popular with her fellow pupils, but without much success. Consequently, she turned to the teacher for recognition and went out of her way to do things that she felt the teacher would notice and like. She was always washing blackboards, collecting papers, emptying wastebaskets, and handing in extra homework. In her particular group, such activities rated low in popularity but high in status-giving hostility. The more things Alice found to do for the teacher the more the class reacted, until Alice finally found herself sufficiently noticed, even though in a hostile fashion.

Joseph P., on the other hand, was in a group that valued the teacher's opinion rather highly. Being new to the group and not finding socially acceptable activities to give him the status he desired, he acquired a high degree of group notice by being argumentative and obstructive. Nothing pleased him; he found fault with everything the group wanted; he annoyed the teacher in every way he could. He succeeded in achieving a certain type of status in the group, even though it was that of active rejection by group members.

The "special enemy" presents a different problem to the teacher than does the child ignored by group. Here it is not merely a problem of helping a child to find behavior of high social acceptability, but of assisting him to overcome the hostility he has already engendered.

This may be difficult to do. It is a job not only of developing acceptance, but further, of breaking down hostilities. Sometimes it is simpler to transfer such an individual to another group where he may have a "fresh start." Obviously, a transfer in itself is no answer, for, if the individual knows no means to achieving status other than through the "special enemy" approach, he will attempt it again in the new group. Under the guidance of an understanding teacher, however, the fresh start may give the child an opportunity to try acceptance techniques without having to break through the rejection he has achieved.

Pet

Another way of achieving status in a group is by becoming a pet of the group. Handicapped children and other deviates often find themselves occupying this role.

Herman was the only Negro boy in a large elementary school. Because he was different he was a great favorite of all, and he thus achieved status without effort on his part. He was occupying the place of "pet" in his group.

Some children go to great lengths to become the pets of their groups. Girls seem to attempt to achieve this more often than boys, probably because it is more compatible with the traditional feminine role. Baby talk, apparent helplessness, giggling, and similar behavior may represent efforts to achieve this status.

There are two dangers in such a status. In the first place, it is an essentially parasitic one. It is a role in which one gets something for nothing, and therefore it is reprehensible. It does not contribute to the good of the group.

The second danger, equally to be feared, is that often the status is only temporary. Herman soon found that having been a pet had its disadvantages when he ran into the real effects of racial intolerance as he grew older. Some handicapped children, because of the pet role that they have assumed, may find that their physical shortcomings have become even more of a disadvantage, while others who so assiduously sought such status may find that changing conditions make them even more lonely and isolated.

One of the major tasks of the teacher is to help each child achieve status in a positive fashion, and to help him avoid the negative or parasitical activities which lead to active rejection or to becoming a pet.

Hidden Links

As was indicated above, we find that status is closely linked with group goals, the group giving status to the individual exhibiting power related to achievement of goals. Sometimes, however, the link may be deeply hidden and can be discovered only after careful analysis.

In a group of senior high school boys there seemed to be status-giving factors associated with low grades. If a boy's report card showed nothing above a "C," other boys referred to him as having "gentleman's grades." It was some time before the teacher was able to discover that grades were associated with "dating power" (a factor of high prestige). Evidently the assumption in the group was that if one gets good grades, one has been spending time in studying rather than in having dates, and anyone knows (so the reasoning went) that if one had a choice, he would choose the date rather than the studying. Ergo, a chap who had good grades had no chance to have a date!

The party giver, the boy with a car, or the pupil with money to spend may wield a power out of proportion to personal qualities because of the ability to provide prestige-giving situations (or to withhold such situations from certain individuals). Sometimes this power is so general as to become a group pattern, and the person who cannot comply with the group cultural expectancy is out of luck.

One teacher, concerned over the plague of "dirty" stories and pornographic art in the lavatories, found that these were means used by members of the group to signify daring in sex experimentation, a status-giving factor. Interestingly enough, those who had least sex information and least sex experience were likely to be the most eager to meet group cultural standards, so felt it necessary to be most expressive through stories and "art."

SHIFT IN STATUS

Realizing that status is *group*-given and is associated with group goals, it is not surprising to find that status shifts as group goals shift. Many factors contribute to such changes, not least of which may be the influence of the teacher. Other common reasons are change in maturity, in group personnel, and in the group view of prestige-giving factors.

Change in Maturity

We have indicated earlier that maturity is an important factor in determining goals of a group; thus it is understandable that goal-linked status shifts as there is change in maturity. The boy accepted as a clown in the sixth grade may find himself rejected in junior high school, as goals shift to those having to do with organized athletics, and dates. The boy who matures early may find that he has status with faster-maturing girls because of similar heterosexual interests, even though he may have been rejected a few years earlier.

The first few in a group to report sex experimentation may find that they have status because of this experience, if it is within the group value

INTERESTS VARY WITH MATURITY.

pattern (although they may be ignored or rejected if the group is disinterested or disapproving).

It is usual to find a whole new alignment of status of girls with boys and boys with girls, as heterosexual interests develop. Even within groups of girls, or groups of boys, there is a realignment of friendships when the maturity rate varies markedly, as is most likely to occur during the junior and early senior high school years. This realignment may prove to be devastating for the deviate, for the one who matures early, or for the one who matures late, particularly the latter. Implications for helping youngsters understand their own development and what it implies, socially as well as physically, seem to us clear and compelling.

Change in Group Personnel

The urge to achieve status, to belong, is never-ending. When a youngster is new to a group, he must find himself in the established status pattern. This is far from easy, particularly if he is the retiring, withdrawn type of person. This situation is multiplied and intensified when whole portions of a group are thrown into new situations. Half-year promotions, which move some members of a class from one group to another, may cause major status dislocations and realignments. How useful to the individual such experience in adjusting to realignment may be, it is difficult to know. Possibly some such experience may be favorable, but more evident to the observer are the number of pupils who, having had difficulty in adjustment, are just beginning to find security when they must go to a new status-seeking situation. It would seem that too frequent need to adjust may give undue emphasis to status-seeking. There are youngsters who seem to spend all their time and energy in this activity, at the expense of other areas of growth.

Ralph was a highly intelligent boy (as measured by I.Q. tests), but shy and retiring and slow to adjust in social situations. In September, he started in the first grade in one school, but because of change of residence, changed to another school at the end of three months. He was placed in a group composed equally of beginning first graders and advanced pupils. In February, the older group moved on to join a second grade class, and another group joined that of which Ralph was still a member. In other words, within six months, Ralph had had three major group adjustments to make. It seemed to be more than he could take. He quit trying. His teacher reported:

"He doesn't seem to care what anyone thinks of him. He just goes his own sweet way. He doesn't bother anyone, but he doesn't join in group activities. He has no close friends."

We have a hunch that if Ralph had been given an opportunity to grow and develop in one group, at his own rate, he might have learned his role as a group member.

The extra move complicated Ralph's case, yet it would seem that for many children the adjustment every half year may be a severe trial, particularly if they are immature or have withdrawing tendencies. In the same way, a change of teacher may be a severe adjustment for many children.

Realization of such need to adjust seems to us to have clear implications *against* plans for half-year promotions for groups or "extra" promotions for individuals, and *for* one teacher's remaining with a group over a period of time. On the other hand, the importance of learning to adjust has implications for the task of the school in providing experiences through which this skill can be learned. It would seem that provision for a "home base" (such as a room assignment in the elementary school, and a general education group with a block of time together in the secondary school) with some opportunity for wider contacts that are planned is definitely in order.

New View of Prestige Factors

As youngsters mature, or as they encounter other changes, they develop new goals and values. We are pleased, of course, to see children developing, but certain changes are difficult to handle. For example, the adolescent who may have been free of any practice of racial discrimination has some extremely difficult choices to make when he begins to have dates. Whether we like it or not, we know that even seemingly liberal adults can take a dim view of equality when their son or daughter suggests the possibility of a social date with a member of another race. Our society has stacked the cards against such association. The easy course is to reject those of another skin color, religion, or nationality background. We should blame society rather than the adolescent, but, wherever the blame, the teacher has a problem to face.

Having worked for acceptance regardless of race, nationality background, or creed, Miss Thorson found it difficult to know how to handle the cleavage which was occurring in her eleventh grade group. She felt that the weight of social opinion was too great for her to fight head-on. She could, of course, hope to develop intellectual concepts which might make for greater liberalism, even if not for complete social acceptance. This she did, with all the skills at her command, but she did not stop here. She tried to find areas in which social taboos would not apply so rigidly. She found that discrimination was strongest in social functions involving boy-girl relations, and not so strong in those less sex-linked. For example, so subtle are the social pressures against interracial relations that social dancing with "mixed" partners was taboo in her community; but folk dancing and much of square dancing did not carry this inter-sex connotation, so were acceptable. This gave her an avenue of approach even in social affairs. The pupils were happy to find an opportunity for retaining the friendships they had built through the years. Moreover, with this evidence that adult pressures did not demand total rejection of other races, relations in the classroom improved. Such a compromise offers no final answer, but Miss Thorson made the most of means available to her in her community. If all teachers did at least this much, we might find we were making progress, even though slowly.

Similarly, with increased maturity boys and girls become more keenly conscious of the power of money and of social class. We were interested to note that the eighth graders with whom we worked listed "seems to come from a good home" as one of the nine major factors by which they measured their friends. When pressed for an explanation, they claimed the phrase meant that the person had acceptable social manners, which, no doubt, was only part of the answer. We are inclined to suspect that social prestige was also implied, and that this was associated with economic status. However, we found that although "seems to come from a good home" was rated as important in choosing friends, when it came to naming friends on the Classroom Social Distance Scale there was no significant correlation of choices with socio-economic status, as measured by the Sims Socio-Economic Score Card. In other words, we feel it is possible that pressure of society operates to a greater extent in verbalization than in action, at least in certain areas of social living.

—maturity and age role

Increased maturity is likely to be associated with the giving of prestige to an ever-widening range of skills. Where at first athletic prowess may have been a dominant factor during adolescence, the prestige base broadens to include a wide range of skills, from that of the girl who can dance to that of the boy who can play the piano, both of whom might have been rejected a few years earlier.

We would be interested in knowing the degree to which such shifts in interests are developmental, the natural result of growing up, and the degree to which they are culturally developed. We shall discuss later (pages 191–194) the cultural influence on sex cleavage. It is possible, we believe, that culturally determined assignments of role by age may be important. There seems to be a tacit assumption that a twelve-year-old boy should be interested in athletics above all else. That he usually is may be an indication either of "native" interest pattern or of response to cultural expectation. It may be possible, too, that this cleavage in age role is associated with sex role. For some unknown reason, it is thought in certain circles that there is something effeminate in the interest of a twelve-year-old boy in playing the piano, yet the same interest in a virile twenty-five-year-old is not so designated. The ten-year-old girl who likes to climb trees may be condemned as a tomboy by the very community which later will make clucking noises of disapproval when this same girl, aged twenty-five, finds housework physically exhausting. It would seem that the culture determines the acceptable means for expending energy. We have discussed what, to us, is the unfortunate role of isolation assigned to youth. Related to this problem is, we believe, the need for a study of the age roles assigned to boys and girls of various ages.

Adjusting to Shift in Status

We have implied above that adjustment in new situations, as status-giving factors shift, may be very difficult for the individual. Reactions are varied and unpredictable. (Again we refer to the pattern which indicates that if immediate goal satisfaction is unattainable, the individual or group resorts to unpredictable detour behavior.) Sometimes the reaction is hostility against the group or rejection of the group. The logic seems to be: "O.K., I've tried, but if you keep changing, why should I bother? I'll go my way, and it doesn't matter whether you like it or not." There may be pathetic overplaying of the old status-giving behavior. For example, Dick, who amused the group by his clowning in the sixth grade, found that the group in junior high school was not amused; but he clowned the harder, hoping that eventually his efforts might succeed. When they didn't, he withdrew from the group. Marjorie, who achieved status at home by getting good marks, thinks the same behavior may win her status in her school group, or, although it gave her some status in the fifth grade group, she finds it does not seem to work in high school; she may nevertheless put more and more energy into achieving high marks.

We have suggested that subjecting boys and girls to undue pressure to adjust to new situations, to find status anew, may be undesirable; but a certain amount of change, such as shift due to maturity, is probably inevitable. It seems to us that the only fair thing is for teachers to guide groups in a frank and searching examination of their group goals, and allow the individual to reject them or to find means to comply with them. A clear acceptance of variation in goals may be healthful, if understood. Moreover, if goals are clarified through discussion, the group may be willing to move to goals acceptable to all.

DEVIATION AND CONFORMITY

Studies have indicated that, on the whole, the person of average mental ability in any group, or one with ability only slightly above average, has the best opportunity to achieve acceptability by the group.

If, then, leaders are chosen on the basis of such social acceptance or friendship (as may be the case in adult as well as child society) it may hold unfortunate implications for the choice of leaders (assuming that mental superiority is important in leadership). This is the way to a mediocre society, we are told. We know that this is claimed, possibly with some justification, by people unsympathetic to democratic forms.

As we see it, this possibility gives tremendous weight to the need to educate groups in their choice of leaders, as discussed earlier (pages 124–127). If leaders are chosen in terms of ability to achieve a particular objective, rather than because of similarity to the group, or because of general good will and friendship, it is the deviate, *because he is a deviate* in a particular respect, and so may have a unique contribution to make to the group, who should be chosen.

It would seem, however, that children as well as adults give weight to conformity. In what respect, then, and to what extent may an individual deviate from the group norm or group ideal and still be accepted by the group? In terms of the factors studied in the groups with which we are associated, it would seem that wide deviation is permissible, *if* (and this is important) the individual conforms in those areas considered the most important (in contributing to goals) by the group. If an individual conforms to behavior expectations in areas regarded by those in power as important, he may deviate widely in other respects and still gain acceptance.

Tom was popular. One would never suspect that he would be, from his mannerisms. He was a perfect example of a "sissy." He even dressed the part, wearing a suit and a necktie when practically all the other boys arrived at school in dirty "cords." Tom waved his hands gracefully when he spoke, tittered like a girl, and, on occasions, was even seen to skip when going down the hall. But Tom was popular and genuinely accepted.

Tom could write and produce assembly programs that were a knockout. His scripts were smooth and polished. His performances had a professional quality. In Tom's school there was great rivalry among classes (Senior, Junior, Sophomore) and among club groups in the production of assembly programs. To be able to outdo the others in presenting an excellent show was one of the most important things in life. Consequently, "sissy" or not, Tom was liked and accepted for the things he could do that had high status-giving value.

Deviation and Status

On the other hand, an individual may conform in most respects, yet if he deviates in that area which is currently considered status-giving by the group, he may be rejected.

Abigail's record might seem to make her a candidate for "Miss Average Fourteen-year-old" in her group. Her mental age was near the median for the group. She was maturing, physically, at a rate comparable with that of most of the other girls. She was neither fatter nor thinner, taller nor shorter, than most of the others. Her academic record was average. She did very well in athletics, but was not outstanding. Her teacher had not discovered any special talents or special difficulties, either in personality adjustment or in academic achievement. As far as she could observe, Abigail did not markedly deviate from the others in social graces. She had neither much more nor much less money to spend than her associates.

If the theory holds that the person nearest average in most things is a candidate for social success and leadership, Abigail should have led the field. But Abigail was not accepted. There was no definite hostility against her. But her name wasn't mentioned when choices were made of people to assume posts of responsibility or prestige. The girls seemed to forget her when they gathered after school to go to the corner drugstore for cokes.

The reason for Abigail's lack of acceptance was not difficult to discover. Whoever chose her clothes had some odd notions about how a teen-ager should dress. The severe, homemade jumper suits and long cotton stockings made Abigail look quite different from her contemporaries. It was interesting to note that this difference in appearance did not seem to bother Abigail; if it did, she was skilled in concealing her feelings.

Her teacher analyzed the situation as follows: Abigail had always been dressed differently from other children, but dress had not been of much importance to the group until early adolescence, when it became very important indeed. Abigail, for some unknown reason, had not developed this interest in clothes and seemed unaware of the shift in group interest.

Abigail, then, serves as our example of the "average" person who is unaccepted because of one deviation, that one deviation being in an area of high prestige.

Although Abigail has served our purposes here as an example, we do not like to leave her here. Even though Abigail did not seem concerned, her teacher was. She felt that sooner or later Abigail would become clothes-conscious, and, even more important, would surely become aware of her growing lack of status in the group. Thus, her teacher felt a responsibility as a teacher to do something about Abigail's clothes—not because she, the teacher, felt clothes to be important, but because she knew that the other girls felt them to be important, and that soon the boys would, too. This matter was far more important in Abigail's general education than that she be able to conjugate a Latin verb correctly.

In this case the solution was not too difficult. It was not complicated by religious beliefs or customs, by ideas of morality expressed in clothing, or by lack of finances, factors which might have made the situation extremely difficult. The teacher found that Abigail lived with her grandmother, a kindly, well-intentioned elderly woman, who did not know how to dress Abigail and welcomed the help of the teacher, and the suggestion that Abigail herself might have more voice in the choice of her clothes.

This example is an easy "success story." Often the task of the teacher is far more difficult, as, for example, when the deviation cannot be changed. The physically handicapped, the child of a different race, or the one who can't "keep up" with the social pattern of the group because of lack of finances, presents severe difficulties.

It is our belief, as implied in the discussion above, that a major task of teachers is to help groups learn to respect and, when appropriate, make use of differences. When the difference makes it impossible for the individual to participate in an activity leading to a major group goal, as, for instance, when a crippled boy cannot play games or an overly fat girl is not asked for dates, it is unrealistic, we believe, to attempt to change the group goal. But at times it is possible to broaden the base of social interaction.

The Job of the School

The school, as a whole, has a responsibility for providing a wide range of activities, so that deviates may find a place in which their deviation is less restricting to their participation, and, equally important if not more so, so that groups may learn that although certain types of differences may limit certain areas of participation, the deviate, as a person, need not be rejected. His deviation is no handicap in some activities, and may even be a resource in others.

In the elementary school, we rely heavily on the individual teacher to provide this breadth of experience. To the extent that the teacher sees his responsibility, this may be a satisfactory arrangement, though we believe it needs examination. In the secondary school, however, it is difficult for one teacher to provide sufficient range of activity, even when he works with a group for a considerable block of time. Moreover, it is just at the age when pupils are in secondary schools that deviations, particularly those restricting social relations, are most keenly felt.

—the "extracurricular" program

The best answer we have found to date seems to be in the "extracurricular" program. Too often, however, scope and participation are left to chance. The extracurricular program may be based on popular demand, which may eliminate the deviate. Most programs of extracurricular activities should be carefully examined in order to determine whether they are meeting the needs of *all* boys and girls.

We wish to repeat that, although the necessity of caring for the deviate himself is usually uppermost in the minds of educators, of even greater importance is the need to help pupil groups learn to accept and respect him. Respect for differences is a fundamental premise of democracy. Unless we can find opportunity for guided experiences of many types, involving people of wide ranges of difference, we fail to teach this respect. And if we fail to teach this respect, we fail in our duty as teachers in democratic society.

Having stated this fundamental premise, we hasten to say, however, that deviation holds no value *merely because it is deviation.* The value, as implied above, is in the contribution which the deviate brings *to the group.*

There are occasions, as we all recognize, when the deviate, by influence of his deviation, can lead the group in undesirable directions. We have told you of Peter, whose deviation in physical strength made it possible for him to "lick" every boy in the room and thus achieve a leadership role which might be envied by any absolute monarch or dictator. This, obviously, is not what we mean when we talk of respect for deviation. The measure of respect, it would seem, is the degree to which the individual contributes to the group by setting goals and working to achieve them. We are convinced that seldom, if ever, is there an individual, however handicapped, whether physically or by community prejudices regarding race, sex, economic status, and so on, who cannot make such a contribution if the setting is appropriate. The provision of such setting is, we believe, a major task of the school.

—using the contributions of all

Unless the school provides a setting in which all can contribute, we are fostering a society which, because some of its members have not learned to discriminate, allows the operations of gangsters and political bosses. The power to discriminate involves an awareness and examination of goals, and the means to achieve them. If skills for developing this awareness and ability to examine are provided in the school, we believe we have little to fear from dangerous or mediocre leaders or from intolerance for deviates.

THE TEACHER AS GROUP MEMBER

In discussing the individual in the classroom group, we should not overlook the fact that the teacher, too, is a group member. As we observed teacher-pupil groups, we were able to identify the general reactions of pupils to teachers as warm, friendly personalized give-and-take, with the teacher accepted as a group member; as apathetic indifference; as active negativism, open hostility; or as fear.

We tried to measure the degree of social acceptance of the teacher in the group by inserting his name in the appropriate alphabetical order in the list of names to be checked on the Classroom Social Distance Scale (page 401). We do not feel, however, that the results were meaningful. Most children gave the teacher top rank, thus assigning him a place above all others in the group. Maybe this was a true evaluation, for we used this method only in groups where we were convinced the relationships were good. (We feel that it is dangerous to use a device such as the Classroom Social Distance Scale unless the degree of rapport of the teacher with the group is high.) On the other hand, it may mean that the teacher was seen as playing a special, different role from that of other group members, and therefore was inappropriately listed with others for evaluation of acceptance.

Thus, though we were unable to measure teacher acceptability with any precision, we are convinced through observation that the range of acceptance is wide.

—what determines the teacher role?

What determines the status of the teacher in the group? We have discussed earlier (pages 92–93) the relation which a teacher's acceptance of group goals bears to his position in the group. We have discussed, too, the expectancy of the group in relation to interaction patterns (page 38). Evidently related to these factors, yet distinct from them, is the role which the group assigns to the teacher, just as it assigns roles to other group members. And, just as with other group members (e.g., the fifth place clown) so the teacher's role seems to vary in status-giving power.

We believe that it is important for a teacher, like any other group member, to be aware of the role assigned him by the group. True, if the group sees the teacher in the same role as the teacher sees himself, this awareness is of less importance. But it frequently seems that the group and the teacher are not in agreement concerning this teacher role. Almost without exception such a situation leads to difficulty.

It is to bring to the attention of teachers the types of roles which may be assigned to them that we present the following descriptions derived from talks with pupils, from statements they wrote concerning "My favorite teacher," and from observation of classroom groups in action. Although the titles we have given these roles may seem facetious, behind each is a picture of a teacher as seen by a pupil.

Enemy

When the teacher is an enemy, he is one to be fought, to be outwitted in battle. Elaborate group campaigns may be directed toward defeat of the teacher-enemy by the group. Fortunately, this role assignment is not often given, it seems, but when it is, the results can be dramatic.

Mr. Houston was a science teacher in Centerville High School. He had gained the reputation for being unreasonable in his demands and unfair in marking. Last fall, pupils who found themselves assigned to his section met in the hall outside his room and held an indignation meeting. When Mr. Houston demanded that they enter the room they complied (for an enemy is to be feared), but not before they had appointed a delegation to go to the principal and protest. The principal refused to do anything about the situation. In fact he threatened to withhold credit for the course from everyone in the group if there was any difficulty. When this was reported to the group, war was declared.

Obviously, the initial designation of role had been made by previous groups, but this group continued it. The weapons of the group were the perpetration of all the major and minor annoyances that could be concocted without getting the group into difficulty. With a common enemy, group cement was strong. Using group strength, it was possible to play all kinds of tricks on Mr. Houston, and of course, no one would admit to any of them. Life for Mr. Houston was not easy.

Kill-joy

A teacher assigned the role of kill-joy is seen as the person who stands as barrier to pleasure-giving activities. Such assignment is given, evidently, when the group sees no reason why the teacher should act as barrier except that he enjoys being a barrier (and perhaps he does, if he is an unadjusted person and uses his power for personal release). Teachers who make a fetish of the "no chewing gum in classroom" rule, giving no reason other than "*I* don't like it," may be assigned this role, at least for the time being. Maybe all teachers assume the role on occasion, for the teacher, too, is a group member with rights. When the teacher's rights are always dominant, this role becomes habitual.

Everyone knew why Miss Bartke had been assigned to the kill-joy role. In the junior high school in which she taught, it was necessary for everyone who wished to play in the band to get a statement from each of his teachers saying that his academic work was sufficiently satisfactory for him to spend time in his "extracurricular" activity. This was a silly rule, of course, but Miss Bartke's reactions were no less unreasonable. She took the position that pupils of junior high school age had no business doing anything but attending to their studies, and she would not give any pupil in her classes a permission slip. The children could see no reason in her actions. She was a kill-joy. (Incidentally, the school finally changed the rule to read that there must be permission "from every teacher of each pupil except those in Miss Bartke's classes"!)

Devil

A devil is a being of power, to be respected to the extent that his particular type of power is respected. Like the devils of primitive religions, teacher-devils, unless placated by certain expected rituals, plague their subjects with misfortunes.

Miss Altman had the power to keep one in at recess, a power to be respected. But if one performed certain meaningless rituals, the devil (teacher) was placated and made powerless. The rituals were many and complicated, but could be mastered if practiced with diligence. They included such things as: writing one's name in the upper left (but never in the upper right) corner of the paper; putting one's name above (but never below) the date at the top of the paper; rising with alacrity when Miss Altman tapped her desk after the bell, and singing out "Good morning" in a voice both loud and clear; never leaning against the desk when standing to recite; holding a book with thumbs upward on either margin (never clutched against one's stomach with hands on top), etc., etc. One wonders what pupils in this group were learning about the relation of cause to effect!

Necessary Evil

A necessary evil is as unpleasant as taxes. Vote against taxation, and highways go untended, police and fire protection is insufficient, and there are numerous other lacks. The citizen may grumble as he parts with his money, but he'll vote for the tax when he sees that it will provide a safer life for him. In the same way, a third grader may find it a nuisance to have to conform to Miss Exton's requirements for behavior, and grumble loudly about her, but is pleased to go to her for help when another third grader pulls her hair, takes her pencil, or calls her names. In the long run, the unpleasantness is worth the protection it affords.

Dispenser of Skills and Knowledge

In talking with some pupils, one gains the impression that a teacher has much in common with a slot machine. If one knows what lever to pull or push, the desired product in knowledge or skill, even as peanuts or chewing gum, emerges. One hears statements such as: "Old Barton may not be so hot in some ways, but you have to hand it to the old girl, she gets you through the College Boards." It may have been a desire to be a teacher of this type which led one teacher to ask the librarian to withhold certain books from circulation to pupils, for, he explained, if these publications were available, pupils might not have much respect for his unique knowledge! He not only wanted to impress his pupils with his "dispensing" powers, but, further, he wanted to be the sole dispenser. It is possible that this role is assigned only when knowledge and skill are seen as secondary to other ends, such as passing exams.

Security Giver

The teacher who is seen as security giver (consciously or unconsciously) is one who is able to convey to the group his faith in them. Another way of saying this, perhaps, is that such a teacher has power to meet the frustrated needs and interests of the group members. When he achieves this power he wields great influence, but if this is the only source of influence he has, he is subject to the dangers of any group leader operating on this level (page 123). This role is flattering to the teacher, but may lead children to be dependent rather than self-directing. Teachers of young children, athletic coaches, and scout leaders seem to be particularly likely to be assigned this role, possibly because they are seen as closely associated with means to group goals.

Steppingstone

Probably more frequently than he realizes, a teacher is used as a steppingstone to a larger goal, quite foreign to the immediate teacher-pupil relationship.

Ralph's father had promised him a dollar toward a bicycle for every "A" on each report card. Ralph wanted a bicycle very much indeed. He recognized the teacher as the one who dictated grades. Appeasement seemed to be in order. He did everything he knew to win approval of the dictator so that he might achieve what to him was the ultimate and all-important goal—attainment of a bicycle.

Similarly, an eighth grade group was well aware that it was within the power of their teacher to procure for them a much-wanted soccer ball for use at recess. The group undertook an appeasement campaign which was very effective.

Goal-Getter

Closely related to the steppingstone, but seen in the light of one who helps the group achieve *for itself* rather than one who merely *gives*, is the goal-getter. A discriminating eighth grade group realized that their teacher had helped them raise their level of group interaction. One of the members of this group said, "She helped us know how to get along together, and how to work together to learn what we wanted to know, and do what we wanted to do." Such a role assignment should offer deep satisfaction to a teacher.

Super-conscience

It is very comfortable to have a super-conscience in the form of a teacher. It absolves one of personal responsibility. While the teacher watches, the conscience is in operation; but when the teacher is not present, there is no law, no guilt. We cited earlier the statement of the eleven-year-old: "Some people think that if they do the right thing around the teacher, they can do the wrong thing away from her."

This role assignment seems to be particularly prevalent in groups of young children where the teacher takes all responsibility for decisions concerning behavior. Miss Peterson was such a teacher of a first grade group. Before starting out on a walk one day, she talked to the group. "We will all stay in line," she said. "We will stay on the sidewalk. We won't touch the flowers or bushes in people's yards. We won't yell or make any other loud noises. We will wait for a signal from the teacher before we cross streets," and so on and on. During the walk, David had great fun kicking Norman who was immediately ahead of him in line. When Norman complained to the teacher, David defended himself by saying, "But you didn't say we couldn't kick people." We can be reasonably sure that David knew he should not have kicked Norman. The point here is that he thought well enough of his excuse to give it voice.

Tone-Giver

It may not take a high degree of discrimination on the part of a group to recognize that the teacher contributes much to the group's emotional tone. Even very young pupils notice it, and say: "When she's here we feel good, but when she isn't, we feel grouchy and mean." A little older, but still too immature to know much of the ways of the world, was a fourth and fifth grade group, which, when told their teacher was going to a meeting and a substitute was coming, said, "Miss Reynolds, why don't you stay with us and send the substitute to the meeting? We're happier when you're here." A junior high school pupil says of his teacher, "Just to have her around makes us feel better. She's swell!"

Certainly tone-giver is a desirable role, but most teachers would want it to be accompanied by some other roles with wider significance for pupil growth.

Hero

It is not unusual for individual pupils to designate a particular teacher as a personal hero. Less common, but not infrequent, is the role assignment of hero given to a teacher by an entire group. The designation seems to be most common when there is unity in group goals and the teacher is seen as a means to goals or as a personification of values. Athletic coaches are often assigned such roles. Attractive young women teachers in secondary school may be assigned the role if the group is sufficiently uniform in maturity, so that both boys and girls find feminine attractiveness to be of value. For some reason, it seems that mere attractiveness is less likely to be the basis of role assignment for men teachers, for those the girls consider "cute" are less likely to be considered heroes by the boys.

When secondary school boys and girls describe their favorite teachers, the statements are full of worshipful accounts which indicate not only their admiration but the goal-linked nature of their reactions:

"She has darling clothes and has a nice hair-do."

"This teacher is a very good sport. She knows when to laugh and when not to laugh. She's wonderful."

"If you wouldn't have had her you wouldn't even know what a good teacher is."

"She is very little and cute and well dressed and nice. I bet lots of fellows want dates with her."

"We'd have done anything she said. I'll bet if she'd said, 'Jump in the river,' we'd all have jumped. I don't know why. That's just the way we felt."

"One of the Boys"

It seems that to be "one of the boys" (or girls) is a role to which many teachers aspire but which few achieve. It is evidently a very difficult role to play, possibly because it violates the expectancy of many pupils. Another difficulty is that it requires that the teacher identify himself with the goals of the group. If any of these are anti-social, the teacher is in a difficult spot (page 31), and may forfeit his teaching role in that he sacrifices his opportunity to help the group raise the level of its goals.

There are teachers, it seems, who think they have achieved this role when actually they are merely held in contempt by the group. As one seventh grader put it, "He thinks he's being a good sport, but we think he's silly." Young, inexperienced teachers seem particularly prone to make this mistake, possibly because they are very much in fear of discipline problems and want to keep the group "on their side." Or, possibly, they feel the loneliness of being adults in a world of youngsters, and sincerely want to be identified with the group. Whatever the motivation, our observation leads us to believe that this role of being "one of the boys" seldom works out well.

Friend

More satisfying perhaps, and certainly more easily attained, than the role of "one of the boys" is the role of friend—albeit (or perhaps because) the teacher is older and wiser than the group. One sixth grader says, "I can talk to her about things I'd never dream of discussing with my chums." A fifth grader, "She works right along with you, but she knows more than you do, so she can help when you get stuck"; and another fifth grader, "She likes us and we like her." We feel that these statements are significant. The friend is more than merely "one of us" ("I can talk to her about things I'd never dream of discussing with my chums"), is cooperative, but has special skills ("She works right along . . . but can help.

. . ."), and the affectional relationship is recognized as mutual ("She likes us and we like her").

We believe that these subtle distinctions between "one of the boys" and "friend" are the rocks which are hazards to many young teachers. Hence we cannot be too emphatic in pointing them out.

The difficulty of achieving the role of friend may be inferred from responses to the question, "If you had a personal problem about which you were worried, to whom would you go outside your family?" (Check Sheet of Opportunities, page 407). In a fourth and fifth grade group only three indicate they would go to the teacher. (Fifteen say they would go to a friend their own age; 5, to grandparents; 6, to an aunt; 3, to an adult neighbor, and 1, to a policeman). In an eighth grade group, one pupil responds, "My teacher," and another, "Maybe a teacher but it depends on what it is about." (Sixteen indicate that they would go to friends their own age; 5 give no answer; 3 respond "no one"; 2 say they would go to adult neighbors; 2, to grandparents; 2, to aunts or uncles; one claims, "I don't know," and one says, "I keep my affairs to myself.")

Factors Influencing Role Assignments of Teachers

The easy answer to role assignment of teachers is that it is determined by teachers' actions. That this is in large measure true we do not deny, but that other factors are operating we are confident.

—tradition

One of these factors is tradition. Somewhere, way back when, a teacher may have made a mistake in handling a group situation. The results of this mistake are handed down from class to class, possibly growing in magnitude as they travel, until a teacher may find himself with a reputation which is totally unrelated to his present action habits. Perhaps Mr. Houston, the "enemy," was caught in this difficulty. Certainly the group had assigned him a role even before they entered his class for the first time.

One teacher, recognizing the force of tradition, took the bull by the horns and announced to all his classes on the first day of school, "I know I have a reputation for being unduly strict. It's true I once was, but I think I've changed. I'd like you to judge for yourselves." In this instance, this approach was successful because the teacher was able to establish rapport, but under other circumstances where there was considerable hostility, it might not have been.

—tradition is strong

Tradition may operate in the opposite direction, too. There seem to be teachers who maintain a reputation for being "good teachers" year after year, even though there is no evidence in their current actions that they are superior in helping pupils to learn or in being liked. Evidently role assignments passed on from group to group may be very strong influences, particularly in the secondary school.

It would seem that in many overly-rigid, restricted schools (secondary schools, at least) there is one teacher chosen by the group as a scapegoat. It may be a sound generalization to state that a thwarted group will designate a scapegoat on which to vent its pent-up feelings. A thwarted society selects a minority group as scapegoat; a thwarted school group chooses a school minority group, one of its own members, or a teacher. A teacher who finds himself the scapegoat has little hope of overcoming the role of enemy until the total school structure is revamped.

—stereotypes

Certain stereotypes may be powerful, too. A common one is that men teachers are more strict, more interested in academic achievement, and less interested in the personal welfare of pupils than are women teachers. The concomitant is that women teachers are "soft," more easily hoodwinked, more apt to believe lies, more easily moved to sympathy by "sob stories" of pupils than are men teachers. These seem to us to be stereotypes because we found it very difficult to discover any sex differences in regard to these factors. Further study might be of interest.

Another stereotype, at least among girls in regard to women teachers, is that young teachers are more "understanding," by which they seem to mean, more sympathetic toward personal problems. As far as we could discover, quite the opposite is likely to be true. The tendency of the young teacher, who usually feels insecure, is to try to maintain strict discipline, and to be more conscious of academic achievement and less of personal adjustment than the older, more experienced teacher. However, perhaps it is well that the young teacher has the support of this reputation.

Other stereotypes are peculiar to particular schools. In one high school, the belief was strong that men who came from a certain university were better athletes than those who came from others. The origin of the belief was not difficult to find in the persons of four men teachers on the staff,

WIDE EXPERIENCE GIVES EVERYBODY A CHANCE TO CONTRIBUTE.

all good athletes and all from that university. However, the stereotype made life complicated for one non-athletic young man from the same university who joined the staff. Other stereotypes had to do with red-haired teachers ("Boy, are they hard to get along with!"), fat teachers (they're motherly, hence kind), music teachers (they're heartless), home economics teachers (they're beautiful and will soon get married), mathematics teachers (if men, they're sissies who try to be tough; if women, they're mannish but have soft hearts). Irrational as these stereotypes may be, a teacher new to a school must deal with them, whether he does so consciously or unconsciously.

—parents are an influence

Parents, particularly parents of elementary school children, can exert a powerful influence over the role assignment of the teacher. One kindergarten teacher, unable to understand the cringing fear of her four- and five-year-olds, discovered that in that community the teacher shared honors with the "bogey man" as the one who would "get you if you aren't good." Certainly the parents who offered a dollar for every "A" on the report card played a part in role assignment.

Teachers who have moved from one type of community to another find variations in parental expectations in terms of economic level. It is not unusual, it seems, to find that parents in the lower socio-economic grouping and those in the upper-upper build the expectation of the teacher's being a friend. As one teacher, transferred from a middle-class area to a school in an underprivileged section, said with surprise, "Why the children in *this* school *like* the teachers." On the other hand, parents of the middle classes tend to assume that the teacher is one to be placated and appeased. No doubt a sociologist could explain this in terms of the hopes for social mobility of the various groups.

Thus, although the role assignment of a teacher (positive or negative) may be justly earned by his own actions, we feel there are other factors operating of which a teacher should be aware, if he is to cope with the assignment successfully.

Fluctuation of Role

We may have seemed to imply that the role assignment of a teacher by a group is static, unchanging, unchangeable, and discrete. If so, we want to correct this impression. Evidently, the role may change rapidly according to situation or goal-change of the group. However, as with general role assignments given to children, such as leaders, pets, popular people, and so on, teachers seem to be given general roles, as we analyzed them above, although subroles may be assigned as circumstances direct. Moreover, it is very possible for a teacher to be assigned more than one of these roles. For example, a teacher may be both "friend" and "goal-getter," or both "devil" and "super-conscience."

What Can a Teacher Do?

It is our belief that any teacher may alter the role assignment given him by the group. One possible exception may be a role assignment of scapegoat, but we believe this to be rare and, even when it does occur, a teacher who knows what is happening may try to use his influence to change the total school pattern. (We are realists enough to recognize, however, that this is never easy!) We repeat, then, that we believe any teacher may alter the role assignment given him. First, however, he must be aware of what his role assignment is. Our experience leads us to believe that many teachers are unaware of their role assignment, that they,

in fact, have never stopped to consider that they have one. Many teachers are concerned about assignment on a range from "popular" to "unpopular," but have not analyzed the factors involved.

Role assignment to any individual is an important aspect of group living, but the teacher's role may be especially important. Thus, we believe
that every teacher should try: *one,* to be aware of his current assignment
(or assignments); *two,* to examine it in terms of his goals and the goals of
the group; and *three,* to take steps to change the assignment if it seems
inappropriate.

We make no claim to have discovered all types of role assignments or
to have explored any one type adequately. But we hope our analysis may
lead other teachers to deeper awareness and keener analysis, and, having
discovered current roles, to examine them and change them if it seems
wise.

IN SUMMARY

The way a person thinks about himself, his sense of personal worth, his
emotional security, is in large measure determined by what he thinks
other people think of him. On the other hand, it is the individual, along
with a number of other individuals, who makes the group. The individual and the group are interdependent.

In our society, the need to belong is a powerful force. Individuals who
do not feel that they belong in their social group may use detour reactions
which may or may not be socially acceptable. It is important, therefore,
for the mental health of both the individual and the group that a teacher
know how to identify lack of belonging and how to adjust the situation
in order that feelings of belonging may be achieved.

In helping an isolate to find acceptance in the group, a teacher may
well ask himself these questions:

Is he rejected?

Does he know he is rejected?

Does he care?

What is the group culture?

To what factors does the group give prestige?

Who can help him?

The group as a group has a responsibility to its members, and should
exercise its power to achieve acceptance of its members.

The group holds within itself a power of great influence—the power to assign status and roles to its members. Leadership, the power to move the group to action, is the most significant assignment of group role. This assignment is made in terms of group goals and, thus, leadership power parallels the factors of goal derivation—identification, thwarted needs and interests, and rational power.

With this power to assign leadership to its members, it is plain that groups should learn to assess their leaders. Moreover, since the assignment of leaders is made by the group, more attention should be given to training groups for this responsibility rather than to lavishing all "leadership training" on individuals.

Other status roles of which a teacher will want to be aware include those of popular person, enemy, and pet.

Shift in status is influenced by a number of factors, including change in maturity, group personnel, and views of prestige factors. Learning to adjust to these shifts is a skill which must be acquired, for some need for adjustment is inevitable. It is possible, however, that some school practices call for undue amounts of adjustment and thus disrupt individual and group life.

Good group living calls for respect for deviation as well as for conformity. Teaching this respect for deviation is a difficult but important task of the school.

The teacher, too, is a group member and is assigned roles by the group. Unless a teacher is aware of the role assigned to him, his actions may seem to the group to be inappropriate, and he is unable to shift the role to one more compatible with his educational philosophy. A teacher's actions are probably the major determinants of role assignment, but other factors, such as tradition or the concept of scapegoat, may be operative, too. Unless a teacher is aware of such factors he is unable to cope with them.

V

Group Structure

Three teachers were talking about the groups of pupils that had come to
them that semester. "I have an amazing group," said Mrs. Turner. "I've
never seen anything like it. No one seems to have anything to do with
anybody else. Why, if I didn't keep working at it all the time, the group
would simply fall apart!"

"I have a surprising group, too," said Mr. Harter. "It's riddled with
cliques and gangs, each strong in itself, but each at the throats of the
others. I'm kept busy trying to keep from having gang warfare in my
classroom."

Miss Bacon joined in the conversation. "I've never had such a cooperative group. The pupils all seem to like each other and enjoy doing things
together."

These are three groups of boys and girls of the same age, in the same
school, yet as different as morning, noon, and night. What makes the
difference?

Classroom groups as well as governments, armies, or business companies have form and structure. The structure of groups in classrooms is
not ruled by constitution, line and staff regulations, or organization tables,
yet may be as clearly organized.

We started early in our investigation to study group structure, through
observation and use of sociometric techniques. We found that this study
raised many questions and directed our attention to problem areas. But
we were unable to interpret what we found until we had made a further
study of group interaction. In fact, the more we studied the more we realized the danger of trying to interpret structure before we had considerable insight into group living. It may be easy, but it is erroneous, for a

[154]

teacher who studies only structure to consider group living as static, or even to allow his findings to create or deepen his prejudices toward certain individuals or subgroups.

We early recognized that findings in the area of structure, such as those supplied by sociometric techniques, cannot be used in evaluation unless accompanied by considerable supporting evidence. In other words, a structural form is not "good" or "bad" in itself, but only as it facilitates or hinders group living. For example, it is commonly implied in the literature that the existence of strong subgroups is unfortunate. Perhaps this is often true, but if a subgroup provides opportunity for security and interaction to some children who might have difficulty in finding themselves otherwise, this organization may be making a contribution to the total group.

—when is a group a group?

We had difficulty, too, in knowing (à la Gertrude Stein) when a group is a group is a group. Our first assumption was that we were studying a group when we were engaged in studying the classroom membership as a whole, but as we worked we began to question the feasibility of this in certain instances. For example, the fact that forty first graders are in one room is no reason to suppose that they should operate as a group. We want the inter-personal human relations to be favorable, of course, but this is not the same thing as creating a group in the sense we have been discussing. It may be that we expect the impossible when we try to mold first graders into groups of more than ten or twelve members. There may be other factors as well as the stage of maturity which indicate smaller groups for some children. By the time boys and girls are ten years old, however, we feel that it is quite possible to go far toward creating a group of the total class membership. Whether the number of people usually thrown together as a classroom group is favorable to good group living, we do not know. There is some indication that even our ten-year-olds might have profited by smaller numbers. It would seem, then, that rather than aspiring to a smaller maximum class size throughout the school, some consideration might be given to graduated sizes, smallest for younger children and gradually increasing as children mature, with special regard for class size for groups having difficulty in adjusting.

Thus, although our attention was directed toward classroom groups, we recognized the possibility that, in some cases, the actual operational groupings were not necessarily those of the total class membership.

ASPECTS OF GROUP STRUCTURE

As we have studied structure, we have found ourselves giving attention to many aspects within the total picture. We have had to *learn* to do this, however. Our first inclination was to look almost exclusively at the position of *individuals* in the group, particularly the most or the least chosen children. This was due partly, no doubt, to our previous training in studying children as individuals. However, with time and experience, we began to realize that the positions of individuals are *group-determined*, and thus we were able to broaden our view to other aspects of structure.

As we discuss the various aspects of group structure, we should like to point to illustrations from a sociogram of responses of eighth grade girls to the question, "By whom would you like to sit?" (Figure 10, page 157).

Degree of Organization

We found wide variation in the degree of organization within groups, with the highest degree among this same group of girls. Contrast this sociogram with that of a first grade group (Figure 21, page 187). We want to emphasize again that we cannot pronounce one "better" than the other without other evidence, but certainly the girls indicate clearer lines of structural relationships and subgroupings than do the younger pupils.

Subgroups

There are two distinct evidences of subgroups in sociogram No. 10. The group at the upper left (subgroup A) is the more dramatic in its structure because not only does it choose within its membership, but, further, no one from "outside" (with the exception of Doris) chooses into the group. Also a subgroup, however, is the group on the right (subgroup B). These four girls choose among themselves exclusively, but in contrast to the other group receive a number of choices from the out-group.

Merely on the basis of this evidence, a teacher might be justified in entertaining the hypothesis that subgroup A is less well group-integrated than subgroup B; that this group would be less likely to conceive or accept common group goals and work toward their attainment. It is possible that a subgroup such as this could operate *against* the group, opposing the goals of the larger group and offering resistance to all group-accepted ideas. When this is the case, there is bound to be difficulty in achieving good group living. We see no way out in such situations except

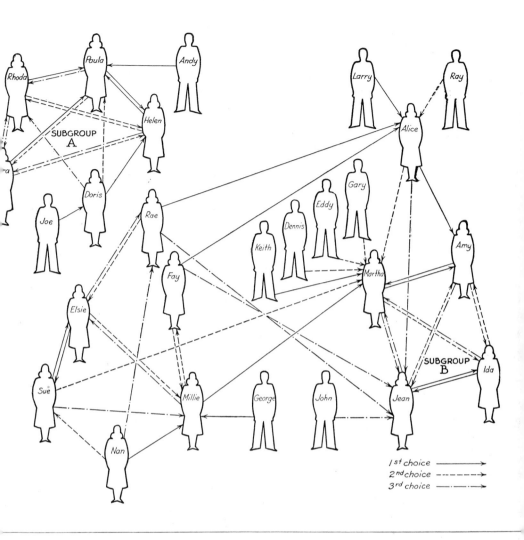

FIGURE 10. 8TH GRADE GIRLS, FEBRUARY—"BY WHOM WOULD YOU
LIKE TO SIT?"

for the group as a whole to try to find areas of agreement, even though
it may mean forfeiting some of the more cherished goals of each of the
subgroups, or, if this fails, operating as separate groups until areas of
agreement are found. This is, in essence, the situation faced by the
teacher, to be described later, who found the girls in the group interested
in studying dolls of other countries, and the boys, in studying aviation.
We suggest that this group attempt to shift the area of study to one

[157]

which may be acceptable to all (for it is futile, we believe, to attempt to *force* the subgroup to accept the group goals, at least in major areas, if there is strong resistance), or to allow the two groups to operate separately, acknowledging, for the time being, that the classroom is composed of two groups instead of one, at least for one particular activity.

A teacher will want to know, too, the strength and cohesion of subgroups. A clique may be a matter of passing fancy, with little group cement, and easily reorganized through a shift in the situation. Another subgroup, on the other hand, may be tightly organized, and strongly resistant to change in its organization. It may have held its autonomy over a considerable period of time. It is this latter type of subgroup, sometimes with antisocial goals, which is commonly designated as a gang. As was mentioned above, any attempt to force the goals of a group on a subgroup is probably futile, but is particularly non-effective when dealing with a gang, for such an act tends merely to develop hostility, hence increasing the gang's cohesion through common resistance.

In the group we are discussing (Figure 10, page 157) the teacher explains that she feels both subgroups are group-integrated (work toward common goals) within the classroom situation. However, all the girls in subgroup A are members of a school organization (the Girls Cavalier Corps), while none of the other girls holds such membership. This common experience has formed the cement which developed the subgroup, but is not such that it interferes with the attainment of group goals. The fact that no one except Doris chooses into the group, however, may indicate that the group in its entirety does not accept the subgroup wholeheartedly. Perhaps it should be pointed out that in this class the girls might be considered a subgroup, with the boys choosing into the group but not being chosen.

Friends

Person-to-person friendships may be considered a special form of subgroup, and studied in terms of similar aspects, that is, degree of group-integration, strength, and the like. We have discovered what seems to be a valid generalization concerning the relation between choices and strength of friendships. When two people choose each other, and then make identical choices of friends for second and third choices, this may be considered an indication that the friendship is strong and tends to be lasting. On the other hand, when the two friends make widely divergent choices of friends other than each other, there is frequently a realignment of these friends, as is indicated on another sociogram made a few months later, unless additional factors are in operation. This seems to be substantiated by observation as well as by sociometric study. In this class group, Martha and Amy, Ida and Jean make identical second and third choices. Sue and Nan, on the other hand, do not.

Stars

People in the group chosen by a number of others, such as, for instance, Martha or Jean, in Figure 10, are designated as stars. During our early study, we assumed that stars were leaders, but further investigation indicated that this is not necessarily the case. We found it desirable to make a distinction between leaders (people who move others to action) and popular people (those who make a special contribution, possibly as entertainers). Stars on a sociogram, it would seem, may be either leaders or popular people and cannot be distinguished except through further study by other means. And if the stars are leaders, the sociogram does not tell on what basis—rational, physical, or in meeting thwarted needs. It does, however, give leads for study. Moreover, it is possible, though it rarely occurs, that a leader who moves the group to action may not be chosen by anyone, hence appears on the sociogram to be an isolate while exerting considerable force in the group life. Peter (described on page 120), the boy who licked the entire group, once went from person to person prior to an election, threatening use of physical force if his name was not written on the ballot. When it was pointed out to him that the ballot was secret, he claimed he would lick everyone if he didn't win, for he'd know some didn't vote for him! Peter won the election. Peter's name might never be mentioned on a sociometric question, in spite of his influence. A disliked though feared social leader may be in the same position.

Isolates

Isolates are people not chosen by others in the group among the three choices of each member. In Figure 10, Nan is an isolate. Doris is, so far as girls' choices are concerned, but she has been chosen by a boy. As we have said earlier, regardless of individual differences in gregariousness, probably no pupil can be well adjusted unless he finds himself accepted by his peer group. Isolates, therefore, are a source of concern to teachers. A sociogram may help to identify isolates, but as we will explain later in connection with the discussion of the Classroom Social Distance Scale, other approaches to study of isolates are more meaningful.

Enemies

Not to be confused with isolates, who are merely ignored, are the people against whom the group shows hostility. It is important for teachers to identify such people (if there are any in the group). Some investigators recommend the use of negative questions, such as "Who are the three people you like least?" in gathering basic material for sociograms. We tried this approach in several groups but found it very difficult to use. Whereas answering the positive question was seen by group members as being an enjoyable experience, when the negative question was asked, there was evidence of considerable feeling of discomfort. In our culture, children are taught that to love thy neighbor is a virtue, and not to like people is naughty. Thus, identifying people who were disliked gave rise to guilt feelings. Moreover, children who suspected they might be named as persons disliked showed increased insecurity. We decided that the harm done to personal trust and group climate through the use of the negative question was not compensated by the added knowledge the result gave to the teacher. It is our experience, however, that hostility against individuals may be studied with less unfavorable emotional reaction and greater precision through the use of other means, such as the Classroom Social Distance Scale.

Thus, for the sociograms we show here, there is no way of knowing whether a person not chosen is so designated because he is ignored, because he is merely overlooked by the group, or because there is definite hostility against him as an enemy of the group.

SHIFT IN ORGANIZATION

It has been our experience that in time organizational shifts occur with all groups. This shifting is greatest and most diffuse (lacking in clear organization) with young children, but gains in stability and organization as the members of the group mature. The group of eighth grade girls we have been observing (Figure 10) furnishes a clear example of organizational shift during the year (Figures 11, 12, and 13, following).

In the sociogram made in September (Figure 11), we find considerable evidence of the existence of subgroups. There is one interesting indication of interlocking subgroups, involving groups B and D, with Jean as the key to the interrelationship.

The only people not clearly members of the subgroup pattern are Elsie,

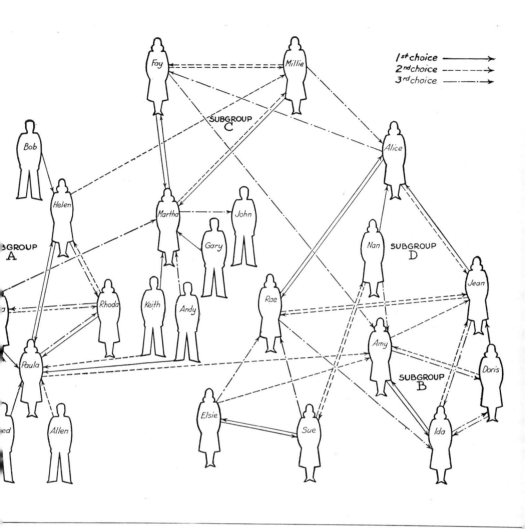

FIGURE 11. 8TH GRADE GIRLS, SEPTEMBER—"WITH WHOM WOULD
YOU LIKE TO GO TO THE MOVIES?"

Sue, and Nan. These three chose among one another but are not chosen
by anyone else. The lack of interchange of choices between Elsie and
Nan, however, indicates lack of organization as a subgroup.

It would seem quite probable that there is an incipient split into two
groups (upper left and lower right). Only four choices cross between
these two major groupings, one being a second choice of Paula for Amy.
The others are third choices.

[161]

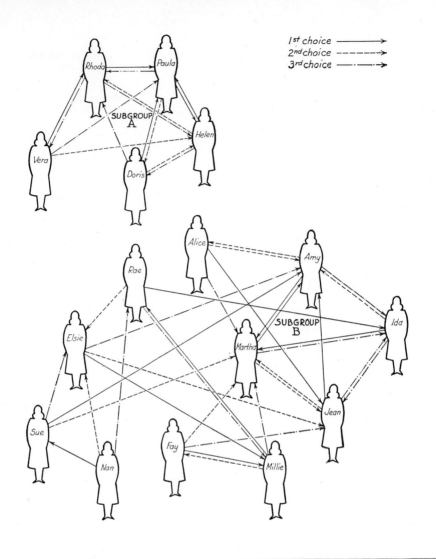

FIGURE 12. 8TH GRADE GIRLS, APRIL—"MY THREE BEST FRIENDS."

—an island

By April (Figure 12), we find clear division of subgroups, similar to the pattern of February which was discussed earlier (Figure 10). Subgroup A is still an island group, with no intercommunication with the main body. Doris, an isolate in February, has been incorporated in the group. Subgroup B has much the same formation as in September, except

[162]

that it has tended to incorporate the former subgroup C. Nan, who formerly identified herself with this group, has shifted to the lower left formation. There is still little organization in the lower left grouping, but April finds closer identification with subgroup B. This realignment gives little evidence of the major split into two equal groups, as seen in September, possibly because subgroup A has completely withdrawn.

It will be recalled that all members of subgroup A are members of an elective girls' organization known as the Girls Cavalier Corps. Membership in this organization is not dependent on academic standing, as is that of many other organizations in the school. Hence, popular girls, regardless of their academic work, are admitted.

—new members

In May (Figure 13) four more girls in this group are admitted to membership in the Corps, and we see immediate effects in group structure. The new members are Alice, Martha, Amy, and Jean. Subgroup A is still relatively exclusive, but, through Doris, is now in touch with the new members of the Corps. Alice, not originally clearly designated as a member of subgroup B, is now definitely "in." Ida, on the other hand, who has been a part of this subgroup from the first, but did not receive a bid to membership in the Cavalier Corps, is now excluded.

The tightening of organization of members of the Corps seems to have further excluded non-members. The lower left group is still not clearly organized, but makes fewer choices into subgroup B—all third choices with the exception of Peggy, a girl new to the group. Millie has become the pivotal person in the group with Fay and Rae as lieutenants, but these last two do not choose each other.

—shift in pattern

Thus, it is possible to see over a period of a year definite shift in the pattern of organization, with membership in an all-school organization exerting considerable influence. Doris presents an interesting study in mobility. In September she was a member of subgroup B. In February she attached herself to subgroup A, and by April she was incorporated in this group. In May she served as the link between subgroups A and B. Perhaps it should be pointed out that different sociometric questions were used as the bases for these four sociograms: "With whom would you like to go to the movies?" (September); "By whom would you like to sit?" (February); "My three best friends" (April); and "With whom would

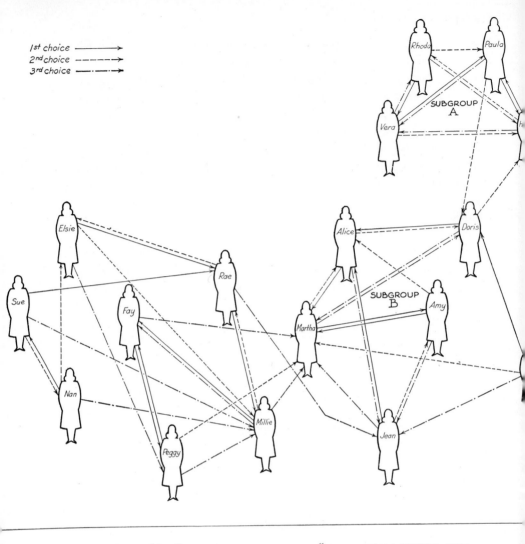

FIGURE 13. 8TH GRADE GIRLS, MAY—"WITH WHOM WOULD YOU
LIKE TO GO TO THE MOVIES?"

you like to go to the movies?" (May). No doubt this variation in question
made some difference in the responses, but, as will be pointed out later,
it is unlikely that this variation was a major influence except for the boy-
girl choices and for the people who had not found themselves in one of
the subgroups.

As has been said earlier, we feel that it is impossible to use the evidence of sociograms alone as a means of evaluation. From this evidence alone we do not know whether it is "good" or "bad" that these shifts occur. Nor do we know whether in subgroups organization is preferable to non-organization, as in the lower left grouping.

The teacher reports that the entire group was group-goal directed on most occasions throughout the year. The split of subgroup A from the major body did not, she feels, serve to disintegrate the group. Moreover, two members of subgroup A may have had reason to cling to this subgroup for security which might have been difficult to achieve otherwise. One pupil was from a home for dependent children, thus handicapped, to a degree, in her social relations with her peers, yet perhaps in need of belonging more than most children. The other was a member of a minority nationality group which is not well accepted in that community. These two chose within the group as early as September, when the separation of subgroup A was less apparent. They were the only two members of the subgroup who were not chosen from outside the group in September. It is quite possible that they contributed greatly to the cohesion of the subgroup because it met their particular needs for a sense of belonging.

—boys' values in group

The boys of this same eighth grade group show an interesting structural shift over a period of time. When all three choices are plotted, the diagrams are so complex as to be almost illegible, so they are not shown here. However, plotting only first choices shows the shift from a number of loosely organized subgroups in September (Figure 14, page 166) to the oddly symmetric pattern in April (Figure 15, page 167). We repeat that we believe it is dangerous to attempt evaluation in terms of the sociogram alone, particularly when only one choice is plotted. However, the implications for further observation are of interest. It would seem that there is greater cohesion in the group in April, yet the suggestion of line-and-staff organization, leading to one or two people, is disconcerting. Gary, the most mature boy in the group, is intelligent, and considered good-looking and "smooth." Sam and Tom are the class athletes. Ray is the leader of the younger boys, but dependent, in turn, on the leadership of the older boys. If it were not that the plotting of second and third choices shows considerable interaction, we might fear that there is a rigid "inner circle" with a number of isolates on the fringe. The teacher, however, feels that the group members were well oriented in group goals.

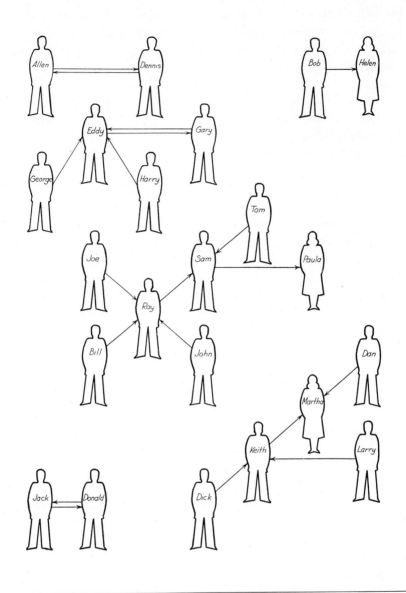

FIGURE 14. 8TH GRADE BOYS, SEPTEMBER—"WITH WHOM WOULD
YOU LIKE TO GO TO THE MOVIES?" (1ST CHOICES ONLY)

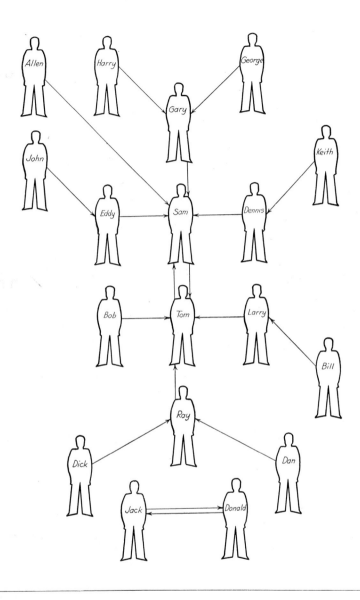

FIGURE 15. 8TH GRADE BOYS, APRIL—"MY THREE BEST FRIENDS."
(1ST CHOICES ONLY)

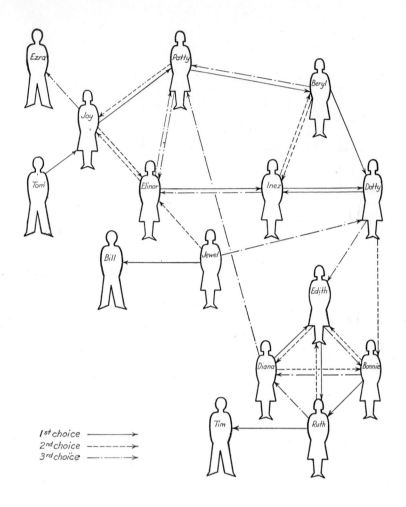

FIGURE 16. 4TH AND 5TH GRADE GIRLS, SEPTEMBER—FRIENDSHIPS.

—shift in membership

Far more difficult to follow are shifts in time of the fourth and fifth grade girls. The organization here is complicated by the increase in numbers in the group from 11 in September to 15 in May. (Figures 16, 17, and 18, pages 168, 169, and 170.)

There are two constants in these sociograms. One is the subgroup Diana–Edith–Bonnie, which appears in all three, growing in strength of "outside" choices as the year progresses. Although in September there

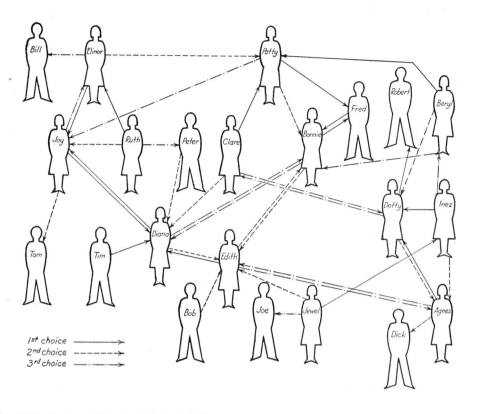

FIGURE 17. 4TH AND 5TH GRADE GIRLS, JANUARY—FRIENDSHIPS.

was indication of several subgroups, other subgroup patterns become less evident as the Diana–Edith–Bonnie subgroup becomes dominant.

These three girls are the oldest in the room. For example, Edith is one year and seven months older than the youngest girl in the classroom group (Beryl). She is the most physically mature girl in the classroom group. This may in some measure influence the choice of her by boys, which becomes quite marked by May. Whether these choices are due to friendships initiated by them or by Edith is not clear, although there is indication that she invites the attentions of members of the opposite sex.

—the isolate

The second constant in these sociograms is the isolate, Jewel. From other records we know that Jewel is not only ignored but is actively rejected by many in this group. Following the usual pattern for such

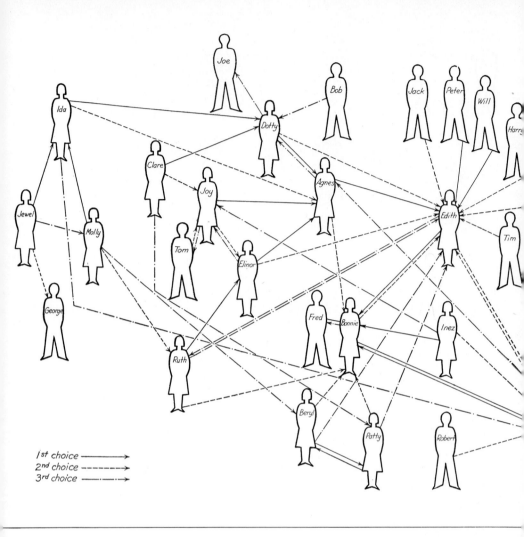

FIGURE 18. 4TH AND 5TH GRADE GIRLS, MAY—FRIENDSHIPS.

children, she attempts to establish relationships in a range of situations. In each case, one of her choices is a boy (not accepted by the group at hand, she goes farther afield, to the boys' group, in her attempt to belong). In September, she chooses Dotty and Elinor, and in January, Edith and Inez. As is so often the case, the two choices are people not closely related to each other. One might almost think that there is a conscious logic, such as: "If I lose out in one place, I still have a chance in an unrelated area. I shouldn't put all my eggs in one basket." In May, she selects as her choices two of the new girls. Again we can almost hear her reason: "These people are new territory. They don't know yet that the others don't like me. Maybe I can get them to take me in." During the course of the year we have seen her aspiration level fall from choices of the most chosen girls to those of the new girls, who are themselves isolated from the group because of their "newness."

PATTERNS OF ACCEPTANCE AND REJECTION

Our first approaches to studying structure were observation, and sociograms constructed on the basis of the usual questions, such as "Who are your three best friends?" and "With whom would you like to go to the movies, eat lunch, play, etc.?" We found the sociograms exceedingly helpful. They illuminated general structure and identified subgroups, cliques, and pal-patterns, and so provided the clues needed to give direction to our observations.

However, we had not been working long before we began to realize that sociograms had severe limitations. They paint a black or a white picture of friendship or choice of associates for certain activities, and give no clue as to the vast realm of shades of gray which we feel must be present between the extremes of rejection and acceptance as first choice. We found from examining our own experience that there are some people we like a lot and some we don't like at all, and that there are many others who are in a middle group and about whom we have distinct variations of feeling. We wondered if some people might not choose a few close friends and yet feel warmly toward many others in the group, while some, after choosing a few close friends, would tend to reject most of the others in the group. We know there are some who have difficulty in finding any close friends. How do such people feel about the majority of the group?

Classroom Social Distance Scale

To find out more about matters such as these, we devised an instrument we call the Classroom Social Distance Scale (Appendix, page 401). The idea is similar to that of the scale devised by Bogardus[1] to measure inter-group attitudes. It allows for a reaction, on a five-point scale, of each youngster to every other in the group. This instrument is most use-

[1] E. S. Bogardus, "A Social Distance Scale," *Sociology and Social Research*, 1933, Vol. 17, pp. 265–271.

ful, in our opinion, in studying responses of each child, when it is used by a teacher who knows his group. However, it is possible, by assigning numerical values to the five items on the scale, to arrive at two types of social distance scores: one, a *self-social-distance* score indicating the degree of acceptance or rejection of the group *by an individual;* and two, a *group-social-distance* score, indicating the degree of acceptance or rejection of an individual *by the group.*

Perhaps the greatest contribution of the Classroom Social Distance Scale to us was to indicate the great range of acceptance or rejection afforded to any one individual in the group. We have examined scores of records of response on social distance scales provided by teachers from coast to coast for their groups, and we have yet to find a record showing a child who is *totally rejected* by everyone in the group, or a record showing a child *totally accepted* by everyone in the group. Even the least accepted children in the group are well received by some, and the most accepted are rejected by some. For example, comparative records for the most and the least accepted child in the fourth and fifth grade group under study, showing the number of checks in each area, read as follows (Table 8).

TABLE 8

RANGE OF SOCIAL ACCEPTANCE OF TWO PUPILS
(IN A GROUP OF 32)

Item on Scale	Checks for Child 1 (Most Accepted)	Checks for Child 2 (Least Accepted)
1. Would like to have him as one of my best friends	20	2
2. Would like to have him in my group but not as a close friend	7	15
3. Would like to be with him once in a while but not often or for a long time	3	4
4. Don't mind his being in our room but I don't want to have anything to do with him	1	3
5. Wish he weren't in our room	1	8

In the entire group of 32 children, only four did not have their names checked on the entire range of five items of the scale (2 were not checked on item 5, nor 2 on item 4).

—"somebody loves you"

The realization that even the least accepted is liked by someone, and the best accepted not liked by someone, made us exceedingly cautious in our interpretation of sociograms. We could see the usefulness of sociograms in indicating general structure of a group, but their limitations in indicating the status of the individual in the group were conspicuous.

We were interested in discovering more exactly the relation of choices on sociograms and ratings on the Classroom Social Distant Scale. First we ranked individuals in terms of number of times they had been "key" people (chosen by five or more children) or isolates (not chosen by anyone) on the nine sociograms made during the year. Comparing this ranking with rank of score on the Social Distance Scale, we found a correlation of $rho = +.48$, indicating that there is little significant relationship. This is easily explained. For example, it might be possible for a pupil to gain a high rank as "key" person by being chosen by five or six others on every sociogram while being ignored by the rest of the class.

—a short-cut

We then studied the number of people in a class who chose a person one or more times. In this way it was possibe to rank individuals in terms of the spread of choices, from the one who was chosen by 22 people at one time or another on the nine sociograms to another who was chosen only once by one person. The ranking, correlated with the group social distance scores, gave $rho = +.655$. This figure indicates greater statistical significance than the one above, but no wonder, for we are merely approaching the general method of the scale. In other words, if there are enough sociograms over a period of a year, the total of responses on all will approach the social distance score. The scale, then, may be considered as a short-cut to finding the place of the individual in the group.

Social Outlook

The Classroom Social Distance Scale provided some indication of the degree an individual accepts the group (self-social-distance). We found, for example, that in this group of 32 there were eleven who checked no names under item 5 (Wish he weren't in our room). Everyone checked at least one name under item 1 (Would like to have him as one of my best friends) but the range was wide—1 to 29. This indicated to us how much is hidden by the usual question, "Who are your three best friends?"

The youngster who said he had but one friend would have to go beyond his real inclination in order to find two more. The youngster who checked 29 would have to limit severely his inclinations in order to name just three.

As was said earlier, we were interested in knowing how people who are accepted or rejected feel toward others in the group. We found that the correlation of self-social-distance (how he rated others) and group-social-distance (how others rated him) was $rho = + .034$, or of little statistical significance. As we examined individual papers, however, we could see interesting patterns of responses. George, not well accepted by the group and keenly aware of the fact, tended to rank everyone high. He wanted friends, so would be a friend to all. Beryl, on the other hand, although likewise not well accepted, seemed to "live alone and like it." She tended to rank many low on the scale. From other evidence we infer that she found considerable belonging in her family and personal satisfaction in her piano-playing. It is possible that contrasts such as these may be a clue to degree of feeling of need to belong in the class-room group.

There were variations among the well-accepted, too. Sam, more mature than most of the other boys, and an athlete, was ranked high by many, but he ranked only a few as high. He tended to rank high only those who approached his maturity and athletic prowess. Edith, on the other hand, a social leader in the group, evidently felt warmly toward all those who liked her—a considerable number.

INTER-PERSONAL RELATIONS

The scores on the Classroom Social Distance Scale made it possible to rank individuals in terms of degree of acceptances by the group, and degree they accepted the group, and then to compare these ranks with other measures which were available to us.

We had measures of chronological age, mental alertness (Kuhlmann–Anderson, Binet, and Otis tests) and socio-economic status (Sims Socio-Economic Scale). Table 9 shows the correlation of these factors with group-social-distance (how others rate him) and with self-social-distance (how he rates others). It would seem that chronological age, intelligence, and socio-economic status have little or no significant relationship to the rating the group gives individuals or to the rating the individual gives the group.

TABLE 9

CORRELATION OF SOCIAL DISTANCE AND CERTAIN OTHER FACTORS
(FOURTH AND FIFTH GRADE GROUP OF 32)

Factors Correlated	Correlation
Group-social-distance and	
Chronological age	+.036
Intelligence quotient	+.480
Socio-economic status	−.337
Self-social-distance and	
Chronological age	−.345
Intelligence quotient	−.026
Socio-economic status	−.09

As can be seen, these results in terms of correlations for the group as a whole indicate little statistical significance. We wonder if some important factors might have been lost in grouping the data. We restudied the material to see if there might be some discrimination between ratings given by children at extremes in each of these aspects. We chose for special study the ten oldest and the ten youngest, the ten having the highest and the ten having the lowest scores in intelligence and in socio-economic status.

Chronological Age

The range in age in this classroom was rather wide, varying from 8 years 10 months to 11 years 3 months.

The ten oldest children made 78 choices as those whom they would like for best friends. Of these, 26 were among the first ten in respect to age, 32 in the middle, and 20 among the ten youngest children. Thus, there seems to be a slight tendency for this group to choose older children.

The ten youngest children made 136 choices as those they would like to have as best friends. Of these, 52 were among the ten oldest children, 42 were from the middle group, and 42 from the ten youngest. It seems that the older children have some advantage here (although the oldest child in the room has the lowest group acceptance score).

It is interesting to note that the ten youngest children made 136 choices of those whom they wished were best friends, while the ten oldest made only 78 such choices. This discrepancy may be of some significance. At least it raises questions as to how secure the younger pupils feel and to what extent they are groping to find status by seeking many friends.

Intelligence

A similar procedure was followed in the analysis of the first choices of the ten with the highest I.Q. rating and the ten with the lowest.

The range in I.Q. of the class was from 83 to 125. The ten children having the top I.Q.'s listed 114 choices in group 1 of the Social Distance Scale. Of these choices 45 were for those in the top ten in I.Q., 48 were for those in the middle, while only 21 were for children having the lowest ten I.Q.'s. Of these last, ten were for two boys, and the other eleven were divided among five others.

Apparently, in this class the children having the highest I.Q.'s seek their friends from among those in the upper two thirds in this respect unless an individual has some other outstanding characteristic.

The ten children having the lowest I.Q.'s listed 124 choices in selecting those they wished to have as best friends. Of these choices, 40 were for children having the ten highest I.Q.'s, 49 were for those in the middle, and 35 were for those having the ten lowest I.Q.'s. The tendency toward the upper two thirds of the class in this respect, though less evident here than in the top group, is still present.

Socio-Economic Status

The first choices of the ten children having the highest socio-economic scores (on Sims Score Card for Socio-Economic Status) were analyzed with the following results. The ten children listed 115 choices of possible best friends. Of these, 30 were for those among the top ten in socio-economic status, 41 were for children in the lower ten, and the remaining 44 were those for children in the middle group. The only indication here is that, in this group, there is a slight tendency for those in the upper ten to choose friends from the middle or lower socio-economic groups rather than from among their peers in this respect.

The ten children having the lowest socio-economic rating listed 99 choices of possible best friends, distributed as follows: 33 in the top ten, 31 in the lower ten, and 35 in the middle group. Since there were 31 children involved in all of these analyses, it is seen that these classifications each contain approximately one third of the boys and girls in the room.

It seems safe to say that there is practically no tendency among these children to choose friends from those with similar socio-economic situations. No pattern is indicated. This would not be very significant if there were not a fairly wide range of scores on the socio-economic scale. As a matter of fact, these scores varied from 1.087 to 2.609. Since it is very unusual to exceed a score of 3 or to fall below a score of 1 on this scale, the range is quite wide and the interpretations may have some significance.

Self-Other Comparisons

The Check Sheet of Opportunities in Human Relations (Appendix, page 407) presents a list of descriptive phrases for checking to describe one's self. The fourth and fifth grade group decided that, having described themselves, they would like to try to describe their friends on the same form. Illustrations of these two types of checking are shown in Table 10.

TABLE 10

DESCRIPTION OF SELF AND FRIENDS ON CHECK SHEET
(FOURTH AND FIFTH GRADE GROUP OF 34)

Describes Self	Describes Friend	
9	22	Find it easy to make friends
8	20	Well liked by most
6	22	Want to be with people most of the time
5	14	More intelligent than most
4	6	More interested in ideas or things than in people
4	16	A leader
4	19	More interested in people than in things or ideas
3	4	Prefer to be alone much of the time
3	7	Wish I had more skill in getting along with people
3	1	Disliked by many
2	5	Not so smart as most
1	4	Not understood
1	4	Shy
1	14	Wish the school would give more help in how to get along with people
0	3	Find it difficult to make friends
0	5	Liked by few, but not many

It is interesting to find that this group had much more to say about their friends than about themselves, but the ratio of one type of response to the other was somewhat constant. We were interested to see that statements of being liked by others were scaled down in the case of one's friends. Not one admitted for himself that he was "liked by few, but not many," while five placed their best friends in this category. On the other hand, three indicated that the more severe statement "disliked by many" described themselves, but only one used it in relation to friends. The most startling discrepancy occurred in the item concerning school responsibility. Only one pupil indicated a wish that the school would give him more help in how to get along with people, but 14, almost half the group, indicated that they felt it desirable for their friends to have this service! "All the world is queer save thee and me, and even thou. . . ."

On the whole, there seemed to be a tendency for the group to use similar phrases to describe themselves and their friends. However, these phrases were quite general and open to a wide range of interpretations. We looked to other sources for more descriptive statements.

Behavior Descriptions and Social Distance

The Social Analysis of the Classroom (Appendix, page 419) offered 37 descriptions of behavior which each pupil could apply to as many or as few of his classmates as he thought fit. We felt it might be fruitful to study the results in relation to scores obtained from use of the Classroom Social Distance Scale.

For the purposes of this study, a child was considered to have been designated by the class as having demonstrated a particular type of behavior if five or more members of the class indicated that a certain description on the Social Analysis of the Classroom applied to him. For example, one of the descriptions on the instrument is, "Here is someone who doesn't like to talk very much, is very quiet, even when nearly everyone else is talking." If five or more members of the class listed John as one to whom this description applies, it was considered that the class had designated him in that category.

The procedure was to list the children who received the five highest Group Social Distance scores and those receiving the five lowest. (Actually, in every case this resulted in more than five names in each category, since there were in some instances more than one individual receiving the same score.) After each name were listed the categories in which the class designated him. The results were then tabulated.

The results of this summarization were analyzed to determine which of the descriptions might be applicable primarily to those having high Group Social Distance scores, and which to those having low scores on the scale.

—people we like

Some items of the Social Analysis of the Classroom (Appendix, page 419) seemed peculiarly descriptive of those who received high Group Social Distance scores, in that they were frequently assigned to such individuals in this group but were never used to describe those having the five lowest scores on this scale. These items were:

Item   9. "Always knows how to start games or suggests something interesting to do, so that others like to join in." (This was listed eleven times as a description of those having the five highest G.S.D.[1] scores and never of those having low G.S.D. scores.)

Item 13. "Always cheerful, jolly, and good natured, who laughs and smiles a good deal." (Listed 9 times)

Item 11. "Seems to have a good time and seems to enjoy everything he (or she) does no matter where it is—in school, on the playground, at a party, everywhere." (Listed 8 times)

Item 19. "Someone whom everybody likes: people are always glad to have him (or her) around." (Listed 7 times)

Item 25. "Can enjoy a joke and see the fun in it even when the joke is on himself (or herself)." (Listed 7 times)

Item 35. "Is very friendly, has lots of friends, is nice to everybody." (Listed 7 times)

Item 27. "This person is very fond of a joke, is the first to laugh and always sees the point." (Listed 6 times)

Item 15. "Someone who is thought to be very good looking." (Listed 5 times)

The general tendency of the class in responding on the Social Analysis of the Classroom was to list names under items which might be considered complimentary, but to avoid use of uncomplimentary items. However, there were some items which were used to describe more than once students having low G.S.D. scores (indicating low group acceptance) but were never applied to those having high G.S.D. scores (indicating high group acceptance). These items were:

Item   8. "Someone who is always worried or scared, who won't take a chance when something unexpected or unusual happens." (Listed 3 times)

Item 18. "Never tries to keep himself (or herself) clean, neat, and tidy looking." (Listed 3 times)

Item 12. "Never seems to have a good time, never seems to enjoy very much anything he (or she) does." (Listed 2 times)

Item 16. "Here is someone who is thought not to be good looking at all." (Listed 2 times)

[1] G.S.D.—Group Social Distance score (how others rated him).

Item 20. "Someone whom nobody seems to care much about: people do not notice when he (or she) is around." (Listed 2 times)

Item 36. "Doesn't care much to make friends or is bashful about being friendly or doesn't seem to have many friends." (Listed 2 times)

In the light of the above analysis, it might be possible to say that, in this group, a child who is thought by his classmates to demonstrate the following behavior will tend to be generally accepted by the group of which he is a member:

He is aggressive and displays a high degree of initiative, especially in suggesting interesting things for the group to do; he is cheerful, jolly, enjoying everything he does; he sees a joke easily and can laugh even when the joke is on him; and he is friendly and goes out of his way to be nice to his colleagues.

By the same token, someone who is judged to be timid, untidy, and afraid, is frequently sad or unhappy; who is unfriendly or too bashful and shy, will tend, in this group, to receive a low score on the Classroom Social Distance Scale.

—areas of indecision

As interesting as these characteristic descriptions are, equally interesting are some of the descriptions which did not seem to apply to either the highly accepted or the less accepted in this group. There are some types of behavior recorded in anecdotes as those which children seem to find obnoxious. For example, children frequently say, "Oh, he talks too much" as a reason for disliking another child. However, Item 3, "Here is someone who likes to talk a lot," was listed as being descriptive of eight of the high G.S.D. group and of only one of the low.

Another fault which children profess to abhor is that of the "bossy" person. Yet Item 33, "Here is someone who is always telling others what to do, bossing them," was said to be descriptive of two pupils with high G.S.D. scores and of only one with a low G.S.D. score.

Thus, in comparing for this group items of descriptive behavior with degree of general acceptance as measured by the Classroom Social Distance Scale, there were some hints of the bases of acceptance and rejection, though not enough to be considered clear evidence.

Opportunity for Interaction

There are teachers who say, "But of course children choose as friends the ones they sit next to in class, or live near, or play with out of school."

If seating is the basis of choice in some classrooms, we wonder about the degree of interaction in the school situation. If the situation is such that children have an opportunity to know only the pupils in the seats around them, there must be a sterile classroom climate. Children in the classrooms where we worked had "home seats" where they kept their personal belongings, and where they sat when not otherwise engaged; but the major "getting to know people" took place in meetings of subgroups or committees, so the seating arrangement could not have had any significant effect, we are sure.

We were not sure about the matter of geography and easy opportunity for after-school play, however. Figure 19 (page 182) shows the location, on a neighborhood map, of the homes of the children in the fourth and fifth grade and the children's first choices of friends after more than five months of association in the classroom. It would seem that geography does not play a dominant part in the choices of the children of the group studied.

—after-school experience

We did come upon some evidence of the effect of after-school experiences in one group, however. The boys and girls came from a crowded apartment-house area, where all were in easy play distance of one another. However, the crowding increased tensions in the inter-personal relations of their parents, and these tensions were reflected in the children. For example, there were two ten-year-old girls whose mothers had been close friends for years and thus the children had spent much time together since their baby-carriage days. The children were seemingly inseparable. One day, however, their teacher noticed that they divided their time between quarreling and ignoring each other. She was finally able to get to the bottom of the matter and discovered that the mothers of these children had had a bitter quarrel. Their daughters were carrying on the family feud. Neither child seemed quite clear about the reason for their quarrels, but evidently they felt "honor-bound" by family ties to continue the fight. The teacher tried to bring the two together on their former friendship basis, but without success. About two weeks later, however, she found them arm in arm and overjoyed to be friends again. It seems that the mothers had patched up their differences and were again on speaking terms! Teachers should realize that factors such as these may be in operation, if for no reason than that they may not feel thwarted and guilty if sometimes their best efforts are met by failure.

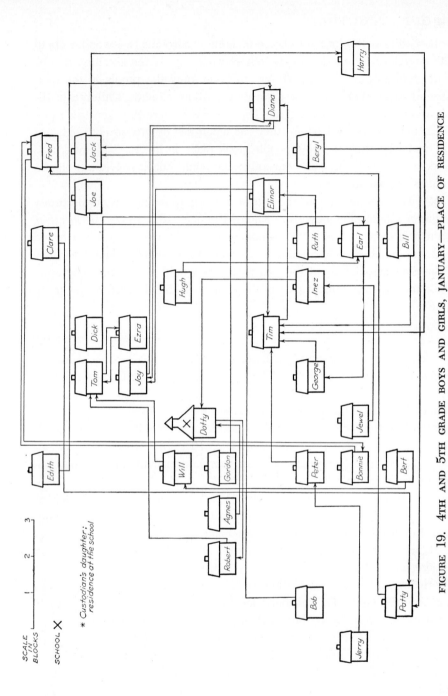

SCALE IN BLOCKS
1 2 3

SCHOOL ✗

* Custodian's daughter: residence at the school

FIGURE 19. 4TH AND 5TH GRADE BOYS AND GIRLS, JANUARY—PLACE OF RESIDENCE IN RELATION TO CHOICE OF FRIENDS (1ST CHOICES ONLY).

UNIVERSITY of SOUTHERN CALIFORNIA
BOOKSTORE—CASH RECEIPT

DATE 2/3/52

NAME (PRINT) Armstrong (LAST) James (FIRST) Fred (MIDDLE)

LOCAL ADDRESS

QUAN-TITY	COURSE NUMBER	AUTHOR	TITLE OR ITEM	CODE	CLASSI-FICATION	QUAN-TITY	UNIT PRICE	AMOUNT DOLLARS	CENTS
		Cunningham	Understanding Group Behavior					3	65
							SUB-TOTAL		
							FEDERAL TAX		
							SALES TAX		
							TOTAL	3	30

FOR VETERAN'S USE WHEN APPLYING FOR REFUND

ALL BOOKS AND SUPPLIES LISTED ARE REQUIRED FOR REGULAR COURSES IN WHICH I AM NOW ENROLLED UNDER THE PROGRAM INDICATED BELOW.
I CERTIFY THAT ANY NON-EXPENDABLE ITEMS LISTED ABOVE HAVE NOT PREVIOUSLY BEEN ISSUED TO ME.
SALES TAX WILL NOT BE REFUNDED.

REHAB. ☐
G. I. ☐
STATE ☐

_____
(VETERAN'S SIGNATURE)

FORM 0816 2-52 100M

RETAIN AS A RECEIPT

Group Judgments

As we studied, it began to look as though it would not be possible for us to find any criteria for boys' and girls' rating of one another on a scale of acceptance and rejection. It seemed clear that the old saying, "Birds of a feather flock together," did not hold in areas we were able to measure through objective means. However, we had one other avenue of approach —the judgment of the children themselves as to their bases of rating.

It will be recalled that early in the year the eighth grade group undertook a study of why they liked people. They first described their best friends, which statements served as the basis for developing a list of descriptive phrases. From the initial list, the group as a whole selected nine items as being the most important. Each member of the class then listed beside the name of each of the other members the key number of the descriptive statement which he felt appropriate for that person. These results were then tabulated, and each person was given a score on each behavior item equal to the number of times he was mentioned by other members of the class as exhibiting that behavior. We then computed rank scores for each member and computed the correlation between rank on each of the behavior items and rank on the Classroom Social Distance Scale. The results of these correlations for each of the characteristics listed by the class follow.

TABLE 11

CORRELATIONS OF DESCRIPTIVE STATEMENTS AND SOCIAL DISTANCE
(EIGHTH GRADE GROUP OF 32)

Descriptive Statement	Correlation with Group Social Distance Score
1. Have fun with him or her	+.862
2. Has other friends	+.847
3. Easily liked	+.839
4. Seems to come from a good home	+.714
5. Is a good sport	+.665
6. Not conceited	+.621
7. Always neat	+.528
8. Does what other people want	+.514
9. Never loses his temper	+.275

It can be seen from these results that there is a rather wide spread between the *rho* scores on items 1 and 9. Apparently, though, the first four or five are criteria which are rather important factors in the choice of one's friends, with the rest being determining qualities to lesser degrees.

It was felt that friendship or liking might be a more complex thing than any *one* of these factors, so the ranks of each individual were averaged and a correlation (Spearman) was obtained among ranks on the Group Social Distance score and rank on the average ranks of the class criteria. The result: *rho* $= + .856$. We can't know, of course, whether these people like those who demonstrate certain behavior; whether, whatever their behavior, it is interpreted as likable; or whether people attribute to people they like the behavior they admire. In any event, the relationship is interesting. Though some of the items are too general to carry much meaning, items such as "Has other friends" carries a message. It seems to be important to this group of adolescents that their friends have a wide range of friends. Is this generally true of this age group? Is it true of other age groups as well?

The first four or five items on the list and perhaps others, and certainly the average for all items, seem to yield an important relationship for this group. In fact, except for "Never loses his temper," all the items hold a higher relationship than did chronological age, I.Q., or socio-economic status.

—talking it over

True, the items listed by the boys and girls are, on the whole, quite general and subject to varied interpretations, so that we may, in a sense, be comparing similar measures when we correlate them with general acceptance. They are specific enough, however, to give some leads. It is interesting, for example, that one criterion for friendship is whether or not an individual "seems to come from a good home," which, as we have indicated earlier, is evidently a way of saying "has social grace, has acceptable manners, etc."

It seems to us that what this study indicates, then, is that a discussion with the group concerning why people are liked tends to give more insight into the bases of inter-personal relations, and the status assigned to an individual by the group, than can be ascertained by statistical analysis of more objective factors. At least this was true of the groups with which we worked. This would seem to give further emphasis to the importance of including boys and girls in the research process, as co-researchers. The curriculum experience of making value judgments conscious and of examining them not only provided rich experience for boys and girls, but further, was more valid (in research language) than the objective testing devices employed.

FACTORS INFLUENCING STRUCTURE

We have implied from time to time what factors seem to influence structure and interaction. Chief of these, in our opinion, is the interaction pattern employed by the teacher and the group.

Structure and Interaction Pattern

It is difficult for us to present precise evidence of the relation of the interaction pattern to group structure. The dynamics of the situation are so complex that it is extremely difficult to study a single variable alone. Moreover, in our investigation we did not set up control groups for precise comparisons, feeling that it was more important to engage in action research with boys and girls as participants, and to put our energies into understanding our own processes, than to make comparisons between groups.

However, with clues throughout as evidence, we can present a number of sociograms from groups which used regularly what to us seemed less favorable patterns (such as adult rule, child obedience). But, as we have said before, we hesitate to use sociograms as instruments of evaluation without a considerable amount of supporting data from other sources. We have some strong hunches, however. When we find that patterns of adult control are frequently accompanied by sociograms which indicate patterns such as that presented in Figure 20 (page 186), we are inclined to believe that lack of interaction tends to concentrate choices to a few key individuals. This further substantiates our view that as group interaction increases there is developed greater discrimination on the part of the group, and the "halo" effect of single strong leaders or popular persons is dispersed. Since our efforts were centered on a range of aspects in few groups rather than in a concentrated study of few aspects in many groups, we present this conclusion only tentatively, and hope it will be tested by other investigators.

Maturity

Also tentative, but somewhat better substantiated by evidence from our experience as well as that of other investigators, is the statement that structure of groups of young children is less organized and more fluid

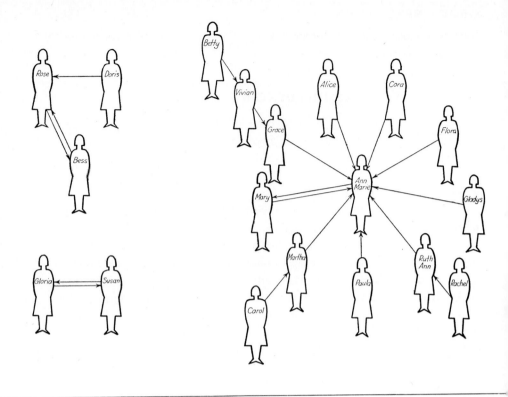

FIGURE 20. 6TH GRADE GIRLS—"BEST FRIENDS" (1ST CHOICES ONLY).
SCHOOL SEEMINGLY HAVING TEACHER RULE, CHILD OBEDIENCE PATTERN.

than that of older boys and girls. The choices of young children may fluctuate widely with the situation. The youngster who is having a birth-day party may be the "key" for one day and forgotten the next. Through observation we were able to substantiate the evidence of other research-ers that young children tend to demonstrate "parallel behavior" (doing things together in space, doing the same thing, or watching one another) but are less likely to cooperate (work together, supplementing each other's efforts toward a common goal). It seems that increased maturity and experience in groups are accompanied by longer periods of social con-tact and more joint action. There is a gradual shift from "doing similar things at the same time" to "doing things jointly." Then there is a shift from "doing things" to "meeting of minds." In other words, there is an increase in verbalization and planning prior to action, and in verbalized exchange of ideas as an end in itself.

[186]

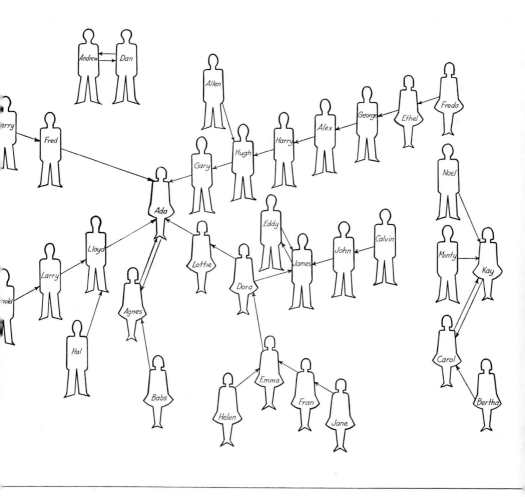

FIGURE 21. 1ST GRADE BOYS AND GIRLS, MARCH—FRIENDSHIPS.

Figure 21, above, shows a sociogram for the first grade group in March, shortly after reorganization for the second term. One of the characteristic aspects of sociograms of groups of young children is the "chain reaction." Note, for example, the chain which starts with Freda in the upper right corner and progresses through Ethel, George, Alex, Harry, Hugh, Gary, to Ada. Although there is some indication of choices of people of the same sex, there are many choices of members of the opposite sex, as is characteristic of boys and girls of this age. As suggested elsewhere, the interaction patterns of young children are quite fluid and tend to change rapidly.

[187]

—maturity and experience

We have said above that changes in structure may be due to maturity and experience. Which of these two aspects is more important in determining the type and degree of interaction we do not know. However, we feel it possible that in some investigations maturity has been emphasized at the expense of experience. If we are correct in our assumption that a high degree of interaction requires skills on the part of the participants, then experience for learning skills of interaction will increase in importance as maturity increases (as the ceiling of possible interaction is lifted through increased maturity). That there may be a ceiling created by maturity we do not doubt. We have cited instances at all levels where we aimed beyond the group's ability, and have attributed much of our failure to the difficulty of immature groups in handling semantics and concepts, and in their lack of ability to generalize, all of which achievements are maturity-linked. However, we found that the skills of the eighth graders were little advanced beyond those of the fourth graders when we began our study. In other words, no doubt maturity is important in the type and degree of interaction, but we believe it to be but *one* of the factors operating, skills gained through experience being a second important factor.

The recognition that maturity is but one of the factors involved gives emphasis to the need for providing experience. Further studies could be significant, we feel.

—unanswered questions

We have a number of unanswered questions in this area. Are there, as some investigators claim, definite "stages" associated with certain ages and maturity levels? For example, is there a "negative phase" of interpersonal relations in pre-adolescence which is manifest through withdrawal from peers and adults? If so, what does this mean for group interaction and group structure for children of this age? To what extent is lack of integration, or even open hostility within a group, the result of an attempt of individuals to adjust to a widening society, as when the younger child moves from adult- to peer-given security or as the adolescent tries to belong simultaneously to childhood and adulthood? What is the effect of age range within a group on group interaction and structure? What is the effect of group acceptance or rejection of the over-aged or under-aged child?

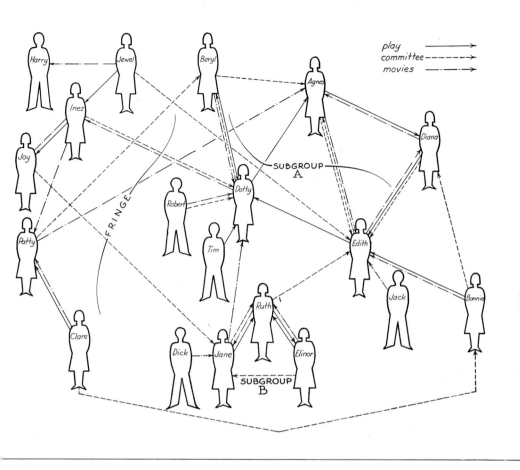

FIGURE 22. 4TH AND 5TH GRADE GIRLS, NOVEMBER—CHOICES
OF COMPANIONS FOR PLAY, COMMITTEE WORK, MOVIES.

The Situation

That structure, as indicated on a sociogram, shifts to some extent with the choice situation is evident. Groups asked at the same time to indicate choices of companions for going to the movies, for play, and for fellow committee members show variation in choice, although the shift is chiefly in terms of realignment of individuals who are not too clearly integrated with a subgroup.

For example, in Figure 22, above, we have superimposed the plotting of three sociograms for three situations. Using first choices only, we first charted choices for "With whom would you like to play?"; then, using the same basic pattern, we plotted choices for "With whom would you

[189]

like to work on a committee?"; then, "With whom would you like to go to
the movies?" If these three sociograms had been plotted separately, we
might have found patterns which appeared to be somewhat different for
the three; but charting in this form brought out the fact that the major
"migration" would have been made by the "fringe" people, who are not
associated with subgroups and are not organized among themselves.

In subgroup A, all choices were made within the "in" group with the
exception of Dotty's choice of Inez for a companion with whom to go to
the movies. Two "out" choices were made from subgroup B to subgroup A.

But fringe people make choices all over the lot—among themselves and
to both subgroups. Although not technically isolates (because they have
received choices from each other, with the exception of Jewel and Clare),
the entire fringe group operates as is usual for isolates, trying to find
acceptance through individuals in widely varying positions.

Bonnie (lower right corner) is an isolate except for a choice from
another fringe person, but she concentrates her choices in subgroup A
and does not migrate, as do other fringe people.

—"halo" effect

We are saying, in effect, that it may be that discrimination per situation is not a strong factor, except for those children who are not clearly
associated with a subgroup. Evidently there is a halo effect which causes
the subgroup to make in-choices regardless of situation. Out-members,
the fringe people, on the other hand, shift considerably in choices according to situations, in a way similar to individual isolates making three
choices in one situation.

It is interesting to note that the question "With whom would you want
to go to the movies?" resulted in many more choices across sex lines than
did other questions. When asked, "With whom would you like to play?"
group members, particularly boys, tended to choose people with athletic
skill, even though some of these children might not be chosen as friends.
Special competence of committee members was recognized, too. For
example, one girl chosen by two others as a playmate is mentioned by
four as a choice for fellow committee member. Another, chosen by
only two as a playmate, is named eight times as choice for fellow committee member.

No doubt the degree of discrimination was heightened when several
questions were asked at the same time. We feel that this is probably a

wise procedure as it directs attention to discrimination in terms of competence rather than allowing halo effect to operate. Thus, even the gathering of basic material for a sociogram may become an instructional experience.

Sex

On all sociograms we found definite sex cleavage, with least in those of young children and in those worded, "With whom would you like to go to the movies?" (Evidently, since one can go to the movies with a date, it is more "respectable" to choose a member of the opposite sex for such activity than as a playmate!)

In the fourth and fifth grade, sociograms made early in the year showed more girls choosing boys as friends or companions for various activities than boys choosing girls, but by the end of the year the opposite was true. In the eighth grade, choices of girls made by boys were much more usual than the reverse. It is probable that the cultural pattern which dictates that boys should do the choosing and asking as they mature was in operation.

—sex in our culture

Our culture is, of course, a strong influence in developing a cleavage between the sexes. Psychologists tell us that young children indicate no innate differences in interest per sex. Little boys enjoy dolls and little girls enjoy wagons—until adults begin to exert their influence through ridicule, or by supplying substitute toys and activities considered more appropriate. As children grow older, there is an increased tendency to impose the adult sex role on children. Traditionally, little girls wash the dishes and little boys carry the wood. In modern apartment house living, where there are no "boy-chores" but where there are still dishes to wash, little girls do more of the work available. When children kept schedules of time-use out of school, these differences were very evident. Two typical time schedules of junior high school youngsters living in a middle class community read as follows:

	Mary		*Tom*
7:00–7:30	Got up and dressed	7:00–7:30	Got up and dressed
7:30–8:00	Helped get breakfast and ate	7:30–8:00	Ate breakfast and read funnies
8:00–8:30	Washed dishes, made bed, packed lunch	8:00–8:30	Fooled around, read funnies, listened to radio
8:30–9:00	Went to school	8:30–9:00	Went to school

It is quite possible, we believe, that this lack of chores for boys may be very unfortunate for the boys, giving them little opportunity to make a contribution to the family and to learn to take responsibility. As long as there are plenty of chores to do, as Mary's schedule indicates, it seems rather stupid to cling to a sex assignment of tasks rather than assign them equally to all members of the family. Yet, it would seem that the assignment of sex role in our culture is so rigid that this situation is maintained in the typical home.

When a committee of the fourth and fifth grade met at the request of the larger group to determine the most pressing problems in human relations for discussion by a jury of group members, one of the fifteen questions proposed was, "How can I stop my sister from being a tomboy?" Even at this age (or is it particularly at this age?), boys and girls are keenly aware of culturally assigned sex roles. The suggestions of the jury reflect further notions of our culture: "Tell her to stay in the house and play dolls" (woman's place is in the home); "Don't let her sell papers" (wage-earning is a male prerogative); "Don't let her dress like a boy" (symbolism, as expressed by clothing is an important means of communicating cultural expectations).

—teacher expectancy

One school staff, in checking the form "Meeting Individual Needs" (see pages 254–257), makes an interesting selection of pupils for study. The directions for use of the instrument suggest: "In selecting pupils for checking try to get a range: e.g., one who is doing well academically, one who is not; one who seems particularly well adjusted socially, one who is not; etc." Each form provides a space for the teacher to indicate his judgment of the pupil selected for study as high, average, or low in respect to intelligence, academic achievement, social adjustment, and maturity in relation to age. Each of the eighteen women teachers of the staff, teaching in kindergarten through the sixth grade, selected three children for study. The distribution of their selections and judgments is presented in Table 12.

It should be no surprise that teachers indicated that the girls selected were more mature in relation to age than the boys, as there is ample evidence for saying that this is characteristic of elementary school children; but responses to the other items raise some questions. The weighting in favor of girls in all areas seems greater than can be attributed to chance alone. It would seem that one of two factors (or both) is operating: *one,*

TABLE 12

DISTRIBUTION OF TEACHERS' SELECTIONS AND JUDGMENTS
ACCORDING TO SEX

	Girls (30)	Boys (24)
Intelligence		
High	14	6
Average	13	13
Low	3	5
Academic Achievement		
High	17	7
Average	8	7
Low	5	10
Social Adjustment		
High	13	5
Average	8	7
Low	9	12
Maturity According to Age		
High	13	6
Average	13	9
Low	4	9

these women teachers may find more which pleases them in the behavior of little girls than they do in the behavior of little boys, and allow a halo effect to influence their judgments in specific responses; or *two*, the school holds to arbitrary standards of attainment in all areas, thus providing a distinct advantage for the more mature girls. In either case, it would seem to be a tough break for the boys. If we are correct in our interpretation of the possible factors operating, then it would follow that the school is contributing to sex cleavage through the favoring of one sex over the other, either directly or indirectly through the program. In other words, is the school set up on the basis of a "little girl" culture to which it asks little boys to adjust? A further investigation of this aspect of school living might be of interest.

—a break for the boys

In some ways, however, the advantage may operate in favor of the boys, if it is an advantage to have fun in the world; and we think it is! We took a quick look through a number of textbooks and other children's books and found some interesting hints as to assignment of sex role. Usually, in these books, boys and girls were pictured in the illustrations as doing similar things, or were assigned adult sex roles (such as little girls with dolls, little boys with wagons). However, and this interested us, whenever there was something quite fascinating going on, the little boy was given the role of participant and the girl was observer. For example, one illustration showed a boy and his father on the floor playing with an electric train, the mother sat on a sofa knitting, and sitting primly beside her mother, hands folded in her lap, was the little girl. The two children seemed to be of the same age, about six or seven. Any teacher or parent knows that no six- or seven-year-old girl likes to sit on the sofa watching when interesting things are going on around her, but this is the role often assigned to her! Our cursory examination of these books may not have yielded a valid impression, but we hope a more thorough investigation of this area will be made and reported. If it is true that, subtly, through illustrations in books, we teach little girls that boys are meant to have all the fun, is it any wonder that girls either dislike or envy boys? And is it any wonder that boys avoid girls, for, if they identify with girls, they might miss out on the fun which is indicated as their right as males?

INTERGROUP STRUCTURE

We decided it might be revealing to study intergroup as well as intragroup structure through sociometric techniques. We attempted this with two groups: one, the ten room-groups of an elementary school, with grades one through six; and two, the seven eighth grade groups in a junior high school. With each we used the question: "What groups would you like to have visit us for a program?" The classroom named most frequently was designated as first choice, next frequently, second choice, and next, third choice.

An Elementary School

We had little idea what to expect in a situation where the age range was from six to thirteen years. We had some feeling that the older groups, the fifth and sixth grades, might carry prestige with all groups. Our findings are presented in Table 13, page 195, and in Figure 23, page 195. As can be seen, the tendency was for a group to choose that next higher group in age and grade. It would seem that prestige of age is less significant than immediate aspiration level, which extended only to the next "higher" group.

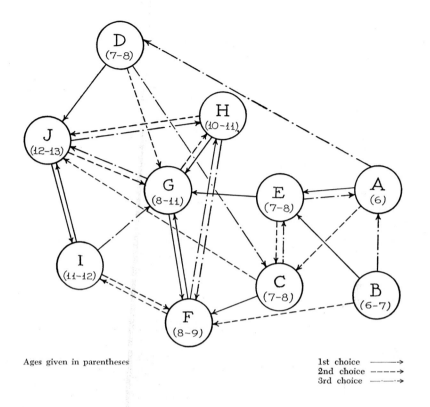

Ages given in parentheses

1st choice ——————→
2nd choice ------→
3rd choice —·—·—→

FIGURE 23. INTERGROUP SOCIOGRAM.

TABLE 13

INTERGROUP CHOICES IN AN ELEMENTARY SCHOOL

Group Making Choice			1st Choice		2nd Choice		3rd Choice	
Group	Ages	Grades	Ages	Grades	Ages	Grades	Ages	Grades
A	6	1	7–8	2–3	7–8	2	7–8	2–3
B	6–7	1–2	7–8	2–3	8–9	3–4	6	1
C	7–8	2	8–9	3–4	12–13	6	7–8	2–3
D	7–8	2–3	12–13	6	8–11	4–5	7–8	2
E	7–8	2–3	8–11	4–5	7–8	2	6	1
F	8–9	3–4	8–11	4–5	10–11	4–5	10–11	5–6
G	8–11	4–5	8–9	3–4	10–11	4–5	12–13	6
H	10–11	4–5	8–11	4–5	12–13	6	8–9	3–4
I	11–12	5–6	12–13	6	8–9	3–4	8–11	4–5
J	12–13	6	11–12	5–6	8–11	4–5	10–11	4–5

The reasons for choices given by the groups are of interest. By far the greatest number claimed that choice was based on the fact that children they knew were in the room group chosen. No doubt acquaintance-ship is a powerful influence, and we took it literally until we realized that there is little reason for knowing people "above" but not "below" (in grade). We concluded that "people we know" included an overtone of "people we admire," with the admiration toned to the level of aspiration.

Other reasons for choices of groups included clues to what children feel to be important in group living.

> They have a good teacher.
> We were invited to their room once.
> They would understand our program even if things went wrong.
> They listen well.
> They do things like us.
> They have nice pictures on the wall.
> They draw good.
> There are lots of Scouts in that room.
> If it (the program) isn't good they will still clap.

When suggesting younger groups, as did happen occasionally, there is almost a note of apology or of patronizing superiority in the reasons given:

> We feel sorry for them; so few choose them.
> We were in that room last year.
> They haven't been going anywhere. They're never invited.
> They are so little.
> They would enjoy it.
> They would get a lot of fun out of it.

Eighth Grade Groups

In the junior high school in which we were working, there were seven eighth grade groups. Five of these were grouped heterogeneously, one on the basis of high intelligence (highest of all eighth grades), and one on the basis of low intelligence.

The choices of these groups are plotted in Figure 24, page 197. The distribution is fairly even, with the exception of the low I.Q. group which was never chosen. The high I.Q. group was neither favored nor ignored over other groups. It is interesting to note that the low I.Q. group chose the high I.Q. group as second choice.

As with the elementary school children, the major reason for choices

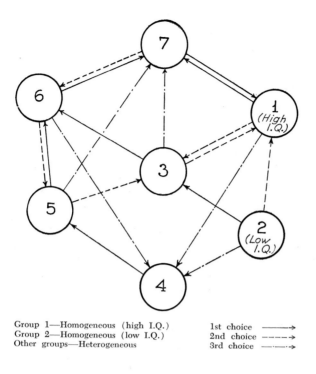

Group 1—Homogeneous (high I.Q.)
Group 2—Homogeneous (low I.Q.)
Other groups—Heterogeneous

1st choice ——————→
2nd choice — — — →
3rd choice —·——·→

FIGURE 24. 8TH GRADES, INTERGROUP SOCIOGRAM.

was acquaintance with members of the chosen group, but frequently this was accompanied by specific statements of opportunity for knowing them, such as: "We're in the same shop class," or "We have gym together."

There was indication that some choices were made in terms of the teachers of the groups. Group No. 7 reached an impasse when all the boys voted for a room with a man teacher, and all the girls for a group with a woman teacher. There were more boys in the group than girls, so the vote was recorded as first choice for the man teacher and second for the woman teacher! Group No. 4, though well favored by choices by other groups, claimed that they knew only one group well enough to vote for it.

If there is as much significance as these boys and girls imply in merely "knowing people," it would seem to add weight to the need to help pupils broaden their social view through their getting acquainted not only within their school but also with groups in their community.

[197]

TEACHER'S JUDGMENT OF STRUCTURE

Teachers frequently say to us, "But why go to all the bother of making sociograms and using the Classroom Social Distance Scale? Doesn't a good teacher know what the results will be before using these devices?"

We were interested in investigating this question. It is difficult to measure a teacher's conception of group structure, but we felt we might inquire into a simpler aspect of structure—judgment concerning the degree of acceptance of individuals by the group. Teachers were asked to list the most and the least accepted individuals, and give their reasons for placing the names on the lists. These listings were made early in the year, prior to the administering of the Classroom Social Distance Scale, but were later compared with the rank in scores on the scale. This type of listing was not repeated, for after seeing the scores resulting from use of the scale, it would be difficult for a teacher to make independent judgments.

For the fourth and fifth grades, we have records of the home teacher (the "regular" teacher of the group) and of one contributing teacher (a teacher who met with the group for one period a day only). The results of their judgments are presented in Tables 14 and 15, pages 199 to 201.

On the whole, it would seem that an observant teacher knows who is most and who is least accepted by the group, yet there are some startling misjudgments. Grace, who the contributing teacher thinks should be accepted because she is pretty and does excellent work, ranks 20 in acceptance in the group of 32 as classed by the group, rather than among the first seven, as the teacher judges her. Seth, whom the home teacher judges to be non-accepted, possibly because his health won't permit him to do some things with other children, ranks 11 in the group of 32, rather than among the lower seven as the teacher judges. Glenn, whom the contributing teacher considers lazy, is not rejected by the group as the teacher believes him to be. Evidently it is easy to attribute to the group one's own judgment of an individual.

For the eighth grade group we had an opportunity to compare several judgments. Although the group was with the general education teacher for a block of time, they went to other teachers for other classes. Six teachers named the boys and girls they felt to be most and the least accepted by the group (Table 16, page 202).

As may be seen, there is a wide range in the judgments of teachers.

TABLE 14

TEACHER'S JUDGMENTS OF PUPILS MOST AND LEAST ACCEPTED
BY A FOURTH AND FIFTH GRADE GROUP

Most Accepted by Teacher	Rank in Social Distance Score (In Group of 32)	Reason for Listing
Carol	2 *	Carol is chosen among the first by both boys and girls for group work and in games. Children gather around her to talk when they have free time at lunch hour or in morning. She finishes her work quickly and has plenty of time to help those who need her and still do her extra work.
Nancy	5	Nancy has a pleasant disposition. She is often chosen as leader of a committee or group. She is willing to help anyone in need of help, including Cora and Faith (non-accepted children). She is seldom alone because children go to her to talk or play at noon or in morning free time.
Ray	13	Ray is boys' captain for three-base soccer. Children take his suggestions well. Both boys and girls like to have him on their teams and in their groups. Has been chosen leader of a birds group.
Jane	5	Children often choose Jane for leader in games or groups. She can go ahead with plans and make children enjoy following her. (Tea Party Hostess.) She likes to play and is active in all games.
Guy	1	Guy is a good reader and the children like his stories (told or read). Guy is always a good sport and has a pleasant smile for everyone. Has been chosen leader of an animal group.
Pearl	21	Some boys have remarked that Pearl is pretty. Children take up for her when she's in trouble. When they hurt her feelings in a group and make her cry they voluntarily go to apologize to her.

* Low numbers, 1, 2, etc., indicate high degree of acceptance by the group; high numbers indicate lack of acceptance.

TABLE 14 (Continued)

Least Accepted by Teacher	Rank in Social Distance Score (In Group of 32)	Reason for Listing
Cora	29	Children do not like to sit near *Cora* in the circle. They laugh at her when she stutters or fails to keep on the subject when she talks. She often gets hit or hits children who try to work with her. She doesn't like to let them use any of her materials.
Faith	30	Children do not like to sit with *Faith.* She is usually the last child to be chosen on a team. Children tell her she can't do her work well.
Seth	11	*Seth* has to sit and watch the children play. He can't dust a table because he is allergic to dust. He can't eat a peanut because he isn't allowed to. He brought gifts to try to do something special for the children, possibly to gain their acceptance.
Belle	30	*Belle* is bossy and quarrelsome with the children when she works with a group. Some children have told me that she bothers them when they are doing unsupervised work and she had "told a lie on them."
Polly	21	*Polly* is always telling on other children when she comes from the lavatory. She told me that the other children copied their stories while she made hers up for herself. The other children accuse her of being a "tattletale." She occasionally slaps or hits the people she is playing with.
Roy	24	*Roy* does very poor school work, has not learned to write so one can read his written work. The children are aware of this and do not choose him on their groups. They are not very pleasant about helping him with work he gets stuck on. He is trying to form a baseball team at home to gain acceptance by his group.

TABLE 15

CONTRIBUTING TEACHERS' JUDGMENTS OF PUPILS
MOST AND LEAST ACCEPTED BY GROUP

Most Accepted by Teacher	Rank in Social Distance Score (In Group of 32)	Reason for Listing
Nancy	5 *	Nancy—Has such a pleasing personality. Happy disposition. Always ready to try. Does excellent work. Nice looking.
Carol	2	Carol—Willing to help at any time. Does excellent work. Wants to please. Good looking.
Jane	5	Jane—Willing to help. Has a nice disposition. Very agreeable when corrected. Dependable.
Ray	13	Ray—Good wholesome boy. Wants to do good work. Has a nice personality.
Leo	5	Leo—Has a nice personality. Just a nice boy that you can't help but like.
Joyce	15	Joyce—Pretty child. Does good work. Lovable.
Grace	20	Grace—Very independent. Let's everyone know she is on her own. Pretty. Excellent work.
Least Accepted		
Belle	30	Belle—Disagreeable. Telling on other children.
Cora	29	Cora—Seems to enjoy getting other children in trouble. Always watching to tell on someone.
Jim	25	Jim—A nuisance. Doing anything but the thing he should be doing. Poor worker.
Glenn	15	Glenn—Lazy. Watching what other children are doing, not working himself.
Polly	21	Polly—I don't feel that I can trust her. Tells on other children.

* Low numbers, 1, 2, etc., indicate high degree of acceptance by the group; high numbers indicate lack of acceptance.

Table 16

TEACHERS' JUDGMENTS OF PUPILS MOST AND LEAST ACCEPTED BY AN
EIGHTH GRADE GROUP*

Named Most Accepted by Six Teachers	Rank in Social Distance Score**	Teacher (each column presents the check by a teacher)					
		1	2	3	4	5	6
Dotty	1				x	x	
Alice	3	x	x		x	x	x
Bob	3	x	x		x		
Galen	3			x			x
Susan	7	x	x				x
Tom	7	x		x			x
Harold	7	x				x	
Joyce	7		x				
Madge	10.5			x		x	
Irene	13		x				
Jim	13		x		x		x
Mary	15.5	x		x			x
Roy	17	x					
Doris	18	x					
Irma	21.5					x	
Marvin	25				x		
Named Least Accepted by Six Teachers							
Olen	35	x		x		x	x
Ernest	34		x		x		
Ralph	32	x				x	
Sheldon	31.5	x	x	x		x	
Mike	31.5	x	x	x	x	x	
Keith	31.5	x		x	x		x
Esther	29		x	x			x
Phyllis	27		x				
Vera	27					x	
Arnold	27						x
Bertha	21.5	x					
Larry	17	x					
May	15.5						x
Nan	10.5		x				
Harold	7		x				

* In group of 35 pupils.
** *Low* numbers (1, 2, etc.) indicate acceptance by group; *high* numbers (35, 34, etc.) indicate rejection by group. Rank is indicated as rank in *total* group. Some pupils in both high and low ranks were not named by teachers, hence the discrepancy in rank intervals.

Out of a group of 35 pupils only five were not named as either among the most or among the least accepted by the group. One, Harold, has the distinction of having his name on both lists. The median rank for this group is 17.5, so on the whole, judgments were correct (as compared with rank on the Classroom Social Distance Scale) to the extent of being above and below the median; but even this was not always true. It is interesting to note that teachers seem to be more accurate in judging rejection than in judging acceptance, possibly because a person, accepted by a subgroup, may thus seem accepted although not well accepted by the group as a whole.

Table 16 seems to us to be a rather dramatic answer to the teacher who says, "Wouldn't a good teacher know, anyway?" Certainly there are many discrepancies in judgments in relation to the ranks on social distance scores, and, even if one mistrusts these scores, the range of judgments among the teachers tells a story.

Perhaps we should add, however, that we are reasonably sure that these judgments would be more accurate as the teachers learned to know the groups better. Thus, an instrument such as the Classroom Social Distance Scale may not reveal more than a teacher would eventually learn, but it may hasten the understanding. Moreover, the use of the scale may indicate early inter-personal relations before the group structure has become defined.

IN SUMMARY

Classroom groups have form and structure which may be recognized through observation or by the use of sociometric techniques. The degree of organization in these groups varies considerably and tends, according to our observation, to be most clearly manifest in groups of older girls.

In any group, there are some children better accepted than others, but in no group that we observed was any child totally rejected by everyone else. The degree to which a child accepts others in the group varies as widely as does the acceptance of him, but the two factors are not in relation. That is, a child who is well accepted may accept either many or few. The same is true of children who are less well accepted.

We found little significant correlation of acceptance with factors such as chronological age, intelligence quotient, or socio-economic status. However, correlations of acceptance with factors stated as important by boys and girls were statistically significant.

There are some clues to factors which influence acceptability in the relation of scores on the Classroom Social Distance Scale to behavior designated as characteristic on the Social Analysis of the Classroom.

We have no clear evidence as to the relation of structure to interaction pattern (though we have some strong clues), but we feel that a study of this relationship is of such significance that we hope it may be carried further by other investigators.

It is evident that maturity of the members influences the organization of groups, but we believe skills in interaction may be of equal importance, with a "maturity ceiling" as the only limiting factor. In other words, we feel that many groups could achieve a greater degree of organization in relation to their maturity if they had the skills. This, too, offers a fertile field for further study.

There is no doubt that sex cleavage operates in groups of boys and girls. We are curious to know the extent to which this is innate or culturally imposed. The culture patterns dictating sex roles, as evidenced in time-use, illustrations in children's books, and teachers' assessments of children, lead us to believe that sex cleavage may be more culturally imposed than is popularly assumed.

Studies of inter-group structure open an avenue to further research. It seems that among groups which vary widely in maturity, inter-group selection is made in terms of admiration for greater maturity, tuned to an aspiration level which is concerned with the next higher "level" (in age and grade). The weight given to "knowing people" in the selection of other groups may hold implications for wider inter-group experiences for groups both within the school and in the wider society.

Teachers may be surprised to discover how often they are mistaken about the acceptance patterns of groups with which they deal, at least until they are well acquainted with the groups. The evidences of misjudgment give emphasis to the desirability of using certain sociometric techniques as short-cuts to greater understanding of groups.

Most important, perhaps, are the implications for group management to be found in a study of group structure. It is possible that the teacher who is unaware of subgroups, isolates, stars, or pal-patterns may have great difficuty in rendering leadership to his group. Conversely, the teacher who understands the group structure may be in a position not only to lead the group more effectively in general learning experiences but also to help the group achieve better group living. The relation of teacher understanding of such matters to group management is deserving of much further research.

*In which we suggest some symp-
toms to examine in studying group
adjustment*

VI

Group Adjustment

It was Friday afternoon. Everything seemed to be going wrong. Billy
had spilled the ink; Sally had had her feelings hurt by Barbara; no one
could remember whose turn it was to water the plants, etc., etc., etc.
Breathes there a teacher who hasn't lived through such a period? It isn't
any one person or any one thing that seems to be wrong. There is just
something the matter with the whole group atmosphere.

Much has been said and written about needs and adjustment of individuals, but little about needs and adjustment of groups. Yet groups, as
well as individuals, have needs. We believe it is possible to recognize
needs of a group: to grow, to find security, to belong, to develop widening social consciousness, to develop increased awareness of goals, to find
increased control of means of achieving goals, and to discover an increased
sense of achievement toward goals.

If these needs are not met, groups, as well as individuals, develop
symptomatic behavior of frustration and maladjustment. If a teacher can
learn to read needs and interpret the symptoms revealed, he has an increased opportunity to guide the group toward development.

All group behavior is symptomatic of a degree of adjustment, but some
types of behavior and reactions to certain kinds of situations seem to be
particularly revealing.

In this chapter we raise questions and cite examples, but throughout
we are well aware that there are few generalizations we dare make.
There is great need for further study in this area.

The following listings are in no sense a check list, but they may serve
as "sensitizers" for group observation, diagnosis, and learning how to plan
to meet needs. Each group may have its unique patterns of "critical"

[205]

reactions, which the teacher must learn to recognize, understand, and adjust. However, our observation prompts us to list the following situations as most revealing in terms of group reaction for the groups we observed.

ADJUST TO WHAT?

Before we get into specifics of group adjustment, however, we have an important problem to face. To what do we want groups to adjust? It is possible to use (misuse, we believe) the knowledge of group adjustment as a means of helping groups adjust to predetermined situations which may be inimical to group growth. We see examples of this daily as teachers struggle to help groups adjust to unsuitable experiences. We hear teachers ask, "How can I help my group adjust to sitting still during an auditorium period?" First, we believe, we must ask whether it is wise to ask the group to sit still; whether there is need for an auditorium period; and, even if these adjustments are wise, whether they are the *most important* adjustments we can help a group learn to make?

There are situations, of course, in which the goals of society come before the immediate goals of the group, and in fact may be a means of developing and lifting them. We are convinced, however, that this conflict between immediate group goals and goals of society occurs less frequently than teachers like to admit. The possibility of such a conflict is often used by teachers as an excuse for imposing a predetermined plan of action, regardless of group needs and goals. We believe that phrases such as "But it's *good* for them," "They *ought* to have this experience," are frequently used as "alibis" for exerting teacher rule rather than operating in terms of group need. (We readily admit that a teacher-rule program can be imposed with less thought, energy, and insight.)

As we look at so-called programs of adjustment, we find seven assumptions in operation. These assumptions are not necessarily mutually exclusive. Two or more may be held simultaneously.

Assumption I:
The Group Should Adjust to Teacher Convenience

In fairness to our profession, we should say immediately that this assumption is not often employed, and when it is, it is likely to be used unconsciously. That it is used at times, however, cannot be denied. As we mentioned above, there are some teachers who employ what seem to them obviously less desirable means to education only because they find the teacher-rule pattern more convenient (easier to apply).

Sometimes merely a small aspect of the program is set up on this basis. One school faculty named pupil tardiness as its major problem. When asked why this was a problem, there was considerable spluttering, but it finally came out that, for some of the teachers at least, it was considered a problem because it was a source of annoyance to them. We wonder how many of the "no chewing gum" and "no talking in the halls" types of rules are in this category. Possibly more than many teachers realize.

The exploitation of teacher interests might come under this category. It is fascinating to find that, although Miss Rogers claims that areas for study grow out of pupils' needs and interests, in her group there is year after year a unit on rocks. In Miss Spearman's group, there is yearly a unit on great art, and in Miss Porter's one on prehistoric animals. It seems a bit strange that these areas of learning should be necessary to the needs of boys and girls year after year.

In this discussion, we are not implying that teachers' adjustments should not be considered; we feel strongly that they should. However, it may be wise to examine the extent to which the needs of the minority (teachers) are allowed to dominate those of the majority (the pupils).

Assumption 2:

The Group Should Adjust to Teacher Inadequacy

A more kindly way of stating this assumption might be: Groups should adjust to teachers' lack of information and critical judgment about teaching and learning. Sometimes this assumption is used with the utmost good will, but also with the utmost lack of understanding of how learning takes place, how children grow, and how society operates. We would place in this category the "sitting still" dictum and the "auditorium period."

There are, no doubt, many teachers who require groups to comply with a program based primarily on memorization and meaningless drill, not because they are "nasty souls" intentionally misusing their power as group leaders, but because they don't know any better. They may believe sincerely that they are "doing what is best." The tide of advance in tested and proved educational practice has swept beyond them, and they are unaware that they are in the backwash. The only answer for providing better group living, in these cases, would seem to be to help teachers learn more about known principles and proved facts of child growth and development.

Assumption 3:

The Group Should Adjust to the Past

It is probable that this assumption is in operation far more than we realize. Many factors help to maintain it. Not the least of these is the often repeated phrase of parents, "Now when *I* went to school—" which assumes that *I* am a perfect product and what made *me* will make a similarly fine product of my child. This is a difficult argument to meet, for it necessitates the establishment of the fact that there might be a more worthy product than the *I* under discussion, or—perhaps an easier approach—that such a perfect *I* can be produced more efficiently.

Subtly different is the "what was good enough for Father" argument. This argument is usually intended to be furthered by some statement concerning "soft" education. There may be, also, a "sink or swim" philosophy, which implies that all efforts of teachers to help groups adjust is contrary to what we know about "survival of the fittest." School people, committed as they must be in a democratic society to the education of all the children of all the people, cannot condone such a stand.

Most influential, however, in maintaining the assumption that groups should adjust to the past are probably the teachers who don't want to change—because they fear the unknown, because they know that "keeping up to date" entails work, because they lack the security necessary to make a change, or because they endorse one of the arguments given above.

We don't find any convincing arguments among this array. In fact, it sounds to us as though people who use them are not thinking very clearly. We are reminded, too, that people who cling to the past, such as the ancestor worshipers of Japan, do not establish patterns we want to use in educating our children in the modern world. Rather than "soft" education, we'd like some further "hard" thinking about this assumption.

Assumption 4:

The Group Should Adjust to "Superior" Wisdom

In school after school, we found teachers who assumed that their major job in group adjustment was to help youngsters adjust to central office demands, supervisory edicts, or "courses of study." Behind this assumption, evidently, is a belief that superior wisdom can foresee adjustment needs of a group. This we doubt.

One first grade teacher, for example, was convinced through observation of her group and conferences with parents that there was need for an after-lunch rest period for the group if she was to reduce fatigue and eliminate tensions inimical to good group living. She finally provided this period but not without considerable trepidation, because she feared she might be criticized for "leaving out" some word drill, phonics, music, or other matter "prescribed" for first graders.

In cases such as this, we believe that the judgment of teachers who have sincerely studied group needs should be given considerable weight. There should be joint consideration of the problem with both the teachers and the central office representatives considering the matter *in its setting* not merely in the abstract wisdom of central office "experts." We cannot condone an assumption on the part of some experts that they can foresee all major group needs out of context of the group situation. This does not mean that there is no place for the expert. Quite the contrary. We believe that an expert who helps teachers recognize group needs can make a significant contribution to group adjustment.

Assumption 5:

The Group Should Adjust to the Demands of Society

That teachers in a democracy have a heavy responsibility to help groups adjust to this society we admit. That teachers may exploit this concept to impose a teacher-dominated, predetermined program we also admit. In other words, in the name of democracy it is possible for teachers to teach undemocratically.

We are convinced that there is a major need for teachers to examine realistically those situations to which they ask groups to adjust—to consider them in the light of what they believe to be the compelling demands of a democratic society, of a technological society, of a world society. Unless there is such examination, and plans are made in terms of its results, there is little hope for a long-term group adjustment.

A variation of this assumption is that the basis of group adjustment should be created by community pressures. A teacher may know better but feel compelled by community demands to try to teach reading to all first graders regardless of maturity or readiness, to try to teach breakfastless children their multiplication tables, to try to teach Latin to youngsters concerned with being wanted or earning a living. A teacher may be convinced that a group is in need of sex information, skills in analyzing labor-management relations, or understanding of the crisis of our relations with Russia, but find it impossible to meet these needs because of community pressures. Our first reaction is to offer our sympathy and to suggest that such a teacher put his energies into community education rather than into futile attempts to achieve group adjustment under such adverse circumstances. A simple answer like this, however, will not suffice.

In our study, we asked parents to meet with us, to state goals, and to plan programs of action. True, we tended to concentrate on areas of agreement, and we left many non-agreement areas untouched. Hence, we do not feel that we found a final means to solution of this problem; but it was a start—a start which any teacher can make with the parents of her pupil group.

In a situation where there is conflict between the community and the schools, the teacher is in a difficult spot, indeed. He dare not operate on the assumption that his way is the right way, not only because he may thus forfeit his opportunity to make his influence felt in the situation, but further, and more important for immediate group adjustment, because he may actually contribute to group maladjustment if he sets up, in the minds of the classroom group, barriers between school and home. The compromise path to be tread while endeavoring to develop better understanding of all involved is one which requires the utmost tact and good judgment. It requires that the individual recognize long-range as well as immediate goals, and be willing to forego some of the immediate aims in favor of more important future objectives—never an easy operation.

Assumption 6:
The Group Should Adjust to the Needs of Individuals

In discussing this assumption, we don't want to be led into the age-old argument of individual *vs.* the group, for we feel it to be a specious fallacy. It seems quite clear to us, as we indicated in Chapter IV, that the individual contributes to the group and the group to the individual. "Johnny helps make the group, and the group helps make Johnny."

We recognize, however, that it is quite possible to give preference to the individual apart from the group. Some programs of education contribute to this assumption. It is interesting to note that in our experience the idea of "helping Johnny get ahead of the others" is most persistently advanced by middle-class parents who see education as a means to class mobility. It seems that in many programs of study in child development, the understanding of the *individual* is the only criterion applied.

Many guidance programs seem to operate on the basis of individual adjustment alone, assuming that a congregation of adjusted individuals will result in a good group. We are convinced that this assumption is erroneous. The group is something more than the sum of its parts, and the achievement of good group living requires special skills and understandings. Moreover, emphasis on individual adjustment alone tends to give emphasis to maintaining the status quo of group life, with the individual the one who must adjust to it. We believe the group has a responsibility to its members and must adjust itself to meet individual needs as well as to better its own living as a group.

Democracy, we believe, cannot condone development of the individual at the expense of the group. Nor can democracy condone development of the group at the expense of the individual. This interrelationship we have tried to emphasize time and time again. The individual contributes to the group. The group must learn to recognize contributions of the individual.

Assumption 7:
Groups Should Adjust to Group Needs

Hand in hand with adjustment to society and to individual needs goes adjustment to *group* needs. Adjustment to group needs cannot be divorced from adjustment to the wider society, for a classroom group is a segment of society growing toward a larger society. Nor can it be divorced from individual needs, for a group is composed of individuals.

Recognizing Assumptions

We are keenly aware that the assumptions stated above are not mutually exclusive. We contend, however, that our society and our education have given undue emphasis to the rights of the individual and insufficient emphasis to the importance of group living. We find some parents deploring the fact that schools have taught the "rights" of democracy but not its "responsibilities." This, we believe, is another way of saying we have overemphasized the individual and underemphasized the group.

Unless teachers, schools, communities are aware of the assumptions on which the educational program is operating, we have little hope for developing better programs. It is our recommendation that as teachers and parents work together for better schooling for children and young people, they critically examine the assumptions above, and others, to determine the basis of their operations. By facing facts, they are in a position to operate intelligently on the assumption understood to be in operation, or to move to a more desirable one. Unless these assumptions are examined, individuals and groups may find themselves in positions of confusion and impasse.

Although the assumptions listed above are not mutually exclusive, and no doubt in the good school several are in operation in subtle combination, the emphasis we are giving here to group living leads us to address ourselves in the following section to group needs only.

SITUATIONS WHICH REVEAL DEGREE OF ADJUSTMENT

Routine

The reaction of the group to the various routines of group living is one indication of the degree of group adjustment. Some routines have probably become habitual and are accepted without question. What are these? Are they routines which promote the general movement of the group toward its goals?

In one classroom, one of the general goals proposed by the teacher and accepted by the group was that everyone should share the responsibility for the care of the room. The teacher felt that in this way each pupil would get real satisfaction from participation, and she hoped that a higher degree of group integration would result. However, the routine schedule was such that only those children who ate lunch at school were able to participate actually in the work of maintaining the room in the desired fashion. What developed was a cozy little club group which was doing the work, and, as a consequence, the amount of group integration was greatly reduced. It was only when the teacher examined the routines to compare them with the goals that this inconsistency was discovered and a new schedule developed (by the group) which provided for participation by all.

Routine has a very important place as a security-giving device. It is much easier to feel at home in a group where many of the casual aspects of daily living have become routinized and are thus predictable. No one feels at home in an entirely strange and unpredictable situation. One of the early tasks in any group is to establish purposeful routines which can provide a partial basis for group security.

However, it would seem that great care must be taken not to use routine and mere precedent as a way to avoid problem-solving. In one

Middle Western high school, it was customary to hold the senior prom in a downtown hotel. It was the established policy of the hotel to exclude Negro guests. As long as the usual practice of holding the prom here was maintained, the members of the senior class were able to avoid facing their responsibility toward their fellow-classmates who happened to be Negroes. In this case, the blind acceptance of precedence of routine was substituted for problem-solving. Incidentally, it is easy for teachers themselves to avoid examining the effectiveness and worth-whileness of their teaching by providing so much routine activity that the real problem is side-stepped. Workbooks, lesson sheets, tests, quizzes, drills, and other potentially very useful devices are frequently employed for this purpose.

In summary, it might be said that a certain amount of routine behavior is necessary for group security. However, the routines employed should be in harmony with the goals of the class and should not be used as substitutes for other more profitable activities, such as a realistic examination of situations and problem-solving.

THIRTY OR MORE PUPILS AREN'T NECESSARILY A GROUP.

Change

It has been our experience that closely related to routine is the problem of group reaction to change. A well-adjusted group should be able to meet change if it is not too drastic. It seems that a less well adjusted group has more difficulty in meeting even simple changes.

If the change is recognized as contributing to the achievement of desirable ends, one of which, by the way, may be relief from monotony, it will generally be welcomed by the group. On the other hand, change which seems to impede the realization of these goals will be resisted.

One fourth grade group had a well-defined sense of what it wanted to achieve. In many ways, it was the most flexible of the groups studied and the most willing to change its behavior. On one occasion, however, when a visiting teacher came into the room while the children were working and said enthusiastically, "Boys and girls, wouldn't you like to come into the auditorium to see a program?" much to her amazement, the answer was a polite but definite "No." The auditorium program offered no possibilities for achieving what the group had in mind. The activities in which it was engaged did. A program at that time had no attraction, though at other times and in different circumstances the group would be eager to attend.

One of the questions which the parents of the children with whom we worked asked most frequently was "What will happen when my child gets back into a traditional school situation? Will he be able to adjust there?" A partial answer was found in the behavior of the eighth grade group. Being in a junior high school, they did not have the same teacher all day but spent part of the time moving from room to room and meeting different types of teaching situations. It was extremely interesting to follow this group from place to place (page 42). It appeared to the observer that they retained their group solidarity and the general group morale seemed to be maintained, but their adjustment to the demands of varying situations was notable. As long as they were able to achieve the satisfaction they were seeking within the requirements of the situation, they operated in the fashion required by the teacher. When they couldn't, they showed resistance.

The same reactions were evident as the groups changed from active work to quiet work, from group work to individual activity. As long as they could see progress toward their ends, the adjustment was good; when they couldn't, resistance was strong.

Change can be a means of fostering growth and development. It can also be disruptive, fostering insecurity. Generally speaking, changes which make for progress toward desired ends will be accepted and enjoyed, while changes that seem to obstruct these ends will be resisted and may be frustrating.

Interference

Probably more teachers consider "ending it all" because of outside interruptions to classroom activity than because of any other one thing that happens in their lives. Groups, too, have these interferences, and if they welcome them with open arms it is likely to be a fairly good sign that they are not engaged in very enjoyable or purposeful activity. Have you ever sat in a group and wished that the fire alarm would ring or that some other equally disrupting event would occur? Children sometimes feel that way, too.

However, when a group is engaged in activities that lead toward achievement, or that are enjoyed for their own sake, there is a strong tendency to resent interference. Thus a teacher is able to judge to some extent the adjustment of the group by its reaction to interferences which occur in even the best of situations. Perhaps it would be well to look at some of these.

The program itself, if not flexible, acts as an interfering factor. Does arithmetic, spelling, or something else always interfere with what the group is doing?

One youngster, reporting in the daily log, again and again made statements such as these: "We got started on our hobby hour, then we had to go to the gym." "We were in the middle of a story, but we had to go to recess." "We were having art, but we had to go get measured and weighed." What a thwarting world our "had to's" can create! One of the characteristics of the usual present-day secondary school is that it is so ordered that sustained activity is impossible.

The principal, a messenger, other teachers, parents and other visitors also provide distracting factors very annoying to a purposeful group. The teacher himself, by his activities, may be a constant source of interference. Talking, moving about, offering unsolicited advice, and similar doings may stand in the way of group accomplishment.

Meeting interference and handling it is a problem for every group. The way in which the teacher responds can very easily set the pattern for group reaction. If he is upset or angry and finds it difficult to get back to work when the interruption is over, the group may follow his example. If he takes interference in his stride, the group's reaction may be the same. This, of course, assumes that the teacher's goals and those of the group are similar.

Organization

Another aspect of group behavior which may be a revealing indication of group adjustment is the type and degree of organization established by the group, and the group's reaction to it. The way in which the group is able to fit into an organizational pattern, or to construct one, gives definite clues to the clarity with which goals are seen and the extent of awareness which the group has of the relationship between current activities and group goals.

Organizations are devised to facilitate the accomplishment of desired ends, and they lose their effectiveness when they become ends in themselves. The way in which a group faces the problem of organization, the type and amount of organizational machinery it establishes, and the purposes expressed for the organization thus become a rough index of group adjustment. Some teachers and classes form committees because it seems to be the popular way to behave. The existence of the machinery for organization may bear little relationship to the jobs to be done, and it is not an uncommon sight to see classes trying desperately to find tasks for a committee to perform. One such class always selected committees at the beginning of an activity, and then sought to find jobs for it. There is nothing quite so futile as a costume committee trying to find a place in a unit on "housing in our town." If first the necessary jobs are clearly seen, and then the organization to do those jobs is provided, the group adjustment is likely to be furthered.

Punishment–Reward

The punishment-reward pattern of a group is another clue to the type and degree of adjustment. The extent to which the group assigns punishments or rewards external to the group situation is one indication. Where children live from one report card to the next, where certificates, badges, honor societies, special privileges, exemptions from examinations, and the like are status-giving activities, one may guess that while some adjustment is being made individually, this is not the type of group-integrated adjustment which we are seeking.

On the other hand, when satisfaction comes from contributions toward

TO BELONG IN A GROUP IS A NEED, TOO.

the achievement of common ends, when the entire group is happy over the contributions of each member, when social pressure from within the group is used to punish those who impede the progress of the group, then a high degree of group adjustment is in evidence.

In other words, when the group provides from within the framework of its own activities the reward-punishment pattern, and does not rely on the teacher or external activities to do so, adjustment is likely to be good.

Intergroup Experience

It is possible that a group may be satisfactorily adjusted within the framework set to achieve its own immediate ends, and yet be completely out of step with the whole-school or community organization.

One teacher had a very interesting, if somewhat painful, series of experiences with such a group. There was in the group with which she worked a high degree of intra-group relatedness and integration. Goals, both major goals and subgoals, were clearly seen and quite effectively pursued. However, in seeking to achieve its own ends, this group lost contact with the rest of the school. They maintained their unity, but it was in hostility and not in friendship toward the others. In class meetings of all the eleventh graders in the school, the antagonism between members of this group and other juniors was very evident. The in-group refused to participate in the activities of the larger group and tended more and more to find their satisfactions within the confines of the small class.

Such a situation is not an uncommon one and emphasizes the need for the group to see itself in relation to the larger society.

Deviates

The ability to capitalize as far as possible on deviates within the group is another indication of good group adjustment. Too many groups over-emphasize conformity and exclude, because of their deviation, many individuals who would have definite contributions to make to group liv-ing. One would not expect a group to find a prominent place on the relay team for a slow, heavy-set individual, but lack of ability to run does not preclude the possibility of other abilities which might promote the welfare of the group. The teacher has a job to do in helping the group to discover individual abilities and ways to use them.

Delegation of Responsibility

Another factor to be examined is the manner in which duties, respon-sibilities, and honors are delegated. Is delegation based on "he's a good guy," "he thinks he's so good," "let's stick her with this," or is it a matter of "he can do this best," "Mary is the best artist we have," etc.? If it is the former, what happens as a result? Does it affect the life of the group in any important way? If, on the other hand, delegation has been made thoughtfully, it probably indicates a high level of group adjustment.

Care must be taken, however, to help the group avoid being in a rut in the delegation of responsibilities. It is so easy always to let Mary do all the art work and thus deprive the group of latent but very signif-icant abilities which others may have.

Group Discussion

In many types of group activity, group discussion plays an important part. Thus the amount and quality of discussion may provide some indication of the type and degree of group adjustment. How the group reacts in discussion situations, whether they stay on the subject or wan-der, the extent to which suggestions are related to the problem under discussion, the degree to which the group breaks up into subgroups or cliques during discussion, the reactions toward those who talk too much or those who never speak, are significant indications of the unity of purpose and clarity of direction of the group.

There are some teachers who give such emphasis to studying the nature of group discussion that they seem to imply this is a sole measure of group interaction. The use of techniques devised for adult discussion groups may be given such prominence that both the teacher and the pupils may overlook other aspects of group life.

It is not our intention to minimize the importance of good group discussion. We feel it to be an important factor in developing desirable group interaction; but it is only one factor among many. It may be that the younger the pupils the less we should rely on verbal aspects alone and the more we should consider the total experiences of groups as means to group living.

REACTION DETERMINANTS

We know that behavior is caused. Behind every act is something which has happened, or is happening, to an individual or group. If we are to understand group behavior, we need to dig as far as we can into its causes. Only as we know what it is that causes groups to react as they do, can we feel that we can guide behavior in the deepest sense. True, we can control behavior, after a fashion, by forcing a change, but significant guidance can be obtained only when we can predict behavior in terms of known causes. We are a long, long way from being able to guide group behavior in this sense, but we are beginning at last to recognize some areas to which to direct our attention.

The School Program

In Chapter II, "Group Interaction," we discussed the relation of interaction patterns to group reaction. In other sections we have discussed the effect of role and status assignments on groups, the relation of group reaction to programs which impede action toward group goals, the effect of group climate, and, above, we suggest some situations which may reveal the degree of group adjustment. It is clear to us that the school has a heavy responsibility for creating situations which elicit favorable responses, which is another way of saying the school has responsibility for teaching good group living *through group experience*. We know that, unfortunately, schools do not always accept this responsibility, or, if they do, they do not always know how to meet it. We have heard schools characterized as "schools for thwarting" or "institutions for creating delinquents." No doubt there is more truth in these accusations than we care to admit. The school program will be discussed further in Chapter VII, "Group Living and the School Program." However, we recognize that there are factors other than school living which play a part. This is not said in an attempt to shift responsibility, but rather to point to the significance of knowing these other factors in order to adjust our programs to meet more adequately needs effected by or developed in out-of-school situations.

Living Conditions

The living conditions of group members seem to make considerable difference in the group reaction pattern. One teacher, studying the after-school time of a group of children, exclaimed in surprise, "Why, they have no place to yell!" This was literally true. If healthy boys and girls have no out-of-school opportunity for the release of tensions, the school has a responsibility to provide for this release. Unless it is provided somewhere, good group living will be difficult to achieve. This teacher and his associates decided it was the job of the school to do something about it, and supervised after-school play was provided. (Prior to this, the rule had been "No children on the playground after school hours.")

Childen who live where there are no others of the same age within easy play distance may need more opportunity for easy, free interaction while they are at school.

Another group of teachers discovered that it was almost impossible for the children to have any privacy. They lived in crowded tenements and played on crowded streets. There was no time or place for anyone to "get away from it all." As an experiment, these teachers set up "privacy corners" in the library, to which children could go to find a few minutes of rest and relaxation. They were provided merely by setting up low screens such as those used between cots in nursery school. The teacher could see into each corner, but children could, by sitting on the floor, be out of the gaze of other children. The corners were pathetically popular. Children went in to cry, to read, or mostly just to "sit and stare."

It may seem paradoxical to suggest being alone as a means to living in a group, and no one can prove, we suppose, that it contributed to better interaction. But we think it is likely that it did.

Another teacher, Mrs. Weston, in a school of similar membership, discovered that her pupils knew no way to use leisure time other than to

INTEREST IS CONTAGIOUS.

go to the movies. Children spent as much as eight hours in a single day, on Saturdays or Sundays, in the movie theater. This fact, she felt, contributed to their restlessness in school, especially on Mondays. Further study and discussion with the pupils indicated that they knew few group games. The games they had learned on the playground at school required equipment, space, or large teams, none of which were available after school. Here was a clear case of group need. She began to teach simple games appropriate to small groups of three, four, or five. This acquisition of skills was not a cure-all, of course, but it helped. The teacher was not sure whether to feel encouraged or discouraged when Tony reported: "When we fight, my mother give us money and we go to the show, but when we play your games we don't fight so my mother don't give us money, so we don't play your games. Now we go to the show."

Miss Tomlinson, in a school of quite different membership, discovered when she studied the use of out-of-school time by pupils in her group that there were many who had almost no opportunity to plan their own time. Piano lessons, dancing school, children's theater, Scouts, and a long list of supervised activities filled their out-of-school hours. She decided that, for good group living, these children needed more opportunity for free choice in school activities. She provided such opportunity and tension decreased noticeably.

[221]

Physical State

We tend to think of physical state as a highly individual matter, but sometimes whole groups exhibit behavior caused by their general state of health. It is well known to any teacher of wide experience that an undernourished, fatigued group may react quite differently from a healthy, robust group, the former being meek and docile or sullen, the latter full of high spirits, highly pleased or equally highly displeased.

Miss Christy, a teacher of a second grade in an unfortunate housing area, discovered that children in her room slept on the floor or as many as six to a double bed, that no one in the family could go to bed until they all retired for the night, and other similar conditions. She then understood the alternate tension and utter fatigue of group members. She provided a lying-down rest (on mats made of paper garment bags stuffed with newspaper) and felt that the general group tone and group interaction were noticeably improved.

Even within a normally healthy group, there are times when the physical state affects the group living. An exciting or fatiguing group experience requires a calming experience as follow-up if inter-personal and inter-subgroup tensions are to be avoided. When rainy days give little or no opportunity for outdoor play, there may be a need to find additional means for releasing tension.

One group of ten-year-olds took on the job of deciding how they could balance their periods of tension and relaxation. First they listed all the activities of a usual school day; then they distributed these under two headings—"Things that make us feel tired" and "Things that make us feel rested." Miss Abraham could foresee where most of the activities would fall in the judgment of the group, but one or two of the items surprised her. For example, art was listed as tiring. On the basis of the two lists the group planned its days, with alternate releasing and tension-creating activities. Incidentally, the teacher made a special study of the activities the group agreed were fatiguing in order to determine whether they caused unnecessary tension. For example, she asked the group to help her analyze why art activity made them tired. Group members claimed that the confusion in assembling, using, and clearing away materials "makes us cross." They set about planning for more efficient use of materials. A few weeks later, the group moved art from the "tired" category to the "rested" one.

Home and Community Mores

One small Spanish-American girl very calmly said to her teacher, when asked if she needed help, "Go to hell, please, teacher." She meant no more than "Thank you, teacher, I'm getting along very nicely and need no help." The words she used were those she heard at home, possibly used as casually and with no more meaning than she gave them. Fighting, spitting, and using language unacceptable to some groups are tolerated and even encouraged in some communities. These are not within the home mores of most teachers, but unless a teacher himself can react with understanding, he may enforce behavior and use control patterns which are meaningless to the pupils, and so contribute to poor group interaction. (This will be discussed further in Chapter VIII.)

Life View

Closely related to the home and community mores, or perhaps part of them, is the view of life held by boys and girls. We get revealing glimpses now and then of things that children take for granted or matters which color their entire lives. Sometimes these life views relate to school matters, such as the statement of the ten-year-old, supposedly writing a log of her day: "Monday we gave our Cinderella play. That's all that was important on Monday." Another youngster, evidently with a stern view of what is appropriate for school hours, wrote: "Monday we had most of the things we should have only in the afternoon we had Cinderella." Another, with a dim view of the value of planning, reported: "We planned what we were going to do and we did not have to work." Still another, recognizing the inevitability of experiences in a modern program, said: "Eddie's dog got in school, so we had a dog discussion."

The items boys and girls choose to talk about in their autobiographies can be quite revealing of ideas which dominate children's lives. This is Robert's complete autobiography:

"I went to kindergarten. I was only 2 ft. 5 inches and weighed 50 lbs. One year I was so little I couldn't go to school, the snow was so high. We will skip from 1A to 6A. I was worried because I only weighed 80 lbs. I am now 8B and weigh 106 lbs. I am 5 ft. 4½ inches and I am very happy."

Tommy, a ten-year-old, after grave thought and careful searching of his past, writes this as his complete autobiography:

"I was born July 2, 1938. I had another mother before this mother I have now. My mother got me when I was one year old and I had a little red cap and if anybody tried to take it off I would cry and I was angry when I was little."

Casual statements may be quite revealing. Jacqueline remarked, "Saturday Mother got her pay so we went to Wards." The relation of getting to spending seemed inevitable to her. "My mother is just a mother" was Joyce's comment after hearing of the jobs held by her friends' mothers.

Children's views of the human relations of adults can be startling. The following statements were made in interviews with primary grade children when they were asked, "What do grown people fight about?" (Reaction to Pictures, Appendix, page 423.)

"Men come home very late. Ladies don't like it."
"The super (superintendent of the apartment building) fights with the people who go out the front door with baby carriages."
"Grown-ups have enough sense not to fight unless they are bad people."
"One grown-up wants twin beds and the other wants a double bed. They fight about it."
"They want to do their work at different times so they fight, or they want to eat different things."
"They fight because sometimes one does the wrong thing like step on the clean floor or make a mess in the bathroom or get ashes all over the house."
"When the children fight the mothers stick up for their children."
"They fight when one wants peace and quiet and the other wants to have a little fun."
"They fight when ladies want to go some place and men won't let them or when both want to go and there's no one to mind the children."
"When husbands won't give wives any money."
"Sometimes husbands and wives fight about the children. My father got it from my mother the other night."
"They fight when they cheat in a card game."

REACTION PATTERNS

We are interested, too, in determining why group reaction takes particular forms. Why do members of one group, when they show hostility, get into fist fights, while members of another group stick their tongues out at one another and call names? The difference is more than degree of feeling (e.g., degree of hostility felt), it would seem.

All reaction has specific form and pattern. We are concerned with observing *all* group reaction, but certain patterns may offer special opportunity for study. Some of the most revealing reactions are those that take the form of hostility, withdrawal, enthusiasm, respect, or contagion.

There is grave need for further research in the causes of reaction patterns. In the following sections we raise questions which seem significant to us, and give some suggestions based on observation, but we do not feel we have adequate evidence to present solutions. There may be value, however, in drawing attention to some of the intricate problems in this area.

Hostility

Does the group often show hostility? How is it shown? Against whom is hostility indicated (e.g., against teacher, against a scapegoat in the group, against adults in general, against certain types of authority, against a particular out-group)? Under what circumstances is hostility shown?

One of the difficulties in tracing causes of hostility is that there may be little or no relationship between the *cause* of the hostility reaction and the person or persons against whom hostility is shown. The scapegoat is a usual example. A group that lost a basketball tournament turned on their cheer-leader, though he had in no way been directly responsible for the defeat. In other words, hostility is not an unusual reaction to thwarting. Having been thwarted, however, the venting of emotion may be quite irrational ("detour" action). Moreover, as we have mentioned before, hostility may turn inward, group members showing hostility toward one another, even though the thwarting has been a group experience.

This discussion is not meant to imply that thwarting is necessarily the only cause of hostility reactions, though it evidently is a common one. "Righteous indignation," fear (which may be a form of thwarting), and other factors may be contributing causes.

Withdrawal

When a group becomes sullen, moody, disinterested, or apathetic, we say it has "withdrawn." It seems probable to us that the causes of withdrawal are the same as those of hostility, only the group has used a different reaction form. It is difficult to analyze why the difference or what the circumstances. Some groups, it would seem, habitually react to thwarting with hostility, while others habitually react with withdrawal. But any one group may use the two reactions alternately. It is possible that withdrawal is an indication that the group accepts the futility of the situation, hence finds no "reason" for expending energy in hostility. It is possible, too, that withdrawal is merely a "waiting" period, and that hostility will finally emerge.

Enthusiasm

It is fascinating to watch the group reaction that takes the form of enthusiasm. When is it shown? What form does it take? What stimulates it? What thwarts it? What happens when it is thwarted? And, most significant questions: How may it be directed? By whom? Under what circumstances? A teacher who can find answers to questions such as these holds a powerful educational tool.

Respect

What or whom does the group respect? What respect do group members show to one another, to school authority, property, their parents, the law, superstition, religion, and so on? How do they show respect? Does the amount of respect seem to the teacher to be appropriate to the object of respect and the occasion? Do the patterns of respect remain fairly constant, or do they shift? If the latter, what causes them to shift?

Contagion

Contagion is one of the most inexplicable phenomena we encountered in studying groups. How it operates is difficult to analyze, but that it does operate is clear. We have seen contagion of irritation, of restlessness, of hostility, of enthusiasm, of resistance, of acceptance or rejection of people, ideas, activities. Sometimes contagion appears to operate as "spontaneous combustion," but sometimes it can be traced as stemming from one or a few individuals.

Contagion seems to operate more freely under certain circumstances, as, for example, when there is high degree of drive toward a goal, or when there is boredom. One might think these circumstances were at opposite poles. This leads us to suggest that contagion operates more freely in times of tension. The group is clearly more susceptible to contagion when under strong emotion, such as fear or joy, or even extreme boredom.

Certainly an aspect of contagion under certain circumstances is a feeling of "strength in numbers." Things no one group member would try alone seem possible when the group as a whole undertakes them. Incidentally, we should like to point out that this may be true in constructive, sometimes complex, learning activity, as well as in blatant infraction of rules. It seems that "strength in numbers" is so frequently associated with misbehavior that teachers are apt to fear it, rather than to see its potentialities for classroom use.

Another aspect of contagion seems to be the "band wagon" response. If everyone is climbing on, "I don't want to be left behind" seems to be the idea behind the reaction. In such response, it would seem that "stars," leaders, or popular people play an important role. It is they who start the wagon rolling. Non-stars may initiate similar or even identical behavior but nothing happens! It is difficult to know whether band wagon response is due to the strength of leadership of the stars, or—and we think this more likely—the strength of the fear of the less accepted members that they may be left behind.

Whatever its sources and mechanisms, contagion is evidently a powerful force and one which deserves much more study.

GUIDING GROUP REACTIONS

The teacher who recognizes that behavior is caused and that reactions are learned is in a favorable position to guide group reaction, to direct it toward desired purposes, toward adjustment and development of the group. This sentence, if taken out of the context of this report, might seem to indicate that we see the role of the teacher as a manipulator, as a puppeteer pulling the strings. This is not our intent. We are not suggesting that the teacher be a Machiavelli of the classroom, manipulating groups to his own ends through knowledge of group or individual strengths and weaknesses.

We have attempted throughout to indicate how a *group itself* may identify its goals, examine them, change them if desired, plan means to attain them, cooperate in the attainment, and evaluate results. However, these processes demand a high level of skills, and these skills must be *learned*. Hence the teacher plays an important role in helping the group attain these skills. There may be, too, a need for the teacher to help the group understand itself. Moreover, we feel it to be the task of the school to provide the setting in which groups may employ the processes mentioned above. These functions—teaching skills, interpretation, and providing the setting—require mature insight and an understanding of the factors involved. It is in this sense that we speak of the "control" a teacher acquires as he gets to understand group reaction.

Although there are many subtle variations, we identified three main approaches to the control of reactions: (1) suppression; (2) re-direction; and (3) creating situations. Perhaps it should be explained that here we are discussing teacher response to reactions, such as hostility, enthusiasm, or withdrawal. The interaction patterns discussed in Chapter II are basic to group structures. It is possible, we suppose, that group reactions may be controlled by the teacher in any of these three ways within any of the five interaction patterns, although some group reactions are more in harmony with certain patterns than others.

Suppression of Reaction Through Adult Authority

Suppression of undesired reaction is commonly used in schools. In fact, in some classrooms one wonders whether the teacher is aware of any other type of control. Signs of hostility are stopped immediately through threat, force, or similar means (at least the attempt is made; it doesn't always work!). Enthusiasm, unless it is for something sanctioned by the teacher, is squelched. No doubt such measures are necessary in "emergency" situations, but it is unlikely, we believe, that teachers are fully aware of the dangers of suppression, for if they were they would not use it so indiscriminately.

Behavior is caused. It seems we cannot repeat this often enough! When there is a cause, there will be a result. Suppression of one reaction (result) has not eliminated the cause, so there will be, inevitably, another reaction. In terms of the discussion of goal-seeking in Chapter III, we might say there will be "detour" reaction. This detour reaction tends to be unpredictable; hence beyond control. Groups find many means of detour reaction when the immediate reaction is suppressed, many of which means may be undesirable. If there is no opportunity to react overtly in the classroom, as, for example, the chance to show hostility, it may take the form of diffuse minor reactions, inter-personal or inter-group hostilities unfortunate for group interaction, or it may find release in out-of-school (hence non-directed) reactions. No doubt you have heard a teacher say, "I'm able to make them mind in school. I can't understand why they're such hoodlums after school." Such an admission is suspect. It is possible that his "making them mind" is the very reason they must be hoodlums out of school.

Pupils moving from room to room in a secondary school or a departmentalized elementary school give evidence of a similar problem. As has been mentioned before, a group frustrated in reaction in one class may find opportunity for release in the next. There is probably no secondary school in which there is not at least one teacher of whom it is said, "I certainly hate to get a class after he's had it. The kids seem to go wild when they get out from under his thumb!"

The use of a scapegoat is still another means of reaction when the initial response is suppressed. This has been mentioned earlier.

Re-directing Reactions

It is often possible for a teacher to diagnose a situation and provide for tension-releasing activity prior to the emergence of undesirable reactions, or as soon as such reactions begin to be manifest. On a simple level, one teacher provides a "pounding block" where any kindergartener who begins to show hostility may go and "pound it out" (release tension). Pounding blocks for an entire group might be somewhat devastating, but other substitute releases can be provided. Primary teachers are well aware of the need for some vigorous physical release on rainy days, when outdoor play is impossible.

On a more mature level, re-direction may be brought about through discussion. Many a wise teacher has suggested that the group pause, bring its reaction urges to the level of consciousness through discussion, and plan appropriate action. Often teachers find that the discussion itself provides catharsis. Thus, even if there is no rational analysis, as when the ten-year-old reported, "We just felt mean," the opportunity to admit one's "meanness" is of itself a re-direction of reaction. A word of caution is in order, perhaps. The teacher who takes a moralistic approach, seeming shocked or reproving at the expression of "meanness," can seldom be successful. On the other hand, if he can be acceptant of expressions of feeling, he may be providing important means to release.[1]

Creating Situations for Reactions

In re-directing reactions, a teacher steps in to do something about a current reaction. On a higher level of control, the teacher sets the stage for desired reaction. This level of control of reactions is that which, recognizing causes of behavior, eliminates undesirable and provides desirable causes. For example, when it was discovered that the "slow groups" (grouped by I.Q.) were a constant source of trouble in Baker School, the matter was given careful study and the recommendation was made that

---

[1] A wide literature is available to the teacher who wishes to go beyond this elementary presentation of group therapy.

so-called "ability grouping" be abandoned. In other words, rather than merely trying to suppress or re-direct unfortunate reaction, the *cause* of the reaction was eliminated.

Similarly, in Johnson Junior High School it was discovered that the troublesome eighth graders were feeling "left out" of school affairs. The faculty was surprised, but on further study came upon the interesting fact that although many programs were provided for incoming seventh graders the student affairs of the school were managed almost exclusively by ninth graders. Planning with the student council led to programs in which both seventh and eighth graders could participate more fully. The cause of the "troublesomeness" was removed.

The teacher in this study working with the first grade group found that creating situations to cause favorable reaction or to eliminate unfavorable reaction was a major means to good group living with young children. The rest program is an example. By providing an opportunity for children to rest on mats on the floor, much inter-personal hostility, plainly the result of fatigue, was eliminated. By replacing the report card and its arbitrary marking by parent conferences, she eliminated another source of group tension. The provision of a more flexible, less exacting reading program had the same effect (and, incidentally, by the end of the year the children were reading as well as or better than might have been expected under the more formal program).

One of the major values in group planning is that it capitalizes on the conscious or unconscious drives of the group in creating situations which will lead to desirable reaction. (Moreover, the planning itself is a form of direction, as discussed above.)

Other means of providing favorable causes are on so simple a level as having adequate supplies, playground equipment, and a program which gives appropriate balance of rest and activity.

In Chapter VIII we discuss further the selection of experiences which provide for good group living.

IN SUMMARY

Groups as well as individuals have needs. When these needs are not met, there is frustration and maladjustment. Teachers should learn to be aware of needs and to interpret symptomatic behavior of groups.

In planning for group adjustment, it is necessary first to answer the question: "Adjust to what?" As we observe school groups, we feel that teachers are operating, consciously or unconsciously, on the basis of seven assumptions: Groups should adjust to teacher convenience, to teacher inadequacy, to the past, to "superior" wisdom, to the demands of society, to the needs of individuals, or to the needs of the group. Recognizing that these assumptions are not mutually exclusive, we have given major emphasis to the last—the needs of the group.

Certain situations seem to offer particularly clear evidence of the degree to which needs are being met, the degree to which adjustments are satisfactory. These situations include the responses of groups to the establishment and maintenance of routine, to change, to interference, to organization patterns, to forms of punishment and reward, to intergroup situations, to deviates in the group, to delegation of responsibility, and to group discussion.

Although the school itself is an important determinant of the degree of adjustment of groups, other factors are in operation too. Among these are the home living conditions of group members, their physical state, the home and community mores, and the life-view held by boys and girls.

Patterns of reactions of a group, the form of reaction to situations, warrant more research. Patterns of particular interest are those that take the form of hostility, withdrawal, enthusiasm, respect, and contagion.

Teachers use several means to guide group reactions. The specific ways teachers behave determine how groups will behave. The specific things teachers do are attempts to suppress group reaction through the use of adult authority, to re-direct behavior, at times through the use of certain types of therapy, and to create situations which foster desired reaction. Creating situations seems to us to be most significant and to hold most promise for developing good group living. It is to this aspect of guidance of group living that we address ourselves in the following chapter.

VII

Group Living and the School Program

"But we offer many group experiences in our school program," says Mr. Green. "In fact, most of us feel that there is too much group experience and not enough individual attention given to boys and girls."

Most of us would like more time to spend with individual pupils. Such time should be provided. The ideal, it would seem, would be to achieve a balance between *meaningful* individual experience and *meaningful* group experience.

The fact that twenty-five to forty pupils are in one classroom is no guarantee that there one will find group living. An opportunity for inter-action is essential to good group living, and looking at the back of the head of the pupil in front and answering questions posed by the teacher is not group interaction. In many classrooms, and entire schools, there is an amazing lack of opportunity for interaction, for group experience. The implication is that the skills of group living are to be learned out-of-school, in backyards, on the street, or wherever children play. That they *are* learned by many through just such means, we know. We also know that unfortunate forms of group living, too, are learned that way.

OPPORTUNITY FOR GROUP EXPERIENCE

Someday someone should make a study of the opportunity, in kind, quantity, and appropriateness of group living provided in the classrooms of the Dead End Kids and other gang members. That many factors are involved in the making of a delinquent cannot be denied; but that the opportunity (or rather the lack of it) for guided group living in school is one factor seems to be strongly indicated.

[232]

We feel that this learning to live in groups is so important to the adjustment of the individual and the development of democratic society that it is dangerous to leave it to chance.

Finding Time for Group Experience

There are teachers who ask, "But when do you find the time? My schedule is so full now that I can't squeeze in another thing!" As we see it, group living should not be something "extra," allocated to a period between 11:00 and 11:40, but should be the essence of all school living. It is the heart-blood of democratic learning and human relations and should pervade the entire program. There must be time for discussion, for goal-setting, for planning, for evaluation.

We are convinced, for two reasons, that "taking time" from other things for such activities need not worry the teacher.

First, we feel that the fundamental values of group experiences transcend subvalues, as, for instance, knowledge of the capital cities of the states. However, unless a teacher feels that such a program is of importance he can easily find excuses for not providing time.

Second, although such a program requires time, it does not require as much time as is often supposed. As Barbara, age 11, puts it, "When we plan it, we understand it and know what to do." Implied in Barbara's observation is the suggestion that if the group doesn't plan its actions, it may not understand and may not know what to do, thus requiring more teacher-time for explanations. Moreover, unless "it" (whatever the "it" is) is understood, there is little chance that it will be learned.

Forms Alone Are Not Enough

A teacher must be aware that even the so-called democratic procedures can be misinterpreted and exploited. We have suggested, for example, that appointment of a pupil chairman is no guarantee of democratic practice. It may be merely a form of delegation of authority by the teacher.

Casting votes and adhering strictly to majority rule are often misinterpreted as "democratic" actions. There is considerable evidence that these forms alone do not contribute to good group living. In the name of democracy, the majority vote is sometimes misused to determine areas of group activity. "I wish there weren't so many girls in my room," remarked Bob to his father. His father, thinking this merely an expression of the usual preadolescent sex cleavage, was not surprised, but nevertheless asked the expected "Why?" Bob's story was that there were seventeen

THE FORM ALONE IS NOT ENOUGH.

girls in his room and fifteen boys. The girls wanted to study about dolls of other countries, and the boys wanted to study about airplanes. A vote had been taken, and the girls had "won." The boys were disgruntled. The group had, according to Bob, a "whale of a row," but the teacher was adamant for majority rule. The group living in this class was sure to be at low ebb, unless the teacher provided for subgroups or shifted the area of study to one for which consensus could be reached.

SPREAD OF GROUP EXPERIENCE

By "spread of group experience," we mean the increased opportunity afforded for more and more pupils to participate in group experience. This might seem to be an anomalous statement. If it is group experience, it includes the group, doesn't it? Isn't the group everyone? Then how can we talk about spread of group experience to everyone?

In terms of the ideal such a statement is inaccurate, but we know that

[234]

many teachers and many schools are just beginning to give consideration to group experience. It is during such transition stages that spread must be considered and watched.

The teachers of one elementary school were concerned about the sense of responsibility demonstrated by their pupils. Their interest in this area was twofold: they felt it important to individual development of pupils, and they saw it as a problem in group living. As a part of their study of the matter, they undertook to discover the experiences of each child in handling matters of importance to the group. They were rather startled to discover that, although they provided a number of opportunities, ranging from committee chairmanship and traffic "safety" regulation to distribution of milk and interclass messenger service, these opportunities were given to relatively few pupils. Moreover, the few to whom they were given were those who had already demonstrated that they could take responsibility. The easy way was to deplore the lack of sense of responsibility of some, while offering all opportunities for experience to those who needed such experience least! (Measures taken to correct this situation are discussed in Chapter IX.)

It is quite possible that frequently the opportunities to develop in group living are given to but few pupils, in a manner similar to that of the "responsibilities" discussed above. "To him who hath shall be given" is the easy rule for a teacher to use in delegating opportunities, for it is simpler to give the experience to the pupil on whose performance the teacher can rely.

It is interesting to note that children in a group are often quite conscious of the need to spread participation. "He hasn't had a turn yet" is Florence's reason for voting for Tom as group leader. We were surprised to find among the statements of evaluation of leaders some such as the following: "He had good experiences," "She wouldn't of learned if she hadn't of done it. Now she's learned and she can do it."

This leads us to the dilemma of whether we are to teach children to select representatives—leaders or representatives for particular posts—for educational purposes (giving each a turn so that all may have a chance to learn) or for reasons of competence. We feel this is not a problem *if* (and this is an important *if*) children recognize the base on which they are operating. We have given considerable emphasis in this report to the need to help pupils delegate responsibility in terms of competence, to choose leaders in terms of goals of the group. Skill in these things is highly important, we believe. Yet perhaps on an even higher level of group awareness is the recognition of need for each individual to develop through experience. Thus, evidently it is desirable to have both types of delegation. The important thing is that the two shall not be confused.

One teacher, recognizing this need to differentiate between competence and opportunity, asked the group who were about to select personnel for painting a mural, "Shall we choose the people who will do it best, or the people who should have a chance to learn?" The group, in this case, decided to ask the "do it best" people to paint the section of the mural for the school lunchroom assigned to them, and to have another group of people "who should have a chance" make a mural for their own room.

As we have suggested, groups of children, particularly young children, are often more aware of the need to spread participation than is the teacher. This, we believe, is a consequence of the high value they place on "taking turns." Perhaps it is fortunate that this value serves as a check to teachers who tend to choose primarily in terms of competence, but it seems to us that it is unfortunate if this is the *only* base for selection. That the "taking turns" philosophy wanes as children grow older shows that it may be merely an indication of acceptance of adult values. If we could maintain that philosophy, lifting it to the level of consciousness of responsibility of the group to its members, at the same time developing discrimination concerning competence, and a conscious judgment of which is appropriate for a particular situation, we shall have achieved a very high level of group living.

EXPERIENCES FOR LEARNING GROUP LIVING

In this section, we discuss experiences in which the attention of boys and girls is focused on other areas, but which, we believe, contribute to learning in group behavior.

Making Choices

An individual (or a group) learns as he weighs values, measures alternatives, and makes selections. If these skills are to be learned, then experience in them must be provided. Experience in weighing values, measuring alternatives, and making selections implies that boys and girls must have the opportunity to make choices. This would seem to be self-evident, yet it is not seen as significant by some educators.

One interesting way to study the patterns of interaction is to follow a group of boys and girls through their school day. A group was followed in this way in a junior high school. In class after class, group members were told when they could open their books, what books they might open and at what page. They were told when they might sit and when they might stand; when they might speak (when called on by the teacher) and when they might not; when they might go to the toilet and when they might get a drink. Bells announced when they might move from one classroom to another. Finally, at long last, in the lunchroom they had an opportunity to make a decision—a choice involving the weighing of values, the measuring of alternatives—and to test it in action. They might choose between a peanut butter or a jelly sandwich!

If this example seems overdrawn in terms of your situation (and we hope it is), try this test. Count the number of choices available to pupils in your classroom and examine each for its significance to learning. Remember that it is the day-by-day experiences which count. In the junior high school described above, there was student self-government through a student council of which the faculty boasted, but to this junior high school group it meant no more than the opportunity, once a year, to cast a ballot for people they didn't know. Democracy to these boys and girls was something far removed from their daily living. Even though the political structure (the student council) might be in existence, their lives offered no opportunity for making meaningful choices.

We are suggesting, then, that for good group living, for democratic living, there must be opportunity for choice of action both for individuals and for groups, and to make these choices meaningful there must be discussions leading to a realization of the bases on which choices are made. This is another way of saying that it is important to bring goals and values to the level of consciousness, for examination, for evaluation, and if desired, for modification. Even though the choices may be in areas far removed from human relations, dealing, for example, with such matters as the amount of dues to be paid for student activities, they nevertheless contribute to favorable group living, if used wisely, to the extent that they teach skills of evaluation and contribute to developing an attitude of respect for individuals and for group action.

Group Planning

That group planning has much to contribute to group living has been noted on several occasions in these pages. It offers an opportunity to develop and practice skills in group living; it is a means to determining group goals and developing ways to achieve them; it may be, of itself, a form of group catharsis. That group planning is an important means to group self-management is evident. A major responsibility of the teacher is to provide expanding areas for planning and action, areas in which group decision will "stick," will be respected and followed.

Dangers in group planning, as we have observed its use, are encountered when a group attempts to plan beyond its skills or the teacher's skills, or in areas in which there is no possibility of group decision, as when a group decides to abolish the grading system when decision concerning this matter lies with the faculty, with the principal, or with the central office of the school system.

Creative or Appreciative Activity

The potentialities for developing good group living through creative activity have not been fully explored. As educators we know, or think we know, that group cement may be hardened in common emotional experience. That creation or appreciation in the arts may be highly emotionally charged, we also know. Groups finding release in creative music, dancing, or other arts have a common experience which, if used wisely, may do much to create favorable group morale. The same is true of groups which

GROUP PLANNING IS IMPORTANT FOR GROUP ACTION.

experience in common emotionally tinged appreciation, such as is sometimes achieved through art, music, or literature.

In the elementary school, where the teacher who leads the group to
such creative experience is present for other activities also, the carry-over
to other aspects of group living may be great. In the secondary school,
however, too often the experience becomes place-linked or time-linked,
furnishing group feeling for the class period of the activity, and is lost
after the experience because the transition to other activities, other classrooms, or other teachers is too abrupt. This, we feel, is unfortunate, and
points to the need for faculty planning for integrated experience, and for
blocks of time with one teacher, so that there may be development of
group unity through emotionally charged creative or appreciative activity, guided, in transition, to unity in less emotionally charged situations.
Compartmentalization of emotion in group experience may lead to compartmentalization of group living. The group which felt itself in unity
in the music class may be disunited in the competitive atmosphere of a
mathematics class. On the other hand, it is possible that any teacher who
recognizes the unifying effect of creativity and appreciation may use
them as a means to good group living, regardless of his area of specialization. For example, creativity and appreciation may be fostered in mathematics and science as well as in the arts.

Games and Sports

Games and sports have long been recognized as means to group unity,
to "team spirit." Often, however, the level of unity is no higher than that
created by hostility toward another team. In fact, this is perhaps always
the level of group unity in highly competitive situations. Such unity may
provide strong cohesion in a group for a short time, but pupils who know
only this type of unity tend to try to "find another guy to be against"
after the competition has passed. For example, note the fights that break
out after an all-school paper drive based on inter-room competition. Certainly short-term unity, born of hostility, is not good group living.

On the other hand, there are reasons why sports should contribute
favorably to group living. They offer an appropriate opportunity for the
self-testing which seems to be important to the development of children
and youth. Moreover, they offer experience in recognizing that the group
can achieve where the individual cannot; that the achievement of goals
depends on using the contribution of each member; and that each team
member needs to be in a position where he can make his unique contribu-

tion. When we are told that wars are won "on the playing fields of Eton," we are inclined to believe that it is factors such as these that are responsible, *in spite of* the competitive elements of the situation. We suggest that there be further studies of value derived from sports in terms of their contribution to group living of the sportsmen and the spectators.

Unplanned Time

We have discussed the use of time planned by the teacher, and of time planned by the group, but there may be still another dimension—time unplanned, left free for spontaneous play or loafing. The value of such free time is difficult to analyze or measure, but the teacher working with a first grade group in this study places high value on such time as a contribution to group living. She feels that the planning done by the group is extremely valuable, but to be realistic and to eventuate in action it must be within areas of experience sufficiently circumscribed for the group to handle. Thus, planning may contribute less to the group living of first graders than it does to more mature children.

On the other hand, she places high value on free time because it offers opportunity for experience in inter-personal and inter-subgroup action leading to an understanding of how people get along together. This type of experience rather than verbalization may be the chief means to group growth for young children. Its importance cannot be overemphasized. Teachers of young children might well examine their programs critically to see if sufficient time for such free activity has been provided.

Not only might more emphasis be given to free, unplanned time for young children, but there is reason to believe that such time-use may have value for people of all ages. There are those who claim that loafing, unplanned bull sessions, and the like, are the experiences which provide the college man with the *savoir faire* with which he is attributed. There are those who point out, too, that the time of children and young people may be so rigidly planned (either by an adult or by the group, under adult stimulation) that there is no understanding of the use of leisure time. It is ironic, in the light of what we say about learning through experience, to visit a class hard at work studying about the use of leisure time! Perhaps some provision for learning by doing might be in order.

Student Organizations

That student organizations of various types may contribute greatly to group living cannot be denied. Nor can it be denied that they are frequently overestimated as a means to group living. Merely because they have student officers is no guarantee that the level of interaction is high or that skills are being learned. The range of interaction pattern may be as wide in organizations as in classrooms, with the same advantages and disadvantages, but with one additional disadvantage—in student organizations there may be less adult help in developing skills.

It is true that in many schools the only opportunity afforded boys and girls to participate in setting goals, in planning, and in cooperative action toward achieving their goals, is found in student organizations. This is less an argument for organizations than an indictment against the school program. We feel that goal-centered activity is of such significance that it should permeate the entire program. Further, we believe that the level of learning is extremely low unless activity is goal-centered.

One hazard to programs of organizations is often a lack of clear understanding of area of function. It is, of course, unrealistic to say to the student council, "Now you may run the school." There are areas in which student council decisions are appropriate, and others where they are not. Unless the boundaries of areas of decision are clearly understood, it is easy for the pupils to step out of bounds and then, on discovering that their decision in this area is not honored, to believe that the whole matter of self-government is a hoax, perpetrated by the faculty at the expense of the student body.

Deciding the boundaries of decision areas is no easy task. It is very likely that in many situations they could be wider. On the other hand, if the boundaries are wider than children of a certain level of maturity and skills can handle, there may be unfortunate results. Evidently the matter needs careful study, with provision for ever-widening areas of decision as pupils mature and gain skills.

One signal contribution of an all-school organization is that it provides inter-group experiences. It may introduce groups to the idea of representation through an individual, hence furnish practice in choosing individuals in terms of competence.

Class Organization

We are not prepared to make blanket recommendations concerning the type of class organization favorable for good group living, but in the groups with which we worked, one of the best-received types of organization was that which provided for subgroup activity in special areas of interest. The boys and girls in these groups had had little experience in this type of organization, and evidently were much impressed with its worth. Over and over in their evaluations of the year's work, they mentioned with favor "group work," by which they meant committee or subgroup activity. They claimed "you learn more," "you get to discuss more things," "you learn to get along together," "you learn to be a leader," and "you learn to give ideas." One youngster, raised in the tradition that all school work must be in "courses," claimed "group work is my favorite course," even though subgroup activity was provided in a wide range of subject-matter areas.

Such organization seems to be so effective and is so simply achieved that one wonders why it is not more widely used by teachers.

One reason often advanced by teachers why such subgroups cannot operate is lack of physical space. In both the fourth and fifth and the eighth grade rooms of the groups in this study, there was little space and seats were screwed to the floor. We regretted these drawbacks, but did not find them insurmountable. Benches made by laying planks across horses or crates, and chairs made from orange crates can be a help. It is surprising how such improvised furniture can be fitted into a minimum of space if the group is really interested in working in subgroups. Five or six children, sitting sideways in their seats and facing one another across an aisle, can carry on a discussion most effectively. The entire class, in groups of four, can carry on effective discussion in checkerboard formation. Extra chairs of almost any size or shape, in a corner of the room or in the hall, can furnish committee space. It may be necessary to move the teacher's desk to a remote corner, but perhaps this is just as well.

—the committee and the group

One thing we found necessary to watch was that a committee should not become removed from the group as a whole. There are several ways in which such a contingency may be prevented. A subgroup may accept an assignment from the larger group, as when one subgroup was charged by the group as a whole to find out the average weekly allowance of its members. This information was wanted by the entire group as a basis for discussion with parents. Or a subgroup may work independently, and then report its findings to the group as a whole. Even more effective, it seems, is the subgroup's combining its report with statements of issues for discussion, as was the case when a committee selected pertinent questions for total group discussion through the children's jury (page 278).

Although we feel it desirable for a subgroup to work on assignments

UNFAVORABLE PHYSICAL CONDITIONS NEED NOT PREVENT COMMITTEE WORK.

delegated by the total group, this isn't always possible. Frequently there are such cleavages in interest that seemingly quite divergent activities are being carried on in the various small groups. An ingenious teacher can sometimes find ways of relating these activities, however, as when one group was interested in careers of athletes, another in health, and a third in self-study of "personality." During the reporting period, the three were interrelated by the teacher so that every member of a group saw the contribution of the report of each of the other two groups to his own area of interest.

Moreover, reporting to the group need not be merely a matter of "telling what we've found out." One group assumed responsibility for organizing a "hobby show" which included exhibits provided by anyone in the entire group who was interested, not merely the subgroup members alone.

—multiple activity

Some teachers fear confusion if various activities are going on at one time. We feel that they have no cause for concern. When the teachers' group visited the fourth and fifth grade room one day, they saw some children painting on a piece of wallboard placed over several seats in the

[243]

MANY THINGS CAN BE HAPPENING AT ONE TIME.

back of the room, and another group rehearsing how they would report to the group what they wanted to say about "manners." A third group was discussing books they had read; another was conferring with the teacher about a play they hoped to present; and still another was reading individually to find answers to science questions. There was a murmur of conversation, but it was controlled and subdued, and quite evidently not sufficient to disturb even those engaged in individual reading and research.

This matter of noise seems to be of major concern to some teachers. We found that as many as six groups of six to ten people each could work in one crowded room without being noisy enough to disturb one another. It is true that it required some self-discipline on the part of group members, but each was so concerned with group progress that it was not too difficult to exercise this self-discipline.

Most primary teachers are accustomed to organizing reading groups (subgroups for oral reading or discussion of reading. Incidentally, we aren't at all sure that these groups need be constituted in terms of reading ability. Groupings based on interest in dog stories, in stories about farms, and so on, may be even more effective). One practice is to provide "seat work" for pupils not in the reading group. We find that reading-group time affords the others a good opportunity for small-group activities, such as playing house, painting, individual reading in the "reading corner," and rearranging the bulletin board. Of course, this isn't possible if the teacher insists on "pin drop" silence, but we find that a normal first grade group, with some help and direction, can learn to carry out a number of activities simultaneously, with satisfaction to themselves and without disturbing others.

A UNIT ON HUMAN RELATIONS

We feel that a study of favorable group living must permeate all activities of the group, but there may be a place for more direct, intensive, organized study in certain specific areas. Both the fourth and fifth and the eighth grade groups undertook units of study in human relations.

The following description of the eighth grade work is summarized from a much more complete report by the teacher.

Introduction

Although the theme of human relations was followed throughout the year as a thread in every unit of study, the unit reported here emphasized those phases of human relations selected by the children as vital to them. It was worked through by the teacher and pupils together in much the same way as other units.

After discussion, the group decided to state the problem as: How can we get along better with people?

Launching

Through class discussion, the class decided that we have human relationships with people mainly at home, at school, and in the community. The children then listed the activities in each category. Sue and Dick volunteered to list them on the board, so that all the class could see them. Samplings from these lists follow.

Things We Do With and For People at Home

Feed baby
Run errands for Mother or Dad
Play games
Have parties
Entertain company
Listen to radio

Things We Do With and For People at School

Work on the school paper
Walk to and from school
Play on teams
Study lessons
Go to social hours
Have elections
Go on field trips
See movies
Work on committees
Talk to friends
Help others with their lessons

Things We Do With and For People in the Community

Go to church
Go to parties and picnics
Go downtown shopping
Play on ball teams
Deliver papers
Baby sitting

When the children saw the lists on the board they thought the activities could be classified under the following headings:

I. Chores
II. Hobbies
III. Safety
IV. Sports
V. Recreation
VI. Work
VII. Personality
VIII. Manners
IX. Use of leisure time

With Gary as the class chairman, the class selected four of these fields to use as guides for study in human relations, and by a vote of hands, they selected Hobbies, Sports, Safety, and Personality. Then on a written ballot each child chose his first and second choice of areas. Gary and Norma, the class secretary, worked out the groups from this ballot.

A chairman and a secretary were selected by each group on the first day it met. The secretary kept a diary of the activity of the group.

Physical Setup of Group Activity

Since the class was working in a limited space (half a normal-sized classroom, with screwed-down double desks for thirty-four pupils), through teacher-pupil planning the following schedule was set up.

The class had a fifty-minute period each day for General Education and Social Science. The period was divided into two parts of twenty-five minutes each. The unit took a seven-week period to complete.

Each day two groups had a part of the period as an activity period in the hall outside the room, while two groups had a discussion period with the teacher. The rest of the time was used for study and research. The schedule was kept by Gary and looked like this:

	Group			
	Sports	Hobby	Personality	Safety
Mon.	Hall	Study	Study	Discussion and planning
	Discussion and planning	Hall	Study	Study
Tues.	Study	Discussion and planning	Hall	Study
	Study	Study	Discussion and planning	Hall

The schedule then repeated itself.

The activity periods always took place in the hall, and the discussion and planning in the classroom. However, the research and study branched out into the library and all other parts of the school as the unit progressed.

Sometimes this program schedule was interrupted for an all-class activity which the various groups presented from time to time. Again it was broken for class evaluation, and for the learning of some needed skills.

Each group spent the first day it met in exploring the field, setting up specific goals, and examining the literature in the area it had elected to study, e.g., sports or safety. As all four groups operated in a similar manner, the report of the Personality group may serve as an example of all group work.

Objectives: To find answers to these questions.

1. How can we make the most of our looks?
2. What should we say on a date?
3. How should we act, and what should we say, when meeting new people?

Activities

1. The group attempted first to try to answer question 1—"How can we make the most of our looks?"

   a. During the study periods they read books, pamphlets, and magazine articles on personal appearance, and took notes on pointers for better looks.

   b. During the planning and activity periods they discussed, and showed pictures illustrating, the care of hair, clothes, teeth; they discussed what foods to eat, and personal cleanliness.

   c. During the activity periods they cut out of newspapers and magazines pictures which brought out the good and bad in making the most of one's looks.

   d. During the activity periods both boys and girls also tried on different colors, using cloth they borrowed from the Art Department. They made a chart for each member of the group, showing his most becoming colors.

   *e. One day they gave pointers to the whole class on the proper colors to wear.

2. Question 2, "What should we say on dates?" was considered next.

   a. In the discussion and planning periods it was pointed out that there are different kinds of dates and the group wanted to know what to say at various times. Kinds of dates listed were:

      1) Boy-girl.
      2) Boy-girl with a few other couples.
      3) Boy-girl at a large party.
      4) Boy-girl with the family.
      5) Crowd of girls.
      6) Crowd of boys.

   b. In study periods the group read of such situations in etiquette books and personality books.

   c. During activity periods they talked over the situations. They also prepared skits illustrative of various situations.

   *d. They chose the best skits and presented them to the class. (They also got some additional hints from the class on what to say.)

   *e. Along with the rest of the class they attended a panel on boy-girl relationships presented by a ninth grade class.

3. Sticking very well to their original list of problems, they attacked question 3—"How should we act, and what should we say, when meeting new people?"

   a. Planning to meet for the first time the following types of people presented problems to the boys and girls:

      1) A person who works with my parents.
      2) Important people.
      3) Children of parents' friends.

* Activities which the group brought to the whole class as a problem to be worked on for the benefit to all.

BOY-GIRL RELATIONS ARE IMPORTANT TO ADOLESCENTS.

    b. Since not much literature was found on this subject, most of the discussion was carried on in the activity period.

4. During the study periods the class worked on a culminating activity—a stick puppet show on the "Do's and Don'ts" for an eighth grader with a good personality. The group members worked in twos, making a pair of figures and preparing a little patter to go with the skit. When all was complete, a stage was borrowed from the Art Department. • Then the group presented the simple puppet show before the class group.

Evaluation

So far as specific objectives of each group went, the activities often took the form of evaluation. For instance, in the Sports group the members identified and evaluated qualities of athletes and the value of sports. The fact that the members wanted to share their findings with others may indicate a growth in the value of sharing.

The Personality group was eager to pass on to the class their findings on appropriate clothing as well as their skits on dating and their puppet show of the "Do's and Don'ts" for developing better personality.

The Hobby group showed their hobbies to the class and asked other members of the class to exhibit theirs. They evaluated their own hobbies when they reported on their worth as a means of making new friends.

The teacher observed some exchange of stamps and material for models after the hobby program.

The Safety group evaluated class participation in the all-school safety program by checking Student Court and bicycle confiscation records of the class group.

At the end of the unit a general evaluation was made through class discussion. The student recorder's report reads as follows:

1. We found some of our own interests and what we liked to do through our room hobby show, by trying out original ideas (such as trying the different colors to determine which were becoming), and by being able to talk things over in our small groups. We also selected what we wanted to study through voting and class discussion when we set up objectives, and sometimes in the Sports group when we changed our objectives.

2. We learned to share more equally when we gave programs for each other, when the Hobby group showed us their hobbies, when the Personality group gave us skits on dating, when the Sports group got the boys and girls from South High School and Denver University to speak, and when the Safety group gave us the questions on bicycle safety. We collected some materials for our hobbies from each other.

3. We had lots of chances to talk things over in the small group. In this way we felt that we could cover more subject matter than if the whole class had been studying the same phase of Human Relations. We listed qualities of good leaders and good group members and tried to live up to them.

4. We think we became more agreeable to each other and especially to teachers. Working in small groups gave us a chance to know some of our class and our neighbors better than we ever had before. We met more teachers.

5. We learned to use better English and to use better language and manners when we gave reports and skits to our own room and to other rooms. We learned how to meet and introduce guest speakers. We learned how to write better and more interesting thank-you notes. We also learned how to use more materials than just books to find information, and how to use the library more than we had done before. Other materials for information are movies, pictures, our own ideas and information, adult speakers, other students for speakers, magazines, newspapers, and the radio.

THE ROLE OF THE TEACHER

As we discuss group living and the school program, we should not overlook the questions of teachers concerning the role of the teacher. There are those who ask: "If we are aiming toward increased group self-management, aren't we trying to work ourselves out of a job? If we are completely successful, what is the need for teachers?" As we have indicated earlier, we see an important role for the teacher in providing the setting, teaching the skills of group interaction, helping in interpretation, and other matters.

Another question is, "Do we abandon all 'formal' lessons?" Our answer would be "No" (depending on the interpretation of the word "formal"). As we see it, the need for a wide range of experiences may demand a wide range of types of learning situations, even the use of the so-called "formal" lesson.

Miss Patterson's second grade group decided it wanted to build a miniature airport in connection with its study of aviation. The landing field, hangars, and other buildings were constructed, but the group wanted to have people also—passengers, pilots, hostesses, mechanics, and other airport employees. They were at a loss how to make these figures. The teacher brought to the group several samples she felt might be appropriate. These were made of spools, pipe cleaners, cut-out paper, and clay. Most of the group felt the clay figures were most appropriate, but they didn't know how to make them. Miss Patterson told them that she would teach anyone interested how to model in clay. As it turned out, everyone in the group decided he wanted to learn this skill; so the next day Miss Patterson taught the whole group. A stranger entering the room might have mistaken this activity for the usual "formal" art class. Everyone was doing the same thing at the same time. The teacher was giving directions and explaining the advantages and disadvantages of the medium. But, although the stranger may have thought it the usual formal lesson, there were differences. The group had a *purpose* in learning this skill. It had *selected* to learn this skill rather than the skills of making pipe-cleaner figures, spool figures, or cut-outs. It knew how this skill was to be *applied* in the attainment of their goals. These factors, we believe, made the formal lesson justifiable and contributed to real learning.

—step by step

This description might seem to imply that it is only under such circumstances that the "formal" lesson may be used. It will be recalled that we suggested teacher security (page 32) as one of the criteria for judging the appropriateness of pattern. There are, no doubt, many teachers now relying wholly on the use of the traditional formal lesson, who would feel insecure if they attempted to abandon this form for group self-management. We have sympathy for such a teacher's point of view and recommend that no drastic shift be allowed to destroy his security. Miss Gaines, an elementary school teacher who believed in group self-management, problem-solving, and teaching and learning "subject matter" in terms of life experiences, but who lacked security for a complete rightabout-face, has solved the problem by planning a series of *steps* in transition as follows:

Step 1: Provide group activity and cooperative planning within usual class periods (reading, spelling, art, etc.).

Step 2: Combine reading and social studies.

Step 3: Provide larger blocks of time.

Step 4: Teach spelling and penmanship together (allow activities in these areas to merge, and grow out of other group activity).

Step 5: Find more opportunity within group activity for developing number concepts (but continue arithmetic "lessons").

Step 6: Teach arithmetic, as opportunity is provided, by experiences in broader areas of living (make learning of number concepts a part of the living experience of boys and girls).

She has now taken five of these six steps, moving from a day scheduled in a series of "periods" devoted to reading, penmanship, spelling, social studies, and so on, to a day scheduled as planned by the group to accomplish its goals. Arithmetic is the one exception. This is still taught as a formal lesson. Miss Gaines moved from one step to the next only after she felt competent in the previous change. Incidentally, for her own security and in order to answer any objections that might be raised by parents or others, she gave standardized achievement tests in language (reading, spelling, language usage) and arithmetic. Moreover, she kept in constant touch with her principal and supervisors, so that all were aware of her attempts to change and could give appropriate help.

Such an approach to providing range of experience is, we believe, more sound than that of the teacher who attempts a total reversal of procedures. A teacher who attempts such a reversal is likely to run into grave difficulties because of limitations of group expectancy, group and teacher skills, and group and teacher security. It is the teachers who try such sudden shifts that are loud to proclaim, "I tried it and it doesn't work."

Teachers' Judgments of Needs

All discussion of *selecting* experiences to meet individual and group needs is futile unless teachers feel responsible for using these needs as a basis of selection and have the opportunity to exercise their judgment in making the selection. In an attempt to discover degree of agreement concerning basic assumptions and judgments concerning the school program, the staff of one school undertook a study of the degree to which needs were being met through the school program. Prior to this phase of the study, the group had made an extensive investigation of individuals and groups, using a wide range of techniques and types of recording. Thus this group of teachers was in a position to know whereof they spoke concerning needs of these children. The eighteen teachers of the staff used the instrument "Meeting Individual Needs" (Table 17, pages 254 to 257), each teacher checking forms for three children (54 children studied).

The directions for use of the instrument state in part (for complete directions see Appendix, page 427): "You will see that the questions have been developed in terms of certain assumptions concerning the job of teachers and the school. You may not agree with these assumptions; many people don't. In order to express your point of view, place a plus (+) in front (to the left) of each question you feel to be important and a necessary responsibility of schools, and a minus (−) in front of those you feel to be unimportant or not the job of the teacher and the school."

—difference of opinion

Figures on the left in Table 17 indicate the value judgments per item (when not designated as − or ?, responses were +). The chief item of disagreement was number 7, where 10 of the 54 responses were minus. In other words, there was a feeling on the part of some members of this staff that it is not important, or not the job of the school, to provide opportunity for individuals (at least for those individuals being studied) to follow certain personal interests even though they may be different from those of others in the group.

Second highest in rejection was item 24. There were 8 minus responses to indicate that it is not thought important, or not the job of the school, to provide opportunity for individuals to work or play in various types of groups (various sizes, with people of various ages, races, etc.).

The third item with several minus responses was number 32: "Is his teacher given a reasonable amount of time, assistance, material, etc., to provide a good school program for him?" In view of the fact that many teachers claim they are not given such aid in adequate amount (see responses in right-hand column), we are at a loss to interpret this negative response. The only possible explanation we can see is that these teachers may read into the word "assistance" a type of arbitrary supervision which they wish to avoid.

TABLE 17

MEETING INDIVIDUAL NEEDS

Teachers' Judgments of Experiences in Relation to Social Adjustment (54 Children; 18 Teachers)

Value Judgment *	Pupil Experiences	High Social Adjustment			Average Social Adjustment			Low Social Adjustment			Total		
— ?		Yes	No	?	Yes	No	?	Yes	No	?	Yes	No	?
	I. FACTORS RELATED TO MATURITY												
	1. Does he have a balance of rest and activity suited to his rhythm of energy use and fatigue?	13	4	1	9	7	0	10	4	6	32	15	7
	2. Are the physical activities provided for him suited to his physical maturity and health?	18	0	0	12	4	0	15	2	3	45	6	3
	3. Is the equipment provided for his use suited to his size and muscular development?	17	0	1	16	0	0	18	0	2	51	0	3
	4. Is his environment suited to his health needs (light, ventilation, physical examination, food, rest, exercise, etc.)?	7	6	5	7	7	2	6	10	4	20	23	11
	II. INTERESTS												
	5. In general, is he interested in the experiences provided for him, and are experiences provided which meet his interests?	18	0	0	13	1	2	12	2	6	43	3	8
	6. Are the experiences he is having broadening and/or deepening his interests?	17	0	1	14	1	1	12	1	7	43	2	9
10	7. Does he have adequate opportunity to follow certain personal interests even though they may be different from those of others in the group?	13	2	3	13	0	3	6	5	9	32	7	15
1	8. Does he have adequate materials with which to work and are they suited to his interests (books, art materials, tools, etc.)?	5	12	1	7	8	1	5	14	1	17	34	3
	III. ACADEMIC EXPERIENCES												
	9. Is the work asked of him suited to his intelligence and maturity (not too difficult nor too easy)?	17	0	1	11	4	1	14	3	3	42	7	5

* Figures in italic at left indicate value judgments per item. When not designated as — or ?, the responses were +.

TABLE 17 (Continued)

Value Judgment — ?	Pupil Experiences	High Social Adjustment			Average Social Adjustment			Low Social Adjustment			Total		
		Yes	No	?	Yes	No	?	Yes	No	?	Yes	No	?
	10. Does the work asked of him help him to solve the problems or meet the situations he encounters in his day-to-day living as a growing individual?	13	0	5	12	2	2	13	2	5	38	4	12
	11. Does he have opportunity to explore academic interests which are not common to others in the group?	11	3	4	9	1	6	8	4	8	28	8	18
	12. Does he know why he is studying that which is required of him?	17	0	1	13	0	3	13	0	7	43	0	11
	IV. SKILLS												
	13. Is he growing appropriately in his ability to think logically?	18	0	0	11	1	4	8	8	4	37	9	8
	14. Is he developing according to a pace adopted for him in academic skills, such as reading, number concepts, etc.?	17	0	1	10	3	3	12	6	2	39	9	6
	15. Is he growing appropriately in his social skills (getting along with others, operating as a group member, etc.)?	16	0	2	8	6	2	0	17	3	24	23	7
	16. Is he developing increasing skill in operating as a free, independent, responsible individual?	17	0	1	10	5	1	6	10	4	33	15	6
	V. EXPRESSION												
	17. Does he have sufficient opportunity to make choices about his daily course of action?	14	2	2	14	0	2	15	2	3	43	4	7
	18. Does he have opportunity to chose from among a sufficiently wide range of media for expression (painting, drawing, modeling, crafts, dancing, music—vocal, instrumental—writing, dramatics, etc.)?	12	6	0	13	2	1	13	6	1	38	14	2
	19. Is he given sufficient time to express his ideas and emotions through the arts and other media?	12	3	3	12	1	3	11	1	8	35	5	14

TABLE 17 (Continued)

Value Judgment —	Value Judgment ?	Pupil Experiences	High Social Adjustment Yes	No	?	Average Social Adjustment Yes	No	?	Low Social Adjustment Yes	No	?	Total Yes	No	?
		20. Is he given sufficient opportunity to express and share his ideas verbally with other boys and girls and with adults?	12	1	5	12	0	4	13	3	4	37	4	13
		VI. GROUP ROLE												
		21. Is he given sufficient opportunity to contribute to the group (help in planning, taking responsibility for chores, etc.)?	18	0	0	16	0	0	19	0	1	53	0	1
1		22. Does he feel himself to be an integral part of the group? (Does he have a feeling of "belonging"?)	18	0	0	12	3	1	8	5	7	38	8	8
		23. Is he given opportunity to practice various roles in his group (leader, follower, performer, audience, etc.)?	18	0	0	16	0	0	18	0	2	52	0	2
8		24. Does he have opportunity to work or play in various types of groups (various sizes, with people of various ages, races, etc.)?	5	8	5	9	5	2	10	6	4	24	19	11
		VII. SELF-NEEDS												
1	2	25. Does he have sufficient opportunity to give and to receive affection?	18	0	0	12	1	3	9	4	7	39	5	10
1		26. Does he feel that he is growing, making progress toward his goals?	17	0	1	11	1	4	6	3	11	34	4	16
1		27. Does he receive sufficient recognition from other boys and girls and from adults to make him feel secure?	18	0	0	9	4	3	5	8	7	32	12	10
1		28. Does he feel that he makes a contribution to the group?	18	0	0	12	0	4	10	3	7	40	3	11
		VIII. ADULT HELP												
		29. Does his teacher know him well enough to be able to plan an adequate school program with him?	15	2	1	11	3	2	10	7	3	36	12	6
		30. Does his teacher work with his parents sufficiently to plan a program suited to his needs?	8	7	3	5	8	3	4	14	2	17	29	8

TABLE 17 (Continued)

Value Judgment	Pupil Experiences	High Social Adjustment			Average Social Adjustment			Low Social Adjustment			Total		
		Yes	No	?	Yes	No	?	Yes	No	?	Yes	No	?
	31. Is his teacher the sort of person who, intellectually, emotionally, and by training and experience, can plan wisely with him?	17	0	1	15	0	1	19	0	1	51	0	3
5	32. Is his teacher given a reasonable amount of time, assistance, material, etc., to provide a good school program for him?	2	10	6	6	8	2	2	14	4	10	32	12
	IX. $64 QUESTIONS												
	33. Is he happy?	18	0	0	11	1	4	10	2	8	39	3	12
	34. Does his total school experience help him grow as an individual, as a member of his group, as a citizen of a broadening social group?	18	0	0	13	0	3	14	2	4	45	2	7
	35. Are his total school experiences meaningful to him? Do they help him meet his day-to-day problems?	17	1	0	11	0	5	8	3	9	36	4	14
	36. Are his total school experiences appropriate to his maturity, his rate of growth, his capacities, interests, and needs?	15	0	3	10	3	3	11	7	2	36	10	8
	37. Is there desirable balance in the types of experiences available to him?	10	5	3	12	3	1	10	8	2	32	16	6
	38. Does his teacher feel that he (teacher) has sufficient freedom (from subject matter requirements, etc.) to plan a program best suited to his needs?	5	10	3	8	6	2	5	12	3	18	28	8
	OTHER AREAS (written in by teachers):												
	39. Is the schoolroom floor space per pupil adequate for his freedom of activity?												
	40. Is there time for teacher-parent contact other than that after school hours?												
	41. Are facilities for extracurricular activities (movies, trips, etc.) available when the need arises?												
	42. Is the teacher-time per pupil (affected by class size) sufficient for his needs?												

HOW CAN WE JUDGE PUPIL NEEDS?

We were interested, too, to find teachers questioning the value to children of the opportunity to give and receive affection (item 25), of feeling one's self an integral part of the group (item 22), of feeling that one is growing toward one's goals (item 26), and similar matters of self-need or group role.

Whatever the interpretation, it seems obvious that this staff may well be talking at cross-purposes as they discuss group living, unless they can come to some agreement on their conception of the role of the school in these areas.

—freedom to meet needs

The columns on the right in Table 17 indicate responses of teachers to the questions for each child studied. The directions state: "If in your best judgment the answer *tends* to be affirmative, circle 'Yes'; if it *tends* to be negative, circle 'No.' (Probably few questions, if any, can be answered definitely as a positive, clear yes-or-no case.) If you don't know which way the situation tends, circle '?'."

These responses were studied in two ways: First, we looked to the total responses, in an attempt to get a picture of teachers' judgments regardless of the children checked; and second, we studied the responses made in terms of children whom teachers had selected as demonstrating high, average, or low social adjustment.

Looking first at the totals, five items stand out as strong negatives: numbers 4, 8, 30, 32, and 38. These all have to do with facilities (for health), equipment, or opportunities for teachers to provide an adequate program. As we said earlier, it is futile to discuss selection of appropriate experiences if teachers have no opportunity to make the selections and to provide the programs. Of these 54 responses, only 18 indicate that, for these children, the teacher feels she has sufficient freedom from subject matter requirements, etc. (item 38) to plan a program suited to their needs! There are, of course, many reasons, some valid and some not, why teachers feel that they cannot meet the children's needs. Among those we consider valid are oversized classes, lack of materials, and "course of study" requirements. Until such restrictions are removed, we cannot hope that even conscientious teachers can do the job required of them. On the other hand, we feel it is possible to do much, though not as much as we would wish, even in the face of these obstacles. The first grade teacher in this study made a tremendous contribution to the group living of her children, even though she worked with as many as 42 in the group, and had a turnover of 20 in the middle of the year! It can be done—we saw her do it—but with great expense of time and energy. It is our hope that other teachers, similarly interested in providing adequate programs for individuals and groups, may do so under more favorable circumstances.

—needs and social adjustment

Since we were interested particularly in programs which provide for social adjustment, we tabulated responses in terms of this judgment (first columns to right of the questions, Table 17). Items which differentiated most clearly between high and low social adjustment were, as might be expected, those in the area of group role (VI) and self-needs (VII). It was interesting to find that teachers felt that they knew unadjusted pupils less well than adjusted pupils (item 29) and needed more time to work with parents of these pupils (item 30), and that the program as a whole was less appropriate to their needs (item 36).

On the whole, it would seem that this group of teachers, knowing their children well, are in agreement on the value of most experiences, but the disagreement in certain areas suggests the need for discussion and clarification. It would seem that to a large extent they feel that they are meeting the needs of individuals, although in every area, with a few possible exceptions, there is considerable need for revision of the program if needs of all pupils are to be met. Teachers seem to feel particularly inadequate or thwarted in those areas in which they feel themselves restricted by lack of materials, time, or freedom.

IN SUMMARY

We cannot expect learning in group living unless we provide opportunity for group experience. The fact that twenty-five to forty pupils are in one room is no guarantee that there is group experience. There must be *interaction*—in the form of planning, discussion, and friendly exchange —if group living is to be learned.

We must be on guard against thinking that there is group process when in actuality there are only forms, such as delegated leadership or misuse of majority vote.

Moreover, a teacher must see that *every* child has an opportunity for group service and leadership. Unless there is conscious effort to spread experience, there is a tendency to provide experience to the few while denying it to many.

Within the school program of the usual school there are many opportunities for learning group values if we but provide them. Of major importance is the degree of opportunity offered to individuals for making choices in a variety of situations. A rigid, adult-dominated program limits the opportunity for learning through choice-making, for individuals and groups. Opportunities for learning group living may be found in group planning, creative or appreciative activity, games and sports, unplanned time, student organizations, and class organization.

Although opportunity for favorable group living must permeate *all* activities, there may be a place for more direct, intensive, organized study in certain areas. A unit of study in the eighth grade is cited as an example of such direct study.

It is important, we believe, to recognize the role of the teacher in the school program for group living. A teacher must be prepared to provide a range of experience in keeping with the needs of the group and the skills of himself and the group. If he lacks the ability to provide complete group experience, he may look to transition steps.

Teachers working as groups to develop better school programs for boys and girls need to have common understanding and agreement as to the needs of children and how these needs should be met. Restrictions due to lack of materials or lack of freedom may be seen as major barriers; but perhaps even more significant barriers are those created by this lack of common understanding. Teachers who want to work toward better group living for boys and girls will need to talk through their differences and achieve good group living for themselves if they hope to provide it for children.

VIII

Selecting Experiences for Group Living

"But how can I know how to select experiences for good group living?"
That's a $64 question. In this chapter we share with you our thinking
about this exceedingly difficult question.

Among the general factors which seem important to consider in selecting experiences are: the learners' maturity, past experience, and purposes; and the sequence and balance of the program. No less important
is opportunity for specific learnings, also discussed in this chapter.

GENERAL FACTORS TO CONSIDER

Selecting Experiences in Terms of Maturity of Learners

There has been much research in the attempt to discover the appropriate maturity level for presenting certain types of subject matter. We
think it possible that there is no maturity level more appropriate than
any other in terms of area of content. Rather, *the scope and depth of the
learning experience, its contribution to problem-solving, to the interests
and appreciations of the learners,* may be the criteria to use. Thus, for
example, there may be no specific time in which to present a study of elec-
tricity. It may be appropriate in the first grade, the fifth, the seventh, the
tenth, in college physics, and in the graduate school. Moreover, if it meets
the criteria suggested, there need be no concern if the study is reintro-
duced time and time again, for at each maturity level the scope and depth
will vary.

Similarly, we feel that no one time in the school life of children is more
appropriate than any other time for a study of group behavior, if the

[262]

scope and depth are appropriate. As we have indicated, we cannot hope to find first graders engaging in profound verbal analysis of their group processes, but they can make a beginning, at their own level, in solving their problems. That an interest in inter-personal relations is present at all levels is evident. The need to "belong" is a need of all, at all ages. The desire for friendship is ever-present. Skill in group action not only gives security, but is the major means to action in our modern society. Thus we see no reason for discussing "grade placement" of experiences in group behavior. Rather, we see much need for such studies at *all* maturity levels, continuous throughout the school life of children and young people.

—*interests are learned*

Determining scope and depth in relation to maturity requires some study, however. Maturity factors are evidently involved in the degree to which various types of goals may be brought to the level of consciousness, and in the ability to grasp concepts of group interaction. No doubt the maturity of the learner is a factor in determining the degree of generalization from experience which is possible.

Interests and appreciations may be maturity-linked, but here we would extend a word of caution. It is quite possible, it seems, to use as measures of interest instruments which do no more than report experiences. As we have indicated earlier, we feel that interests may be *developed;* hence there is danger in expecting a predetermined array of interest in relation to maturity. For example, if the teachers in this study had approached their groups with the question, "Would you be interested in role-playing?" there is no knowing what the answers would have been, since none of the children had ever experienced role-playing. An authentic indication of interest, however, is the statement of one boy at the end of the year, "My favorite (experience) was role-playing." In other words, we feel it is quite legitimate for a teacher to introduce a new experience to a group, using the reaction to the experience as a measure of interest more meaningful than a statement of interest prior to the experience. This means, it seems to us, that an introduction of experiences designed to further group living is a duty of the teacher, whether or not the group expresses interest. If the group rejects or responds unfavorably to the experience, after having sampled it, we may conclude that the particular experience was ill-chosen in terms of the maturity-linked interests of the group.

Selecting Experiences in Terms of Past Experience of Learners

That past experience has a profound influence on learning cannot be denied. As was indicated above, it may be the basis of interests. Moreover, it is a powerful determinant of needs, values, and goals. Thus children used to playing since infancy in groups of their peers will require quite different experiences in group living from those needed by children who have seldom seen other children until they entered school.

Interestingly enough, it is the two extremes of living, the isolated rural area and the crowded apartment-house district, which most frequently furnish examples of children lacking in group experience. Most suburban children start school with considerable experience in small, intimate play groups, and continue to keep up these groups after school all through their school careers. The rural child may lack this opportunity because of geographic isolation and because of decrease in family size. Where once the rural child found companionship in brothers and sisters, he suffers today, not as drastically as his city cousins but in some degree, from the limited social contacts offered by small families. He may continue to lack this social experience, even through high school, unless the school makes special provision for his needs. The apartment-house child may lack experience with other children because his mother is afraid to let him out of her sight, or because she has failed to provide for supervised social contacts, or because she fears the "contamination," physical or psychological, of such social intercourse. This isolation may continue during after-school hours, even after the child has entered school, until such time as he exerts his independence (if he is healthy and normal) and demands the right to play with others.

—isolation of children

The first grade teacher in this study, aware of the isolation of many of her children, provided for them special after-school playtime on the school grounds. Fourth and fifth grade teachers in apartment-house areas may expect, it seems, the tears of harassed mothers who claim that "Johnny won't mind me any more. He doesn't come home after school the way he used to." Teachers have a job on their hands explaining to such mothers that their sons (or daughters) are merely expressing the normal desire of children of their age to have free play time with their peers.

This discussion may have taken a turn which makes it seem that it is a "fault" of mothers and fathers that they have small families or live in crowded apartment houses. We are inclined to place the blame on our modern society, which makes such conditions necessary. But, more important, we see the added responsibility which is placed on schools if educators are to do their duty in providing for the individual adjustment, the group living, and the democratic education of their pupils.

Selecting Experiences in Terms of Purposes of Learners

We have discussed at considerable length our belief in the importance of determining group goals, helping groups evaluate them, and finding means to achieve them. Responses on the Check Sheet of Opportunities in Human Relations (page 407) give us some indication of the degree to which we are providing opportunities for experiences felt to be of value by boys and girls. A sampling is given in Table 18, which is read as follows: To the item "Take part in community affairs" the eighth grade group assigned a rank of 9 in value (in a list of 40 items) but a rank of 32 in frequency of opportunity; thus the difference in ranks was 23. In other words, the boys and girls felt that the experience was of considerable value, but that opportunity for it was seldom provided.

TABLE 18

ITEM WITH VALUE RANK CONSIDERABLY HIGHER THAN OPPORTUNITY RANK
(IN A LIST OF 40 ITEMS)

Experience	Value Rank	Opportunity Rank	Difference in Rank
Eighth Grade (group of 32)			
Take part in community affairs	9	32	23
Be a member of a club	9	28	19
Do work for the community without pay	16	35	19
Observe adults engaged in various types of work	7	20	13
Visit communities other than my own	13	24	11
Fourth and Fifth Grades (group of 34)			
Visit communities other than my own	2	37	35
Be a leader or a representative of a group of people my age	2	24	22
Work or play in groups in which adults are members (not including teachers or youth leaders)	21	37	16
Meet people who come from outside my community	15	31	16
Talk with adults engaged in various types of work	13	28	15
Take part in community affairs	8	22	14
Be a member of a group which makes its own rules	19	31	12

It is rather a severe indictment of our school programs that children and young people see value in these selected activities which we, too, feel to be important, yet they feel that they have little opportunity to find experiences in them. It is interesting that these items in which there is a wide difference between value rank and opportunity are heavily weighted toward broadening experience beyond immediate school life. Provision for some of these experiences considered important by boys and girls, such as visiting other communities, might involve much planning and expense, but many of the other experiences could be furnished easily through group-teacher-community cooperation. Why should any community deny children and young people an opportunity to be of service to the community, without pay? Shouldn't there be a way in which these boys and girls can take part in community affairs? Couldn't any teacher provide opportunity for her group to observe or talk with adults engaged in various types of work? If we mean what we say about meeting needs and interests, about goal-centered activity, about helping pupils learn that which is important to them, about widening social experience, we will find a way.

—meeting objectives

The eighth grade group in this study attempted to take steps toward meeting at least one of these objectives. Adults with varied experiences came to the classroom to talk to the group. Statements of evaluation indicated that this was appreciated. "We got a lot out of Mr. Oldham's talk." "Hearing people who have had experience is better than reading." The fourth and fifth grade group planned that when they were fifth and six graders they would begin community service by being of service to the school community. Activities discussed included helping on the playground, reading to younger children, assisting younger pupils at lunch time, and the like.

Also of interest are listings of experiences which boys and girls claim to have frequently but in which they see little value. Table 19 gives a sampling of these, and is read as follows: To the item "Work or play with people of the opposite sex" the group assigned an opportunity rank of 5, but a rank in value of 25; thus the difference in rank is 20. In other words, the boys and girls felt that the opportunity for the experience was considerably less than its value. (This is the reverse of information given in Table 18, in which opportunity was considered higher than value.)

TABLE 19

ITEMS WITH OPPORTUNITY RANK CONSIDERABLY HIGHER THAN VALUE RANK

Experience	Opportunity Rank	Value Rank	Difference in Rank
Eighth Grade Group			
Work or play with people of opposite sex	5	25	20
Work or play with people of differing national backgrounds	5	20	15
Work or play with people whom I consider to be considerably smarter than I am	7	22	15
Work or play with people who are considerably more wealthy than my family	20	33	13
Work or play with people whom I consider slower thinking than I am	23	35	12
Work or play with people of differing	17	28	11
Work or play with people who have considerably less money than my family	24	35	11
Fourth and Fifth Grade Group			
Work or play with people who are considerably more wealthy than my family	18	40	22
Work or play with people whom I consider to be considerably slower thinking than I am	14	36	22
Work or play with people whom I consider considerably smarter than I am	7	28	21
Work or play with people of differing religious belief	4	24	20
Work or play with people of opposite sex	14	31	17
Discuss boy-girl relations	10	24	14

There is difference of opinion among the group as to the interpretation of these findings. There are those who claim that if rankings of opportunity are greater than those for value it implies social sensitivity. If one is highly social-conscious, one will claim that it isn't important whether one plays with people of differing races because *the difference is unimportant.* This point of view is strengthened by the indication that the experiences of this nature are high in opportunity. Another interpretation is that the boys and girls see no value in such experience, even though they have it frequently, and that they might even feel it desirable to eliminate it. In other words, the use of this instrument in this way lends itself to two divergent interpretations and needs the support of other evidence. We are in total agreement that the areas opened up for interpretation are significant and require further study.

—value assignments

When we found on examining Table 19 that fourth and fifth graders feel they have more frequent opportunity for experiences in discussing boy-girl relations than they think is of value, we decided we should examine the age and sex differences in value assignment to experiences, and Table 20 evolved. This table is read as follows: In response to the item "Work for pay," a sufficient number of boys of the eighth grade marked it important to give the item first rank. Boys and girls of the fourth and fifth grade group and girls of the eighth grade did not designate it as important a sufficient number of times for it to be in the first ten items in rank.

TABLE 20

RANK OF VALUE ASSIGNMENTS OF EXPERIENCES
IN RELATION TO SEX AND AGE

(Items rated by the most boys and girls as being important)

Experience	Fourth and Fifth Grade		Eighth Grade	
	Boys	Girls	Boys	Girls
Work for pay	*		1	
Visit communities other than my own	6	1		5
Work or play in a group of thirty to fifty people	1	3		
Work or play in a group of four or five people	6		9	1
Work or play in a group of ten or twelve people		7		
Work or play with people much older than I am (five or more years older)	6	7	5	
Be a member of a team for some sport	6		5	
Be a member of a club	4	3	9	5
Be a leader or representative of a group of people my age	6	1		5
Be a member of a group which elects its own leaders	2		9	5
Talk with adults engaged in various types of work		3	2	1
Observe adults engaged in various types of work		7		5
Spend leisure time with friends of my own choice		7	2	5
Discuss with others my age what is going on in the world	6		5	4
Discuss boy-girl relations				5
Discuss sex problems				5
Take part in community affairs	2		9	5
Work at home (do chores) without pay		4		1
Do useful work for the community without pay				5

* Blank space indicates item was not within first ten in rank.

As may be seen, sex differences are more marked than age differences. For example, boys of both age groups (but not girls) indicate the importance of being on a team, while girls of both age groups (but not boys) feel that doing chores and observing adults at work are of importance. Certain items are both age- and sex-related. For example, eighth grade girls feel that it is important to discuss boy-girl relations and sex problems, but boys of both age groups and younger girls do not. Older boys and girls seem to feel much more strongly than do younger people the importance of time with friends of one's own choice (fourth and fifth grade girls give it a rank of 7 and the boys of this age do not give it a rank within the first ten).

Rather than attempt to draw generalizations from these data, we should like to point to the importance of two further steps which need to be taken: one, much wider studies by many more groups to discover whether there are common elements according to sex, age, and other factors; and two, similar investigations on a limited basis, as in the present one, by teachers working with boys and girls in studies of group behavior. It is to this latter type of study that we feel emphasis must be given if experiences are to be selected in terms of the goals, values, and purposes of specific groups of children and young people.

Sequence of Experiences

As we discussed the selection of experience in terms of the maturity of the learner, we indicated that we believe that the sequence of experience grows out of the situation and the meaning it can have for pupils. Thus there is little basis for allocating experiences to grade levels. However, there is one aspect of sequence to which we want to give special attention. In our modern world, we want people to be worthy group members of families, of communities, of nations of the world. We claim these relationships to be important for many reasons: They contribute to mental health, for both the individual and the group, to social health, to good citizenship, to world understanding. The logic in teaching these relationships might seem to be to teach each in turn, starting with home membership, moving on to community, then to national, and finally to world membership. The logic is based on what we know of a child's growing concepts (which makes sense) but also on a "serial" concept of learning (which we question). When these various relationships are treated as "steps," each examined and then set aside in favor of the next, there is grave danger of failing to teach the relationship of each to the others. We have ample evidence of adults who have "stopped" on one of the steps, and are unable, seemingly, to mount the next. This is particularly true of those who have "stopped" on the step of national membership, and are unable to achieve world membership. Adults who are unwilling to see the U.N. flag flown beside the flag of the United States may be in this category.

What we are suggesting is that instead of conceiving these relationships as steps in a sequence, we recognize them as concentric circles. This would mean that, at any one time, a child is encouraged to see his relationship in all aspects. True, the focus may need to be in terms of the concepts of the child; but we believe that every teacher, no matter what the age of the learners, has a responsibility to help develop concepts in terms of all the relationships. The teacher of young children may give primary focus to home membership, but needs to stress the relationship of this to the community and, as far as possible, to the nation and the world. The high school teacher, on the other hand, while developing concepts of world membership, has a responsibility of pointing to the relations of this to family and community membership.

Our plea, then, is that we abandon the idea of a sequence of steps, and substitute a concept which gives major emphasis to the interrelated factors of various types of group living, from family groups to world groups.

Balance in the Program

We believe there are many areas of experience which must be balanced if we are to create good group living.

—*rest and activity*

The first grade teacher in this study has been most insistent that balance of rest and activity makes a difference in group living. If there is imbalance, there is inter-personal hostility and subgroup friction. No doubt such factors as these, closely related to basic needs, are more important at all ages than we realize.

—*individual and group*

Certain aspects of balance within group living are brought to our attention on many occasions. The need to balance individual-centered and group-centered activity is one of these areas. In our emphasis on group living we do not wish to overlook the need to consider purely individual activity. In fact, unless there is this balance, group activity may suffer. It will be recalled that group living seemed to be benefited when "privacy corners" were provided for children who lacked an opportunity for individual-centered activity. It became evident, however, as we visited classrooms, that the preponderant time and energy was of the individual-centered type. There were classrooms in which this was so true that even speaking to one's neighbor or looking at his work was considered a crime. We were surprised at the number of children in the groups with which we worked who seemed amazed that there was no law against speaking to one's neighbor ("I like the way our teacher lets us talk to each other") or helping each other ("Our teacher lets me help my friend when he gets stuck"). Thus, although we believe a favorable balance of individual- and group-centered activity is desirable, we believe, also, that most teachers err in the direction of overemphasizing the individual-centered activity and could do much, much more in the area of group-centered work before imbalance would occur.

—immediate and long-range

A second aspect of balance has to do with experience centered in *immediate* group experience in relation to that which is directed to *widening* social experiences. We find it difficult to discuss this type of balance because we feel that most teachers err in favor of the widening social experience they *think* they are teaching, although, we fear, without success. There are dangers in assuming that one is leading a group toward widening social consciousness when, in reality, one is merely creating misconceptions and indulging in meaningless abstractions. We think it possible that much of the teaching of social studies is of this nature. It seems appropriate to urge teachers to give more attention to immediate experience so that the wider experiences may have greater meaning. To us this implies the need for more attention to group interaction which, in turn, may contribute to the understanding of wider group processes.

—release and control

A third aspect of balance is also difficult to discuss. It has to do with the relation of tension-releasing activities to those controlling or disciplining. This is a relationship on which many teachers have "taken sides," as though on an "either-or" issue. In terms of group living, we feel the releasing experience is important because, unless emotional release is provided, the tensions created may take the form of inter-personal conflicts, so damaging to group interaction. Controlled or disciplined activities are important also, for unless the individual is willing to find reason beyond himself, he is feeling an autonomy incompatible with group living. Perhaps the major point of difference here is the source of the authority which disciplines. In our view, the group goal is the major

disciplinary factor. A group which has determined a goal will not condone the actions of the individual who thwarts its attainment. It will
exert pressure to urge the individual to contribute to goal attainment. It
is this type of discipline of which we speak—group-imposed in terms of
group goals. We hasten to add, however, that it is sometimes the duty of
a teacher to protect the deviate or the minority from domination by the
goal-centered majority. The autocracy of a majority may be as devastating to the development of the individual or subgroup as a teacher autocracy is to that of the total group

—goal-centered and non-goal-centered

We wish to draw attention to one further aspect of balance, that is,
the balance between goal-centered and non-goal-centered activity. We
have given considerable emphasis in the preceding pages to the importance of group goal-directed activity because we feel it to be important
and because we have observed in many classrooms so much *teacher*-
directed (rather than goal-directed) activity. The balance we wish to
indicate is not that between teacher goals and group goals (for we feel
that activity is futile unless group goal-directed) but between goal-
directed activity and non-goal-directed activity. We feel there is a place
for many activities totally unrelated to goals, and desirable purely for
enjoyment, for appreciation, for recreation. Listening to music, painting
a picture, or dancing may have little relation to a predetermined goal,
but may have value nevertheless, and the balanced program will find a
place for such activities.

LEARNING AND GROUP LIVING

Learning is a unified experience. There are teachers who see the value
of interaction during a planning period for about one-half hour a day,
but seem to give it little concern beyond this period. Not only is this time
allotment meager, but the idea that good group living can be achieved
through the planning, yet denied in the execution of the plans, is, we
believe, fallacious. Eleven-year-old Caroline, after considerable experience in working toward favorable group interaction, is astute enough to
see a relation between planning and execution. She recommends, "Before
you stop (the planning) be sure everyone knows how to get started on
what you've planned to do." In other words, "democratic" planning without related democratic execution is meaningless.

Further, the assumption that group living can be relegated to a particular school period just doesn't make sense in terms of what we know about how learning takes place. Such a concept is as foolish as the one implied in the school program which listed "rational thinking" as a course, to meet from 11:00 to 11:40 each day. Neither rational thinking nor group living can be thus segmented. Unless good group living is to be a part of the total living of children and young people, we are defeated before we begin when teaching democracy. Learning about group living must be a part of the total school program.

Thus, although we deny the possibility of segmentation of learning, for the sake of discussion we present in the following pages a series of considerations having to do with learning the three R's, problem-solving, developing concepts, and evaluation.

Learning the Skills of the Three R's

A major problem confronting us as we began to experiment in the area of group living was the fear of parents and teachers that this emphasis might interfere with "regular learning"—meaning learning to read, write, spell, and compute.

There is evidence in the literature[1] that, in programs which allow for a degree of flexibility and pupil planning, achievement, even in the three R's, is as much as would be expected—or even more—in a rigid, teacher-directed program. It is not possible for us to present conclusive evidence in this area. However, we found no evidence that growth in academic learning suffered, even when there was intensive experimentation in group living. Table 21 indicates fall and spring test results in reading for the fourth and fifth grade groups. Midyear promotion is practiced in this school. Although the group remained stable during the year, it was composed, in the fall, of children in grades 4B (beginning fourth), 4A, and 5B, and in the spring, of children in grades 4A, 5B, and 5A.

These figures should speak for themselves, as they indicate for each group gains in reading achievement far beyond what might be expected in terms of norms on the test.

Problem-solving

A study of group living presents many opportunities for developing skills in problem-solving. A description of a situation in which role-play-

[1] Paul Leonard and Alvin Eurich, *An Evaluation of Modern Education.* New York: D. Appleton–Century, 1942.

ing was used will serve to illustrate one approach to problem study and solution. Three little girls in the fourth and fifth grade group were having trouble getting along with one another. This problem was significant in

TABLE 21

ACHIEVEMENT SCORES IN READING*

	October 10 Form B	June 10 Form A
Grade 4B		
Grade norm	4.1	4.9
Average for group	5.2	6.8
Range	2.9–7.1	3.5–7.3
Average growth per 8-month period		1.8
I.Q.[1] range	72–122	
Median I.Q.	110	
Grade 4A		
Grade norm	4.6	5.4
Average for group	4.7	5.9
Range	2.3–5.9	3.6–6.9
Average growth per 8-month period		1.2
I.Q. range	86–120	
Median I.Q.	104	
Grade 5B		
Grade norm	5.1	5.9
Average per group	5.7	6.9
Range	3.7–7.0	3.4–7.0
Average growth per 8-month period		1.2
I.Q. range	84–125	
Median I.Q.	108	

* Progressive Achievement Test, California Test Bureau, Los Angeles, California.
[1] Kuhlmann–Anderson Test, Educational Test Bureau, Educational Publishers, Minneapolis, Minnesota.

itself, but was intensified because other group members were taking sides. The situation was well on its way toward causing major group disruptions.

—defining the problem

First the immediate participants in the difficulty analyzed the situation. One wrote a statement as follows:

"I like Susan and so does Betty, but Betty and I don't get along. Susan likes Betty and she likes me too. The reasons we don't get along is Betty is too bossy and silly, and she gets tired of one thing too fast, she doesn't like to play things that I like to play, she's a Tom-Boy just like my sister. But she's a nice kid."

—gathering evidence

The teacher suggested that three other people play the part of the three having difficulty, showing how the situation looked and how the difficulty might be resolved. The pupil recorder of the log for the day reports:

"Susan, Betty and Gloria are having trouble with friendship. Susan, Betty and Gloria chose people to have a play. Jean is Betty. Sharon is Susan. Nan is Gloria. They are deciding how they are going to spend the evening. They are deciding what they are going to play. They started to argue so they planned how they were going to quit arguing."

—suggesting solutions

After the role-playing, pupils in the class wrote their evaluation of the solutions suggested by the role-players, and made recommendations on how the difficulty should be resolved. The most frequent suggestion had to do with taking turns and the mechanical means for determining these turns.

"If I were Susan I would let them take turns. Let the first one there start the game then if each one didn't get a turn to be first let them start the next day."
"I think they ought to flip a coin or draw straws, or Susan could play with one girl one day and another the next day."
"I think they should play 'work-up' and 'the potatoes' to be first. And if the other person is up don't get mad."

We were interested to find that next to the recommendation of taking turns, the suggestions most frequently offered had to do with some type of arbitration:

"If I was Susan I would go over to Gloria's one day and go over to Betty's another day. And if that did not work, I would call each one up and talk it over."
"Well if I was in Susan's place I would call both Gloria and Betty up and have a meeting and figure some way they can play together without fighting."

Several boys and girls suggested the necessity for continuing attempts to get along together:

"They should play together because if they don't they'll never be friends."
"I think they should be together more so they would learn to like each other."

We must confess we don't know how to classify the following remark, but we were interested to note that children may see that a single incident can have wide implications.

> Well when they fight they should go home and don't. That's how wars start."

Several tried to get at the source of the difficulty, suggesting that the games played were the source of the problem.

> "I didn't like the games they played. I would have played soft ball."
> "If I were them I would play a little more childish games."

Others, however, recognized that the motivation of the individuals under discussion may not be the same as their own.

> "If I were these girls I would play more quiet games but I like quiet games and maybe they like other games."
> "I don't think I would play like that but if thats the way they want to play, O.K."

One pupil suggested resorting to higher authority.

> "I would try to get the mothers together."

Some suggested that attitudes during play should be modified or that certain acts might resolve conflicts.

> "They get too excited. They should be more calm."
> "I think they should shake when they get in a fight."

One sympathetic soul suggested a responsibility to the unfortunate.

> "I think Betty should call up Gloria and play with her because Gloria doesn't have anyone to play with but a boy."

We present these reactions only as an indication of the types of responses to a role-playing situation created by a group of nine- and ten-year-olds who are trying valiantly to think through a problem in human relations. The characters themselves state their conclusions:

> SUSAN: I think we could play all together and not argue. I think if I was playing with Betty and Gloria didn't like her, I think she still wouldn't have to play with her. And I think we could all play something really fun and we could go to school together and have a lot of fun together.
> GLORIA: We should take turns playing at each others houses. We should have more and better games to play. We shouldn't play the same games like Susan and I do, we either roller skate or ride my bike. We shouldn't argue either.

ALL THE WORLD IS OF INTEREST.

—testing solutions

Having seen the role-playing and heard the suggestions of their class-mates, one of the three participants asked for an opportunity to show the class how they might get along together. The group granted this permission. The teacher's log reads:

> Our plans called for Betty, Susan and Gloria to show the way they felt they could play together better. They had watched three disinterested children play it out yesterday and Barbara had asked for them to have a chance to show the class how they would really play, showing how they felt they should play.

—evaluation in changed behavior

The three girls then put on a demonstration of how they could play amicably together. Evidently the opportunity to "see themselves as others see them," the suggestions of their classmates, and the effort to get along well afforded by the opportunity to play the role of themselves as good

[277]

friends were sufficient to effect a change in their inter-personal relations. We don't know which factor or factors had the most influence; perhaps it was the combination of factors that was important. Whatever it was, the experience inspired the three girls to prove they could get along together, and they did. Not only was the difficulty among the three resolved, but further, the group, no longer needing to take sides, regained its unity and happy integration.

Another example may be drawn from a committee report prepared by a fourth and fifth grade group. The process of problem definition is not specifically indicated but is easily inferred. Other processes are clearly indicated: suggesting solutions; testing; evaluation; provision for further suggestion, retesting, and so on. The following is the report of the pupil recorder:

OUR PLANS

We talked about how can we play together better.

1. Don't argue.—Jean
    (a) You waste your time arguing about rules when you don't know them yourself.—Polly
2. Learn to play for enjoyment and exercise. Don't worry too much about the way others play.—Janice
3. Appoint captains and assistant captains to help get you started.—Roy
4. Learn to be a good sport when you win or lose.—Tom
5. Cooperate with other rooms to help solve our problem.—Gerald
6. Be sure to choose a captain that knows the rules.—Anna

The teacher asked Jane (the chairman) if we knew how we could get started and Jane told Miss Roberts how we can play better on the playground. We went out to play and had a nice time. Jane said she would make a list for playing and for a good sport and she will let us know who talks all the time. We discussed it after we came in.

—jury panel discussion

Another approach to problem-solving grew out of the use of one of the instruments described earlier (Check Sheet of Opportunities, page 407). The boys and girls of the fourth and fifth grade group had each listed three things about themselves they wanted to improve. The teacher listed these items anonymously and reported them back to the class. The group decided they wanted to discuss how to achieve improvement in the kinds of behavior itemized, but realizing that the list was too long for the discussion of each item, they asked a committee to prepare a list suitable for discussion by a jury group. The teacher's report of this activity follows:

The committee worked out lists of problems which they felt were important and had many interesting discussions among themselves as well as some very interesting sharing periods for children in the room and for one of our parent meetings.

The answers which are given below are the answers given at the parents' meeting in answer to the questions prepared by the committee for use on this particular program. They were taken down by three secretaries from fourth and fifth grades. The pupil reporters caught the gist of the responses, but things went too fast for them to record the entire discussion.

We expect to use this technique in other ways next year in order to define, evaluate and discuss problems of our class. The children liked the technique and hope to be able to use it more.

It has more appeal than the usual type of panel discussion for children of this age.

We tried a similar idea without microphones when we were coaching our representative, Susan, for a wire recording program on safety. We asked her questions, giving her first chance at answering them, then opened each for limited class discussion. We could open our jury discussion to the entire class, making still another variation.

Our Children's Jury Questions and Answers

(as reported by the pupil recorders)

1. *How can we play ball better?*

   I think you can learn to play ball better if you don't argue with the umpire.
   I could play ball better if I was a good sport.
   Don't cheat. Be a good sport.
   Practice more.
   Don't fight.

2. *How can I get along better with my sister?*

   Be nice to her.
   If she's little, don't boss her.
   Don't kick her and pull her hair.
   Share things.
   Don't kid her—don't kid her about playing with dolls.

3. *How can I get people to like me?*

   Don't call them names.
   Treat people as you want them to treat you.
   Share things with them.
   Don't fight and argue.
   Don't make fights with them.

GROUPS CAN LEARN TO SOLVE PROBLEMS.

4. *How can I stop my sister from being a tomboy?*

> Take guns away from her and give her girls' toys.
> Don't play boys' games.
> Don't let her dress like a boy.
> Don't let her sell papers. Don't let her play ball.
> Tell her to stay in the house and play dolls.

5. *How can I get more friends to play with?*

> When you're going to some other place be friendly with the children there.
> Treat others as you would be treated.
> Play well.
> Be friendly.

6. *Is it all right for children to read mystery stories or listen to them on the radio?*

> Gladys says yes.
> You might get nightmares.
> You might dream.
> You might be afraid of the dark.
> I listen to them all the time and I can't see where they hurt me.

7. *How can I get along with my brother?*

> Don't fight with him. Be kind to him. Don't pull his hair.
> Don't tease him.
> Share things with him.

8. *I'm new in the room. How can I make friends?*

> Don't bother people when they are working.
> Share things with people. Be friendly with them.

Developing Concepts

We believe it to be our duty to teach pupils that good group living may apply in situations ranging from friendships and family relations to world affairs. In much of this report we have concentrated on the classroom living of boys and girls. We believe this to be but a beginning, however. Unless the lesson is taught so thoroughly that it is seen as applicable to *all* human relations, we shall have fallen far, far short of our objectives.

Such broadening of concepts may be related to maturity. It is our experience that group living is best taught to six-year-olds in appropriate settings for good group living, thus providing direct experience. There is a beginning, however, in learning to play together, to take turns, to "play fair," to help one another. We are not belittling this beginning. Far from it. We feel it to be extremely important. However, as was indicated earlier, asking six-year-olds to make a rational analysis of their interaction may be inappropriate.

Ten- and eleven-year-olds are capable of insightful analysis and evaluation of their own group processes, but it is possible that the broad concepts of time, space, and complex human interaction to which they are often subjected in studies of history and geography are too mature or too unrelated to their living to be grasped by them in meaningful form.

Perhaps a word of caution is in order. It may be easy for us to think we are making a transition from immediate group understanding to broader understandings when there is no such transition.

A committee of the fourth and fifth grade group decided it was interested in learning more about human relations through a study of great men. The teacher was much encouraged. This seemed to be an excellent opportunity for boys and girls to broaden their vision beyond their immediate interaction. The committee set to work with a will, and wrote a series of descriptions of people they had selected as "great," such as Washington, Chopin, Eisenhower, and Franklin D. Roosevelt. They gave some details of the lives of these men, and then attempted to describe them as people. The descriptions were full of terms such as "courageous," "loyal," and "daring."

—real meaning

In discussions with the group, the teacher attempted to ascertain how much this meant to the boys and girls by asking how they would act if they acted like these great men they described. The responses were deflating to her enthusiasm. It was evident that the group members were not only vague as to the meaning of the words they had used, but saw little relation between their study and their own lives. It is possible that another approach might have made the children realize this relationship, but we think it probable that both semantics and concepts were being strained. We need to remember that this is the group which stated as a goal, "Don't be a coward," and then defined it as, "Means not to be scared of mice," and, "Don't pick on little kids then be afraid to start something with your size and age." To the group these latter concepts are real, and the words have meaning. Is it possible, however, that the courage of a statesman and the daring of a general are too far removed from reality for ten- and eleven-year-olds to grasp? If so, what futile time and energy must be spent in much of the history teaching we try to do!

This does not imply that wide, important concepts cannot be learned by boys and girls. When, in a discussion of how to get along together on the playground, Donald suggests, "We should ask the other rooms to work with us to decide," he is voicing the basic idea underlying the U.N. A discussion of world cooperation growing out of this concept can make sense to Donald and his classmates. A discussion without this experience in examining real, immediate problems in inter-group relations may be meaningless.

—seeing wider relationships

Thirteen- and fourteen-year-olds, it would seem, are capable of appreciating the relation of their own group processes to wider social issues. As Alvin, a fourteen-year-old, states (in evaluating the year's work), "We learned about how to get along together, to work in groups, also about how people in other countries get along together and they get along just like we do."

To the Donalds and Alvins who appreciate the reality of world affairs, because it is seen as being as meaningful as their immediate experiences, we entrust with confidence the future of our world.

—understanding motives

The number of times children ascribed to adults motives of children their own age, when asked why adults fight (Reaction to Pictures, page 423), leads us to question the extent to which children can understand motives they have not experienced. If children interpret the adult world in terms of their own motives, what strange notions are we teaching—of war, for example? Are wars a matter of "he called me names," "he took something of mine"? On second thought, perhaps the children come closer to a real interpretation than those who speak of wars to make the world safe for democracy or to achieve the four freedoms. Correct or not in interpretation, what must children think of adults who give their lives for "he called me names," yet tell children it is naughty to take a punch at a guy for the same reason? The apparent inconsistency may well cause confusion in their minds.

[283]

—what do children see?

It seems to us that this notion that children may attribute their own motives to others is deserving of further study. We made the beginnings of such a study when we asked pupils of various ages to react to pictures of children fighting, asking why five- and six-year-olds fight; why ten- and eleven-year-olds fight; why boys in junior and senior high school fight; and why adults fight.

First graders tended to suggest similar reasons for fighting, regardless of the age of the fighters (with the possible exception of adults). The reasons for fighting suggested by first graders were (in this order of frequency):

> Defending possessions—("The one boy took the other boy's ball so he socked him then they were fighting.")
> Not abiding by rules of play—("One boy didn't play fair.")
> Being rough—("This one guy here pushed this other guy here so they started fighting.")
> Name calling—("He called him a bad name." Incidentally, the range of vocabulary of first graders in designating what constitutes a "bad name" was interesting. It ranged from "bum" to that which would ban this book even beyond Boston. The degree of "badness" seems to be culturally dictated, however. In one group being called a "goat" was the height of insult, even though more colorful language, often heard at home as well as on the playground, was dismissed as less damaging to one's honor.)

The motives attributed to adults are a possible exception, though we doubt it. That most frequently mentioned was "They fight about their children." We feel it possible that this is a mere extension of the idea of defending possessions, in this case the children being the "possessions" of adults. As described earlier (page 224), the specific examples may be revealing. "Grown people fight like my mother and daddy when my daddy takes money out of my mother's pocketbook." Again, this may easily be seen as an extension of the notion of defending possessions, on the same level as one boy taking another's ball. Or a first grader says, "They fight about when ladies get home at night. My mummy comes home late and my daddy gets mad and they have a fight." Does this mean any more to a first grader than "playing fair" in hopscotch? We doubt it. As children see it, adults may have strange codes of "playing fair," but they are to be respected, as is the rule in hopscotch that one may touch one's toe to the ground only once, and only in certain designated areas.

—understanding motives of others

When asked why five-year-olds fight, ten- and eleven-year-olds seem to be quite realistic in their interpretations. They agree with the younger children that the major reason is defense of possessions (marbles, toys, and so on). In second place they put "tattling." Apparently the tattletale can expect that telling on someone will result in a physical effort to get even! This factor was not rated high in the list of reasons given by the younger children, but is given often enough to indicate that ten- and eleven-year-olds have a fairly accurate insight into motives of those younger than themselves.

The ten- and eleven-year-olds list these reasons why boys their own age do battle:

Decisions in play—"Who won the game?" "Whether he touched first base." ("Might makes right" seems to be an accepted philosophy in settling disputes. Or the assumption may be that the best batter is also the best battler, hence has the right to defend his skill in sports through use of his fists. This may well be an extension of the "play fair" idea of the younger children.)

Defending possessions—(Not as strongly indicated as with younger children, yet frequently mentioned, was the need to protect what is yours, even if you "gotta" fight for it. It will be recalled that in stating goals, the fourth and fifth graders agreed that "if someone takes something away from you it's o.k. to fight.")

In listing reasons why older boys fight, the ten- and eleven-year-olds put first "fighting over a girl," and second the need to defend possessions. We suggest that the girl in this case may be classified as a "possession," just as children may be seen as possessions of adults. Evidently the ten- and eleven-year-olds do not consider girls as possessions worth fighting for, but, admitting the peculiar taste in possession of older boys, they understand the motive for fighting!

Eighth graders, responding to the same questions, seem to have lost the zeal for defending possessions and to have gained respect for verbal insult. They gave a place to "name calling" on the list of reasons for fights for young children, for ten- and eleven-year-olds, and for boys their own age. In addition, they listed "tormenting" as a reason why young children fight, using the word to apply both to verbal teasing and to physical pokes and pushes. They frequently suggested "Fighting over a game" as a reason why ten-year-olds fight, thus agreeing with the ten-year-olds themselves.

—interpretation and experience

From this preliminary study, it would seem that one often, perhaps always, attributes to others only those motives known through one's own experience. Moreover, the nearer the experience, the clearer the insight. Fourth and fifth grade boys and girls came closer to interpreting motives of young children, in terms of young children, than did the eighth graders. It seems likely, too, that the setting and semantics of the reaction need careful study. It may be easy to read an understanding of maternal love into the statement, "They fight over their children," or an understanding of sex attraction into the statement, "They fight over a girl." We are suggesting that this is not necessarily the case; there may be discrimination per age concerning the type of "possessions" desired, but the motive may be thought to be merely the defending of one's property, whether girl or marbles, against theft.

Certainly our evidence is insufficient for wide generalization, but it opens up a question about the selection of learning experiences which should be of great concern to educators. Is it possible that boys and girls understand only those motives they themselves have experienced? If so, what are the implications for our teaching of history, literature, or, for that matter, anything having to do with adult motivation? Can motives be taught? If so, are they to be taught through reading and discussion? Can an immature fifteen-year-old boy see in Romeo and Juliet anything beyond a misplaced fervor for possession? In fact, may we be teaching that love is merely a form of possession? Can motives be taught through experiences which give rise to them?

We can't answer these questions, but we believe it is important that studies be made which will throw light on them. Until answers are provided, it would seem advisable to be extremely critical of the learning experiences we provide for boys and girls, asking ourselves whether we are presenting concepts beyond their comprehension, or possibly developing unfortunate concepts on their part.

Evaluation

Evaluation is, of course, but an aspect of problem-solving. We use the term here to apply not to immediate testing but to the larger aspects dealing with major factors in program development. The general framework in which we worked included the following processes:

1. Developing goals for group living by parents, teachers, and pupils,

in terms of group *behavior* (not mere verbalization of generalizations).

2. Developing suggestions on how to achieve these goals.
3. Testing suggestions through tryout.
4. Evaluating results by measuring them against goals.

—developing goals

In Chapter III, "Group Goals," we described how parents, teachers, and pupils developed lists of goals for group living. The initial listing was but a start, however. In each classroom, the list of goals was posted, frequently discussed, and interpreted in terms of behavior; and often additions were made.

As maturity and ability to verbalize increased, there was a growing awareness of goal shifts and the reason for such shifts. The ten- and eleven-year-olds with whom we worked were conscious of increased scope as the year wore on.

—a playground fight

There had been a playground fight. Billy was convinced that there was nothing wrong with the use of a certain word. His older brother used it. Sam was equally convinced that it was wrong. His father said so. Knowing no better way to settle the dispute, the two took to use of their fists. Their group mates were interested, but knew no better solution at the moment than to watch the matter decided by physical might. "Might makes right" was the best technique of evaluation they knew. They brought the problem into the classroom, however, and discussed it with their teacher.

After a half-hour of calm discussion they added two items to their goals: "Be able to decide between right and wrong," and "Know where authority lies." Their teacher explained that even adults were frequently at a loss to know right from wrong, and how to judge authority, but knowing the issues involved was a help.

Such statements are no guarantee that other fights over similar matters will not occur on the playground. Many of the group members, however, were thereafter more aware of the elements of the situation and were in a better position to avoid such fights if they themselves were involved, or to arbitrate if others were participants. In other words, these boys and girls were becoming increasingly aware that goals change and broaden as experience grows.

In the statements of goals made by the group of parents of the first graders, there were dramatic shifts during the year from "I want him to be well liked" to, finally, "We want these children to get along with each other."

—we look at ourselves

We, the authors of this report, were well aware of our changing goals as the experiment proceeded. We can chart our progress by looking back at the outlines we prepared from time to time and at the records of our discussions.

What we are saying is that, although we talk of goal-setting as part of the process of evaluation, we do not imply that it is something to be achieved in the beginning only. Goal-setting and goal-revising are constant processes throughout a study.

—proposing solutions

The major portion of this report is in terms of suggestions which we have tried out as a means to attain goals in group living. We have presented these in many forms, from hints or hunches to relatively well defined hypotheses. We have given many more suggestions than we were able to test, in the hope that others may find them useful in further problem-solving in the area of group living.

—testing suggestions

The testing of suggestions we have carried out was on many levels. Most of our tests were made in a relatively limited situation, involving few people. Therefore, the results of the testing are primarily in terms of possibilities, rather than generalizations which we would claim to hold for all groups and all situations. We do claim, however, that through certain relatively precise tests made in some areas, we can make generalizations which we claim to be sound *for the groups with which we worked.* We hope other teachers will undertake similar tests with their groups.

From the first, as we have previously explained, we asked boys and girls to join us as co-researchers. This approach took the study out of the realm of adult observation and made it a curriculum experience of pupils. We are convinced that this procedure did much to develop attitudes, understandings, and skills in the area of good group living.

We were all partners in an exciting enterprise, none knowing the answers but all interested in developing greater understanding. When, on occasion, techniques were used the results of which were not reported to the group (such as intelligence tests or sociograms) the group accepted the situation as part of an understood plan.

We are sometimes asked, "But didn't the use of all those techniques and instruments make the boys and girls self-conscious and resistant?" Far from it; they welcomed them and suggested further use of the ones employed or devised additional ones which hadn't occurred to us.

For example, after the fourth and fifth grade group had written statements about "My best friend," they were discussing what it was about people that made for liking when one youngster said that his best friend was a grown person, and that "the things you like are different when you're a grown-up." The group members thereupon decided to discuss their relations with adults as well as with one another.

—adults, too, as friends

The list of things they liked about adult friends (several named mother and father) included the following items:

They like to play ball with you sometimes.
They are nice to me.
They treat you right.
He and I always go to the movies together.
My mother and father knows best, not me.
My mother, she is kind, gentle, loving, helpful and does things for me.
She leaves me alone, my mom.
Well, they take you places and let you have fun.
They understand me.
I like my parents because they are adults. They do anything you ask them to do.
I like mother and father because they let me have things I want. I love them and they love me.
My best friend is my aunt. She is silly. She likes me, too. She takes me places. She has good ideas and is fun. She lets me do a lot of things.
They play cards with me.
An adult tells you things that you didn't know before and things like that.
She lets me do things that I like.

This listing served as a basis for discussing "how kids get along with their mothers and dads and other grown-ups."

As an extension of one of the instruments used (Check Sheet of Opportunities, page 407), Ann asked if she could make her own check list to describe her mother. Her teacher told her to go ahead. She used the

sixteen items on the original form, and added two of her own, and this
was the result:

1. ____ finds it easy to make friends
2. ____ finds it difficult to make friends
3. ____ wishes she had more skill in getting along with people
4. _x_ well liked by most
5. ____ liked by few, but not many
6. ____ disliked by many
7. ____ shy
8. _x_ a leader
9. ____ not understood
10. ____ not so smart as most
11. ____ more intelligent than most
12. ____ prefers to be alone much of the time
13. _x_ wants to be with people most of the time
14. _x_ more interested in people than in things or ideas
15. ____ more interested in ideas or things than people
16. ____ wishes the school would give more help in how to get along with
        people
17. _x_ is truthful
18. _x_ is honest

Ann, on her own initiative, added items 17 and 18 to her original check
sheet, evidently because she felt that the omission of these items was a
serious oversight.

One youngster, evaluating the year's work, said, "I liked best the Institute Tests." Another mentioned "tests and things about ourselves." No
one mentioned dislike for use of these instruments.

—resistances

There were some minor resistances, however. When Jean, a popular
girl in the eighth grade, discovered that the physical examination was to
be given by a man doctor, she decided she would have none of it. Many
of her friends decided to follow her example. Their teacher spent much
of one day and all of the evening talking with the girls, individually and
in groups, and with their parents, describing the examination and explaining its purpose. Finally, Jean and her friends decided to give it
a try. When the examination was over, several took occasion to thank
the teacher for making it possible. As one girl stated, "I'm glad to know
I'm healthy and normal." (From this statement we think that the resistance may have been due to a fear that one is not "normal," a fear which
seems to be not unusual in adolescence.)

It might be advantageous if we could present precise objective data concerning the value of a study of this nature in terms of the changed behavior of boys and girls, teachers and parents. We have presented such evidence for certain aspects of the study. However, perhaps our most meaningful type of over-all evaluation is to be found in the thoughtful testimony of pupils, parents, and teachers as to the value of the program.

Such evaluations, either by individuals or by groups, and in terms of the total programs or of certain aspects of it, were part of a continuous process throughout the year. Evaluation of results was not something that happened only at the end of the year. However, some of the year-end statements are of particular interest.

Boys and girls gave explicit statements concerning their evaluation, as exemplified by the fourth and fifth graders who said:

"We've improved a lot in liking each other and not arguing, but sometimes I still want the biggest piece."

Implied, though less direct, were statements of other fourth and fifth graders who said:

"I liked the people in my room. I like arithmetic but not too much."

"I like the way we got to go on trips and have the mothers and different people in. And we got to have plays and group work and hobby hours and planning and having movies and having our picture taken and the way we got to choose different people for different things and the way everybody got a chance to do different things."

"I liked group work. I liked to be able to do things I wanted to do. I liked the trip to the museum. I liked to read what I wanted to read. I liked to know I was an important person as all the rest of people. I liked the way we could all be able to be a officer in group work. I liked the way all of us was some kind of a leader. I liked the way we got to be a planning leader. I liked the way we got to have plays. I liked to be able to give suggestions without everybody laughing at you."

IN SUMMARY

How to select experiences for good group living is the crux of the problems discussed in this volume. There seem to be some bench marks that can help us. It is obvious that if experiences are to be valuable and meaningful, they must be selected in terms of the maturity of the learners, their past experiences, and their purposes. Sequence appears to be of importance only as it is significant to these criteria. Balance of experience, however, assumes importance as we consider such matters as release and control, and goal-centered and non-goal-centered activity.

Learning is a unified experience. Hence, learning in the three R's is not to be overlooked as we examine learning in group living. It seems clear that, with the groups with which we worked, there was no lessening (and possibly some acceleration in the three R's) when group living was given major importance.

The processes of problem-solving can be applied to the areas of interpersonal relations as well as to any other area. In human relations, as in any other area, pupils may learn to define the problem, gather evidence, suggest solutions, test hypotheses, and evaluate the hypotheses in terms of results. In human relations, results are measured in terms of changed behavior; hence the emphasis on actual behavior rather than mere verbalizations in regard to behavior.

One measure of the effectiveness of studies of group behavior is the development of concepts. Educators know far too little about the relation of personal motivation to concept development. It is possible that children are able to understand only those motives which they have experienced. If this is true, it raises profound questions concerning the teaching of adult concepts to immature learners. This possibility suggests the need for much more research in this aspect of learning.

Evaluation of experience must be considered an integral part of the experience itself. Evaluation involves the conscious development of goals, the development of suggestions on how goals may be achieved (hypotheses), the testing of these means to achievement, and the assessing of results in terms of changed behavior. That these processes are within the possibility of even young children we are confident, and we believe that we have presented evidence to substantiate our confidence. It is also our belief that unless such evaluation takes place, no experience— and particularly no experience in group living—has achieved its full potential.

IX

Organizing to Study Group Living

In the preceding chapters we have told you much about how we operated in our study of group behavior. In this chapter we shall focus directly on the role of teachers, parents, and others in such studies, and shall tell you more of our experiences. We hope it will be understood, as we describe how we operated, that we are not suggesting that our ways of working are the only ways, or necessarily the best ways, of studying group behavior. We share our methods with you, not to suggest patterns but in the hope that our experience may be useful in helping you to find procedures appropriate to your problems. No doubt you will discover better ways of working and will find means of avoiding other mistakes.

As we have explained, the major work in this study was undertaken by three teachers, working with a first grade group, a fourth and fifth grade group, and an eighth grade group. These teachers undertook to explore group behavior, to discover the problems it involves, to test some means of studying these problems, and to examine their significance for curriculum development. Also involved, however, were a number of individuals and faculty groups or committees who worked in special areas of the study. The suggestions and recommendations in the following pages, therefore, are the result of the experiences of many people working in a variety of relationships.

WHOSE JOB IS IT?

It is our conviction, as the result of our experience, that there is more likelihood of the success of a study if *all* involved play a part—pupils, parents, teachers, administrators, and people of particular competence in certain areas—although there should be differentiation of function or role.

The Role of Teachers

As we have said before, it is our conviction that teachers, as people who can know groups of boys and girls and plan with them, are the key people in studies such as this one. It is they who must carry the major responsibility, through their day-to-day contacts with groups, through their role as group leaders, and through their observation and record-keeping. It is difficult, however, for teachers to work alone.

The Role of Pupils

We found that pupils could be able co-researchers, entering into the study of group behavior with zeal and insight. Their participation made of the study an experience in action research with children, and we feel that the results have amply justified our confidence in young people. Moreover, their work as researchers provided them, we believe, with valuable curriculum experiences.

This statement does not intend to imply that pupils carried the total load of the investigation. There were areas in which teachers operated as observers apart from the group; but when this was the case, pupils understood the purpose and gave willing cooperation.

The Role of Parents

We know that parents, deeply concerned with the welfare of their children and in a position to work with them in a wide range of situations, can be of invaluable aid in such a study. We know, too, that this same concern can cause them to wreck a research program if they misunderstand or mistrust it. No parent wants to feel that his child is a guinea pig. The very word "experiment" may cause sparks to fly. In the case of the three groups with which we worked most closely, the parents were asked to join the program from the beginning, and with all other groups parents were brought in at an early date. As soon as they understood the purpose of the study, we found parents enthusiastic co-workers. The specific ways in which they cooperated will be discussed later.

The Role of Administration

We found that the principal and the members of the central office staff could do much to facilitate or to hinder a program of investigation. Their

TEACHER GROUPS NEED TO LEARN GOOD GROUP PROCESS.

encouragement or their lack of interest made the difference between our working happily or working against discouragement. It is possible that administrators underestimate the importance of their role in this respect. We found it to be of great significance.

In many situations, particularly where teachers worked as a faculty group, the principal furnished the leadership and coordinated the study, or made it possible for such leadership to emerge from the faculty group.

One important function of an administrator in studies such as this is to act as facilitator, furnishing security, free time, materials, and suggestions for procedures, and providing for cooperation among teachers or between teachers and parents. It may be difficult for a teacher or a group of teachers to achieve these conditions unless the administrator is willing to be of help.

The Role of Other Community Members

Although we feel it to be important, we did little to work with community members other than parents of the school children. The exceptions were when people from the community were invited to open parent-teacher meetings (few came), when individuals came to classrooms on special invitation to talk to pupil groups, or when groups took trips in the community. We believe that school-community relations could be broadened considerably beyond those we were able to achieve. We plan to develop them further and hope that other teachers will experiment in this type of cooperation.

The Role of the Consultant

This study was undertaken as a cooperative venture, between an agency of an institution of higher education (Horace Mann–Lincoln Institute of School Experimentation, Teachers College, Columbia University) and several public school systems. In this study a consultant from the Institute worked with administrators, teachers, parents, and pupils in defining problems and suggesting procedures. The teachers claimed that this type of cooperation was helpful in providing them with incentive, insight, and immediate assistance in problem-solving. Perhaps it should be emphasized, however, that the problems were those growing out of the situation as seen by the people involved. The consultant served as a resource.

More specifically, in this study the consultant met with faculty groups, parent groups (or groups of teachers and parents), and pupil groups, for discussion, planning, and evaluation. Work with the three teachers who undertook the over-all approach involved meeting with the groups of teachers, with individual teachers, with parents, with pupils, with principals and supervisors. The consultant and the group cooperatively determined areas of investigation and means of study. The progress of the study was discussed at various stages of development, and the final report is published under joint authorship.

It would seem that there are certain advantages in providing for the cooperation of colleges with schools in studies such as this, or in other investigations. The representative of the college, the consultant, may bring to the situation certain skills and interpretations which may be a valuable resource to teacher-researchers.

ORGANIZING FOR STUDY

The basic groups for a study of group behavior, the classrooms, are already organized for work. The pupils of a class, their teacher or teachers, parents, and administrators can easily be organized as a working team if they care to be so organized, for the "machinery" is at hand. True, parents of a group may not be organized except through an all-school parent-teacher organization, but it has been our experience that parents of one classroom group of children welcome the opportunity to meet as a group, for they find much in common in their concern for the group experiences of their children.

An individual teacher can take the initiative in forming a team, if there is no objection from the administration, but it seems that there is much to be said in favor of groups of teachers working together. Groups may be made up of committees of interested people from one school or from several, or of faculty groups comprising the staffs of departments, of divisions, or of the entire school. The stimulation and professional support given to each teacher through these group approaches do much to commend such cooperation. There is advantage, we feel, in operating as a faculty group of a school unit. Such organization makes it possible to see as a whole, and with time, in perspective, the school living of boys and girls.

Although we feel that teachers working in groups may operate more effectively, we hasten to say that we believe that any teacher can do much to study group behavior with the pupil group with whom he is associated. And this is true, even though he may find it necessary to work without the cooperation of other teachers.

GETTING STARTED

Finding a point of initial attack in an area as broad as group behavior is sometimes difficult. Everyone may be enthusiastic about getting started, but unless there is some center of focus, the group may "ride off in all directions," thus dispersing the energies of the group and leading to frustration and disappointment.

Achieving Consensus

It is probable, we believe, that any problem area presents many aspects for initial focus, a number of equal promise. It is thus difficult or impossible to select the problem for initial attack on the basis of merit of the aspect alone. That there shall be consensus on the point of initial attack is, then, of major significance, even though other problems might hold equal promise, or, in the view of some, more promise.

There are many means of achieving this consensus. It is difficult to identify one or another as superior to others, but any one may be measured by criteria we believe to be important. It is our conviction that the means to consensus must result in a center of focus:

1. Which is understood by all.
2. Which is accepted by all.
3. Which is no threat to status or security of any.
4. To which each individual in the group can see his relationship.
5. To which each can recognize his potential contribution.

Unless these criteria are met, there is little hope, we believe, of attaining the maximum teamwork needed for a major undertaking. This means that all those involved must have a part in determining the point of initial attack. We found that various forms of preliminary studies or of problem census-taking were helpful in achieving this goal.

Preliminary Studies

Some type of preliminary study is particularly helpful when people disagree as to the nature of the problem because they have various interpretations of it. It is quite possible for a group of people to view a problem as the blind men who studied the elephant—each bringing his interpretation based on his individual experience. This may easily be the case when a faculty group composed of teachers of various experiences and backgrounds and teaching children of various ages meet to determine the problem for study. A preliminary investigation offers common experience which lends itself to common interpretation and thus to unanimous acceptance of the problem.

—surveys

There are many types of simple surveys which may give information about the school-community living of boys and girls. The following are but a few examples.

Teachers of one elementary school made a survey of the home living conditions of the boys and girls of their school. Finding that rest and cleanliness facilities in the children's homes were meager, they decided to focus on the health program of the school.

Another group of teachers made a survey of the family status of children and discovered that a large proportion came from broken homes, or from homes in which both the mother and the father were working.

A teacher in a secondary school made a study of the pupils who had left school before graduation and was able to report to the faculty the relation of drop-outs to participation in extracurricular activities, failure in courses, and other factors of personal adjustment in group living, faced by the pupils of the school.

A group of parents of children in another school went with their children to the various eating "joints" in the neighborhood and made a report of their findings in regard to where the children ate, what they ate, and how they spent their time during the noon hour.

—studies of the school program

Looking to the current school program may afford another starting place.

Teachers of a school in a metropolitan area studied the programs of their children in order to discover points of tension and relaxation, balance of rest and activity, and other factors.

A group of teachers in another school studied the school program in order to discover the opportunities offered to children for self-expression through language and the arts.

Teachers of still another school studied the number and kinds of daily interruptions of classroom activities caused by announcements, messengers, drives, campaigns, and other factors.

Studies of Children

Though the studies above are indirectly studies of children, a preliminary step may involve a direct study of children through observation, or with the use of such instruments as personality tests or sociometric techniques.

Teachers of an elementary school, after using the California Test of Personality, decided on the basis of their findings to focus on a study of means to develop a sense of self-direction for the children in their classroom.

In another school, teachers studying the children's leisure-time activities found that some spent as much as eight hours a day at the movies on Saturdays and Sundays. With the help of parents and children, they then surveyed the community in order to discover the recreational opportunities for boys and girls of various ages.

As implied above, several types of study may be undertaken simultaneously, or one may lead to another, as was the case when the study of leisure-time activity led to a survey of recreational opportunities.

Getting into Action

We think it is important to point out some possible dangers in the use of preliminary investigations. Groups may become so intrigued with the study that they cease to regard it as a means to better program development and it becomes an end in itself. This danger is particularly acute when a group launches into a study of children. Such a study is, of itself, one of such breadth that it may be difficult to move from it to the action phases of the research program. True, the study may cause teachers individually to effect changes in their classroom procedure, but unless teachers as a group determine what changes are to be made, and how, the program rather than being a group venture breaks up into individual studies.

Moreover, a preliminary study which is too extensive and too time-consuming may lead to a sense of frustration. We often hear teachers say, "We do a lot of talking, but nothing ever happens." We feel it important that the group get into the action phase of the program soon after initiating their group endeavor. This means that one of two things must happen. One, the preliminary study should be so circumscribed that it may be terminated, and the results studied and appropriate plans for action undertaken, within a brief span of time. For example, plans were developed for the study of what children do with their noon-hour recess, the survey was made by parents, and plans for providing a lunch-room and supervised noon-hour play were initiated, all within one day. The study of children's use of leisure time and plans for a classroom program to help children find means of recreation other than the movies were developed within a span of one month.

Another possibility is to plan for some type of action during the progress of the preliminary study. Teachers in one school initiated a rest program for children in the primary grades, as a result of their early studies of the children while continuing a longer-range program of child study.

Taking a Problem Census

The taking of a problem census might be considered a type of study, but it is treated separately here to distinguish between studies which eventuate in objective data and those which, as in a problem census, pool the judgments of the researchers. The procedure is to collect from individuals their opinions of the problems in the situation, and then, after group discussion, to arrive at a consensus in regard to the area most suitable for initial attack because it is most pressing, or most prevalent, or lends itself most easily to immediate study and action. This census may be made by teachers, pupils, parents and other community members, or by a group which combines these categories of people.

Ideally, the group making the problem census should include all those involved. However, this is not always practicable. Taking the census and arriving at consensus as to the point of departure is an extremely complex and difficult process. Unless there is high rapport and wide experience in working together, the process may be too difficult for a group representing a diversity of interests. This does not mean that all may not have a part to play, or a contribution to make. The sequence of census-taking of the teachers in this investigation may serve as an example. First, the teachers met to determine the problems of human relations which they might consider in their study. They then asked parents to indicate the problems they considered to be important and the goals of human relations they held for their children. At the same time, teachers took a problem census with children, again in the form of goals in human relations. Later in the year, the pupil groups invited parents and other community members to meet with them in a discussion of youth-parent relations; in other words, to conduct a problem census of problems within a particular segment of the larger area. Thus, we believe, the principle of involvement was preserved although there was consideration for the particular contribution of each, achieved within the setting most favorable for each.

We should like to repeat here a statement made earlier: We are convinced that it is of major importance to find a center of focus understood by all, accepted by all, and to which each individual in the group can see his relationship and to which he can recognize the contribution he can make. Obviously, no quick listing, voting, and tabulation can achieve these results. Each problem presented deserves careful consideration. The process of arriving at consensus cannot be hurried. If it should be hurried, it may be spurious.

—of teachers

We would hope, eventually, in every case, to provide a broad base for the problem census. But since teachers are the people who must carry the burden of the research program, it is their problem census which must be given primary consideration.

—of parents

As we discussed earlier, parents, meeting as parent groups, may conduct a census independent of that taken by other groups. Parents of all three groups in this study met to discuss the problems in human relations which they felt their children meet, and the objectives they held for their children. It is interesting to note that the problems stated by parents parallel those stated by teachers, although they are less comprehensive.

One group of parents and teachers, accustomed to joint action, had no difficulty in arriving at consensus. These people had a long history of meeting together to discuss common problems. It is probable that parents and teachers in general see eye to eye more frequently than is realized, and that joint meetings could be arranged with greater freedom and frequency than is now usual.

—of pupils

One teacher of a junior high school group conducted a census of problems in inter-personal relations as seen by boys and girls in the seventh and eighth grades, and arrived at a series of problem areas which served as a basis for both course content and teacher-group consideration. Teachers of another junior high school conducted a census through the question, "How can we make this school a better place in which to live?" Another group, working with younger children, conducted a census through the questions, "What do you like best at school?" and "What do you like least or dislike most?" The areas identified by boys and girls served as the basis for focusing the point of attack by teachers.

—of common problems

It may seem that there has not been sufficient distinction in the above discussion between the process of problem census and that of reaching consensus. It is our belief that the two processes should be closely related. As we have said earlier, the people involved should have a sense of commonality of problems. Although a problem census of groups not involved in the planning may serve to broaden the vision of the planning group, we believe it should be used with extreme caution, for there is nothing more frustrating than being asked to state one's problems, and then find that nothing has been done about them. We feel strongly, therefore, that those who are asked to state problems should be in on the decision concerning which problems are to be attacked.

Although there is danger of seeming repetitious, we want to re-emphasize the importance of moving quickly from study or discussion to action. Whether attempting to reach a focus for initial attack through a preliminary study or through problem census, there is grave danger of bogging down in the focusing process. Moving from the process of focusing to the process of action is crucial, and cannot be delayed too long if frustration and disappointment are to be avoided.

PROBLEM DEFINITION

Even after finding a center of focus through preliminary study or problem census, there may be a further difficulty in reaching agreement on what to do about the problem. The problem may seem too big or too small.

When the Problem Seems Too Big

Having successfully reached consensus as to the focus of initial attack on the problem, there is still the problem of knowing how to proceed. This is particularly true when the problem looms too large in area to be manageable. The following example may serve to indicate a way of proceeding when the problem area is too big for people to "get their teeth" into it.

Teachers and parents of one elementary school made a study of the home status of pupils, and reached consensus that the question to be answered was: "What can we do for children from broken homes?" This question was too general for the group to know where to begin. Members of the group, parents and teachers, took the following steps.

1. They asked, "Why is this a problem?" They made a further study of children, and decided this was a problem because the children from broken homes were insecure and tense. Further, they discovered that children from such homes had inadequate opportunity for after-school play, for supervised lunch-hour activities, and for rest. As one teacher stated, after studying the survey of use of time, "Why, they have no time or place to yell." Incidentally, the study of children from broken homes was soon expanded to include almost all children of the community, as they came from homes which were crowded and lacked facilities for privacy, rest, and recreation.

2. Starting with specific problems indicated by the original survey and

certain subsequent substudies, the group planned for and provided a lunchroom, rest periods during the school day, and supervised lunch-hour and after-school play.

3. The group undertook further study of child development in general, and of their particular children as individuals and groups, to determine how to provide a sense of security and to release tensions.

4. The group studied its current school program in order to identify the school experiences which were tension-creating, and planned means for eliminating such experiences.

5. Finding that there were social experiences of importance to children which, however, were not provided for in the current curriculum, the group made a further study of needs identified in the original survey and in the study of the groups, and revised the social studies curriculum in order to meet these deficiencies. The group gave time to re-thinking the type of total school experiences which needed to be provided for children as individuals and groups if there was to be satisfying group living.

Thus, starting with a broad problem of what to do for children from broken homes, the group began to identify component parts of the problem and to cope with them one by one—by providing rest, a lunchroom, and after-school play. Further, the school offering in curriculum content was re-examined and revised in terms of the needs identified.

When the Problem Seems Too Small

Sometimes consensus is reached concerning a problem which some might consider too small or of insufficient significance to merit study. Frequently the people who feel that the problem is "too small" are the status leaders of the group—the principal, the supervisor, or the consultant—who are sorely tempted to use the influence of their status to alter the decision of the group. We are firmly convinced that arriving at consensus by the group is of far greater significance than *anyone's* opinion of the importance of the problem. An attempt to shift the problem because it seems insignificant to a status leader violates the criteria stated earlier—that the problem be understood, that it be accepted, that each see his relation to it, and that each see the contribution he can make to its solution. No matter how insignificant the problem may seem, if it has been arrived at through consensus, we believe that it should be the point of departure. For example, one school group decided by consensus that the major problem in group living in the school was that of the tardiness of the pupils. There were those who felt that this was an indication of a symptom rather than of a major problem, but the group as a whole did not agree. The group attacked the problem of tardiness, and before long, as they studied reasons for tardiness, they were concerned with community living and the school program. Thus, no matter how insignificant a problem may seem, we believe that it must represent consensus of the group and, further, we are sure that any point of departure will lead a group into more significant consideration of fundamental problems if the problem is pursued in terms of the insights and convictions of group members.

As we examine this problem of getting started, and explore means of determining a point of departure, such as preliminary studies and a problem census, perhaps it should be pointed out that determining the focus and delimiting the problem are merely first steps, though significant ones. It is of major importance that the people involved shall see themselves in relation to the problem. This does not mean that the point of departure or the early steps necessarily determine all subsequent action. The shifting of problems, their expansion and spread, may be a sign of growth. In fact, in most situations, we feel that there is something wrong if the problem does not shift with growth and increased insight on the part of the group.

MAKING A STEP-WISE PLAN

After determining the point of initial departure we believe it is important that the group see specific procedures and direction in their further plans. We give two situations as examples.

A group of teachers determined by consensus that their major problem was that of the tardiness of pupils. They set up the following plan and followed it step by step.

1. Determine why it (tardiness) is a problem (other than that it annoys the teacher!). The teachers decided that the problem was real because the children were developing unfortunate habits which were detrimental to the general social adjustment of individuals as well as to the group living in the school.

2. Members of the group asked: "To what extent does the problem exist?" They made a study to determine how many children were tardy and how often. They discovered that certain chronic cases had colored

the thinking of group members, but that the occurrence of tardiness was sufficiently widespread to be of concern.

3. Members of the group asked: "What are the causes of this behavior (tardiness)?" They checked with the tardy pupils, their brothers and sisters, and their parents. The school social worker helped by making studies of home situations. A number of revealing facts came to light. For example, there were more pupils tardy on foggy days than on bright days. Investigation showed that many pupils had no clocks in their homes and depended on one on a department store tower some blocks distant to show the time. The tower could not be seen on foggy days. Children's responses included statements such as these: "I didn't get up in time. My mother wasn't home, and I went to bed late last night." "My mother had to iron my clothes. Both my dresses were in the wash." Studies of special cases revealed home responsibilities prior to school time, health deficiencies, and immaturity and low mentality accompanied by lack of time-sense.

4. The group asked itself: "What procedures can we try in our attempt to lessen or eliminate the difficulties?" The problem was discussed in classes; the social worker and the teacher discussed the problem with parents. Several suggestions were made and tried out; for example, jobs which held prestige with the group were assigned for the first thing in the morning.

Having taken these steps, the group met to review outcomes. They found that there was considerable decrease in tardiness, but, more important perhaps, the teachers, having learned about children's problems and needs, felt that tardiness was no longer of major concern. They shifted their interest to revising some basic aspects of the school program to meet the needs they had discovered through their study of the problem of tardiness.

In another school the teachers, having given the California Test of Personality, decided by consensus that the major problem was how to help children develop a sense of responsibility. Following are the steps they planned:

1. Teachers will list the names of pupils who in their judgment have best developed a sense of responsibility, and of those who have least done so.

2. For each pupil named above as high or low in a sense of responsibility, teachers will make brief comments concerning his characteristic behavior.

3. Teachers will compare the comments concerning behavior they have made in step 2 (above) and will make a list of behaviors which characterize children who demonstrate a sense of responsibility or lack of it. Thus there is developed a catalogue of items under each of the headings: "A child who demonstrates the lack of a sense of responsibility is one who . . . ." and "A child who demonstrates a sense of responsibility is one who . . . ."

4. Teachers will list the types of situations in which a child is able to practice the behavior characteristics listed in 3 (above).

TABLE 22

SAMPLE CHECK LIST OF OPPORTUNITIES FOR RESPONSIBILITY

Names (listed in order of demonstrated sense of responsibility)	1. Hall Monitor	2. Milk Monitor	3. Ball Monitor	4. Student Council	5. Errands	20. Color Guard	21. Class Officers	22. Library Assistant	23. Bulletin Board Assistant	24. Hospitality Committee
1. Philip	x	x	x		x	x	x		x	
2. Bernice		x		x	x		x	x	x	
3. Marie		x			x		x	x		x
4. Victor	x		x	x		x			x	
5. Ralph	x		x	x			x			x
6. Frieda		x	x		x			x	x	
7. Rhoda	x				x		x	x		
8. Norman	x		x			x			x	
9. Vera		x			x					x
10. Martin			x		x	x		x	x	
31. Louise					x				x	
32. Allen					x	x				
33. Alice										x
34. Charles								x		
35. Gerald					x					
36. Rose		x			x					
37. Gilbert						x				
38. Mary										x
39. Albert			x							
40. Leonard					x					

5. Using as a check sheet the list developed in step 4, teachers will check the opportunities provided for each child to practice taking responsibility.

Table 21 (page 307) is a sample of the use of this check sheet. Pupils' names on the left are listed in order of the teachers' estimate of the sense of responsibility of the child, the ten "most responsible" heading the list and the ten "least responsible" at the end (see step 2, above). The opportunities for practicing responsibility as listed in step 5 (above) are across the top of the page. In most cases, teachers assigned pupils to these activities. Checking each child in terms of the opportunities offered him gave dramatic evidence that "to him who hath shall be given." In other words, teachers realized that they were providing many opportunities to those pupils whom they considered capable, but giving very few chances to the less able to gain skills in taking responsibility. Incidentally, developing the list of situations for practicing responsibility offered a chance to teachers for shared experience, so that each saw possibilities beyond those of his own list. The joint listing they compiled was broader than that of any one teacher. The project also brought to light the degree to which teachers were dominating their classroom situations, and plans were made for ways of working that would allow for more pupil participation in determining individual and group action.

With the evidence before them, teachers readily agreed that there should be wider spread of opportunity for responsibility. In fact, it seemed logical to give additional opportunities to those pupils who had little skill in taking responsibility. The teachers planned more activities, such as group planning and committee work, and planned that *every* child should have a chance to participate.

To supplement the sequence of steps above there were a series of concomitant studies:

1. Teachers listed the situations in which children failed to demonstrate a sense of responsibility, and attempted to discover *why* in each case. After developing hunches as to why, they discussed means to correct the situation. For example, it was decided that Mary shows no sense of responsibility because her older sister "babies" her, never giving her a chance to act for herself. It was decided that the teacher discuss this with Mary, her parents, and the older sister in an attempt to work out a program of independent living for Mary.

2. Teachers observed children in an attempt to identify factors related

PUPIL-TEACHER RELATIONS ARE IMPORTANT.

to a sense of responsibility. For example, they asked, "Are children who show a lack of a sense of responsibility those who fail to secure personal satisfaction or group recognition for classroom achievement? If so, how can satisfaction and recognition be provided?"

3. Teachers and parents discussed how home-school cooperation might provide suitable opportunities to children for taking responsibility.

4. Teachers discussed with boys and girls the behavior which demonstrates a sense of responsibility, why it is difficult sometimes to accept the responsibility expected of them, and what can be done about it.

The program was evaluated through a recheck on a form, such as that used in Table 21, in order to discover whether there was provision for wider participation; and teachers examined their records, such as anecdotes and case studies, to see if there was evidence of any change in children's behavior. It was difficult to achieve precise measurement through these methods, but teachers were convinced that progress had been made. Perhaps of even greater significance than such measures, however, was the change in point of view of the teachers, who as a result of their study, decided there was a need to examine wider aspects of living in the school and launched forth into a revision of the social studies experiences being offered to the boys and girls.

[309]

We believe that certain principles of planning may be seen in these illustrations:

1. The development of certain specific steps gives a sense of security and direction. This sense of security is of particular importance to those who have had limited experience in problem-solving in group situations.

2. Specific plans give everyone a chance to make a contribution.

3. When everyone follows the same steps, there is opportunity for common experience, sharing, and broadening vision, though supplementary studies offer a play of individual initiative and a recognition of the various competences of people in the group.

EVALUATING THE PROGRAM

Evaluation of the program, as well as its planning, is a cooperative job and must involve all those who have worked on the program. We have described earlier (Chapter VIII) some of the means used by pupils in evaluating the program in terms of their progress. Teachers, too, evaluated the program, usually in cooperation with parents and pupils, but sometimes independently. It is this independent evaluation by teachers which we report in the following sections.

Evaluating Pupil Experience

Each of the teachers engaged in this study prepared at various intervals statements of their judgment as to the advantages and disadvantages of such a study in terms of pupil experience.

The teacher of the fourth and fifth grades summarizes her final judgments as follows:

> The children have gotten from this study many things which have been of value. They have benefited greatly from program changes which have given them chances to have larger blocks of time and to plan for things which they consider important. They have been able to improve their group living through the solving of problems which are meaningful to them. They have had more variation in their experiences than they had ever had before.
>
> They have been able to manage a great many of their affairs which they had not been able to do before. They have learned how to carry on the group process from actually having experience working in various sized groups and committees. There have been many more chances for leadership. Children have learned to get things down on paper and to think through group planning in a logical manner, beginning with "What do we do first?" and leading to "Let's get into action" and ending with "How did we do?"

They have learned to have goals and purposes for what they do and have found the importance of delegation of responsibility in getting jobs done. They have learned to use unanimous consent more often in deciding things. They have been able to work in groups on things which they have chosen because they are interested in solving problems in that area.

They have learned to be quite skillful in evaluating their own processes. They have learned to respect opinions and ideas of other people. They have found that it is a good idea to capitalize on special abilities of children in the group in order to have better quality in their activities. They have learned to budget their time so that they can make the best possible use of their time together, and yet have a balance of rest and activity. They have learned that everybody can do something well.

Values to Parents

This same teacher looks back on many experiences in which parents and teachers have cooperated and discusses values to parents:

The parents have had an active part in our study from the beginning. I interviewed each parent in order to find out more about the background of the child.

We had parent meetings at which we discussed children's goals, children's behavior, etc.

The mothers saw to it that each child had physical examinations and immunizations.

Parents gave many interesting verbal reports regarding the planning and activities that the children have been undertaking as a result of this work. One incident was about a child planning with her mother for a dinner with her violin teacher, and another about children working out a community library this summer and lending books to their friends.

Some of our parents even went so far as to keep anecdotal records on some of the children.

One mother who started observing her child objectively recorded her behavior. She started by listing affirmative and negative behavior traits. After I had a conference with her she decided to try to go even further and write down exactly what happened in anecdotal form. Many of the parents have been enthusiastic about our work. One mother this year insisted that we not only have group meetings but that parents continue to have conferences with the teacher in order to take up the individual problems of various pupils.

Values to Teachers

Teachers have been enthusiastic in expressing their personal reactions to programs of investigation in the area of group behavior. Of particular interest have been their "before" and "after" responses to certain questions.

—schedules

Elementary though it may seem, the very matter of scheduling may give important clues. Periodically throughout the study each teacher recorded her current daily schedule, and the schedule she would like to employ if it were possible. Inevitably there was considerable disparity between the two. If these teachers are any true sample of the usual, then teachers feel that there is more they would like to do than they dare try. Many obstacles stand in the way of change. Fear of supervisors and administrators cannot be underestimated, even when people in these positions profess a willingness for experimentation. And fear of the opinion of fellow teachers may be a serious barrier. When a teacher is sensitive to their opinions, the "extra work" inevitably involved in undertaking investigation may be a barrier to rapport with the others. No teacher wants to incur the ill will of other teachers by seeming to be an "eager beaver." It is possible that such inter-personal relations are more influential than most curriculum workers care to admit.

But vision, too, may be a determinant of what a teacher wants to do. For example, there is the teacher who early in the study said she would like to have more "outside people as visitors in the classroom," and by the end of the year of working toward better group relations claimed a much broader interest, to develop "better adult-youth relations in the community." Mere verbalization may not convey the deep shift in conviction from merely "having visitors" to "developing better relations," but the growth in vision was clear to an observer.

—changes made

Of more significance than scheduling are the actual changes in the program as a result of studies of group behavior. Statements by teachers concerning these include the following:

I have provided more flexible organization within the group, with subgroups and committees. As a result of this change, I feel that boys and girls are more able to take responsibility, to get along together, and to make suitable use of materials.

Since starting to make use of anecdotes, sociograms, and other devices, I have become more sensitive to youngsters and their needs, and consequently I handle them better.

Meeting the mothers has given an insight into youngsters' lives, and I have learned to know youngsters better.

—learning

Even teachers of experience have expressed appreciation of what they have learned while engaged in a program of investigation in group behavior. To quote from some:

> I have always been interested in individual reactions, but I have learned to look for the "whys" of behavior, and to give more attention to *group* reactions.

> I have learned the fun of exploring and experimenting.

> I have learned that teaching is more interesting when one knows more about the group. Problems become challenges.

> I have learned to what a great extent a group can handle its own affairs if it is given an opportunity.

> I have learned that a group can be constructively critical of its own behavior.

> I have learned to feel greater skill in teaching; more competence in working with children.

And perhaps less explicit, but more expressive than any of the other comments, is the statement of a teacher of thirteen years' experience: "I am just beginning to learn how to teach."

IN SUMMARY

In this chapter we have focused directly on the role of teachers, parents, pupils, administrators, and others in studies of group experience.

The basic unit for study, the classroom, is easily organized for work through the teacher, the pupils, and the parents of boys and girls in the room. An individual teacher can take the initiative for forming such a working group, but there is much value in creating teams of teachers, who may stimulate and support one another.

Finding a point of initial attack is not easy. Consensus of opinion concerning the point of attack is essential. Means to consensus must result in a center of focus which is understood by all; which is accepted by all; which is no threat to the status or security of any; to which each individual in the group can see his relationship; and to which each can recognize his potential contribution.

Unless these criteria are met, there is little hope, we believe, of attaining maximum teamwork needed for a major undertaking.

Preliminary studies, such as surveys, studies of the school program and studies of children, may be a definite aid in focusing the area for investigation. A problem census, whether developed by teachers, parents, pupils, or others, or by various combinations of these people, will help in reaching consensus.

Problem definition is no easy job, even after consensus has been reached. Sometimes the problem is too big and needs further analysis before it can become a practical basis for attack. Sometimes the problem may seem to be too small for consideration. We are convinced that no problem is too small. If it is attacked conscientiously, its significance is sure to grow as people see its many facets.

Having reached consensus and defined the problem, it is desirable next to determine a step-wise plan. Such a plan is important, whether the problem be large, or small, and should meet the criteria stated for determining a center of focus.

Although team research creates the most favorable atmosphere for the study of group behavior, any individual teacher who is sincerely convinced of the importance of investigation in this area can do much to study his group and to create programs in terms of group needs.

Evaluation of teacher growth in such studies is of major importance. Some significant leads to such evaluation may be found in sincere answers to periodic questions, such as: "What is your current class schedule?" "What would you feel to be the ideal class schedule for your group?" "What changes have you made since undertaking this study?" "What have you learned from this study?" Not least among the many aspects of evaluation is the satisfaction felt by teachers, their increased vision, and their renewed enthusiasm.

X

Parents as Co-Researchers

SCENE I—*A Parents' Meeting*

MRS. B: I want my child to learn to read and write.

MRS. T: I do, too, but I want him to learn to get along with people, also.

MRS. B: I agree, of course.

MR. S: I think we all want both. Let's list them both, "reading and writing" and "getting along together," as goals.

SCENE II—*A Parents-Children Panel*

BOBBY: We of this group feel that boys and girls our age should be allowed to stay out until seven-thirty in the evening.

MRS. R: Does that mean you run out after supper without helping to wash the dishes?

BARBARA: We didn't discuss that, but maybe if we helped with the dishes we could stay out until eight o'clock.

MRS. F: But it's dark by then in winter. Do you think you should be allowed to stay out after dark?

We could go on with scenes III, IV, V, and many others in which parents cooperated with us in our study of group behavior, working with one another, with teachers, and with the boys and girls—working as co-researchers.

We consider work with parents an important aspect of cooperative research for several reasons. First—we repeat this—cooperative research implies the involvement of all who have a stake in the outcome, and certainly parents have a major stake in the educational programs developed for their children. Second, we found that parents could contribute significantly to the thinking of the group. Their statements of goals, analyses of situations, and suggestions for action added much to our study. Many aspects, such as the investigation of home-school re-

[315]

PARENTS, TEACHERS, AND PUPILS CAN HELP ONE ANOTHER.

lations and lunch hour activities of children, could not have been studied without them. Third, the enthusiasm of parents for what we were trying to accomplish did much to bolster the morale of hard-working teachers. It also gave prestige to the program in the eyes of the administration. This was the positive aspect of their cooperation. Stated negatively, we know how easy it is for a group of parents who don't understand what is going on to wreck a program of investigation.

No series of reports can tell the whole story of such cooperation of parents, teachers, and children; so as you read the material in the following pages, we hope you will see between the lines and catch glimpses of the sincere interest of teachers and parents, their tact and insight, the time they spent, the immediate benefit to children, and the long-range furthering of research.

The first report we present here tells of the work of one teacher in organizing a parents' group and working with mothers and fathers as individuals and as groups. The second is the report of a teacher committee on the work of a school staff in cooperating with parents. And the third is a description of a program given to demonstrate to the public the work of the school and prepared cooperatively by parents and teachers of one school.

[316]

PARENTS OF A FIRST GRADE

In the school described here, there was a whole-school parent-teacher organization but no meetings of parents of children of any one group. The teacher of this first grade group felt that she needed the cooperation of the parents of the children with whom she worked, so she set out to organize such a group.

Getting Started

Early in the year the teacher and her group invited parents to a meeting at the school. The following note was mimeographed, signed by each child, and taken to his parents.

October 1

Dear Parents:

Please come to our little program Friday at 2:45 p.m. We would like to explain to you what we are doing and what we would like to do throughout the year.

We would like for you to stay for a short discussion after school.

Someone will take care of me on the grounds while you meet.

Your child,

_____

Teacher

The next meeting was called by the teacher and the principal. The following note was sent to each parent:

October 7

Dear Mrs. ——————:

The discussion group of mothers of children of the 1B class will have their second meeting Friday, October 18, at 2:45 p.m. We shall follow the same procedure as at last meeting. We shall meet with the children at 2:45, and dismiss the children at 3:45 for organized play on the playground while the mothers remain for a meeting in the room.

We appreciated very much the fine response to our last meeting and are grateful for your attendance. Will you please come again?

We believe that it is very helpful to your child and to our whole school program.

(Signed) ———————

Teacher

_____

Principal

At these two initial meetings, parents discussed their goals for their children, organized with a parent chairman and secretary, and planned for individual parent-teacher conferences. Each parent was given an opportunity to sign, on a schedule prepared by the teacher, for a half-hour conference to talk over his child's progress and plans.

Subsequent meetings of the group were called by the parent chairman of the group. The following is an example of the notices sent by the chairman.

First Grade Discussion Group

THURSDAY, JANUARY 16   ANOTHER OBSERVATION MEETING, to see the children in action, demonstrating their progress under the special education[1] plan in Grade 1.

The topic to be discussed is vital to your understanding of what is being done in Grade 1.

(Signed) ———————————
                                                           Chairman

Parents expressed interest in study as well as discussion. A parent committee was charged with preparing a selected bibliography of helpful material available in the nearby public library. This bibliography accompanied the notice of one of the meetings. Perhaps we should add that parents in this community were not highly educated. Few had been to college, the majority had had one to four years of high school, and some had not completed even their elementary school education.

The bibliography included easy-reading articles from periodicals, such as *Parents Magazine, Hygeia,* and the *New York Times Magazine,* and bore such titles as "Getting Them Off to School," "Little Guests Can Be Pests," "When Parents Disagree," and "This Matter of Spoiling." The bibliography was accompanied by directions for reaching the neighborhood library and how to obtain materials.

Physical Examination

In January, through the cooperation of the central office of the school system, thorough physical examinations by a physician were given to the boys and girls in the three groups with which we worked intensively. (We were interested in investigating the relationship of health to group behavior.) Each child of the first grade group was accompanied to the examination by at least one parent. Some parents came at great incon-

---

[1] This refers to the study of group behavior. Parents felt that this study was providing something "special" for their children.

venience, as, for example, the mother who had her much needed pay check cut because of this absence from work.

The parent, the teacher, and the school nurse were present during the physical examination. The teacher kept a record of all suggestions given by the physician.

Parent Conferences

As might be expected, not all parents attended the meetings. The matter of attendance was particularly difficult in this school community as many of the mothers worked. To give parents who had not attended meetings an opportunity to schedule conferences, the teacher sent out the following letter. Note the evening hours suggested for those who were not free during the day.

December 31

Dear Parents:

I have had an opportunity to have a conference with almost all of the parents of children in my room. As yet I have not had the opportunity to talk with you.

Will you please see me or call me at my home, No. 7654, between 6 and 8 P.M. and I shall be glad to arrange for such a conference when and where it will be convenient to you.

We believe that such conferences with parents promote more growth on the part of their children.

(Signed) ——————————

Teacher, Grade 1

We presented earlier some of the teacher's reports of conferences. Other examples follow:

Mrs. Albert came to talk with me about Donald. She was very, very timid and shy. She said she would come to the discussion meetings. She was happy that Donald was doing so well. . . . She said Donald had been after her to come to school. . . . She said Donald played with older people more than children his own age. She said her husband's brother (about 20) played with him a lot but that she would try to see that Donald played with children his own age. . . .

Sometimes one of the parents came alone, sometimes they came together, and sometimes both came, but separately. This last was the case in conferences with Peter's parents, who were separated. The father took his day off to be with his son.

September 3. Peter's mother (Mrs. Charles) brought him to school the first day. She asked to have Peter bring his lunch because she works. She said the charges at the nursery were more than she could afford.

December 4. Peter's father brought him to school. I made an appointment to see him the next day.

December 5. Peter's father and I looked over Peter's records. He seemed much interested. He said Peter disliked school and was always offering excuses or trying to fib about not having to go . . . I recommended that he be given more opportunity to play with children his age. Mr. Charles, Mrs. Charles, and I are making a special effort to get at the bottom of his reason for disliking school.

January 2. Found a note on my desk asking me to call Mr. Charles. He said Peter had been sick again and wanted to know how he might help him with school work. I told him not to worry; that we were doing a good deal of individual work and that I would give him special attention when he came back, and that we should be interested only in his getting well and strong now. He thanked me and seemed pleased that we took so much interest in the youngster. He said to please call him at any time I felt the need to see him.

January 9. (6:45 P.M.) I was invited to Peter's house to see his mother. When I got there Peter and his grandmother, but not his mother, were at home. Peter showed me a book he and his father had made. Peter's mother came in saying she had had to work late at the office. . . . Peter's mother seemed affectionate to him, kissed him goodnight, but she said she felt Peter had "just been lazy" and that was why he was slow in walking and talking. She said he was often quite proud of himself for a minor accomplishment and would tell her about it when she came home. . . .

April 3. Went to report to Peter's grandmother (she takes care of Peter while his mother is at work). She talked about Peter being so much like his father (daydreaming). She said she felt this was the reason for the parents' separation.

   She asked about Peter's milk. She said she had sent 25¢ before spring vacation and again on Tuesday.

   The next morning I looked at my record and found Peter had not turned in either quarter. When I asked him what he had done with them he said, "I don't know," and smiled. . . .

April 7. Mrs. Baker, the landlady where Peter lives, called to ask about Peter's progress and to ask if it would do much harm if he had to change schools. She said she expected to start eviction charges but wanted to know that it wouldn't do serious harm to Peter.

April 17. A note was sent from the office asking me to call Mr. Charles, Peter's father. He told me Peter was in the hospital . . . He had bought Peter several pre-primers but he seemed worried about his spelling. Said he believed I had made a "Christian" out of Peter: that he could read better than he expected.

April 18. Peter's father stopped by after school. I talked to him awhile, and in the course of the conversation, asked him about the eviction. He said it had been taken to court . . . but he knew a fellow, so got by with a box of cigars.

Sometimes conferences can be initiated almost casually. Though not planned, they may be very significant.

October 10. I saw Mr. Roberto in the hall helping Don put on his coat and overshoes. I spoke to him and he asked about Don. I told him Don was very quick but that it seemed hard for him to relax . . . He thought that perhaps they should cut out listening to the radio. I said I thought it would be worth trying. (It seems he listens to the radio almost continuously.)

December 4. Mrs. Roberto (who had come to school for a meeting) and I went to her home for a conference. Mr. Roberto was there. We looked over Don's records and work. Mr. Roberto is very proud of Don . . . His mother and father are quite interested in their children and live with and for them. She supervises their play and keeps an eye on them at all times . . . They are Catholics and she says they are criticized terribly for sending their children to public school. She says she feels she can give them their religious training at home and by taking them to church . . . She says Don can sit for long periods of time working on things but that his smaller brother often disturbs him . . . Mrs. Roberto is not interested in pushing him but likes to find things for him to do.

December 30. I was invited to see Don's Christmas tree. Father, mother, and kindergarten brother were all there. Don and his brother looked at books quietly as we (adults) talked . . . Evidently both Mr. and Mrs. Roberto enjoy their children and give them much time. . . .

These reports represent but brief excerpts from the records of three children. The teacher kept extensive records of parent conferences, using a separate folder for each child.

At first glance, such records might seem to be highly individual in nature, and to have little relation to group living. It will be recalled, however, that this teacher reached the conclusion that the best means to good group living for young children was the providing for release of tension and for opportunity for practice of social skills. Through parent conferences she was able to identify tension-creating situations, sometimes working out with parents solutions for better home programs for children, as well as to plan for what was necessary in the school program.

The same dual purposes were achieved in the area of opportunity to develop social skills.

Who can miss the range of individual differences in background represented by even these few excerpts, and the special problems they represent to the teacher who is trying to create good group living for forty-two first graders:

> "Mrs. Albert . . . was very very shy."
> "Donald plays with older people."
> "She works" (and can't get his lunch).
> "They were separated."
> "She expected to start eviction charges. . . ."
> "Mr. Roberto is very proud of Don. . . ."
> "They enjoy their children. . . ."

What teacher can ever again be the same in her attitude toward children and the means she uses to create good group living after learning something of their background?

This teacher of young children feels that with youngsters this age the understanding of the teacher, leading to better provision for group needs, may be the most important factor in developing better group living. Further, she feels that parent conferences are an important factor in developing such understanding. Thus *individual* parent-teacher conferences were an important aspect of the *group* program.

Planning Play Programs

At parents' meetings as well as during individual parent-teacher conferences there was considerable discussion of the progress of boys and girls in group living. It was found that in this crowded apartment-house area there was little or no opportunity for children to have free play time together after school hours. The school provided a playground supervisor after school, but he was occupied largely in directing games with older boys and girls.

Teachers and parents felt that some additional supervision for younger children was in order. The teacher agreed to stay after school to supervise such a play period once a week, and a notice to this effect was sent all parents, with a slip to be signed if they wished their children to participate in the program. The teacher felt so strongly that this experience was important for the boys and girls in her group that she was willing to donate her time to this activity. One might wish that there were extra compensation for such extra expenditure of time and effort. The teacher expressed her feeling as follows: "Of course I wish there could be some adjustment of my schedule or salary, but, honestly, this time does so much to make my teaching easier that I guess it's worth it."

Many parents took advantage of this opportunity for play experience for their children. Both parents and children appreciated the chance for after-school play. The teacher felt it was contributing to better group living.

At a parents' meeting in late May, parents raised the question of how this play program could be continued through the summer months. The mothers decided to carry it on themselves, even though the teacher would not be available to help. As a result of the pool of opinion, the following provision for play was made and reported to the parent group.

Summer Playground Schedule

The school grounds will have supervised play for all the children of our school from 12:30 until 8:30 P.M. during the summer months, every day except Sunday. However, the mothers of our Discussion Group feel the need for special attention to our smaller children. Therefore, we will try to have a mother from this group on the playground from 9:00 to 11:00 A.M. and 3:00 to 5:00 P.M. every Tuesday and Thursday of each vacation week.

PLAYING TOGETHER IS A WAY TO LEARN SOCIAL SKILLS.

Evaluation

By March it was felt desirable to take stock of the program in a some-what more formal way. The following questionnaire was presented and discussed at one of the meetings that month. Those present answered it during the meeting, and the form was sent home to parents who had not attended. (Responses are reported on the form below.)

EVALUATION QUESTIONNAIRE

We wish you would respond to this questionnaire as a means of evaluat-ing our work. This will help us in formulating plans for the future.

	Very Valuable	Of Little Value	No Value
1. Parent Conferences with Teachers	23	1	0

Would you be willing to let these conferences take the place of a grade card this first period (6 weeks)?   Yes *16*   No *8*
Second period   Yes *13*   No *8*
Semester marking   Yes *11*   No *9*

	Very Valuable	Of Little Value	No Value
2. Parent Study Group Discussion	19	2	0
3. Observation of Children at Work in the Classroom	20	1	0
4. After-School Play	18	2	0

Do you think this play important enough to use 30 or 45 minutes of the school day for play, say 2:30 to 3:15?   Yes *20*   No *5*

	Very Valuable	Of Little Value	No Value
5. Nap or Rest Period	16	1	0

Do you think this is important enough to use 20 minutes a day for it?   Yes *23*   No *1*

	Very Valuable	Of Little Value	No Value
6. Individual Reading*	23	1	0
7. Discussion and Interest in One Another's Experiences (among pupils in the classroom)†	23	0	1

* Rather than group reading only, an innovation in this school.
† Telling experience, planning, and evaluation, also an innovation.

In other words, once they understood what we were trying to do to create better group living for their children, parents heartily endorsed the teacher's procedures toward this end. They seconded the teacher's belief that release of tension and opportunity for practicing social skills are important for group living. The significance of this endorsement must be understood in terms of the change of program implied. As indicated, group reading and "telling" experiences were innovations in this school community. The generalization we'd draw is that parents who understand the purposes of a program for group living will give it their support even though some of its aspects are contrary to tradition and to what we tend to assume parents will demand.

Reporting to Parents

The teacher of this group had been conducting parent interviews throughout the year. In fact, it was doubtless this experience that gave parents the awareness of the value of such conferences—a value sufficient to suggest that conferences replace report cards (see parents' evaluations, page 324). One needs to know the community tradition to understand the significance of this decision (although it could probably be duplicated in many communities). One parent made a protest against elimination of report cards, because if they weren't furnished, she said, there would be a blank place in her child's baby-book!

The teacher felt that these conferences with parents, replacing report cards, were of such value that she gave hours of her time to conducting them. At each conference, she showed the parents samples of the child's own work, and pointed out the improvement made over a period of time—a kind of "before and after" evaluation which put emphasis on growth of the individual child rather than on competitive marks. The conference gave her an opportunity, too, to get to know the children better through knowing their parents, and to discuss and plan individual programs, especially in the area of social adjustment.

Moreover, the teacher felt that elimination of the report cards had done much to lessen tension among the children and so had contributed to good group living.

Parents were enthusiastic about this type of reporting and mutual planning, but decided that they wanted something in writing as the final report of the year. In compliance with this request, the teacher wrote notes to each parent concerning the progress of his child. The following is an example:

Dear Mr. and Mrs. Brown:
Lois is always neat, clean and attractive looking. She has grown ½ inch since she has been in our room and she now weighs 52 pounds. She is trying to learn to relax during our rest periods and she usually does a good job of it.
She takes good care of all her things. When she has been given opportunities to help in the room, she always does her duties well.

She has a very soft speaking voice and sometimes she is a little shy about sharing her experiences but usually has interesting things to tell. She enjoys art and spends much time with it. She sings well and seems to like it. She was able to do all our number work on a recent review check.

She reads fairly well, but she seeks a good deal of help and has little faith in her own ability. She does some outside reading on her own.

She seems to get along well with the children and she enjoys her play.

Sincerely,

(Signed) ———————————

Teacher

———————————

Principal

. . . .

PARENT'S REMARKS

———————————

PARENT'S SIGNATURE

A Continuing Program

Perhaps the best evaluation of the parents' interest in this program was their enthusiasm throughout the year and their plans for continuing their classroom organization. We have already described their plans for taking responsibility for continuing the play program throughout the summer.

The parents felt so strongly that their association had been valuable that they made plans for continuing the organization, even though many of the children would be with another teacher the following year. At the final spring meeting, on the parents' initiative officers for the next school year were elected, and tentative plans were laid for programs for the fall.

It is possible that next year parents of the first and second grades may meet together with the three teachers of these grades, and that the teachers may cooperate to the extent that they will operate as a primary unit, combining groups for certain activities. It is felt that this may make it possible for young children to participate in groups of various sizes. There is, too, a very practical consideration. The teacher we have been discussing conducted all conferences, wrote all letters, and attended all meetings *after school time*. Three teachers cooperating may make it possible for one or two to relieve the third for some of these activities during the school day.

DEVELOPING BETTER PARENT-TEACHER RELATIONSHIPS AND UNDERSTANDINGS

The preceding report told of the work of one teacher in developing parent-teacher relations. The following is a report of a faculty group working cooperatively to this end.[2]

When the first Horace Mann–Lincoln Institute meeting was held, parents were invited to be present to help plan and discuss the program with the school people, and they were invited to all other meetings held with the Institute.

Another type of activity receiving impetus from the Horace Mann–Lincoln Institute study was study groups of parents of children of one room. Although there had been a study group for kindergarten and first grade for a year and a half, by the spring of the following year *all* rooms had organized such groups. In these study groups the parents tried to solve common problems concerning the growth and development of their children.

Several teachers had felt for some time that a report card did not serve the purpose of insuring better adjustment of the child. Sometimes the child's card was compared in the home with that of his brothers and sisters, with dire results. Reports of neighboring children were compared. Johnny's mother became quite concerned if Susy, who lived next door, had a better report. Some parents objected to the card by saying that it didn't tell enough. To try to do away with these difficulties three teachers decided to try individual conferences with parents.

Parents were asked to fill out a questionnaire prior to the conference. Not all parents complied with this request, but the ones who did did a good job. Parents of this group tended to be highly intelligent, well-educated people. The following is an example of parents' statements of aspirations and evaluations of a child's performance. (The form was prepared by the teachers; the comments were provided by the parents.)

Child's name: *Billy Brown*

I. *School Experience*

In addition to the academic skills, we want him to develop the proper

[2] This report was prepared by a committee of teachers, Mary Alice Elliott, Mildred Farran, and Irene Gunkle, all of University Park School, Denver, Colorado.

social attitudes and cultural gains in order to become a worth-while, mature citizen in the years to come.

II. *Physical Adjustment*

We feel at the moment that five full days of school a week are too much for Jack. He is entirely worn out by the end of the week.

III. *Social Adjustment* (at school and home)

Jack seems better adjusted to first grade than he was to kindergarten. He is a very friendly little boy, is well liked and has many friends both at school and in the neighborhood. He has a good idea of fair play and enters wholeheartedly into games, etc.

He is still too dependent upon his mother and shows a great deal of resentment toward his younger brother.

IV. *Emotional Stability* (mental attitudes, approach to work, ability to take suggestions)

We think he is making progress along these lines. His tendency is to be mentally lazy. He has a good mind (really unusual reasoning ability if along a line he is interested in), but is very apt to resort to guessing or a hit-or-miss method, rather than thinking his school project thru. His approach to work is therefore not good. We think he is able to take suggestions well, although he is easily discouraged (being very sensitive), and if spoken to harshly after making a mistake, the entire project would be lost. If he is given any special responsibility and can feel that confidence is placed in him, he responds well and will work like a little trooper to accomplish the desired end.

V. *Special Abilities* (hobbies, outside interests)

He loves outdoor sports (horseback riding, skiing, etc.), loves animals and all phases of ranch life.

VI. *Academic Skills*

He is slow in developing interest in letters, etc., and therefore may be lagging in his academic work. If his health problem can be solved, I think he will progress much more rapidly along these lines.

(Signed)   *Emily Brown*
PARENT

Each teacher had a difficult job to do before each conference. She had to review the information she had about the child's background, his brothers and sisters, his place in the family, and his school adjustment. She needed concrete evidence of the child's social development as well as academic progress. She had on hand a folder containing samples of the child's work.

When the parent arrived, the teacher really had to be a combined counselor, psychiatrist, and educator. Sometimes the parents came in fear and trembling about why they had been asked to come. Sometimes they thought their children were behavior problems or were not doing good work. After the first task of putting the parent at ease had been accomplished, the conference was off to a good start.

The shortest conferences were from fifteen to twenty minutes. The longest lasted for two hours after school.

One of the most interesting and fruitful parts of the conference was the parents' replies to the question, "What do you expect your child to get from his school experiences?" Out of one class of twenty-nine fourth grade children, twenty-two parents mentioned as their first or second choice the desire for their children to work and play well with the others. Only seven parents mentioned as first choice acquiring academic skills or merely "to learn" or "to learn to concentrate." It would seem that possibly the study groups were having their effect on how the parents answered this question.

Parents were asked if they thought this type of reporting was better than a report card. For this same group of twenty-nine the results were as follows:

Liked the conference method better or thought conferences were a wonderful idea.	24
Liked both ways. They wanted a written report to show Dad.	3
Would like it, but her time was limited. She had five children.	1
Didn't know.	1

In the sixth grade, the teacher experimented with a type of report to parents different from that used by other teachers. The children themselves wrote letters telling how they thought they were getting along in school. Below are samples of the children's letters. There were no directions on what was to be included, and the letters indicate the freedom with which each child reported his own progress.

Dear Mother and Dad,

We are writing notes telling how we are getting along in school.

I know that all of my work could be improved and I think I am too slow in all tests and in some of my work. In social science I think all of us have done O.K. and I understand all of our social science very well. Arithmetic seems to come fairly easy for me and I like to read a lot. One of the reasons I like all my work and do fairly well in it is because of the nice teacher I've had during this school year.

I think I should practice being more courteous and helpful, too. But in general I guess I'm pretty good.

With love,
Doris

Dear Mom and Dad,

I am writing a paragraph on our school work, and how I'm getting along. In spelling I used to miss a lot of words, but now that I have been studying harder, I haven't missed so many. I have been getting a hundred the last few Fridays. In reading I enjoy it very much except answering questions. I don't answer many questions because I don't like to talk in front of the class very well. In arithmetic I was missing quite a few, but now that I understand it better and I am used to it I don't miss so many problems and examples. In our Aviation study we had a lot of fun. We built our airport and went to the airport and saw many things. Art is the subject I enjoy most. We all have a lot of fun. We finger-paint, work with clay, airplanes and other things. In gym we play baseball and run races and also "Jump the Brook." I enjoy school very much except getting up in the morning. I think I am doing well in all of the subjects and I am trying to read well.

Love
Sam

After each child had taken his letter home, his parents were scheduled for a conference in much the same manner as that described above. The sixth graders accompanied their parents to the conference, and pupils as well as parents expressed their appreciation of the conferences. The teachers felt they were contributing to better group living for children at home as well as at school.

Parents in rooms where no conferences were scheduled heard from other parents about the value of such conferences. Some telephoned the teachers to ask for appointments. The interesting fact about these requested conferences was that usually the matter for concern was social adjustment rather than scholastic progress. (Parents want good group living for their children.)

Values of this program of developing better parent-teacher relationships seem to be:[3]

I. *To the Parents*

    A. Parents were in on the planning meetings for the Horace Mann–Lincoln Institute study. They developed a sense of sharing in the school program.

    B. Through visitation of a class demonstration new techniques of teaching and new aims and objectives for teachers and children were explained.

---

[3] May we remind you that this report was written by the teachers themselves, not by an observer who might have preconceived ideas of what the values might be, or should be.

C. The freedom with which parents visited the rooms all year long indicated an interest in the school's program—and in the children's growth.

D. The telephoning done by the teachers to find the causes for extended absences, etc., helped to foster a good feeling between parents and teachers.

E. The report letters written by the teachers or by the children themselves were appreciated as a means of developing mutual understanding.

F. The study groups that were formed for every age level did much to help the parents understand child growth and development. How the school was adjusting its program to meet the needs of the children at the various levels received much attention.

G. The parent-teacher conference as a means of reporting was invaluable to parents in the following ways:

　　1. It helped the parent to become clear in his own mind as to what he wanted his child to gain from his school experiences.

　　2. The parent was given an opportunity to explain any pertinent facts about the child that would enable the teacher to work with him more effectively as an individual and as a group member.

　　3. Any maladjustment of the child at school was pointed out. If there was a difficulty at home, the parent and teacher were often able to find tentative means of solution for this mutual problem.

　　4. The parent was assured of the fact that he was welcome at school at all times.

II. To the Child

A. The child felt more secure in the school situation in which his parent took an active part.

B. When the parent understood the school program better, he was less apt to frustrate the child by demanding too much of him academically.

C. Where the parent conference entirely replaced the report card, the child was freed from any fear of the evils of report cards, i.e., being paid for grades, comparison with brothers and sisters or neighbors' children, punishment for lack of achievement.

III. To the Teacher

A. A better understanding of the whole child was gained as a result of learning about the home background and the aims and aspirations of the parents.

B. The improved attitude of the parent toward the school program and the teacher, due to active participation, helped in the development of a better school curriculum.

C. A feeling of oneness was developed among the parents, the teacher, and the children in working together for the good of the children of the group.

We recommend that the various ways mentioned in this paper as a means of fostering better parent-teacher relationships be continued.

We should like to insert a word of caution, however. Parent conferences are very exhausting to teachers. If scheduled for out-of-school time, they become almost too time-consuming. Therefore, because these conferences are of unquestionable value, we recommend that substitute-teacher time be given to the teachers willing to engage in this activity.

FACULTY AND PARENTS REPORT

There is a story behind the following report, and a sequel. When the Horace Mann–Lincoln Institute started to work with this school, parents were invited to all planning meetings. As might be expected, not all parents came, and some who did come misinterpreted what was being planned.[4] Word got abroad among the uninformed that children were being used as "guinea pigs." A few parents called a public meeting of indignation and expressed their doubts and fears. There were those present who tried to explain that the program was designed to better the social adjustment of boys and girls as well as to further their academic achievement, but the final results of the meeting were inconclusive. The faculty and parents who understood the program felt that a report to the parents and the public was in order. On the following pages are excerpts from the dramatized report prepared cooperatively by parents and teachers, and presented at an open meeting. Roles were taken by teachers, the principal, parents, and members of the staff of the central office.

The sequel is that after this public report there was no further opposition from parents. In fact, the support for the program increased as understanding among parents spread and was deepened.

The parents and teachers gave no title to their cooperative report other than "The Play."

THE PLAY[5]

> SETTING: Principal, teachers, and representatives of parents sit in panel facing the audience.

---

[4] Perhaps this is an indication that we did not do as competent a job of group living among adults as we might have wished, yet the following report by parents and teachers substantiate our belief in group action. The parents who participated with us in our planning and evaluation were active in planning the dramatic skit we report.

[5] The script for this presentation was prepared by a committee of parents and teachers of University Park School, Denver, Colorado.

(Mother approaches principal, carrying a paper in her hands.)

MOTHER: I know I shouldn't interrupt at this time, but I am so worried I feel that I must ask you some questions. You may be planning to answer some of these questions; but if I wait until all of you have talked, it may be too late for me. Please sir, will you listen? I am so troubled about my three children who attend school here.

PRINCIPAL: Certainly, I shall be glad to help you, and the members of the panel will be happy to add their comments, too.

MOTHER: First of all, people have been talking about a new man—a Horace Mann. They say he is having too much influence on the work in our school. Who is he anyway, and why is he interfering at our school?

PRINCIPAL: We have a guest here tonight who is well qualified to answer that question. She is a supervisor from our city schools.

(Supervisor gives description of aims and program of Horace Mann–Lincoln Institute, Teachers College, Columbia University, New York.)

MOTHER: Well, I'm glad to know that Horace Mann isn't really here. How about our school, though? Who chooses the problems for this school to work on?

TEACHER 1: The teachers of this school with the help of the principal, set up the problems for our school to study. The faculty decided that a fine opportunity for improving the curriculum was being offered. They decided they would like to work out the best possible curriculum for the daily living of our boys and girls. Later, after we got started in the study, the emphasis of the primary teachers shifted to that of developing self-reliance in children and providing opportunities wherein self-reliance could be developed. The upper grade teachers analyzed their programs and put special emphasis on reducing tensions through ample opportunity for self-expression. Parents were present at all planning meetings. The parents, teachers, and the principal determined the directions of the Horace Mann–Lincoln Institute study at our school.

MOTHER: I am relieved. Some of us thought that people from New York had been telling you what to work on.

I hardly know how to state my next question. One of my children said his teacher asked him who his best friends were. When I went to school no one cared who my friends were. Why is it so important now?

TEACHER 2: It is just one of the many ways we have used to help us identify the needs, interests, and concerns of the children of our school and to help them get along together in their groups. Some of the other techniques we used are: The California Test of Personality, the tests of achievement in various subject fields, and the use of anecdotal records.

We learn to know children on the playground, before school, at recess, and during activity periods when there is special opportunity to observe their interests, needs, and concerns, as well as during all the school day.

We observe the children's responses and reactions to specific situations which give clues to our understanding them, and we try to help each child learn social skills as well as to help the group learn to know itself as a group.

We consult with parents about the interests, needs, and concerns of their children. We use records of development as outlined on cumulative cards, report cards, and appraisals of former teachers. We use objective evidence gained through scores on standardized tests, such as Kuhlmann–Anderson, Pinter–Cunningham, Monroe Reading Readiness, and Progressive Achievement Tests. We consult studies regarding the growth and development of children.

In identifying the needs, interests, and concerns of the children, and in adjusting to them, we seek to guide our children to better personal and social living.

MOTHER: Nowadays, my first grade boy isn't too tired when he comes home from school. When I ask him to rest, he says, "Aw, Mother, we rested at school." Is he telling the truth? Is resting part of your program?

TEACHER 3: In reviewing the needs and interests of the children in our school, the group of primary teachers in the school felt that one of the needs for the children in grades 1, 2, and 3 was a more adequate health program. During the school year, a program was launched to help meet the health needs as we saw them. It was felt that there was a great deal of tension in the children and that many of them did not know how to relax and that they were overstimulated much of the time. In order to meet this need for relaxation, and to help children get along better in the group we felt that our program should be evaluated and revised so as to help the children to find means, and periods of time, for relaxation.

One place where we felt children were especially fatigued was in the first grade, where they were adjusting to a full day at school and to longer periods of concentrated study. We arranged to allow more time for free activities. Formal reading in the afternoon was replaced by more informal reading situations growing out of the unit of work. Playtime was given in both mornings and afternoons.

The above rearrangement of time allotment also applied to the other primary grades and was worked out in each classroom by the teacher.

In order to supplement this schedule, it further was decided that a program of rest might well be initiated. Various plans were tried; resting with heads on desks, resting by lying on the tables, and resting on mats provided by the home for this purpose. These mats were kept clean by the home also. Each teacher explained the rest program to the mothers of the children in her group, and worked out a suitable plan for storing the mats.

The time allotted for rest varied in the individual classrooms. In some rooms this was at the same time every day. In some rooms the time varied from day to day. The rest period came once a day or twice a day as the teacher wished it. There was quiet, or playing of the victrola or music boxes, or soft singing by the teacher.

The teacher also took the time to relax for a few minutes. The school nurse was called into the picture for guidance and in some cases talked to the children about the importance of relaxing, how to relax, and when to relax.

In order to further evaluate the success of the rest program, a questionnaire was sent to the parents to ask them to help us evaluate the program. By an overwhelming majority, both parents and pupils favored the program.

PRINCIPAL: Perhaps the first grade teacher could be of further assistance in explaining why the first grade children don't get so tired as they used to.

TEACHER 4: For a long time it has been felt that the first grade program should be changed to meet the needs of the children. This year the first grade teachers were faced with these problems as they tried to meet the needs of individuals and provide better group living:

1. How to keep a free and spontaneous atmosphere with the first graders and at the same time maintain certain standards necessary in 1B.
2. How to provide for the physical needs of the 1B children so as to minimize fatigue and restlessness.
3. How to provide for the needs of all the children when there was a range of 100 points in I.Q.
4. How to provide sufficient free choice and activity periods, and at the same time not slight the basic subjects being introduced.

We have tried many things. The following are some of the ways which seemed most fruitful toward solving these problems:

1. By initiating rest periods each day.
2. By using the morning for basic subjects and by spending more time in the afternoons for free choice and activity periods.
3. By having conferences with the principal before the innovation of new methods and procedures of teaching.
4. By using individual parent conferences as a means to better understanding of the individual children—also better understanding of the school program by parents.
5. By checking all pupil records, keeping anecdotal records, and having conferences about some of the children with their former kindergarten teacher.
6. By studying social structures in groups through the use of sociograms, and other means.

We recognize the fact that there are many more things that might improve the first grade program, but we do feel that we are making progress in making it (first grade program) better fit the needs of the six-year-olds, both individually and as a group.

MOTHER: Oh, so that's what you are doing. Of course I can't grasp all the implications of what you have said, but I'll think about it. But is it true that you let children weave, write newspapers, make up songs, and even give plays here?

TEACHER 5: In the beginning our group explored the possible problem areas which might aid in the relief of nervous tensions and the emotional instability of our boys and girls. We decided to test the hypothesis that more satisfying self-expression would ease these tensions. We asked ourselves:

1. Does every child have ample opportunity toward richer and more abundant growth by means of self-expression?
2. Does every teacher find enough time in the curriculum to further such expression?

At the outset we attempted to get some evidence of the tensions and emotional stability of our children through tests such as: California Personality Test, the Wishing Well Test, Sociograms, Reading and Arithmetic Tests. Next we endeavored to discover the opportunities for self-expression then offered to our children. We did this through anecdotal records of group and individual activity over a given period of time. Also, each teacher examined the general program of her group.

We have examined and are continuing to examine these records in order to determine the extent of opportunity for self-expression as to *time, value, satisfaction, balance in program, relief of tensions,* and so on.

We are attempting to re-evaluate all through:

1. Re-testing (spelling and language tests) for two reasons: one, because progress in the fundamental skills is of great concern to parents and teachers: second, to discover any relationship between progress in these areas and emotional adjustment.
2. Sociograms.
3. Teacher-parent-pupil adjustments.
4. Class demonstrations in various subjects.

MOTHER: How I wish I could have gone to this school when I was young! A few weeks ago my children came home enthusiastic about helping me with spring cleaning. One day they worked in the basement, clearing out papers and magazines. One day it was front yard day: the next, back yard day. Did the school have much to do with this interest?

TEACHER 6: Yes, it is quite possible that the school had much to do with this interest. Throughout the year our school has capitalized on community service as an integral part of our curriculum. There have been many such campaigns. A few of them are: the Red Cross drive, paper drives, and Community Chest drive.

Perhaps there is no campaign that receives more interest from the children than the Clean-Up, Paint-Up, Plant-Up, and Fix-Up Campaign. This year Room 205 was in charge of the campaign. Much interest was aroused in individual and group projects for cleaning up at home and at school.

MOTHER: Oh, I almost forgot. With all these things going on, how do I know my children are learning to read, write, and spell? What assurance have I that they are up on their fundamentals?

PRINCIPAL: We have an expert here from the Instruction Department of our public school system. He is especially interested in testing. He has some information that may interest you.

SUPERVISOR OF RESEARCH: I have a tabulation sheet here showing the standing of children in this school in the fundamental skills. If you will study this sheet, you will see that the median for the school is above the national median in all cases except one. In that case, the median is exactly equal to the national one. (Shows results of standardized tests in reading, arithmetic, language, and spelling, indicating score in grade level, range, and median for each grade.)

MOTHER: What I wonder about now is how the teachers find time to do all these things. Teaching is so much more than the teaching of reading, writing, and arithmetic—the way it used to be.

I do thank you for explaining your program so well. I'll probably have more questions, but I will know that you people are really interested in doing a better job of understanding my children. I do hope I have asked questions that were pertinent to the discussion we were to have tonight.

PRINCIPAL: As it happens, your questions have been the very ones we were planning to attempt to answer. We appreciate your coming to us. Please feel free to come at any time.

WHAT IT MEANS

It seems to us that these reports bring us several significant lessons about parent-teacher cooperation:

1. Any teacher, even though she operates alone in her school, can do much to provide parent cooperation.
2. Parents want what we, as teachers, want—including good group living for boys and girls—as we find out when we give them a chance to express themselves.
3. Parents can be creative people contributing to a program of investigation if we as teachers but provide the opportunity for them to make themselves heard.
4. In times of stress, as when "the public" questions the school pro-

gram, parents who have had a part in planning for better school programs become towers of strength in interpreting the change.

We Need Parents

Perhaps these three approaches (the individual teacher and the parents of her group of children, the teachers of a school, and the cooperative parent-teacher effort) are another way of saying that we *need* parent cooperation if we are to develop good group living for boys and girls.

If good group living is as important as we have implied throughout this report, then we need the help of parents and other laymen in terms of ideas and support. Our belief in boys and girls demands that we bend every effort to achieve the cooperation of adults who believe, as we do, that good group living is important to the individual, to the community, to the nation, to the world.

IN SUMMARY

We believe that the cooperation of parents is an important aspect of studying group behavior. Parents are deeply concerned with the social development of boys and girls and have an important contribution to to make in the analysis and planning of better group living.

Probably the easiest starting point in working with groups of parents is the organization of a study group of the parents of children in each classroom. Parents find common interests in the similar problems of children of comparable age. Moreover, there is the possibility for active participation, such as in the statement of goals and in the development of plans for immediate programs and evaluations. The evaluation of the parent conferences and the plans for continuation of the play program of the first grade group described serve as examples.

Physical examinations, observation, reporting to parents, and pupil-parent discussions are further examples of opportunities for participation.

Parents appreciate the opportunity to learn of the progress of their children, and to help in the planning of programs for them when given a chance.

Parent participation in planning means extra work for teachers; but teachers who have worked for such participation feel that it pays dividends in increased service to children and in personal satisfaction. The last report in this chapter is evidence that parents may be a help in interpreting a program of experimentation to other parents and to the public in general.

That parents and teachers see the same goals for children if given an opportunity to get together and to look at problems jointly, is evidenced throughout these reports. Moreover, that such joint study and planning can be achieved is the major thesis of these descriptions of parent-teacher cooperation. We believe that parent-teacher-pupil cooperation is well worth the effort involved in the creation of better group living for boys and girls in our classrooms.

XI

Techniques for Studying Group Behavior

"Mm-m," mused Mrs. Thompson as she looked over recorded responses of boys and girls to a set of questions. "I'm surprised at some of these results. I had a hunch about some. But whether I foresaw them or not, they give me clues to watch for as I study my group." Clues for further observation—these are the major contributions of techniques and devices.

No technique or device is of itself "good." It is valuable to the degree that it is appropriate to the ends desired—that it helps to find valid clues to questions. In our investigations we were faced by many questions, and we were in great need of illumination on the problems we undertook to study; consequently we made use of a wide range of techniques. These are described in the following pages not because we recommend, necessarily, that other teachers use them, but in order to give a clearer picture of how we studied and to provide suggestions for teachers who feel that these techniques might help them to find answers to *their* problems.

Few of the techniques used in this study were original with us. In some cases we found ourselves faced by problems for which we knew no techniques, so we either devised appropriate ones or adapted some originally designed for other purposes. Many of the techniques were intended by their orginators for use in the study of *individuals*. When we used these, we attempted to interpret the findings in terms of *groups*. Some techniques lent themselves to such interpretation more successfully than others.

Most of the techniques have been mentioned earlier in this report in relation to questions to be answered or in connection with findings reported. It should be understood that we now are examining them out of context, in a sense, and thus we wish to re-emphasize the fact that we are not recommending any one for itself, but only as it may be helpful in solving problems with which teachers must cope.

We have one further word of caution. It is quite possible, of course, to regard the findings which result from the use of some of these techniques in the spirit of "back-fence gossip," allowing them to create or to deepen personal prejudices. No professional teacher would regard them in that way, but he may fall easily into the error of employing them in a spirit of idle curiosity, merely learning for the sake of learning. This attitude, we believe, is as unprofessional as that of the gossip, though it is often condoned in the name of research. We believe that any teacher who undertakes to use techniques or devices to understand groups or individuals has a moral and a professional obligation to use the findings for creating better living for the people studied. When dealing with human beings, mere observation and recording is not enough. Unless a teacher is prepared to do his utmost to develop educational programs better suited to individuals and groups because techniques have helped him know them and have given leads to development of better programs, he has no business using the techniques. No professional teacher, we believe, can divorce individual child study or group study from curriculum development.

COOPERATION IN RESEARCH

Bringing into the study as co-researchers the people involved in the study—parents, teachers, administrators, and pupils—was perhaps the most significant approach to the solution of problems. To those people interested in action research in community study, we should like to point out that we believe the way we worked is an application of such research technique, with children as the principal participants. The problem area evolved as we studied, molded by the participants, and the researcher became a part of the research situation as it developed. For children, this was curriculum experience; for parents, an experience in home-school cooperation; for teachers, in-service education and means to curriculum development. For all, it was an exciting adventure into the unknown, undertaken with the realization that it could be successful only if there was cooperative effort, and that answers were to be found only as hunches and suggestions *of the group* were tried out and then evaluated *by the group*.

EXPERIENCE—THE BASIC APPROACH

That discovery and learning are achieved through experience was a major premise of the study. Moreover, realizing that this was true for everyone involved, all made an attempt to provide broadening experiences for pupils, teachers, and parents.

Teachers took first responsibility for developing this experience. This meant creating an atmosphere favorable for experience, such as planning rest periods and time for free play for young children; for more mature pupils, it meant offering opportunity for discussion and action, for making choices and for making mistakes; and, further, it gave a chance for common experiences in creative and appreciative activities for boys and girls of all ages.

Providing experience took various turns. One teacher in a school in a metropolitan area helped a group within her classroom plan Saturday excursions to zoos, exhibits, museums, parks, and other places of interest. We have told you of the group which took responsibility for informing others in the school of out-of-school opportunities. Thus, as we use the term "experience," it means not only school experience but out-of-school time use as well. (Other aspects of experience are discussed in Chapters VII and VIII, pages 232 to 292.)

Providing opportunity for parents meant that teachers made it possible for parents to meet, observe, and discuss. When teachers provided opportunity for themselves, it meant long hours of discussion with one another, study, observation, and record keeping. Though time-consuming, all agreed the results justified the expenditure.

Discussion

Although we are keenly aware of the great importance of direct experience, we are aware also that in this verbal world words are a major means to inter-personal communication—and hence to group living. As was mentioned above, discussion was used as a means to understanding among parents, teachers, and pupils. These discussions served many purposes.

A special aspect of discussion is bringing goals up to consciousness, setting goals, and communicating goals. "Talking it out" in this sense is a means to bringing goals "out in the open," to be recognized, examined, and, if desired, changed. With the emphasis given in this study to recog-

A LIVING SOCIOGRAM.

nition of behavior as goal-directed, this function of discussion was exceedingly important.

Discussion made it possible to develop plans of action to achieve goals. A high level of discussion was reached when a group was able to arrive at a step-wise plan. (Several such plans made by teachers are described in Chapter IX.) Pupils, too, achieved such planning, as when a group decided that the list of items concerning "how to improve myself" was too long, charged a committee with responsibility for developing a revised list, which list was then to be discussed by a jury and finally by the group as a whole. And it was achieved when a group agreed that qualities of people that made for liking were of importance, and decided to write descriptions of best friends from which a list of qualities to be used as a check list could be distilled, then tabulated and reported to each individual.

Closely related to planning and problem-solving discussions are those of evaluation. A major means of evaluating group living is the reaction of the group itself, and a major means of discovering this reaction is through discussion. Moreover, the evaluation becomes a learning experience on which to base further planning. Thus an upward spiral of growth is started. Many opportunities for evaluation were used—an incident on the playground, a day's interaction, an activity of a planning period, the year's work together. Each evaluation, we believe, served the dual purpose of providing learning experience in relation to the matter evaluated, and providing insight into how group living is achieved.

Sometimes discussion was used as a means of catharsis, allowing group members to "get it out of their systems." As discussed earlier, this was a means to directing reaction—allowing emotion to "spill" rather than take the form of antisocial action destructive to group living. It is probable that discussion served this purpose more often, for more people, and with deeper significance than we realized.

RECORDS OF EXPERIENCES

Anecdotes

Any research program must, of necessity, involve a certain amount of record-keeping. There seems to be abroad in the land a myth that teachers abhor record-keeping. Perhaps this abhorrence is not totally mythical, for it is evident that many teachers strongly resist keeping records which are merely routine, or worse, meaningless. In this study, however, we found teachers willing and eager to keep records if records were seen as meaningful and contributing to teacher-determined ends. In other words, the behavior of teachers, as well as that of pupils, is goal-determined, and if the goal is not clear or is not understood, record-keeping may be a chore. On the other hand, if the goal is also that of the teacher, record-keeping attains meaning and significance. The main aspects of this report are based on teachers' records of experience.

A major technique in our study was observation of group behavior and recording of it in the form of anecdotes. This was not as easy as it sounds. We found much in the literature that was of help in directing our attention to the need for objective and precise observation and recording, but all, or most of it, referred to anecdotes describing a situation or event in which an *individual* was the central figure. We found we had much to learn about how to look at *groups* and *group behavior*, and how to describe what we observed.

We did not question the need for anecdotes. We knew that such objective recordings could provide a picture of something which might be forgotten, or an image which might be distorted by subsequent events. We knew we needed such descriptions to provide evidence of change in group living. But there are so many interesting things happening in every group every day that it is difficult to decide what to record. Moreover, a conscientious teacher may find himself so involved in the "paper work" of recording that he has neither the time nor the energy to do anything about the very problem he is investigating. What started as an interesting adventure in research may become a boring routine task with very little, if anything, resulting other than an accumulating stack of papers. We have perhaps overdrawn this statement. No doubt there is value in observing in order to record, but we wanted to take a step beyond this.

We decided, therefore, that to be most effective in group study, observation (and anecdotes) should be pertinent to the particular questions under consideration. For example, at one point, the teachers decided to focus attention on the group acceptance and group rejection of children. The consultant made the following suggestions:

Suggestions for Writing Anecdotes of Observation of Group Behavior

Needless to say, you will want to make your records as objective and meaningful as possible. You will find many helpful suggestions for writing anecdotes in the early chapters of *Helping Teachers Understand Children* (Teacher Education Commission, American Council on Education). In reading this material, keep in mind that our major concern is group rather than individual behavior as stressed in this book. However, most of what is said can apply here.

As we mentioned at our meeting, you may want to review Part II of *Discipline for Today's Children and Youth* by George Sheviakov and Fritz Redl, for examples of how group behavior may be recorded.

You, as the teacher living with your group, will know better than anyone else what behavior is significant in a study of acceptance and rejection. No predetermined list of items should be allowed to cramp your style. The following suggestions, therefore, should be considered merely as "brain teasers" and not as rules for recording.

Two approaches are suggested. One focuses on certain children, and the other on certain types of behavior. No doubt you will want to try both.

Approach I: Focus on Certain Children

Through various means, we have identified certain children as being the most or the least accepted by their peers. Giving some special attention to observing these children, record instances of their behavior in the group *and the reaction of other children to this behavior.*

Sample: Mary (an isolate as indicated by several sociograms) fell and skinned her knee while playing on the playground with eight or ten other girls. She dropped out of the game and started to cry. Susan left the game and went to her. The others continued the game. Alice called, "Come on, Susan, we want you in the game." Susan left Mary, still crying, on the side of the playground and rejoined the group. When the bell rang, Susan, Dorothy, and Gloria went to Mary and walked into the building with her. Susan explained to the teacher about Mary's accident (the first part of this action was observed by the teacher from the window of the classroom).

Approach II: Focus on Certain Types of Behavior

From our general knowledge of children and of group behavior, we have come to recognize certain types of behavior as symptomatic of acceptance or rejection. Records of instances of these types of behavior (descriptions of the setting and of what happened) should be significant. Below are a few examples of symptoms for which you may wish to watch. No doubt you will find others and will be able to amplify this list as you study your group.

CAUTION: Listing behavior under headings, as is done below, may seem to imply that this behavior always indicates the suggested relationship to acceptance or rejection. We know this is not necessarily true. No one item of behavior should be taken as evidence. This business of acceptance and rejection is exceedingly complex, and we must not expect to find easy answers through simple analysis. The complexity of our problem makes it all the more important for us to record what happens exactly as it happens, avoiding personal bias as far as possible, and indicating certain statements as interpretations rather than as records of observation.

A. Symptoms of group rejection of an individual or a subgroup:
   1. Ignoring (paying no attention to; not listening to; obviously excluding from group, from conversation; not selecting in choice situations, etc.).
   2. Ridiculing (laughing at, to face; laughing about, when not present; making side comments about, to others who giggle or laugh; malicious teasing, etc.).
   3. Showing aggression toward (fighting, pushing, elbowing out; malicious name-calling; derogatory remarks about, etc.).

B. Symptoms suggesting that an individual or a subgroup feels rejected by the group:
   1. Withdrawing from group ("I didn't want to be with you, anyway." "I'd rather be by myself." "I won't give you a chance to snub me." "I'll be mean to you, just as you are mean to me").
   2. Showing aggression toward ("If you won't be friendly toward me, I'll make you." "I'll make you sorry you're mean to me").
   3. Showing off ("I'll *make* you notice me").
   4. Seeking adult approval ("If the kids don't like me, I'll get recognition from the teacher").

C. Symptoms of group acceptance of an individual or a subgroup:
   1. Singling out for recognition (selecting for desired position; electing to posts of leadership; naming to represent group, etc.).

2. Choosing to be with (spending time with; sitting beside; working with, etc.).

3. Giving or asking favors (giving or asking help with work; sharing opportunities, possessions, etc.).

4. Praising (complimenting achievement, clothes, etc.; speaking favorably of, etc.).

5. Emulating (copying behavior, mannerisms, etc.).

6. Agreeing with (accepting suggestions, submitting to leadership, stating other's ideas as own, etc.).

> Note: Keep in mind that this behavior may also indicate that there is rejection and that the people employing it are trying to gain acceptance.

D. Symptoms indicating that an individual or a subgroup feels accepted by the group:

1. Acting as equal (contributing to group discussion; joining groups naturally, etc.).

2. Taking leadership (forming groups; making suggestions for group action, etc.).

3. Seeking peer approval (asking for opinion and criticism of other children, but feeling free to disregard it; preference for peer approval to adult acceptance).

E. Questions to ask in looking for symptoms of group structure:

1. Does group organize as gangs or subgroups?

2. How does group react to punishment or praise of leaders by the teacher? Of non-leaders?

3. How does group react to newcomers to the group?

4. How does the group react to new situations?

5. Does group as a whole ever "gang up" on one person? On subgroup? On teacher?

6. How does group react when certain leaders are absent?

7. Does group, or certain sections of group, wait for reactions of certain individuals before giving own reactions?

8. Is there tattling to the teacher? To pupil leader?

9. To what degree does group accept rules made cooperatively?

10. To what extent do classroom friendships and gangs operate after school hours?

11. Are there boy-girl friendships as well as boy-boy and girl-girl? If so, how does the group react to these friendships?

12. Does group show markedly different reactions to different teachers?

We have learned much since this list of suggestions was made, and many of the questions raised in earlier chapters of this report may be more significant than the ones raised in this list. But these are the ones which started us on our way.

Time Sampling

Another type of observation and recording may be in the form of time sampling. The following is a section of a record made by a student teacher attempting to observe Tommy's relations to the group during a two-hour period.

Observed: *Tommy S., Grade 1*   Observer: *Mary Dunbar*
Date: *January 8*   Time: *10:00–12:00 A.M.*

10 : 00—Asks Diane if he may use her crayon. Exaggerates walking on tip-toe when he goes to get paper.
10 : 01—Scribbles on paper with pencil. Looks at partner's paper.
10 : 02—Wanders about. Looks at others coloring. Sees Terry at painting easel so walks over.
10 : 03—Asks Phil what he is doing. Phil tells him to go away.
10 : 05—Sits down, then walks over to see Phil again. Leans on Phil's desk.
10 : 06—Sees boys at crayons. Follows them over there, then goes back to seat.
10 : 08—Colors (without pattern) for a time.
10 : 09—Walks over to see what Phil is doing.
10 : 10—Sees someone else at crayon table. Gets a crayon and goes back to seat.
10 : 16—Climbs up on own desk. Watches Terry.
10 : 17—Sits with feet on chair.
10 : 18—Gazes around room for about five minutes.
10 : 23—Goes back to crayon table because someone is there again.
10 : 25—Tosses two crayons in own desk. Goes over to reading desk where others are.
10 : 26—Stays at desk. Flips through several books while gazing at other boys.
10 : 30—Back at own desk. Paper falls on floor. Stuffs it into desk. Stands on chair and gazes around the room.
10 : 31—Sits gazing around room. Picks up Dolores' paper which fell on floor. Smiles when he hands it back.

Log of Activities

The log of activities is a record of daily experience kept by the class, the teacher, or both. The purpose is to record what is done in an attempt to describe the situation, and to aid in the interpretation of shifts in group interaction from time to time. When very marked shifts in the group pattern are noted, it is helpful to know what factor may have brought about the change.

In the upper grades, the pupils can share the responsibility of keeping the day-to-day record of activities. In the lower grades, the teachers or some other mature observer will need to do this. Parents have been used in this role and in many cases have been most interested and helpful. One of the great advantages of pupil-parent-teacher cooperation in research is that, in addition to combining the intelligence and insight of all, it makes possible a division of labor which keeps the burden from falling in an unbearable way on the shoulders of one or two individuals, and gives everyone a chance to participate.

One of the difficulties in keeping logs is that frequently much that is recorded is not found applicable to the specific problem under investigation. On the other hand, if one knew what was applicable, there would be no reason for investigation. The decision on the amount of time and effort which can be devoted to keeping a log is one that will have to be made by the teacher and group involved, in the light of all the conditions. The teachers who worked on this study started by keeping lengthy, time-consuming logs, but found themselves devoting less and less time to the task as time went by because the results didn't seem at the time to justify the effort needed. However, there is some question of the wisdom of lessening the time devoted to this activity.

Another dimension of log-keeping was discovered by accident. Logs kept by children helped us to see the school day as children see it. For example, for one such day we have these divergent entries by two pupils who had the same experiences:

> SUSAN: We had our Cinderella play. That was all that was important on Tuesday.
>
> LARRY: Tuesday we had everything we should have, except in the afternoon we had the Cinderella play. (Evidently the usual daily routine constituted the "should have," as Larry saw it.)

Thus, although logs kept by children may not always be accurate or complete records, they may serve to indicate the reaction of children to their experiences.

Time Use

Some of the questions to which we sought answers in this study were: To what extent is there free choice of companions out of school hours? If choice is free are companions chosen on the basis of generalized friendship, in terms of specific activity, or largely on the basis of proximity and availability? To what extent are school companions out-of-school companions? What out-of-school activities contribute to, or negate, good group living? How much group experience do youngsters have after school hours? With whom? etc.

To secure answers to questions such as these, pupils supplied information concerning their use of leisure time, either as free records of "My Day" or "My Week End" or as a schedule of activities. A time schedule might look something like this:

Time	What I Did	With Whom	Where
4:00–4:30	Rode bicycle	Joe and Tom	Around stockyards
4:30–5:00	Chores	By myself	Home
5:00–6:00	At supper, did dishes	Mother and Daddy	Home
6:00–7:00	Played with electric train	Pete and Alec	At my house

No teacher or group of pupils could overlook the individual differences in experience in a group when faced with two before-school-time schedules such as these:

Margaret		Bertha*	
5:30–6:00	Sleep	5:30–6:00	Get up, dress, clean room
6:00–6:30	Sleep	6:00–6:30	Clean washroom
6:30–7:00	Sleep	6:30–7:00	Clean washroom
7:00–7:30	Sleep	7:00–7:30	Eat breakfast and work in laundry
7:30–8:00	Sleep	7:30–8:00	Work in laundry
8:00–8:30	Get up, dress, and have breakfast	8:00–8:30	Work in laundry and get ready for school
8:30–9:00	Read funnies and go to school	8:30–9:00	Go to school

* Bertha lives in a home for dependent children.

Through this comparatively simple device we learned a great deal about the play and work habits, about opportunities for group participation, and about the home life of boys and girls.

Autobiographies

One very effective way of securing information on the values held by members of the group is to have each individual write his autobiography.

Some preliminary discussion of what constitutes an autobiography, as well as the reading of an interesting autobiographical sketch or two, is probably necessary preparation. However, the experience of the teachers in the study was that those autobiographies written without recourse to any formal pattern or outline were much more revealing and valuable than those directed toward specific information.

The major significance of these unstructured autobiographies was in the factors which children chose to report as happenings in their lives which they considered to be their most important experiences. It was also found necessary to allow the children ample time because the newness of the situation caused them to work slowly.

Young children may be asked to "tell the story of you," while the teacher or other adult transcribes it. What children consider important enough to report is revealing.

Peter, a first grade youngster, reported in his "story of me" that there was a new baby in the family. A few days later, the teacher had occasion to call his mother and congratulated her on the new arrival, only to be told that such "arrival" had not taken place and was unlikely to. Evidently Peter was impressed with the attention given to children who announced that they had new baby sisters or brothers and decided to try the technique himself (to the subsequent embarrassment of his teacher). His flight of imagination, even if in wishful thinking, was significant in itself, however, and suggested to us that he felt he wasn't getting the attention he desired.

We discovered that many boys and girls of all ages reveal preoccupying ideas, as did Robert (page 223), whose whole autobiography was concerned with height and weight. A rather startling autobiography was written by a son of a Marine officer who had traveled widely. He reports:

> When I was in Shanghai, I was 2 and took drinks from people's cocktails. In Panama, I was 5 and sat on the stairs when my dad got tight. Boy, was he mad. At Quantico, I drank some beer and all the people laughed because I couldn't walk straight. When we went somewhere in South America, I used to snitch from the bottle. I had lots of fun. Then my dad went away on active duty because of the war and I don't drink now until he comes home, maybe next month.

After talking with him further, his teacher decided that this boy identified himself strongly with his father, who, it seemed, made much of his drinking. Whether or not the boy had the experiences he described is beyond the point. It is probable that he was trying to say, in a language he knew and felt comfortable in using, "I love my Dad."

In other words, although we have listed autobiographies under the heading of "Records of Experiences," perhaps more significant than the experiences reported are the hidden clues to values to be found in children's statements of what to them are events or impressions important enough to report as a part of their life histories.

STUDIES OF CHILDREN'S REACTIONS

In addition to discussion as a means of helping a group examine itself and its own processes, certain technical devices were employed. Sometimes results obtained from these techniques (often compiled by the teacher and reported anonymously) were the basis of group discussion.

Classroom Social Distance Scale

One of the most revealing devices we used was the Classroom Social Distance Scale (Appendix, page 401). Results of the use of this instrument gave us insight into the wide range of acceptance the group extends to individual members as well as the range of acceptance individuals feel for the group. Moreover, giving numerical weight to ratings and then placing scores in rank order gave us a basis for studying the relation of acceptance to other factors.[1]

Check Sheet of Opportunities in Human Relations

The major purposes of this Check Sheet (Appendix, page 407) are to discover the range of activities in which an individual engages, and the values he places on them. There are also opportunities for the individual to indicate his opinion of the degree of adult control, to show to whom he would go for help with personal problems, and to give his opinion of himself as a group member. The responses on this instrument were helpful in gaining insight into the relation between children's experience and individual differences, age, sex, and between opportunity for an experience and its value. Of even greater significance, however, was the relation of adult values to those of children, revealed when parents and teachers were asked to check the value of experiences for pupils of a particular group.

Check Sheet for Describing People

In several groups boys and girls devised lists of descriptive statements which could be used as check sheets for describing one another, heroes, historical or fictional characters. (One such list, developed from descriptions of "My best friend," is presented on pages 17 and 18.) We found this technique very useful in bringing values to consciousness and thus in

[1] Only ranked scores were used as a basis of correlations because it was realized that there is no reason to suppose that the five points of the scale are of equal intervals. See Appendix, pages 401 to 404, for description of scoring techniques.

developing insight into group interaction, *if* the atmosphere was such that boys and girls felt they could be honest. When only the expected, adult-instigated responses are forthcoming, we doubt the value of this activity.

As a variation of this technique, eighth grade girls and boys were asked to answer the question: "Like what two people would you like to be? Why?" Answers ranged from Tarzan ("because he's so strong and has a good shape") to José Iturbi ("because I want to play the piano like him. I love music very much. It would be my favorite way to get rid of extra energy"). It was interesting to examine these responses in relation to statements of "Things I want to improve about myself" (Check Sheet of Opportunities). Almost without exception the same ideas shone through. The youngster who wanted to improve her skating wanted to be like Sonja Henie; the ones who wanted to make friends chose to be like Bob Hope or Red Skelton; those who worried about "looks" or personality chose movie actors and actresses. Well-known athletes and the President of the United States ("because he gets whatever he wants"—he'd be glad to know it!) were popular choices. Few people personally known to group members were chosen, although one girl mentioned a teacher, one "My Dad," and one a contemporary in the group.

"Things to Improve About Myself"

The opportunity to express the three things to improve about themselves was offered to pupils through the use of the Check Sheet of Opportunities for Human Relations. With the groups with which we worked most intensively, this single item proved so revealing that we decided to use it with certain other groups, independent of the scale. With some groups it was indeed revealing, but with others, where rapport was low or academic goals and those of behavior conformity were strongly stressed by both parents and teachers, we found child after child making statements such as these:

   "Improve my arithmetic."
   "Not to talk unless called on."
   "Mind my teacher."
   "Do better in my studies."

When we found responses such as these, we considered them more revealing of the teacher and the interaction pattern he employed than of the pupils. Comparing these with statements presented on pages 69 to 71, we feel they reveal acceptance of teacher-dominated goals rather than self-determined goals of boys and girls.

"Complaint Box" and "Letters to the Teacher"

One teacher concerned with the number of tattletales in her group started a complaint box, where any pupil who felt the urge to tattle could deposit his complaint. Once a week the teacher reported, anonymously, complaints made, and the group discussed whether the matters reported were real causes of complaint, and, if they were, how the behavior which caused the complaints could be eliminated. It is obvious that this technique could be misused as a means of "sniping" against fellow classmates. It should be employed with extreme caution. However, if used wisely it may offer both catharsis (in the writing of the note) and intellectual analysis (in the weekly discussions).

A variation of this technique is the "Letters to the Teacher" used by another teacher. Any member of the group could write a note to the teacher, expressing his concern about a problem he might have. He could mark the letter "Confidential," in which case he had a private interview with the teacher. If the letter was not so marked, the matter was brought before the class for group problem-solving.

Springfield Interest Finder

Although devised as a means to discover individual interests, we found the Springfield Interest Finder (page 418) an important tool to discover range or conformity of group reactions. The fifth grader who wished:

"To be with God."
"To lead a good life."
"To go to heaven."

was understood by his teachers to be a child with an unusual preoccupation, and probably with a problem. Prior to use of this form they had been concerned with his lack to achievement in reading and arithmetic. The number of children who reported "Work with my group" as the most interesting experience of the week gave further evidence of the importance of organization of subgroups in terms of interest areas as identified by boys and girls.

Social Analysis of the Classroom

This instrument (page 419), is a modification of the "Guess Who" type of tool. Each member of the class was asked to list those members of the group who, he believed, could be described by each of the thirty-seven statements on the form. If no one was described by any one statement, he said so. Also, if he felt that any description fitted him, he put down his own name.

The examination of the papers was most meaningful to the teacher who knew the group. For purposes of group study and analysis, however, we considered that if five or more members of the class indicated a certain statement as being descriptive of an individual, that fact was significant enough for the statement to be listed as a class description of him. In recording the group results of the use of the Analysis, a somewhat clumsy but quite revealing form was used. What was done was this:

A chart was prepared with the names of the members of the group listed on the left-hand side, while across the page were double columns for each of the items on the instrument. One column was for checking the class reaction (if any), and the other for checking an individual's inclusion of his own name. Table 23 is an example of this type of record for the group.

TABLE 23

CHART OF SCORES FOR SOCIAL ANALYSIS OF THE CLASSROOM

Name	1 Class	1 Self	2 Class	2 Self	3 Class	3 Self	4 Class	4 Self	5 Class	5 Self	32 Class	32 Self	33 Class	33 Self	34 Class	34 Self	35 Class	35 Self	36 Class	36 Self	Total Class	Total Self	Agreement
Gregory	x						x														4	5	0
Susan				x			*	*							*	*			*	*	9	8	7
John	x				x				x						x				x		12	0	0
Thomas													x								1	3	0
Alfred			*	*																	3	2	1
Mary								x						x				x			0	9	0
Etc.																							

x = choice (class or self).
* = agreement between class choice and choice by self.
Class = 5 or more members.

This form would be read as follows (from the part reproduced): Gregory was selected by five or more members of the class as being the kind of boy that statement 1 on the form would describe. Gregory did not agree,

TABLE 24

GROUP RECORD OF SCORES: CALIFORNIA TEST OF PERSONALITY

SECTION 1A — Self-Reliance

	Allen	Agnes	Andrew	Arnold	Barbara	Bertha	Calvin	Caroline	Catharine	Charlotte	Dan	Dennis	Dorothy	Eddie	Emma	Frances	Fred	Gary	George	Harry	Helen	Hugh	Inez	Irving	Jane	Joe	John	Keith	Larry	Molly	Rhoda	Totals
1. Would you rather plan your own work than to have someone else plan it for you? (No)	x		x					x				x	x			x		x					x	x				x				10
2. Do you usually apologize when you are wrong? (No)			x		x				x		x											x										5
3. When you have some free time, do you usually ask your parents or teachers what to do? (Yes)																					x	x			x		x	x		x		6
4. When someone tries to cheat you, do you usually try to stop him? (No)												x								x			x				x			x		5
5. Is it easy for you to recite or talk in class? (No)		x		x	x	x	x	x	x	x	x	x	x	x		x	x															14
6. Do you like to meet new people or introduce them to others? (No)											x								x		x						x					4
7. Do you usually go to bed on time, even when you wish to stay up? (No)								x			x	x	x	x			x	x		x			x	x	x	x	x					13
8. Is it hard to do your work when someone blames you for something? (Yes)	x	x	x	x	x	x	x	x	x	x	x	x	x	x		x		x		x	x	x	x	x	x		x			x	x	25
9. Do you usually eat food that is good for you, even if you do not like it? (No)	x		x					x			x	x		x		x		x					x							x		10
10. Do your parents or teachers usually need to tell you to do your work? (Yes)										x					x		x		x		x						x					6
11. Do you get excited when things go wrong? (Yes)	x				x	x	x	x	x	x	x		x			x		x					x	x	x	x	x	x	x	x	x	20
12. Do you usually keep at work until it is done? (Yes)																													x	x	x	3
Scores in Section 1A	8	9	9	9	8	9	8	6	9	8	6	7	7	8	10	7	10	7	10	8	6	6	7	8	9	9	5	10	10	8	10	

x Indicates lack of adjustment in this area.

but thought that statement 3 described him. Class members listed four statements as being descriptive of Gregory. He listed five as being descriptive of himself, but Gregory's own selections did not agree with the class choices in any instance.

Susan thought that items 4, 34, and 36 described her, while the class listed items 2, 4, 34, and 36. All in all, the class listed nine as descriptive of Susan. Susan listed eight for herself and they agreed with the class choices in seven cases.

The interpretation of the data will depend, of course, upon the items checked and the general pattern of response.

PERSONALITY TESTS

We used both the California Test of Personality and the Wishing Well (when appropriate to the ages of the groups).

California Test of Personality

Although devised as a test of individual personality, we found this test[2] most valuable when scored as a group measure. That is, the score for each item was computed for the group instead of for each pupil (Table 24). This made it possible to identify *group* problems. For example, when asked, "Is it easy for you to recite or talk in class?" fourteen out of thirty-one pupils answered "Yes." We thought this a sufficiently significant number to justify considering this factor as a problem of the total group.

A method for tabulating both group and individual scores is suggested in Table 24. Questions from the test are listed on the left. Immediately following each question is the response (Yes or No) which, according to the key provided with the test, is an indication of lack of adjustment. Under the name of each child a check is made if the child gives this response. At the right are the totals of such responses for each question. These totals may be considered the scores for the *group*. At the bottom of the table, below the name of each child, is his individual score for the section, scored according to the key developed by the author of the test. Thus the group score for question 8 is 25 (many unfavorable responses) while the individual score for Rhoda, say, is 10 (indicating above average adjustment in this area).

[2] The California Test of Personality is available from California Test Bureau, Los Angeles, California.

Wishing Well

The Wishing Well [3] was helpful to us in discovering children who felt a lack of feeling of belonging (page 111). As with the test described above, we found the major value in group scores. This test is devised to be used without names of individuals, but because of the use we made of it, we found it was more valuable when pupils signed their names. When rapport is high there is no reason for not using names. If good rapport has not been established, the results will be valueless in any event.

TESTS OF INTELLIGENCE, READINESS, AND ACHIEVEMENT

Intelligence and achievement tests were used with all groups, and with the first grade group readiness tests were used as well. We are frank to admit that these tests were used less as measures than as "insurance" against the insecurity of teachers, parents, and administrators. As stated earlier, we suggest that all teachers undertaking experimental programs use such tests, for they are respected by parents, administrators, and teachers and may forestall the criticism that experimental programs are detrimental to learning in basic skill areas. Our experience, like that of other investigators, indicates that scores for the three R's as measured by standardized achievement tests are as high (or higher) for groups engaged in a wide range of activities as are those of children in non-experimental programs, with the possible exception of the results for grades 1 to 3. In the primary grades, achievement tests may have been standardized with groups in which emphasis was given to reading and number work regardless of readiness. Thus it is difficult to measure groups with more flexible programs through tests standardized with groups which employ other methods. When parents are aware of the concept of readiness, and realize that it is not associated with I.Q. (*this is important*), they are usually willing, we find, to accept an approach based on readiness and experience rather than one based on arbitrary achievement standards per grade. The usual argument, which still works, is to point out that we don't measure "normality" by age of walking or eruption of teeth, so why

---

[3] The Wishing Well is available from Division of Evaluation, Bureau of Educational Research, the Ohio State University, Columbus, Ohio. The more recent form of this test, designated as Personality N, will be available soon from School of Education, New York University, New York City.

measure it by reading? Parents, on the whole, are understanding people if we give them a chance to review the facts of the case.

The use of intelligence tests gave us an opportunity to see that we were dealing with typical public school groups as far as I.Q. range was concerned. The range of I.Q.'s in the groups with which we worked most intensively was 92 to 112 (Kuhlmann–Anderson[4]) for the first grade group; 83 to 125 (Otis[4]) for the fourth and fifth grade group; and 76 to 123 (Otis[4]) for the eighth grade group. Thus the criticism that programs of experimentation are undertaken with selected groups could not be made against our work with these groups.

Moreover, we were interested in discovering the influence of I.Q. on group acceptance. That it had some, though not dominant, effect has been indicated (page 176).

PROJECTIVE TECHNIQUES

We found some projective techniques very helpful; the value of others we question. We have an uneasy feeling that we did not use others to the extent of their potentiality.

Rorschach Tests

At considerable expense and as the result of very fine cooperation from the administration of the Denver Public Schools, Rorschach tests were administered to all the members of the eighth grade class participating in the investigation.[5] This test can be given and interpreted only by a highly trained and competent psychologist. Examples of the types of analysis furnished follow.

Raymond Donovan

Intellect: Raymond is functioning at a normal intellectual level for his group. His ability to synthesize is slightly less than the average. Intellectual energy is low. Spread of interests and background is impoverished.

Emotional Life: The boy's emotional rapport with his surroundings is suffering from a severe shock of the neurotic variety. At present he is resisting strenuously any tendency to respond emotionally. Furthermore, he is exhibiting a marked anxiety in connection with this situation. To say he is blocked is understatement. Phantasy, life and imagination are nonexist-

---

[4] Individual Binet examinations were given in a few instances when group tests scores were seriously questioned by the teacher.

[5] We are indebted to Frank Vaughn, Counselor, Emily Griffith Opportunity School, Denver, a competent administrator of Rorschach tests, for the fine cooperation he gave.

ent in his present state. He is extremely constricted, blocked, and tense. He shows much more than the normal desire to conform. This is the only clue to his anxiety. As a matter of conjecture we could reason that his tension is probably caused by parental rigidity or overcontrol. There are no inferiority feelings.

Conclusions: A boy of average intellect but poor background, exhibiting marked symptoms of tension and anxiety, and unable because of this to engage in normal emotional give-and-take.

Robert Stevens

No analysis as to intellect and emotional life.

Conclusions: Suffice it to say that the individual is suffering (according to the record) from a typical pre-schizophrenic psychosis. He is out of contact with the world. There is an extremely high potential intellect, but the boy is on the verge of a complete breakdown. Any reactions within the group must be interpreted in the light of the fact that he is mentally ill. There is but a thin bridge left between him and reality.

Tommy Ingersoll

Intellect: Tommy is functioning on a slightly less than average intellectual level for the group. He is attending to the obvious at the expense of overall thinking. He has a regular approach to his problems. Intellectual energy is high, however, which may more than compensate for any lack of innate ability he may possess. He is utilizing every bit of his capacity. His intellectual background could stand bolstering.

Emotional Life: The boy is responding emotionally on a normal adolescent level. He is maintaining a balance between extraversion and intraversion. A normal phantasy life is present. He is slightly constricted.

Conclusions: A normal healthy adolescent boy, using his abilities to their fullest.

The psychologist administering these tests admits that it is difficult to interpret reactions because of paucity of standardized results for normal boys and girls of this age. The teacher feels that the results were helpful, but that they gave new insight in *degree* rather than *kind* of reaction. In other words, she knew from other sources of study the type of reaction reported by the Rorschach analyst, but had not, in some instances, recognized it as being as significant as the analyst indicated.

Our general conclusions are that, although Rorschach reports can be illuminating they are probably not worth the time and expense involved in being administered to an entire group. They may be very helpful, however, in interpreting reaction of *individuals* whom the teacher finds difficult to understand through other types of investigation.

Reaction to Pictures

We felt that it was important to devise some way of ascertaining how boys and girls regarded certain situations and activities—what motives they ascribed to different types of behavior for people of different ages, and the like. One method used was to show children pictures of various sorts of situations (page 423) and to ask for their reactions. It was responses to these situations that made us question whether boys and girls can understand motives they have not experienced. Our investigations were concerned largely with reactions to fighting and to teacher-pupil relations, but we feel that there might be some possibility in extending this to a number of other situations, such as various types of teacher-parent relations, employer-employee relations, relations with police, boy-girl relations, attitude toward new baby in the family, relations with people of minority groups, and so on. (In one of the photographs used the fight is between a Spanish-American—who might be mistaken for a Negro—and an Anglo-American. In only 2 per cent of the cases was this difference in skin color mentioned as a reason for fighting.)

The pictures we used (pages 283 and 363) were posed and photographed by a professional photographer. We feel this approach gives the most exact information in terms of the reactions desired. However, that such formal procedure was not necessary was proved by the teacher who cut pictures from current periodicals and asked appropriate questions, such as: "What do you think this father is saying to his son?" "How would you feel if you were this girl?" and "What would you do if this happened to you?"

One picture, cut from an advertisement in a current magazine, shows a child and her mother talking to a teacher in the classroom. The teacher mounted the picture and wrote under it, "This is a little girl coming into the room for the first time. Would you like to be this little girl?" Some of the responses read as follows:

> "I would not like to be the girl because nobody knows you and you don't know them. Sometimes you get acquainted fast. But I never do."

> "No I wouldn't like to be her because I always feel so funny when I just go in to the rooms in the school. I don't know how I would feel if I had to go in another school where all the children are new. I would feel like just crawling away because they might think that I'm just not their type or something like that. When I go someplace like that my stomach feels like it has butterflies in it and it turns around."

"No! Because I wouldn't know anybody and they would have new ways of teaching."

"Yes, I would like to be this little girl. She is meeting lots of new friends. I like to go into a new room and meet new friends."

"I would think that everyone hated me and they are all so new and everyone with mean looks on their faces.[6] I don't have any friends when I first went to school."

The motion picture film is an extension of this device, with the advantage of showing a situation developing in time.

Many of the situations suggested would lend themselves to role-playing. The advantage of a photograph, a picture cut from a periodical, or a motion picture film is that it can introduce particular situations, the discussion of which might not otherwise be introduced into the classroom.

Unfinished Stories

Not so different from the reaction to pictures is the reaction to the unfinished story.

To find indications of a feeling of belonging to the family we used unfinished stories devised by others.[7] Equally or more significant for our purposes were much less complex situations devised by teachers. For example, one teacher merely stated, "Here is a girl (or boy) alone on the school ground. What do you think she (he) was thinking?" Among the responses were these:

"Maybe her mother and father had a quarrel and the little girl isn't happy."

"She must be lonesome but if she tried to get in the games she would have lots of fun. The other children probably like her but she doesn't think so."

"I think that the little girl is thinking about how much she would like to be playing ball or jumping rope with the other children but no one wants to play with her because she doesn't have nice clothes like them."

"She might be fat and she has no friends because they might not like the girl like they don't like me in the same ways because I'm fat but I don't have bad manners."

"I think she is wondering why she doesn't have any friends and other children have a lot and how children get so many friends and why she doesn't have any."

[6] Only the back of children's heads could be seen in the picture.
[7] Zucker, H. J., *Affectional Identification and Delinquency*. Archives of Psychology, No. 286. Columbia University, 1943.

"He could be thinking about having millions and millions of friends. He could be thinking of ways of making friends."

"He is thinking about when he is old enough to get a job."

"She is thinking about her report card. Maybe she didn't pass."

"She might be thinking what fun it would be to have friends."

Role-playing

We have reported to you two instances of role-playing. One, the attempt to discover expectation in interaction pattern (the "playing school" incident), was unsuccessful. The other, based on the quarrels of three little girls, we feel was quite successful.

Dramatic play of young children may be considered a type of role-playing. An extension of the usual values ascribed to role-playing is the fact that it may give the teacher additional insight into home living. A teacher in an underprivileged area, anxious to know more of the home responsibilities and eating habits of her group, prepared a simple ques-

WHAT WOULD YOU DO IF YOU WERE THERE?

tionnaire to be filled in by the pupils. One of the questions was, "Who sets the table for breakfast?" A variety of answers was given, which the teacher carefully tabulated. A few days later the teacher was observing the children "playing house." The scene was the kitchen of the home in early morning. The mother was busily heating a big pan of beans on the stove. She placed bread on the table, then called the children one by one. Each child entered, took a piece of bread, spread beans on it, and went out the door. This was breakfast. The "table setting" comprised putting bread on the table. It is probable that in many of these homes the family rarely sat down at the table for meals, and even then it was not supplied with the usual table service. Watching these children act out their daily lives did more to enlighten this teacher than could the most carefully tabulated responses to questionnaires.

We feel that it is quite possible that we could have used role-playing more widely than we did. As we used it, it was primarily a means of providing common experience as a basis for group discussion. Enthusiasts for role-playing give emphasis to its value as therapy. No doubt there is this value when it is employed by a skilled therapist in situations highly emotionally charged. We do not doubt that some group therapy was provided even in the less highly charged situations we introduced. However, we feel that there is grave potential danger when untrained people attempt to use role-playing as a means to group therapy in situations of emotional tension.

Creative Arts

Creative arts—painting, modeling, crafts, music, drama, writing, and dancing—were an important aspect of the programs of all groups with which we worked. We were extremely hesitant, however, in using art *products* as a basis for interpretation. No doubt such interpretation may be of value, but we did not feel sufficiently skilled to employ it. We were interested, however, and extremely so, in the *approach* to the arts made by individuals and groups. In observation of children engaged in painting and modeling, for example, we asked ourselves questions such as these:

Does he seem to have ideas he is eager to express?
Does he have the techniques for expressing his ideas?
Does he work with absorption or is he easily distracted by those about him?
Does he seem satisfied with the results of his work?
Does he stick to his work until he considers it finished?

Does he work well with others in group projects?

What is his usual role in group art work?

Does he tend to use one or a few media or does he employ a wide range? Which media does he prefer?

Does he enjoy exploring the use of new media?

Does he have certain recurring "themes" of expression (e.g., horses, flowers, war scenes, etc.)?

Observations were recorded as anecdotes of individuals or of the group.

When children wished to do so, they were encouraged to tell or write the "story of my picture." Samples of such stories written by nine- and ten-year-olds are given below.

Ronny, insecure in both his home and his school relations, and wanting to be "owned," to "belong," tells this story of his picture of a truck:

> Once there was a truck that was sad because nobody owned him. While he was sitting in a parking lot, Jimmy the dump truck came along and said, "Why are you crying, Billy?" Billy the truck said, "Nobody owns me." Then Jimmy said, "Yesterday I saw a person who needed a truck like you. Why don't you go find him?" Billy found him and the truck had an owner.

Peter had painted a battleship, complete with crew and plenty of black smoke coming from the stack. This is Peter's story of his picture, entitled "The Ship on the Sea":

> The ship on the sea reminds me of my uncle in the army. When he came back from the army he told us about his adventures. Now he doesn't like to tell us about it because we are getting old and we will soon be in the army and he will think if we hear about it we will not go in the army. (And to think that this revelation of cultural forces is in the picture of a ship!)

Gloria, aged 10, finding that one art form leads to another, expresses her feeling in verse:

Spring Is Here

Spring is here,
Spring so dear.
When leaves on trees grow,
And little plants grow row on row;
When people feel so gay,
Today and every day, and in every way.

The art products of children, though difficult to interpret and often impossible to interpret without supporting evidence from other sources, nevertheless may serve to furnish valuable clues, particularly when the child artist aids in the interpretation.

RECORDS OF HEALTH AND PHYSICAL MATURITY

A physical examination, more thorough than that usually provided by the public schools, was offered to every child in each of the three groups with which we worked intensively. The notice of the eighth grade group reads as follows:

Dear Parents:

We are having a physical examination for your child during the week of January 27th.

This examination is to be given in conjunction with the Columbia University study to determine the correlation between physical characteristics and various aspects of human relations. There is no charge for this service.

The examination will be more helpful to both child and school if the parent can attend.

The decision as to whether the examination is given your child rests entirely with you.

Please return the attached slip,[8] indicating whether you desire that your child have this examination by January 23.

You will be notified of the time of your appointment later.

We shall appreciate your cooperation.

$$\text{(Signed) } \underline{\hspace{3cm}}, \text{ Principal}$$
$$\underline{\hspace{3cm}}, \text{ General Education Teacher}$$

All children in the first grade and in the fourth and fifth grade group were examined, with the exception of a few absent for valid reasons and one whose parents objected for religious reasons.

Most of the eighth graders were examined, although there was almost a walkout when one of the girls discovered that the examining physician was a man (see page 121).

Reasons given by parents of the eighth graders for not allowing the examination ranged from that of one mother who claimed school doctors did not know their business (one doctor had once diagnosed a seeming heart murmur for one member of her family) to that of the mother of a seriously handicapped boy, who said, "He's been to so many doctors."

In all groups, there was discussion prior to the examination concerning why it was given and what would happen during the examination. With this preparation, there was no evidence of nervousness on the part of the six- and seven- and the nine- and ten-year-olds. Eighth grade pupils went to the examination room in two's and three's, if they cared to, each wait-

[8] See "Notice of Health Examination," Appendix, page 431.

HEALTH RECORDS ARE A MEANS TO UNDERSTANDING BOYS AND GIRLS.

ing in the anteroom while the other was being examined. This seemed to put them more at ease than if they had gone individually. Parents accompanied all first grade children and many of those in the fourth and fifth grade group.

The examining physician was aware of the purpose of the examination, and asked a few questions concerning personal adjustment, likes and dislikes, use of leisure time, and the like. The questions themselves gave little information not already known to the teachers, but the first grade teacher, present for the examination, was interested in seeing children's reactions to such questioning by a stranger. Moreover, she reports that she found valuable the opportunity to watch mother and child together while she played the role of observer. She had seen them together before, but only under circumstances in which she was a participant in the happenings. (See Appendix, page 433, for form of report to parents of results of examination.)

The eighth grade teacher was able, from the physician's report, to make a rough four-point scale of maturity based on records of amount of axillary and pubic hair and date of first menses.

A grip test was administered to pupils of the group, but the results were not found to be meaningful or useful. Perhaps if they had been studied further in relation to other factors there might have been more significance than we realized.

As reported earlier, we could find little concrete evidence of the relation of general health and maturity alone to group living. The boy who the teacher felt might not be well accepted because his health made it difficult for him to do some things with other children was, according to the Classroom Social Distance Scale, well accepted. There is some indication that the more physically mature are better accepted and are assigned roles of leadership, but the many exceptions in these groups make this difficult to state as a generalization. In the eighth grade group, Sam, one of the most physically mature as well as one of the oldest boys, was a dominant leader of the group; but Don, equally physically mature and older by a month, was not well accepted by the group. Although there are many exceptions, it would seem that skill in sports, related to some extent to physical maturity, is more significant than the maturity itself, at least with children of certain ages. This hypothesis has interesting implications for grouping.

If boys are "held back" because they lack academic achievement, are we providing as leaders of younger boys the ones we "fail"? If we, knowing that girls mature more rapidly and at an earlier age than boys, "hold back" boys, is it possible that we are providing to girls, as the first objects of romantic interest, the boys whom we won't "promote"? There is food for thought here, we believe.

In terms of individual adjustment, *rate* of growth may be of equal or more importance than state of physical maturity at any one time. The monthly height-weight records kept by teachers, even for only one year (though preferably over a longer period of time), can give a rough measure of the place of an individual on the growth curve, thus providing an estimate of physical maturity.

In the eighth grade, many of the girls were at or near the top of their growth spurt, but even among these girls there were dramatic differences. Figures 25 and 26 give the height records of two eighth grade girls from October to June, and show Ruth still growing, with Doris having passed the growth spurt.

The physician's notations for Ruth read (Figure 25), "Regular menstruation, pubic and axillary hair, well developed, mature," and for Doris they read (Figure 26), "No menses, no axillary, slight pubic hair, im-

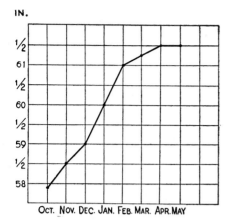

FIGURE 25. RUTH.

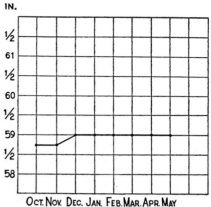

FIGURE 26. DORIS.

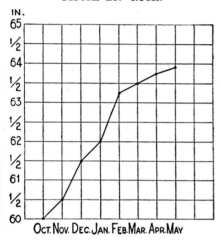

FIGURE 27. HERBERT.

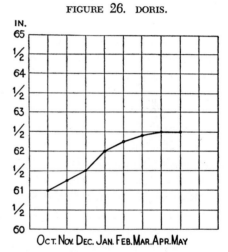

FIGURE 28. PETER.

GROWTH RECORDS

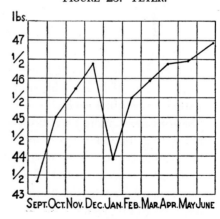

FIGURE 29. SUSAN.

mature, underdeveloped." Not all cases show as clear a relationship of growth to maturity, but the growth rate may be an indication at least.

We should not leave the statements above without pointing to the dangers of interpretation on the basis of short-term records. In Figures 27 and 28 we find Herbert growing rapidly and Peter showing little growth. On the basis of this small amount of evidence, we might be led to believe that Herbert is reaching the end of his growth spurt (probably true) and that Peter has passed the growth spurt. However, on the basis of the teacher's estimate and the physician's report for Peter (moderate pubic hair, no axillary hair), it may well be that Peter has merely reached the "slow-down" stage prior to the major growth spurt. The dangers of possible mistakes, such as those suggested above, lead us to re-emphasize the need for *continuous* height-weight records for boys and girls of all ages, but particularly for ages eleven to eighteen. Moreover, it points to the need for boys, girls, and teachers to be aware of how growth takes place, particularly during the preadolescent and adolescent periods, and to know how to interpret records of growth. Of all times, this knowledge is most important in junior high school, when worries about growth are most prevalent. Such information given to boys and girls during junior high school will forestall the worries of the slower maturing, who may apply the information concerning growth spurt during their senior high school years.

Records like Figure 29 for Susan, a first grader, showing sharp drops in weight, may furnish the teacher a signal that a further health check is needed. Incidentally, weighing, measuring, and making graphic records of height and weight for young children may be an excellent opportunity for school service, as well as for learning experience, for older boys and girls.

We are not recommending that, in studying group living, records of height and weight replace the physician's examination. We are suggesting, however, that the height-weight record may be helpful to teachers, and that it is easily available under circumstances where the physician's careful examination is not.

Studies much more carefully made than ours give ample evidence of the relation of maturity to *individual* adjustment. Further studies of *group* adjustment in relation to range of maturity, rate of growth, and similar factors would be of value.

Still unanswered is the question of group reaction in terms of general health of group members. We have pointed out earlier that it seems evident that undernourished, fatigued groups respond with listlessness and easy conformity, while groups with robust health respond with vigor and spirit. More precise studies in this area should be made.

STUDY OF SCHOOL PRACTICES

One of the most revealing activities in which the teachers engaged was that of looking at the generally accepted, everyday practices which they employed in the management and operation of the classroom. In every school and in every classroom within a school there are ways of working so firmly rooted that they seldom intrude on the level of consciousness. Whether we are aware of them or not, they play an important part in determining the reactions of the boys and girls. Many generally unrecognized group routines have much the same effect.

It was very revealing to both teachers and groups to see occasionally just what they were doing, and what possible effects these habitual ways of working had on their subsequent behavior. Needless to say, many changes were made, and many other practices were being closely examined for their effects, rather than being accepted without question. Among the practices thus examined by the teacher, the group, or both were:

Grouping	Delegating responsibility
Class organization	Competition
Student government	Rewards, Awards
"Extracurricular" activities	Conforming to rules
Group planning	Deviation from rules
Grades, Reports	Selection of experiences
Promotion practices	Interaction patterns
Methods of choosing leaders	

We have discussed many of these in Chapters VII and VIII. We are far from "knowing the answers" as to how situations such as these should be handled, even for the groups with which we worked. Available in the literature are reports of a number of precise studies in several of these areas (studies of the effect of competition, for example), but we cannot be sure that the conclusions reached in the rigidly controlled experimental situations in which most were conducted, apply to those where the variables are many. We made no attempt to eliminate variables, but rather attempted to study the variables as well as the factors being scrutinized. It is our conviction that this research approach has promise, and should be explored further.

THE TEACHER AS OBSERVER

In many of the techniques discussed, the teacher may play the role of an observer, but in most, the group as well as the teacher may participate. There are occasions, however, when the teacher may consider himself more observer than participant.

Responding to Forms Used by Group

The teacher, apart from the group, may make responses and record judgments on forms also used by the group. Among these are the Check Sheet of Opportunities (page 407) and Social Analysis of the Classroom (page 419). The listing of most and least accepted children might be considered an extension of this type of activity. Use of these forms may furnish the teacher with a basis for a comparison of his judgments with those of the group, to be used as a check of accuracy in interpreting group reaction, or as a means to discover difference in values.

Instruments for Teacher Use

It is probable that the value of instruments used by teachers is primarily in directing attention to certain factors rather than in measurement. The Identification Sheet (page 416), Study of Group Composition (page 425), Meeting Individual Needs (pages 254–257), and Guide for Group Observation (page 413) are of this nature. Attention having been directed to certain aspects of group living, these aspects can then be studied by other means. As in the case of any techniques of this type, there is danger in relying on them too heavily. We feel they should be supplemented continuously by less circumscribed observations recorded as anecdotes.

TEACHER-DEVISED INSTRUMENTS

It is possible that when teachers devise instruments, a major value lies in the devising itself. The importance of this fact cannot be overlooked, we believe. The teacher group which created the Guide for Group Observation brought to it the experience of group observation which might not otherwise have been crystallized for them or easily communicated to other teachers.

We do not mean to disparage the value of the instruments themselves, however. When a teacher has a problem to which he wants the answer, and no standardized instruments are available, we feel that the instrument he devises may be extremely important for his purposes. One such creative teacher decided that she wanted to know more about the playground reaction of her second and third grade group. After some initial observation of the group, she devised a list of nineteen items to observe, a number of which are given here:

1. No interest in playing old games of past year.
2. Not interested in learning new games.
3. Interest span very short.
4. Unsocial acts that disrupt other groups.
5. Throwing sand.
6. Quarreling about rules or score.
7. Bragging or boasting.
8. Pouting and sulking over defeat.
9. Selfish in sharing "turns" on swing.

Her report states:

Procedure: With a colored pencil I checked names on the seating chart for each of the headings listed. Later, when I had more time, I wrote the child's name after the proper heading. I watched for only one or two things each day.

I used the unsocial acts of behavior as teaching situations, so that after the second week many of the things checked were no longer a problem. (Examples 4, 5, 6, 7, 8 are improved.)

The Three Wishes test (Springfield Interest Finder, including a sociometric question) given later shows that the first eleven items in this observation test were peculiar to children not liked or chosen by others, and *also* to children well liked but immature in physical development.

Children who are having trouble in adjusting to school life or who are problem children with problem parents fall under the first eleven items.

The record form for checking looked like this:

Names (2A–3B)	Points Observed																		
	1	2	3	4	5	6	7	8	9	10	11	12	13	14	15	16	17	18	19
Robert B......	x									x	x								
Anthony.....												x			x		x		
William......												x	x	x				x	x	x
Robert F.....				x		x		x					x							
Janice........											x	x	x	x		x	x		
Barbara......											x		x	x		x	x		

The teacher provided additional information for certain children, such as "Negro boy," "Very immature," and "Heart ailment."

There are those who might question some of the items on the 19-point list as difficult to interpret. Maybe they are; but this teacher was interested in answers to *her* problems, and she found them in terms of her interpretations. This, we believe, to be of major significance in teacher-devised instruments. If they can be so devised as to be useful to other teachers and lend themselves to wider use, all the better.

We feel it important that teachers share with one another their research findings, which means that there must be sufficient objectivity to furnish common interpretation; but if a teacher is discouraged from trying to know his group because of the rigidity of research techniques, it is better to overlook the rules and to encourage the teacher. There are too few creative teachers and it would be a pity for us to shackle them with rigid rules. If, after trying the less objective approaches, a teacher shows signs of being interested in more precise measures, then is the time for those measures to be developed.

Another group of teachers decided that they had many unanswered questions about the needs and interests of boys and girls in their group. After considerable study of children and practice in use of other techniques, they devised a questionnaire for children. The following items are samples of the questions asked:

Do you like to have the teacher or someone else tell you how you can make your work better, or would you rather work it out by yourself?
Do you feel you should be successful in everything you do?
In art, would you rather think up a new picture or design, or would you rather copy a picture or design from a book?
Do you ever make up stories or poems for a friend or for your brother or sister?
What do you like to make up stories or poems about?
When were you the most excited in your whole life?
What did you do at that time?
Are you tired after any of your classes?
Which one?
Would you rather work alone or with a group?
Does it worry you if you are left to take care of a younger child?
When were you the most afraid?
Do you have a fear of anything?
Is there anyone at home or at school that you are afraid of?
Would you rather write the timetables or make up problems?
Do you like to go to school?

What would you be doing if you could not go to school?
Do you think boys and girls need to go to school?
Do you like to be with the children in this section?
Would you rather be with some other group of children?
Is there anyone in another section that you wish were in this section?
Do you like to dress like other children or do you like to be a little different?
Do you think your teachers are fair?
Do you think they are kind?
Do you think they like you?
Do you wish they were a little different in some way? How?
What do you do at home that is fun?
Is there something you would like to do at home that you are not allowed to do? What is it?
Do you have fun with your brother or sister?
Do you have fun with mother and daddy, or do you feel they are too busy?

We see two dangers in this type of instrument. First, it probes into areas of high emotional charge, and unless the teachers who use it are equipped to handle the possible emotional disturbance to children (these teachers were), there may be a major disruption in group living. Second, such techniques as this lend themselves to the "knowing for the sake of knowing" error we discussed earlier in this chapter. Teachers who undertake to use forms of this type should be willing and able to provide more appropriate programs as a result of their findings. This is easily said, but not so easily achieved. For example, if a child indicates on the form that he does not think his teachers are fair, are his teachers sufficiently objective to take this statement as an honest expression of opinion, and are they willing to examine possible causes of such opinion?

SURVEYS

In Chapter IX we discussed the use of surveys by parents and teachers—surveys of community living, home status, use of lunchtime, use of leisure time, learning opportunities, interests and concerns, high school drop-outs, and the like. In most of these surveys, children as well as adults participated. We are convinced that surveys can be valuable as a preparation for developing plans of action and for evaluation. There are innumerable opportunities in any school and community for boys and girls to learn through study of real situations, with the survey as an important part of this study. Because such surveys imply, usually, the investigation of the way of life of people, their relation to studies of group living is clear.

Socio-Economic Status

Although not strictly a survey, the use of the Sims socio-economic scale[9] might be considered to be in this category. It attempts to discover, on the basis of a number of questions concerning home living conditions, the socio-economic status of pupils. We chose this scale as more appropriate than others for the fourth and fifth and the eighth grade groups because it can be understood by pupils of these age groups. It is possible that the scale might be administered to a first grade group through interview, but rather than try this, the first grade teacher made a rough scale from her observations in visiting homes.

We found little relationship between socio-economic status as measured by this scale and group acceptance (page 175), but further studies might be of interest, starting not with the items of a predetermined scale but with prestige items as indicated by pupils.

GRAPHIC PRESENTATION OF DATA

Whenever it seems to add meaning, we have employed graphic presentation of data.

Sociograms

Plotting data in the form of sociograms has been most helpful in the study of group structure. In fact, without such plotting, the data indicate primarily status of the *individual*, and only with difficulty can it give indication of general *group* structure. (The use of this technique is discussed at length in Chapter V.)

Maps

The map presented on page 182 in connection with choice of friends was helpful in the study of the relationship of locality to friendship. Since all the children in the group studied lived in a relatively small area, it did not tell us much beyond the fact that friendships are not on a "neighbors only" basis. We would be interested in knowing whether similar results are found in relation to other types of school programs and in other types of communities where there is greater cleavage according to socio-economic status.

[9] The Sims Score Card for Socio-Economic Status is available from the author, School of Education, University of Alabama, University, Alabama.

Topological Presentation of Ideas

In Chapter III (pages 58 to 62) we attempted the application of some rudimentary topological principles in presenting ideas of field, force, and group action. Enthusiasts for topology might accuse us (with much truth) of merely presenting in graphic form preconceived ideas rather than making a true topological analysis. We feel it quite possible that further investigation in use of topological interpretation might be a definite aid in studies of group living. We recognize that we have made only a beginning, but hope our initial efforts may suggest further studies to other investigators. The exploratory ventures we have made may suggest directions for further research for others interested in this area.

Graphs and Charts

Our chief use of graphs and charts in this study has been in presenting height and weight data. It is quite possible that presentation of other data, particularly those which lend themselves to graphic comparisons, may be of value.

Much of our data might have been presented in chart form. It seemed to us, however, that in most cases descriptive or numerical presentation was sufficiently clear for our use, and therefore little chart-type material was prepared. There were exceptions, however.

Figure 30 (page 378) gives examples of profiles charted to show various patterns of group rating of individuals. Such profiles were plotted for each individual in the eighth grade group. Three widely divergent profiles are given as examples in this figure: The profile for Dorothy was most consistently high; that for Charles was most consistently low; and that for Eddie had the widest range (Eddie was rated as the most conceited boy in the class, yet he was accorded top rank in neatness and in control of his temper).

In Figure 31, page 379, are charted the relationships between group and self social distance scores. For the visual-minded, such a chart might show more clearly than rows of figures that there are wide individual differences in the relationship between how a group rates an individual and how the individual rates the group, but that there is a considerable tendency for those rated low by the group to rate the group high, and a slight tendency for those rated high to rate the group low.

Such means of interpreting and communicating findings can be valuable, and should be explored further.

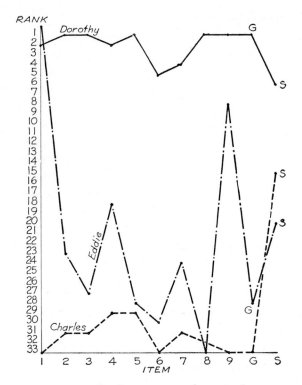

1   Always neat   7   Seems to come from nice home
2   Have fun with   8   Not conceited
3   Has other friends   9   Never loses temper
4   Does what people want   G   Group social distance (what others think of him)
5   Good sport   S   Self social distance (what he thinks of others)
6   Easily liked

FIGURE 30. PROFILES OF RATINGS ON 8TH GRADE CHECK SHEET.

GROUP RECORDS

In the groups with which we worked, each teacher kept a folder for each child. Individual test results, samples of work, such as spelling, arithmetic, art, and other such materials were kept in this folder. Examination of folders made it possible to get pictures of individuals and the group.

Sometimes, however, it is helpful to see records for the group as a whole. Each teacher drew up what was called a "Comparison Sheet," which made it possible to see at a glance certain records for the entire class. The notations included name, age, I.Q., achievement scores, data about family, scores on instruments such as the California Test of Personality, Classroom Social Distance Scale, and similar data.

Other groups of teachers have devised group records to show range of interest and ability in groups. One record, on one large sheet of paper, indicated for each pupil in the group such information as the following:

Health (above average, average, below average)

Muscular coordination (above, average, or below)

Interest in physical education (high, average, low)

Reading (score on achievement test)

Academic ratings in reading, spelling, English, social studies, and arithmetic (each ranked as high, medium, or low)

Major interests in academic subjects (e.g., art, gym, reading)

Acceptance by the group (high, medium, or low)

Sportsmanship (high, medium, or low)

Hardest subject (e.g., music, spelling, arithmetic)

Subject worried about (e.g., arithmetic)

Reaction to success (pleased, embarrassed, makes him want to do it again, etc.)

Reaction to failure (doesn't matter, worried, will do better next time, etc.)

Reaction to criticism (embarrassed, wants to improve, argues, etc.)

Reaction to excitement (laughs, cries, "shaky," etc.)

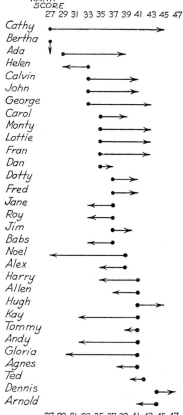

FIGURE 31. RELATION OF GROUP SOCIAL DISTANCE SCORES TO SELF SOCIAL DISTANCE SCORES.

Creative work (prefers "copy work," imaginative, plays piano, composes music, etc.)

Group work (likes to work in groups because "it isn't lonely," more fun in group, prefers working alone, etc.)

Responsibility (not too quick to accept responsibility, does not like to do
tasks in room, tries to do what he should, accepts it well but is worried for
fear of not doing things right, etc.)

Fear (afraid of dark, of getting lost, of meeting new people, etc.)

Routine work (likes routine, wants change, likes to make own decisions, etc.)

Attitude toward school (would rather play football, likes school, doesn't like
to go to school)

Attitude toward classmates (wishes his best friends were in the group, likes
this group, etc.)

Attitude toward teachers (they're friendly, teachers are nice most of the
time, thinks some teachers don't like him, etc.)

Attitude toward home and family (says happiest day was when Dad came
home from army, enjoys playing with brother, feels parents too busy to
play with him, etc.)

Talent (swimming, poetry, piano, art, mechanical aptitude, etc.)

Hobby (stamps, dog pictures, violin, etc.)

Information for many of these items was drawn from the questionnaire
described on page 374. Admittedly, many of these items are subjective.
The chief value of this chart, we believe, is that it presents for easy reference a record for an entire group, thus directing observation to further
aspects of behavior of the individual and the group.

JUDY, A GROUP MEMBER

The study we undertook was an investigation of group behavior, but
as we progressed we realized that, although the focus was the group, we
were learning much about each individual in the group. As an illustration
of what is learned about an individual through the study of a group, may
we introduce Judy.

The records for Judy will serve also to show how the various types of
information gathered through the use of techniques and devices are
interrelated and how they supplement one another.

There is no particular reason for choosing Judy instead of any of the
others in the group except that she is a girl who in many respects might
be referred to as "an average person." She does not stand out in any
particular way. She could very easily be overlooked in a teacher's preoccupation with deviates whose very conspicuousness compels attention.

The following account was written not by her teacher, but by a person
who did not know Judy, from an examination of the teacher's records of
her group. Comparable information was available for each child in the
group.

Judy as a Vital Statistic

Judy was born on August 25, 19—. When school opened in the fall of last year she was just past her tenth birthday. There were seven children in the room older than Judy. She was 53½ inches tall and weighed 58 pounds, being 10 pounds underweight for her height and age. However, the physician's examinations showed that she was well built, had a good muscular tone, and gave no evidence of impending physical maturation. Her right eye vision is 20/70 and that of the left eye 20/50. This defect is corrected by glasses so that her vision with her glasses is 20/20 in each eye.

Judy's parents have been divorced. She lives with her mother, stepfather, two younger brothers, and a younger sister. Her stepfather is custodian of an apartment house. Her mother is a housewife. The socio-economic score for Judy, as determined by the Sims Socio-Economic Scale, is 1.7773. This is 17th in rank in the class of 31.

In June, Judy completed the first half of the fifth year in school. Her grade placement, therefore, was 5.5. At the time, the Progressive Reading and Language tests gave the following grade placements:

Reading Vocabulary	6.7
Reading Comprehension	6.4
General Language	6.6

Her I.Q. is 107, 16th in rank in the class of 31.

The results of the California Test of Personality placed her in the 55th percentile in self-adjustment and in the 70th percentile in social adjustment, with a total adjustment in the 60th percentile.

Judy as the Teacher Sees Her

Using the Identification Sheet (Appendix, page 416), the teacher on October 7 classified Judy in the following ways:

Usually conforms to and accepts classroom regulations.
Regular in attendance.
Apparently bright and is doing well.
Particularly well coordinated.

Since the teacher in this case used only four of the ten possible descriptive categories, Judy apparently was not a conspicuous character.

This same identification sheet was re-used on February 10. Judy this time was described as follows:

Usually conforms to and accepts classroom regulations.
Works steadily on assigned work.
Spontaneous in contributing ideas.
Apparently bright and is doing well.
Popular with other children.
Usually seems happy.
Attendance regular.

Later in the spring, on the third use of the Identification Sheet by the
teacher, Judy was described as follows:

Usually conforms to and accepts classroom regulations.
Works steadily on assigned work.
Spontaneous in contributing ideas.
Apparently bright and is doing well.
Appears tense; easily upset.

It should be remembered that the teacher in this case was completely
immersed in a study of ways of contributing to group living and was using
the Identification Sheet as a group-centered device. As the year wore on,
her insights became keener and she had an ever more abundant background of information on which to draw.

As one examines the descriptive phrases applied to Judy in the three
instances, it is easy to notice the growth in discrimination on the part of
the teacher. The first time, there is the obvious description of the inconspicuous child. The second time, the teacher has dropped the "particularly well coordinated" item as not being applicable but has added
"works steadily on assigned work," "spontaneous in contributing ideas,"
"popular with other children," and "usually seems happy." Obviously
she is becoming more aware of Judy as a participant and an integral part
of the group.

A further acquaintance with Judy leads the teacher to conclude (the
third time) that Judy seems tense and easily upset, and has caused her to
question Judy's popularity with the other children.

Obviously, then, the teacher saw Judy first as an inconspicuous average
child, then as an important and apparently happy, effective, popular
group member, and finally as one whose contributions are sound but who
faces personal problems of some magnitude.

Three other instruments used by the teacher give indications as to how
the teacher sees Judy: the Classroom Social Distance Scale, the Study of
Group Composition, and the Social Analysis of the Classroom.

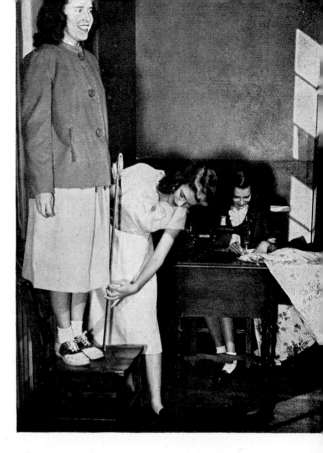

EVERY INDIVIDUAL HAS A RIGHT
TO RECEIVE HELP IN SOLVING HIS
PROBLEMS.

On the Social Distance Scale (Appendix, page 401), filled out by the teacher in the fall of the year, Judy was placed in Group 2 (Glad to have him in the room). By May, when this scale was used again, Judy had dropped, in the teacher's opinion, to Group 3 (Would like to be with him once in a while but not too often).

A device entitled Study of Group Composition (Appendix, page 425) was filled out by the teacher in May. There are sixteen aspects of group living listed here, with an opportunity for the teacher to list those having each quality to a large extent or a small extent. Judy's name does not appear.

In May the teacher filled out the Social Analysis of the Classroom form (Appendix, page 419). Judy was placed in the following categories:

Here is someone who can work very quietly without moving around in her seat.

Here is someone who plays active games like football and basketball a great deal, or who likes to run and jump and so on.

[383]

This is someone who never seems to have a good time, who never seems to enjoy very much anything she does.

Here is someone who always tries to keep herself neat and clean and tidy looking.

Here is a girl who is interested in boys. She likes to go to parties or dances.

Here is someone who can never appreciate a joke when it is on herself.

Here is someone who enjoys a fight; she often fights rather than let the other person have his (or her) way.

This is someone who is always telling others what to do, bossing them.

We not only have recourse to formal instruments to discover how the teacher sees Judy. From the anecdotes written by the teacher concerning Judy, the following are selected as examples:

Judy is very talkative and offered to help with many things. (9/23)

Judy does very good school work but is not too well adjusted socially. (9/27)

She is practically in tears at just the least reprimand, but is soon pleasant and busy again. (9/27)

Judy mentioned both of her dads without seeming to be embarrassed, but often seems to imply that she'd like to see her first dad. (1/14)

Judy spends most of her spare time talking with Peter S. (1/21)

Judy has improved more than anyone else in the room socially in the last two or three weeks . . . She is a motherly little person and is very helpful. (1/21)

Judy has developed a suspicious attitude and acts as if things weren't aboveboard with her. (2/28)

Judy was unwilling to cooperate with me in counting votes today. She seemed sorry that she'd been so cross and was very good the rest of the day. (4/22)

Judy has been leading Catherine into being unfriendly with Susan, and had difficulty a few weeks ago with Betty. In the interview she said this has happened every winter. She just likes to start things. She said at her former school she and her cousin told the kids that a child had its head cut off. They got into a lot of trouble. She seems to think that to tell these wild stories are just "jokes." She claims she likes to tease. (5/9)

Wednesday, when we were in a ball game, Judy said that all that mattered was who won and that all the other kids felt that way, too. (5/9)

Judy stayed with me from 3:15 till 5:00, helping to get things ready for our supper. She was a good helper. (5/23)

(Incidentally, it is of interest to note that the teacher showed improvement in objective reporting.)

On the last day of the school year, the teacher made the following comments, among others, on Judy's cumulative record card:

Judy has made rapid progress in trying to get along with other people, both children and adults. She still can improve a lot, but seems to recognize the need to be better understood in order to make her ideas more effective, and has worked hard to control herself.

Judy as the Group Sees Her

During the first few days of school, the teacher suggested to the group that they might be interested in writing some statements of first impressions of one another. The group decided to try this. Thirteen people in the group commented on Judy. Ten of these remarks were favorable, ranging from "Judy is a nice little girl" to "Judy looks like a good playmate." Two, however, one boy and one girl, indicated that they had the impression that "Judy thinks she's smart." One boy bluntly stated, "I hate Judy."

On the Social Distance Scale, Judy received a group social distance score of 3.5. This placed her 21st in rank in the group of 31. The distribution of her ratings on this instrument was as follows:

	No. of Children
Group 1—Would like to have him as one of my best friends	12
Group 2—Would like to have him in my group but not as a close friend	8
Group 3—Would like to be with him once in a while but not often or for long at a time	2
Group 4—Don't mind his being in our room but I don't want to have anything to do with him	2
Group 5—Wish he weren't in our room	7

Apparently many of the group like Judy, some dislike her intensely, but very few are lukewarm about her.

On the nine sociograms, Judy was designated a key person (chosen by five or more pupils) on four. On all three of the sociograms constructed in November she was given this designation, also on the "movie" sociogram ("With whom would you like to go to the movies?") in April. Judy never received key-person designation on the friendship charts, which may indicate a certain aloofness in the group attitude toward her. She was not an isolate on any of the sociograms.

In the Social Analysis of the Classroom, the group indicated that the following nine statements were descriptive of Judy:

Here is someone who can work very quietly without moving around in her seat.

Here is someone who plays active games like football and basketball a great deal, or who likes to run and jump, and so on.

Here is someone who is always worried or scared, who won't take a chance when something unexpected or unusual happens.

Here is someone who waits for somebody else to think of something to do and always likes to follow the suggestions which others make.

Here is someone who always tries to keep herself neat and clean and tidy looking.

Here is a girl who likes to read boys' books, play boys' games, or would prefer to be a boy.

Here is a girl who is interested in boys. She likes to go to parties or dances.

This person is fond of a good joke, is the first to laugh, and always sees the point.

Here is someone who is very friendly, who has lots of friends, who is nice to everybody.

Even a cursory perusal of the above gives the impression that the description of Judy by the group is very different in some important respects from the description of Judy by the teacher, although similar in the more obvious aspects. It would seem to indicate that the group and the teacher do not always look at an individual through the same-colored glasses.

One of the important positions in Judy's group is that of planning leader. The planning leader is essentially an assistant teacher. He conducts the planning sessions, writes the plans on the blackboard, assigns tasks, and acts as person in charge when the teacher is not in the room.

Judy served as planning leader for one week during the year. At the end of that time, as was customary, each member of the group wrote an evaluation of "Judy As a Planning Leader." Indications of the group's impression of Judy may be gleaned from these evaluations. A few of the comments were as follows:

Judy As Planning Leader

She is just about perfect.

I liked the way she took over the class when Miss Roberts was out of the room.

She planned good and the people minded.

She gave her suggestions as well as she took ours.

She asked questions very good. She didn't show off and she was very good in front of the room.

The teacher had to help her a little, but aside from that she was good.

She was always up there on time.

It is interesting to note that Judy received no unfavorable comments, although most of the pupils who served as planning leaders did.

Judy as She Sees Herself

On most of the devices used in the study an opportunity is provided for each individual to include himself. This gives us the chance to ascertain how an individual sees himself in the group setting.

On the Classroom Social Distance Scale, Judy was one of the few who did not rate herself, so we have no indication here as to her concept of her place in the group.

On the Social Analysis of the Classroom, Judy listed three categories as being descriptive of herself. In all three of these there was agreement between Judy and her group. In only one case was there agreement with the teacher. The statements that Judy felt were self-descriptive were:

> Here is a girl who likes to read boys' books, play boys' games, or would prefer to be a boy.
> Here is a girl who is interested in boys. She likes to go to parties or dances. This person is very fond of a good joke, is the first to laugh, and always sees the point.

The Springfield Interest Finder reveals more about the way in which Judy sees herself. Her three wishes are (1) to be a singer, (2) to have a fountain pen and pencil set, (3) to take tap dancing. She likes best outside of school to have friends to play with, and dislikes most having to stay in on cold days. She doesn't like story time in school, but favors the music periods. Apparently she does not take too seriously her mother's remark to the teacher—"I think the (my) children are such ugly little things sometimes that I wonder if they'll ever grow up to be useful people."

Judy's responses on the Springfield Interest Finder used several months later were:

> My three wishes:
> 1. I wish I could be a singer.
> 2. I wish I had a five-dollar bill to buy my mother a set of new dishes.
> 3. I wish I had a "one" (high grade) in music this year.
> What I'd like to learn more about at school: (no response).
> What I don't care to study about: Reading.
> What I like best at school: Music.
> What I like best outside of school: Piano.
> What I like least or dislike most at school: Nothing.
> What I like least or dislike most outside of school: To not have people to come over (not to have visitors).
> What I want to be or do when I grow up: A singer.

The most interesting thing I have done at school during the past week or so:
Is we have lots of fun.
One of the places I especially like to go to in Denver: Shows.
One of the happiest days in my life: Was when I was going horse riding.

On the Check Sheet of Opportunities in Human Relations, Judy describes herself as:

Finding it easy to make friends.
Wishing she had more skill in getting along with people.
Well liked by most.
A leader.
More intelligent than most.
Wanting to be with people most of the time.
Being more interested in people than in things or ideas.
Wishing the school would give more help in how to get along with people.

On the same instrument Judy said she wanted to improve herself in the following ways:

Get along with people.
I would like to be interested more.
Have more friends.

She says she seldom or never:

Plays with people much older.
Spends leisure time with friends of her own choice.
Works for pay.

On the other hand she thinks she frequently:

Plays with children younger.
Plays with boys.
Plays with wealthier people.
Is a member of a group which elects its own leaders.
Is a leader of a group her own age.
Spends her leisure time alone.
Works at home without pay.

Judy would go to her mother or grandmother if she were worried about a personal problem. She thinks there is too much adult control of her in both home and school.

When Judy wrote "My Story" (her autobiography) in September, soon after the opening of school, she found little to tell other than the names, ages, and birthplaces of herself, her mother, her father, her sister, and her two brothers. She adds to these coldly factual statements these sentences: "My father is the janitor. He works pretty hard. My mother she works hard too. I enjoy my family and home. That is the end of my story."

"The Story of My Life," written in May, toward the end of the same school year, is much more revealing. She reports:

> I was born in Denver Colorado in the St. Joe General hospital. When I was 6 years old I was in California. I went to a school that had just two rooms, first, second and third grade in one room and fourth, fifth and sixth grade in the other. We lived right across from the ocean. My dad was in the Navy. There was sort of a little cabin where the sailors stayed and I used to go up there and the sailors were always teasing me. I came back to Denver and I went to a home for two or three months. I went to another home and stayed a while. Then I went to another home and stayed 2 years. My mother came back and she got a home.[10] When I was 3 years old we lived out on Arnold Street. One Sunday they had an orchestra playing and I got up and started dancing to the music in front of the crowd.

Thus it would seem that Judy sees herself as a leader, and as happy, useful, and artistic. She finds home satisfying, wants to be with friends, and is eager to have more. She is interested in musical activities and has vocational plans in that direction.

The Group as Judy Sees It

In checking the Classroom Social Distance Scale, Judy indicates the following degrees of acceptance of people in her group:

	No. of Names Checked
Group 1—Would like to have him as one of my best friends	12
Group 2—Would like to have him in my group but not as a close friend	12
Group 3—Would like to be with him once in a while but not often or for long at a time	4
Group 4—Don't mind his being in our room but I don't want to have anything to do with him	4
Group 5—Wish he weren't in our room	0

These designations give Judy a self social distance score of 4.0, which places her 12th in the class of 31. From this it would seem that Judy leans very heavily toward accepting her fellow classmates, without absolutely rejecting any.

---

[10] Now we know the significance of Judy's September statement, "I enjoy my family and home."

An examination of her choices on the sociograms may also be some-what revealing:

Of the nine choices that Judy made on the three friendship charts, she listed seven different names. She evidently did not find a clique within the group to which she became attached.

On the November sociograms she was apparently much interested in Roy and chose him first on all three activities. Her other choices were varied in terms of the suggested situation. However, in May she chose the same three names for all three activities, indicating somewhat greater identification with the people of her choice.

In filling out the Social Analysis of the Classroom form, Judy mentioned all but four of her classmates as fitting one or more of the descriptions. This was a considerably larger number than most of the other members of the class mentioned, and probably shows a fairly high awareness of the capabilities or incompetencies of her classmates.

Judy says that she "likes the way my best friends play. They play fair in games practically all the time. Except one girl. She plays fair all the time." Apparently Judy looks at the group in terms of how fairly they play. She also seems willing to overlook occasional lapses from the standard.

In the evaluation discussion at the end of the year, Judy made the following statements about the progress of the class toward the goals they had established:

> We do not have so many arguments.
> We have learned that the "safeties" are our friends.
> I think we have improved our playing together.
> We get along working together better.
> We have friends now.
> There is not so much arguing.
> We have improved by not being so selfish.
> There are just a few rude ones, so I think we have improved.
> We have improved on being greedy.
> We all have healthy bodies.

These statements have that strange vagueness which so often creeps into discussions of goals and evaluations of progress. In this class, however, the goals were made specific by examples (Appendix, page 427), so that the fact that Judy considered improvement to have been made may be more meaningful than her statements indicate.

Summing up, we might say that Judy is well aware of the group in which she works, is conscious of the potentialities of its members, varies from time to time in her "at homeness" in it, but feels that, as a whole, progress is being made toward the accomplishment of the group toward its stated goals.

The Teacher as Judy Sees Her

Our one indication of Judy's attitude toward her teacher is given in the following brief statement which was appended to a description of her favorite teacher. (Judy chose to describe her kindergarten teacher as her favorite.)

> If I was a teacher I would not be cross if I did not have to. Some teachers have to be cross, or some kids would think they could get away with things they want to do that are not right. The teacher I have now is o.k. in some cases when she does not get cross. She does not get cross if some one does something that would be right. She does not get cross very often. Because this morning I was having help from Jane and she thought I was doing something wrong and when she scolded me it sort of hurt my feelings. But I do think it was my fault for half of it.

The World as Judy Sees It

We have no clear indication as to how Judy regards the wider society beyond her own immediate environment. There may be clues, however, in the two instances cited below.

The first of these is her remark: "The important thing in a game is to win. All the kids think so." Such a remark may indicate a highly competitive attitude toward others, and as such is a clue to her "life view."

Again, when she was asked to tell the story of her picture of a cabin on a high mountain, she spun a fanciful tale of an evil man hiding helpless people who were in his power and compelling them to do his bidding. However, in some way (Judy doesn't say how) right triumphs over might, and the deserving people, after putting the evil one in jail, retire in peace to "live happily ever after in the little cabin up so high."

It would be possible to spin out the story of Judy for many more pages. In these excerpts from her teacher's records, we have hoped to show that, although the study has been focused on the group and group living, we have gathered a great deal of information about even an "average" individual as she operates in a group setting. Such information is important and necessary. The individual is important and we must work with him. However, we don't do so in a vacuum, and seeing the individual as a participating member of the group is most helpful.

IN SUMMARY

No technique is "good" in itself. It is valuable or not in terms of the light it throws on problems. The research techniques we found most revealing were those involving boys and girls, parents and teachers, in "action research"—research in which all those concerned help to set the problem, suggest procedures, and evaluate results.

Certain supplementary devices may speed understanding and give clues to further action. We were particularly interested in certain response forms, such as the Classroom Social Distance Scale, Check Sheet of Opportunities in Human Relations. Teachers, as well as pupils, may employ with profit some of these devices.

Records of experience, written as anecdotes, may be helpful in studying groups as well as individuals. The techniques for observing group behavior are not easily acquired, but they can be learned with practice.

Boys and girls may contribute to records of experience by keeping logs, diaries, and records of time use. Autobiographies may contribute to records of experience, but they are most helpful in revealing the values held by boys and girls as they record what to them have been the most important events of their lives.

Personality tests may indicate areas for further investigation. Answers to questions in such tests may be recorded so as to indicate *group* responses, providing *group* as well as *individual* scores.

Tests of intelligence, readiness, and achievement may provide information about individuals and the group which is of interest if studied in relation to other factors of group living.

Projective techniques, particularly of the more informal type which may be used by a teacher, offer many avenues to further understanding of individuals and groups. Reaction to pictures, unfinished stories, and role-playing seem to offer great promise.

Records of health and rate of growth are of great significance. Records of rate of growth in height can be of particular meaning during pre-adolescence and adolescence, when stage of maturity may be intimately linked with the pupil's position on a curve of growth.

Studies of the reaction of individuals and groups to certain school practices can be helpful in understanding group behavior. Many such studies have been made in circumscribed laboratory situations, but the results may or may not apply to classrooms. There is need for further studies, in which the many "normal" variables of school situations are studied in relation to one another as the point of special interest is investigated.

Teachers, even those with little research training, can demonstrate creative insight by devising ways of studying group behavior. Although some of these techniques may lack the precision dear to the experienced researcher, we believe they can be very helpful to teachers in finding both personal satisfaction and clues to problems. We hope that these more or less informal approaches will be encouraged.

Surveys provide an important aid to the understanding of the backgrounds of group living. Teachers, parents, and pupils may find surveys a means to problem identification and increased insight.

When appropriate, graphic presentation of data may be helpful. Sociograms, maps, topological presentations, graphs and charts were found useful in this study. Some of these graphic presentations were of the usual type, such as bar graphs and charts, and some were "invented" to meet the needs of the situation.

We wish to repeat that we feel a device or technique is "good" if it helps to solve a problem or if it provides clues to further study. We believe that those who employ techniques to understand children have a moral and professional obligation to use the knowledge so derived for providing better programs of living. Child study or group study cannot be divorced from curriculum development.

Epilogue

For so many pages we have been immersed in the discussion of the affairs
of boys and girls and the practical matters of how teachers may operate
in classrooms that we may appear to have lost sight of the significance
of our job. Before we close we wish to restate our purposes and beliefs,
our vision of the ends to be achieved.

Franklin D. Roosevelt, at the time of the Bretton Woods Conference,
said, "The point in history at which we stand is full of promise and of
danger. The world will either move toward unity and widely shared
prosperity, or it will move apart into necessarily competing economic
blocks. We have a chance, we, the citizens of the United States, to use
our influence in favor of a more united and cooperating world. Whether
we do so will determine, as far as it is in our power, the kind of lives our
grandchildren can live."

It may be that before the children in our classrooms are grown fateful
decisions will have been made, and, depending on these decisions, Barbara, now wide-eyed and pigtailed, may be asked to say "Yes" or "No"
to bombings which can wipe out whole cities of men, women, and children. Tommy, freckled-faced and restless, may be the man to drop that
bomb, or David, struggling now with 10 + 2, may live to help wield a
force greater than atomic energy—the force of peoples united for a world
at peace. What can we do so that boys and girls can learn to use their
power, as group members, to ends both sound and just?

It is matters such as these which have concerned us as we have discussed the seemingly small affairs of classroom living, for from things
such as these grow the affairs of moment for individuals, groups, nations,
the world. They are the seeds of all tomorrows.

There was a time, perhaps, when man complete and individual could
stand alone against the wilderness and rule his destiny. That day has

ON THIS THRESHOLD WE HAVE A CHANCE.

passed. Today he lives because his neighbors will it so. He lives by merging his life with that of others in joint effort. Or he dies because he and his neighbors are at war. The pivot of the force which moves our world has become multiple, changing from the individual to the group. Moreover, the group is more than a mere aggregate of individuals. "We" is something above and beyond the sum of "me's." The group is a unit of human energy, operating as a body, and its behavior, as is that of the individual, is governed by its goals. The power of groups is now the ruler of our collective destinies.

What does this mean for schools? Where once we saw our job as educating each to his individual capacity (though, perforce, within a group), we now must see the responsibility for educating *groups* for group action, and for the development of group members. This means that grouping on the basis of individual needs or capacities alone is not enough. Studying and knowing individual needs and interests alone is not enough. Providing programs (curriculums) to meet these individual needs and interests alone is not enough.

These are not enough either to serve the individual who in our modern society is a member of the group, or to serve the group as a whole.

[395]

To meet this grave responsibility of educating groups and directing group dynamics, we need to know so very much. This need to know has been an important motivation as we have worked together.

In the study of some aspects of the problem, we pushed through in a systematic manner to marshal data, interpret and evaluate our findings. In the study of many other aspects, however, we found that we were opening such vast fields for research that we merely put down markers along the way to indicate areas in need of further study, and pushed on to probe other areas. Thus in many places in this report we raise questions, and sometimes suggest approaches to problem solution that we think might be helpful, but do not carry the investigation through to its conclusion. In a number of important areas, we have attempted to formulate working hypotheses, even though we have insufficient data to substantiate the postulated statements. Our major objective has been to explore the whole field and discover the problems it involves.

There may be readers who feel that we have been naive or superficial in our studies. Perhaps we have. We do not wish to make claims beyond our achievement. On the other hand, we wish to express the deep satisfaction it has given us, working as a group, to realize the significance of the studies we have made. They are studies which any group of teachers can make. We know, because we, a group of teachers, have done it. We are not anthropologists, sociologists, psychologists, or psychiatrists. We are teachers. We had the help of consultants and specialists, to be sure, but the things we report here are things we did in our classrooms with our groups of children. Any other group of teachers could do the same, or more.

The few beginnings which have been made in studying group structure, group reaction and interaction, and selection of experiences for group living, are but beginnings. We hope our studies have made some contribution, however small, to the growing stockpile of knowledge in these areas. But more than this, we hope our efforts may have pointed to the significance of the problems, the need for more studies, and the great contributions teachers working with boys and girls can make.

These phrases ring again, "The point in history at which we stand is full of promise and of danger. The world will either move toward unity . . . or . . ." But most significant to us, as teachers, is this further phrase, "We have a chance . . ."

Appendix: Instruments and Exhibits

On the following pages are the forms for some of the techniques and devices used in this study, and in some instances the instruction sheets accompanying them.

We are grateful to Gertrude P. Driscoll for permission to reproduce the Identification Sheet and to Arthur T. Jersild for the Springfield Interest Finder. We wish to express our appreciation to the Denver Public Schools for permission to reproduce the Notice of Health Examination.

Every means has been used to identify the authorship of the form, Social Analysis of the Classroom, found in the files of the Bureau of Research of the Denver Public Schools. It had been used in Denver in connection with an earlier research project; the people associated with that project recall using it, but disclaim authorship. We thought it might be an adaptation of Who's Who in My Group,* but the people who employed it state that it was used prior to the publication of that form. To some unknown author, we present a deep apology for not providing the credit due, and a sincere expression of gratitude for developing an instrument which we have found very useful.

For permission to reproduce forms originated by the Institute, write to: Horace Mann–Lincoln Institute of School Experimentation, Teachers College, Columbia University, New York 27, New York.

* Issued by Ohio Scholarship Tests and Elementary Supervision, State Department of Education, Columbus, Ohio.

HORACE MANN–LINCOLN INSTITUTE OF SCHOOL EXPERIMENTATION
TEACHERS COLLEGE, COLUMBIA UNIVERSITY

DESCRIPTION OF CLASSROOM SOCIAL DISTANCE SCALE

PURPOSE

The purpose of this instrument is to discover the social tone of a group as a whole, and the degree to which individuals and subgroups are accepted by the group and accept others in the group. It is devised to extend the usual sociometric approach, which allows a limited number of responses (e.g., three friends), to include an opportunity for every child to give a reaction to every other in the group.

ADMINISTERING

As the responses requested are of a highly confidential nature, this instrument is valid only if honest responses are given. It should be used only in situations where the teacher has achieved a high degree of rapport with the group. If there is resistance on the part of boys and girls either to using the instrument or to signing their names, it is probable that it should not be used. Obviously, it should be used only by teachers with a professional point of view and a genuine interest in knowing more about children in order to provide more adequate programs for them.

It is recommended that this scale be used only with children over 9 years of age. If the teacher has good rapport with the group, he will have little difficulty in introducing it. His explanation may be that he is interested in knowing how people in the group feel about each other so he may know how to help the group get along together and enjoy each other.

The teacher's name may be inserted as a group member, in the appropriate alphabetical position.

SCORING

It is probable that a careful study of each paper with special reference to interpersonal responses is more meaningful than a numerical score. However, if numerical scores are desired, it is possible to calculate them by giving arbitrary weighting to the items. Thus for each child the score is the sum of the number of times his name is checked for each item. For example, the name of John Jones in a class of 30 was checked 5 times in column 1 ("Would like to have him as my best friend"); 8 times in 2; 11 times in 3; 5 times in 4; and once in 5.

$$
\begin{aligned}
5 \times 1 &= 5 \\
8 \times 2 &= 16 \\
11 \times 3 &= 33 \\
5 \times 4 &= 20 \\
1 \times 5 &= \underline{5} \\
& 79
\end{aligned}
$$

John's *group* social distance score is 79. (Note: The lower the score, the greater the acceptance by the group—the less the social distance.)

We are interested also in John's feeling toward the group, his *self* social distance score. Examining John's paper, we find he checked 2 names in column 1; 5 in 2; 8 in 3; 10 in 4; and 5 in 5.

$$2 \times 1 = 2$$
$$5 \times 2 = 10$$
$$8 \times 3 = 24$$
$$10 \times 4 = 40$$
$$5 \times 5 = 25$$
$$\overline{101}$$

John's *self* social distance score is 101. It would be inferred that John's feeling for the group is less than the group's feeling for him. (*Self* social distance is greater than *group* social distance.)

INTERPRETATION

Examining responses and calculating scores are beginnings, not ends. Results should raise questions rather than answer them. Too little is known about group psychology of boys and girls to allow generalizations to be drawn from data provided through the use of an instrument such as this. Perhaps the greatest value in an examination of results is that it directs attention to certain aspects of inter-personal relations which lead to further observation of individual and group behavior. Such observations, carefully reported as anecdotes by teachers who are sensitive to problems of group relations, can make a great contribution to knowledge in this area.

REPORTING

Forms for the Classroom Social Distance Scale are being provided on a limited basis by Horace Mann–Lincoln Institute of School Experimentation to teachers who are willing to share results with the Institute. If you wish to cooperate in this study, you are asked to:

    a. Check the attached form headed "Characteristics of the Group."

    b. Return to us the original papers or the scores (see score sheet attached) or both.

Address materials to: Ruth Cunningham, Box 120, Teachers College, Columbia University, New York 27, N. Y.

HORACE MANN–LINCOLN INSTITUTE OF SCHOOL EXPERIMENTATION
TEACHERS COLLEGE, COLUMBIA UNIVERSITY

CHARACTERISTICS OF GROUP
(To accompany Classroom Social Distance Scale)

Teacher's name ....School ....
City ....State ....
Grade ....Age range .... to ....
Boys .... Girls ....

PART I

In a few sentences, describe what you consider to be characteristics of this group (e.g., wide range in ability; many isolates; overage or underage children; high or low morale; gangs, cliques; fighting; generally irritable, etc.).

PART II

On the basis of your experience with other groups of boys and girls of the same grade level, check each item to indicate whether you think this group is above or below average, or about average. Note that this check represents your impression of *the group as a whole.*

1. AGE: older.... younger.... about average.....
2. DEVELOPMENTAL PHASE: more mature.... less mature.... about average.....
3. SOCIO-ECONOMIC BACKGROUND: more favorable.... less favorable.... about average.....
4. DEGREE OF ACCEPTANCE OF EACH OTHER: more acceptance.... less acceptance .... about average.....
5. DEGREE OF PARENTAL ACCEPTANCE: more accepted.... less accepted.... about average.....
6. ACTIVE-LETHARGIC: more active.... more lethargic.... about average.....
7. INTELLIGENCE: more intelligent.... less intelligent.... about average.....
8. PHYSICAL SKILL: more skilled.... less skilled.... about average.....
9. INTEREST RANGE: more interests.... fewer interests.... about average.....
10. INTEREST INTENSITY: more interested.... less interested.... about average.....
11. HEALTH: higher physical tone.... lower physical tone.... about average.....
12. CONTROL OF TEMPER: higher degree of control.... lower degree of control.... about average.....
13. GROUP LIFE: more enjoyment of group life.... less enjoyment of group life.... about average.....
14. ATTITUDE TOWARD ADULT CONTROL: greater acceptance of adult control.... less acceptance.... about average.....
15. OPERATIONAL GROUP PATTERN: more democratic.... less democratic.... about average.....
16. CHARACTERISTIC OUTLOOK: happier, more cheerful.... more tense, worried, unhappy,.... about average.....

HORACE MANN-LINCOLN INSTITUTE OF SCHOOL EXPERIMENTATION
TEACHERS COLLEGE, COLUMBIA UNIVERSITY

SCORE SHEET FOR CLASSROOM SOCIAL DISTANCE SCALE

Teacher_____ School_____ Grade_____

Name	Group Social Distance	Self Social Distance

HORACE MANN–LINCOLN INSTITUTE OF SCHOOL EXPERIMENTATION
TEACHERS COLLEGE, COLUMBIA UNIVERSITY

CLASSROOM SOCIAL DISTANCE SCALE

Name .... Date ....
School .... Grade ....

We don't like all of our friends in the same way. Some we like more than others. There may be some people we don't like at all.

The check list on the next page will give you a way of telling how close an acquaintance you would like to have with other boys and girls in your room. Under each name listed across the top of the page, put a check in the space opposite the statement which most nearly describes your feeling about the person. Of course you are to substitute "her" for "him" in your thinking when checking a girl's name.

When you come to your own name, check the space which describes how you think most of the boys and girls feel about you.

No one in your room will see this paper but your teacher.

TURN TO THE NEXT PAGE

CHECK SHEET: CLASSROOM SOCIAL DISTANCE SCALE

Name																
1. Would like to have him as one of my best friends.																
2. Would like to have him in my group but not as a close friend.																
3. Would like to be with him once in a while but not often or for long at a time.																
4. Don't mind his being in our room but I don't want to have anything to do with him.																
5. Wish he weren't in our room.																

HORACE MANN–LINCOLN INSTITUTE OF SCHOOL EXPERIMENTATION
TEACHERS COLLEGE, COLUMBIA UNIVERSITY

CHECK SHEET OF OPPORTUNITIES IN HUMAN RELATIONS

Name.......................... Age..... Grade..... Boy..... Girl.....
     (Sign your name if willing)
School................................ City or County.................

You are asked to check this sheet to help in a study of how young people get to know each other and people in the community. This material will be treated as confidential. Sign your name if you are willing to do so, but do not feel that you must.

Directions: Read the statement under the heading "Experience." Then for each statement give the following information:

1. *How often?* How often do you have this experience? Check (√) in the appropriate column, as frequently, sometimes, or seldom or never. If you honestly do not know whether you have this experience or how often, check ?.

2. *How valuable?* How valuable do you feel the experience is to you? Check (√) in the appropriate column as important, O.K.—good but not important, or unimportant (might well get along without experience). If you honestly cannot decide how valuable the experience is, check ?.

TURN TO THE NEXT PAGE

CHECK SHEET OF OPPORTUNITIES IN HUMAN RELATIONS	HOW OFTEN?				HOW VALUABLE?			
EXPERIENCE	Frequently (almost every day)	Sometimes (once a week or so)	Seldom or never (not more than once a month)	?	Important	O.K.—good but not important	Unimportant	?
1. Be a member of a team for some sport.								
2. Be a member of a club.								
3. Be a member of a gang.								
4. Work or play with people of differing religious belief.								
5. Work or play with people of differing race.								
6. Work or play with people of differing nationality background.								
7. Work or play with people who are considerably more wealthy than my family.								
8. Work or play with people who have considerably less money than my family.								
9. Work or play with people whom I consider to be considerably smarter (quicker thinking) than I am.								
10. Work or play with people whom I consider to be considerably slower thinking than I am.								
11. Work or play in groups in which adults are members (not including teachers or youth leaders).								

CHECK SHEET (*Continued*)

EXPERIENCE	HOW OFTEN?				HOW VALUABLE?			
	Frequently (almost every day)	*Sometimes (once a week or so)*	*Seldom or never (not more than once a month)*	*?*	*Important*	*O.K.—good but not important*	*Unimportant*	*?*
12. Be a member of a group which makes its own rules.								
13. Be a member of a group which elects its own leaders.								
14. Be a leader or representative of a group of people my age.								
15. Be a member of a group of people my own age where there is no adult control.								
16. Meet adults who are considered leaders in my community (other than teachers and youth leaders).								
17. Meet people who come from outside my community.								
18. Visit communities other than my own.								
19. Talk with adults engaged in various types of work.								
20. Observe adults engaged in various types of work.								
21. Spend leisure time with friends of my own choice.								
22. Spend leisure time alone.								
23. Discuss with others my age what is going on in the world.								

CHECK SHEET (*Continued*)

EXPERIENCE	Frequently (almost every day)	Sometimes (once a week or so)	Seldom or never (not more than once a month)	?	Important	O.K.—good but not important	Unimportant	?
	HOW OFTEN?				HOW VALUABLE?			
24. Discuss boy-girl relations.								
25. Discuss sex problems.								
26. Discuss marriage, home and family living.								
27. Discuss my vocational choice.								
28. Discuss local politics.								
29. Have dates with individuals of the opposite sex.								
30. Take part in community affairs.								
31. Work for pay.								
32. Work at home (do chores) without pay.								
33. Do useful work for the community without pay.								
34. Work or play with people much younger than I am (5 or more years younger).								
35. Work or play with people much older than I am (5 or more years older), not including teachers or youth leaders.								
36. Work or play with people of opposite sex.								

CHECK SHEET (*Continued*)

EXPERIENCE	HOW OFTEN?				HOW VALUABLE?			
	Frequently (almost every day)	*Sometimes (once a week or so)*	*Seldom or never (not more than once a month)*	*?*	*Important*	*O.K.—good but not important*	*Unimportant*	*?*
37. Work or play in a group of four or five people.								
38. Work or play in a group of ten or twelve people.								
39. Work or play in a group of thirty to fifty people.								
40. Work or play in a group of fifty to one hundred people.								

41. If you had a personal problem about which you were worried, to whom would you go in your family? _____
To whom would you go outside your family? _____

42. How do you feel about the amount of adult control of you by your family? (check one) too much _____ about right _____ too little _____.
How do you feel about the amount of control of you by your school? (check one) too much _____; about right _____; too little _____.

43. Put a check in front of the words or phrases which you feel describe you:
_____ find it easy to make friends.
_____ find it difficult to make friends.
_____ wish I had more skill in getting along with people.
_____ well liked by most.
_____ liked by few, but not many.
_____ disliked by many.
_____ shy.
_____ a leader.
_____ not understood.
_____ not so smart as most.
_____ more intelligent than most.
_____ prefer to be alone much of the time.
_____ want to be with people most of the time.

_____ more interested in people than in things or ideas.
_____ more interested in ideas or things than in people.
_____ wish the school would give more help in how to get along with people.

44. The three things I most want to improve about myself:

45. My three best friends in my room, home room, group, or section (boys or girls):

GUIDE FOR GROUP OBSERVATION

(Adapted from guide prepared by College Study in Intergroup Relations)
American Council of Education

Group (grade or age) .... School ....
Group activity observed ....
Date of observation .... Time (hours and minutes) ....
Number of participants: Boys .... Girls .... Total ....
Teacher .... Observer ....

Group observations: This is not an evaluation form in the sense that it measures "good" or "bad" group action. It is an attempt to guide observation and recording of what *is* in group process, rather than what ought to be. It is possible that there is a time and place for many or all of the behaviors listed under each heading. It is hoped that with sufficient practice in observation and greater understanding of group processes, an observer may be able to determine with greater validity what behavior is most appropriate to a group and its goals at a particular time. However, for the present the major purpose of this form is to help in making objective observations of what actually happens in the group.

From each group of behavior descriptions below, check the one which most nearly describes the group behavior during your observation. If none of the descriptions fits the situation, write your description under "Other." There is space provided at the end of this form for any explanation you may wish to make of your checks, and to record any unusual happenings to the group.

1. GENERAL TYPE OF GROUP ACTIVITY
   a. I cannot determine .... a......
   b. Very formal, such as lecture, sitting still and watching or listening to
      teacher, question-answer recitation, extreme "order" .... b......
   c. Rowdy, noisy, unmanageable .... c......
   d. Informal, group situation, "comfortable" but not active .... d......
   e. Active participation yet with control: vigorous play, discussion, work e......
   f. Other .... f......
      ....
      ....

2. GROUP REACTION TO TEACHER
   a. I cannot determine .... a......
   b. Warm, friendly, personalized give-and-take .... b......
   c. Fear of teacher .... c......
   d. Apathetic, indifferent atmosphere .... d......
   e. Active negativism, open hostility toward teacher .... e......
   f. Other .... f......
      ....
      ....

3. INTER-PERSONAL RELATIONS
   a. I cannot determine .... a......
   b. Group members willing and anxious to help each other .... b......

   c. Keen individual competition, "me first" .... c......
   d. High group spirit and helpfulness within subgroups, but keen competition among subgroups or teams .... d......
   e. Range of responses within competitive situation: some engaged in cut-throat competition, others disinterested .... e......
   f. Other .... f......
       ....
       ....

4. GROUP STRUCTURE, INTERRELATION OF UNITS

   a. I cannot determine .... a......
   b. Unorganized, no indication of common goal .... b......
   c. Loosely integrated but with everyone working independently ..... c......
   d. Extremely disunified, marked tensions, conflicts .... d......
   e. Well understood and accepted group goal, definite division of responsibility .... e......
   f. Common goal understood but no effective division of responsibility f......
   g. Other .... g......
       ....
       ....

5. CONTROL PATTERNS

   a. I cannot determine .... a......
   b. Adult rule, child obedience .... b......
   c. No plan apparent, "catch as catch can" control .... c......
   d. Teacher plans with individuals .... d......
   e. Adult dominated group planning .... e......
   f. Group self-management through group planning .... f......
   g. Other .... g......
       ....
       ....

6. LEADER CONTROL DEVICES

   a. I cannot determine .... a......
   b. Uses threats, scolds, "bawls out" .... b......
   c. Places stress on praise, rewards, friendly "pats" .... c......
   d. Controls chiefly by expressing personal approval or disapproval .... d......
   e. Resorts to action, such as isolating individual from group, physical punishment .... e......
   f. Children participate in formulation of guides to behavior .... f......
   g. Other .... g......
       ....

7. AVERAGE GROUP MEMBER ROLE, GENERAL ATTITUDE

   a. I cannot determine .... a......
   b. Strained, fearful, marked tension .... b......
   c. Indifferent, pleasant, but a shade cool .... c......
   d. Warm respect for others, comfortably friendly .... d......
   e. Confidential, intimate, not inhibited .... e......

f. Definitely unfriendly, irritable, selfish, unsocial .... f......
g. Other .... g......
....
....

8. THE SOCIAL ISOLATE

a. I cannot determine .... a......
b. Group badly divided into high and low rated persons, pairs, cliques b......
c. Some children who do not seem to value good will of group ...... c......
d. Some children who are rejected by group .... d......
e. No apparent isolates, general participation by all .... e......
f. Other .... f......
....
....

9. STATUS DETERMINANTS OF LEADERS

a. I cannot determine .... a......
b. Status due to favoritism by adult, appointment to leadership position
   by teacher .... b......
c. Status due to general alertness, social ability, or likable personality c......
d. Status due to physical strength, daring, or bravado .... d......
e. Status due to sympathy aroused in others: crippled, etc. .... e......
f. Status due to particular competence in special area .... f......
g. Other .... g......
....
....

10. LEARNING ACTIVITY DURING OBSERVATION PERIOD

Note: If several types of activity were evidenced in sequence, give estimate of
minutes per activity in space at right. If there was wide range of activity at one
time, give estimated number of children engaged in each.

a. I cannot determine .... a......
b. Largely memorizing .... b......
c. Practicing skills through rote drill .... c......
d. Individual problem-solving or research .... d......
e. Group problem-solving, planning discussion .... e......
f. Creative activity through arts, writing, constructive .... f......
g. Appreciation, enjoyment; reading, looking, listening "for fun"...... g......
h. Other .... h......
....
....

Remarks:

Write below whatever comments you want to make in explanation of your checks
above. Key remarks to number and letter when you can. Report any special happening, dramatic incident, general reaction of group, or impression you have received
which may help in understanding this group.

IDENTIFICATION SHEET*

School...................... Grade........ Teacher......................

To Teachers:

On the basis of your daily work with the children in your class, write under the following behavior items the names of children who rather consistently show this behavior. Place as many names as you think appropriate in each category, or no names.

-1-

a. Usually conforms to and accepts classroom regulations.

b. Needs frequent reminders about classroom regulations.

c. Unpredictable in response to classroom regulations.

-2-

a. Works steadily on assigned work.

b. Easily diverted from assigned work.

c. Seeks undue amount of help and attention from teacher.

-3-

a. Spontaneous in contributing ideas.

b. Never contributes unless called upon.

c. Inconsistent in contribution.

d. Self-conscious in contributing ideas.

-4-

a. Apparently bright and is doing well.

b. Appears slow in comprehension.

-5-

a. Popular with other children.

* Prepared by Professor Gertrude P. Driscoll, Teachers College, Columbia University.

b. Avoided or ignored by other children.

-6-

a. Continually seeks contact with other children.

b. Seeks undue attention from adults.

c. Seldom initiates contact with other children.

d. Ignores advances made to him by other children.

-7-

a. Usually seems happy.

b. Appears tense; easily upset.

c. Has nervous habits:
    a. Nail-biting
    b. Sucking small objects
    c. Facial twitching
    d. Masturbation
    e. Lapses into daydreaming

-8-

a. Attendance regular.

b. Absent frequently for minor illnesses (state general character of absences).

c. In school but seems listless, fatigued, pale, or unwell.

-9-

a. Particularly well coordinated.

b. Obviously awkward.

-10-

Has speech inaccuracies:
    a. Poor enunciation (baby talk)
    b. Lisping
    c. Stuttering or stammering
    d. Substituting letters

SPRINGFIELD INTEREST FINDER*

My three wishes:

What I'd like to learn more about at school:

What I don't care to study about:

What I like best in school:

What I like least or dislike most at school:

What I like best outside school:

What I like least or dislike most outside school:

What I want to be or do when I grow up:

The most interesting thing I have done at school during the past week or so:

One of the places I especially like to go in ....:
                                                        (name of city)

One of the happiest days in my life:

My three best friends in my room (boys or girls):

* Developed by Arthur T. Jersild and members of the staff of the Springfield, Missouri, Public Schools.

SOCIAL ANALYSIS OF THE CLASSROOM

Name .... School ....
Grade .... Room .... Date .... Age........

Directions

Below are some word pictures of members of your class. Read each statement and write down the names of the persons whom you think the descriptions fit.

Remember:

One description may fit several persons. You may write as many names as you think belong under each.

The same person may be mentioned for more than one description.

Write "myself" if you think the description fits you.

If you cannot think of anyone to match a particular description, go on to the next one.

You will have as much time as you need to finish. Do not hurry.

Now You Are Ready to Begin

1. Here is someone who finds it hard to sit still in class; he (or she) moves around in his (or her) seat or gets up and walks around.
   ....
   ....
   ....

2. Here is someone who can work very quietly without moving around in his (or her) seat.
   ....
   ....
   ....

3. Here is someone who likes to talk a lot, always has something to say.
   ....
   ....
   ....

4. Here is someone who doesn't like to talk very much, is very quiet, even when nearly everyone else is talking.
   ....
   ....
   ....

5. Here is someone who plays active games like football and basketball a great deal, or who likes to run and jump and so on.
   ....
   ....
   ....

6. This person seldom plays active games like football and basketball, but prefers to read or sit and play quiet games.
   ....
   ....
   ....

7. Here is someone who is always ready to take a chance at things that are new or unusual, and is never worried or frightened.

....

....

....

8. Here is someone who is always worried or scared, who won't take a chance when something unexpected or unusual happens.

....

....

....

9. Here is someone who always knows how to start games or suggests something interesting to do so that others like to join in.

....

....

....

10. Here is someone who waits for somebody else to think of something to do and always likes to follow the suggestions which others make.

....

....

....

11. This person always seems to have a good time and seems to enjoy everything he (or she) does no matter where it is—in school, on the playground, at a party, everywhere.

....

....

....

12. This is someone who never seems to have a good time, who never seems to enjoy very much anything he (or she) does.

....

....

....

13. This is someone who is always cheerful, jolly, and good-natured, who laughs and smiles a good deal.

....

....

....

14. Here is someone who always seems rather sad, worried, or unhappy, who hardly ever laughs or smiles.

....

....

....

15. This is someone who is thought to be very good-looking.

....

....

....

16. Here is someone who is thought not to be good-looking at all.

....

....

....

....

17. Here is someone who always tries to keep himself (or herself) neat and clean and tidy looking.

....
....
....

18. This is someone who never tries to keep himself (or herself) clean and neat and tidy looking.

....
....
....

19. Here is someone whom everybody likes; people are always glad to have him (or her) around.

....
....
....

20. Here is someone whom nobody seems to care much about; people do not notice when he (or she) is around.

....
....
....

21. Here is a girl who likes to read boys' books, play boys' games, or would prefer to be a boy.

....
....
....

22. Here is a boy who prefers girls' books or girls' games, or would prefer to be a girl.

....
....
....

23. Here is a girl who often goes out with boys, or a boy who often goes out with girls. He (or she) likes to go to parties or dances.

....
....
....

24. Here is a girl who isn't much interested in going out with boys, or a boy who isn't much interested in going out with girls. They do not care to go to parties or dances.

....
....
....

25. Here is someone who can enjoy a joke and see the fun in it even when the joke is on himself (or herself).

....
....
....

26. Here is someone who can never appreciate a joke when it is on himself (or herself).

....
....
....

27. This person is very fond of a good joke, is the first to laugh and always sees the point.

....

....

....

28. Here is a person who doesn't care much for jokes or who has to have them explained before he (or she) sees the point.

....

....

....

29. Here is someone who enjoys a fight; he (or she) often fights rather than let the others person have his (or her) way.

....

....

....

30. Here is someone who never fights but lets the other person have his (or her) way.

....

....

....

31. This is someone who is always trying to get others to watch what he (or she) can do or to listen to him (or her) tell about all the things he (or she) can do.

....

....

....

32. Here is someone who does not care whether or not he (or she) is the center of attention.

....

....

....

33. This is someone who is always telling others what to do, bossing them.

....

....

34. Here is someone who does not mind being told what to do, who does not mind being bossed.

....

....

35. Here is someone who is very friendly, who has lots of friends, who is nice to everybody.

....

....

....

36. Here is someone who doesn't care much to make friends or who is bashful about being friendly, or doesn't seem to have many friends.

....

....

37. Here is someone who is one of my very best friends in this room.
(*Note:* Most people think that about three names is enough to include the very best friends. If you really feel that this is not enough you may write as many as five names, but not more than five.

....

....

HORACE MANN–LINCOLN INSTITUTE OF SCHOOL EXPERIMENTATION
TEACHERS COLLEGE, COLUMBIA UNIVERSITY

REACTION TO PICTURES[*]

To the Teacher:

The purpose of asking children to react to these pictures is to discover leads to children's attitudes toward their group culture.

For children under nine or ten years of age, responses may be given orally and recorded by an adult. Older children may be asked to write their responses. Both boys and girls are asked to respond to questions about all pictures.

It is important that boys and girls have an opportunity to react frankly and honestly. This means that the teacher will want to avoid communicating to children his personal attitudes concerning the situation pictured. Children should be told there are no "right" or "wrong" answers.

If answers are oral, it will be necessary to show the pictures to children individually and record their responses. (Parents or high school boys or girls may be able to do the questioning and recording after some preliminary training by the teacher.) If answers are to be written by children, it is suggested that the questions be written on the board, and the pictures circulated and then put in a prominent place where they may be reexamined by individuals. It is probably wise to suggest that some start with A, others with B, etc. It is suggested that each pupil write at the top of the page on which responses are to be recorded his name, age, grade, school, and whether boy or girl.

The questions, keyed to the number of each picture, are:

A. Most boys and girls get into fights sometimes.
   1. What sorts of things do boys and girls your age fight about?
   2. What do you think grown people fight about?
   3. What do little kids (four- or five-year-olds) fight about?
B. 4. Why do you think these boys are fighting?
   5. What would you do if you were one of the four boys watching this fight?
   6. What would a teacher do if she saw this?
C. 7. What do you think the teacher is saying to this girl?
   8. What is the girl thinking?
D. 9. Tell the story of this picture.

For the purposes of this study, teachers are asked to collect individual responses first. However, group discussion of the situations may follow. If group discussion is used, teachers are requested to record the main ideas expressed, using children's words as far as possible. If pictures C and D only have been used, questions for A and B may be the basis of group discussion. Older children may be able to discuss *why* certain responses have been made.

[*] See pictures of fighting boys, A and B, pages 283 and 363.

HORACE MANN—LINCOLN INSTITUTE OF SCHOOL EXPERIMENTATION
TEACHERS COLLEGE, COLUMBIA UNIVERSITY

INFORMATION SHEET TO ACCOMPANY
"REACTION TO PICTURES"

Teacher .... School ....
Address ....
Groups (grade or age) .... Date ....

I. How did the children react when asked to respond to these pictures?

II. Did the responses of the children give you any new ideas or deepened concepts about how your children think and feel? If so, what were these ideas or concepts?

III. May we have your suggestions concerning other types of situations, other questions which might be used, different procedures, or other comments.

Note: We'd appreciate marginal comments or notes on the back of the children's papers giving any information about the child which will help to interpret the responses.

HORACE MANN–LINCOLN INSTITUTE OF SCHOOL EXPERIMENTATION
TEACHERS COLLEGE, COLUMBIA UNIVERSITY

STUDY OF GROUP COMPOSITION

School .... Grade ....
Teacher reporting ....

PART I

Place under each category the names of the children in your group whom you feel to be outstanding in the characteristic. Place as many names as you think appropriate in each category, or no names.

1. AGE
   Oldest   Youngest

2. DEVELOPMENTAL PHASE
   Most mature   Least mature

3. SOCIO-ECONOMIC BACKGROUND
   Most favorable   Least favorable

4. DEGREE OF ACCEPTANCE BY OTHER CHILDREN
   Most accepted   Least accepted

5. DEGREE OF ACCEPTANCE BY PARENTS
   Most accepted   Least accepted

6. ACTIVE-LETHARGIC SCALE
   Most active   Most lethargic

7. INTELLIGENCE
   Most intelligent   Least intelligent

8. PHYSICAL SKILL
   Most skilled   Least skilled

9. INTEREST RANGE
   Many interests   Few interests

10. INTEREST INTENSITY
    Vitally interested   Mildly interested

11. HEALTH
    High physical tone; much alive   Low physical tone; lacks vigor

12. CONTROL OF TEMPER
    High degree of control of temper   Lacks control of temper

13. ATTITUDE TOWARD GROUP LIFE

Enjoys being in group   Resents need to be in group

14. ATTITUDE TOWARD ADULT CONTROL

Accepts adult control   Resists adult control

15. OPERATIONAL GROUP PATTERN

Acts democratically   Acts autocratically

16. CHARACTERISTIC OUTLOOK

Happy, cheerful, unworried   Tense, worried, unhappy

PART II

On the basis of your experience with other groups of boys and girls of the same grade level, check each item to indicate whether you think this group is above or below average, or about average. Note that this check represents your impression of *the group as a whole.*

1. AGE: older.... younger.... about average.....
2. DEVEOPMENTAL PHASE: more mature.... less mature.... about average.....
3. SOCIO-ECONOMIC BACKGROUND: more favorable.... less favorable.... about average.....
4. DEGREE OF ACCEPTANCE OF EACH OTHER: more acceptance.... less acceptance .... about average.....
5. DEGREE OF PARENTAL ACCEPTANCE: more accepted.... less accepted.... about average.....
6. ACTIVE-LETHARGIC: more active.... more lethargic.... about average.
7. INTELLIGENCE: more intelligent.... less intelligent.... about average.....
8. PHYSICAL SKILL: more skilled.... less skilled.... about average.....
9. INTEREST RANGE: more interests.... fewer interests.... about average.....
10. INTEREST INTENSITY: more interested.... less interested.... about average.....
11. HEALTH: higher physical tone.... lower physical tone.... about average.....
12. CONTROL OF TEMPER: higher degree of control.... lower degree of control.... about average.....
13. GROUP LIFE: more enjoyment of group life.... less enjoyment of group life.... about average.....
14. ATTITUDE TOWARD ADULT CONTROL: greater acceptance of adult control.... less acceptance.... about average.....
15. OPERATIONAL GROUP PATTERN: more democratic.... less democratic.... about average.....
16. CHARACTERISTIC OUTLOOK: happier, more cheerful.... more tense, worried, unhappy.... about average.....

HORACE MANN–LINCOLN INSTITUTE OF SCHOOL EXPERIMENTATION

TEACHERS COLLEGE, COLUMBIA UNIVERSITY

MEETING INDIVIDUAL NEEDS

Meeting the needs of ....

(name of pupil)

Sex: M.... F..... Age.... Grade.... School............................

Intelligence: High.... Average.... Low.....

Academic achievement: High.... Average.... Low.....

Social adjustment: High.... Average.... Low.....

Maturity in relation to age: High.... Average.... Low.....

Teacher......................................

This check list is designed to help teachers think through some of the problems in providing for the individual needs of boys and girls. It is suggested that you select from your group several (three to five) pupils and, for each, attempt to answer these questions as honestly as you can. Use a separate check sheet for each pupil.

In selecting pupils for checking, try to get a range, e.g., one who is doing well academically, one who is not; one who seems particularly well adjusted socially, one who is not; etc.

If in your best judgment, the answer *tends* to be affirmative, circle "Yes"; if it *tends* to be negative, circle "No." (Probably few if any, can be answered definitely as a positive, clear, yes-or-no case.) If you don't know which way the situation tends, circle "?."

You will see that the questions have been developed in terms of certain assumptions concerning the job of teachers and the school. You may not agree with these assumptions; many people don't. In order to express your point of view, place a plus (+) in front (to the left) of each question that you feel to be important and a necessary responsibility of schools, and a minus (−) in front of those questions you feel to be unimportant or not the job of the teacher or the school. There is space at the end for additional items you feel should be considered.

Check importance as

plus or minus   *Circle your answer*

I.

.... 1. Does he have a balance of rest and activity suited to his rhythm of energy use and fatigue?   Yes   No   ?

.... 2. Are the physical activities provided for him appropriate to his physical maturity and health?   Yes   No   ?

.... 3. Is the equipment provided for his use suited to his size and muscular development?   Yes   No   ?

.... 4. Is his environment suited to his health needs (light, ventilation, physical examination, food, rest, exercise, etc.)?   Yes   No   ?

II. INTERESTS

.... 5. In general, is he interested in the experiences provided for him, and are experiences provided which meet his interests? Yes   No   ?

.... 6. Are the experiences he is having broadening and/or deepening his interests?   Yes   No   ?

.... 7. Does he have adequate opportunity to follow certain personal interests even though they may be different from those of others in the group? Yes No ?

.... 8. Does he have adequate materials with which to work and are they suited to his interests (books, art materials, tools, etc)? Yes No ?

III. ACADEMIC EXPERIENCES

.... 9. Is the work asked of him suited to his intelligence and maturity (not too difficult or too easy)? Yes No ?

....10. Does the work asked of him help him to solve the problems or meet the situations he encounters in his day-to-day living as a growing individual? Yes No ?

....11. Does he have opportunity to explore academic interests which are not common to others in the group? Yes No ?

....12. Does he know *why* he is studying that which is required of him? Yes No ?

IV. SKILLS

....13. Is he growing appropriately in his ability to think logically? Yes No ?

....14. Is he developing according to a pace best *for him* in academic skills, such as reading, number concepts, etc.? Yes No ?

....15. Is he growing appropriately in his social skills (getting along with others, operating as a group member, etc.)? Yes No ?

....16. Is he developing increasing skill in operating as a free, independent, responsible individual? Yes No ?

V. EXPRESSION

....17. Does he have sufficient opportunity to make choices about his daily course of action? Yes No ?

....18. Does he have opportunity to choose from among a sufficiently wide range of media for expression (painting, drawing, modeling, crafts, dancing, music—vocal, instrumental, writing, dramatics, etc.)? Yes No ?

....19. Is he given sufficient time to express his ideas and emotions through the arts and other media? Yes No ?

....20. Is he given sufficient opportunity to express and share his ideas verbally with other boys and girls and with adults? Yes No ?

VI. GROUP ROLE

....21. Is he given sufficient opportunity to contribute to the group (help in planning, taking responsibility for chores, etc.)? Yes No ?

....22. Does he feel himself to be an integral part of the group? (Does he have a feeling of 'belonging')? Yes No ?

....23. Is he given opportunity to practice various roles in his group (leader, follower; performer, audience; etc.)? Yes No ?

....24. Does he have opportunity to work or play in various types of groups (various sizes, with people of various ages, races, etc.)? Yes No ?

VII. SELF-NEEDS

....25. Does he have sufficient opportunity to give and to receive affection? Yes No ?

....26. Does he feel that he is growing, making progress toward *his* goals? Yes No ?

....27. Does he receive sufficient recognition from other boys and girls and from adults to make him feel secure? Yes No ?

....28. Does he feel he makes a contribution to the group? Yes No ?

VIII. ADULT HELP

....29. Does his teacher know him well enough to be able to plan an adequate school program with him? Yes No ?

....30. Does his teacher work sufficiently with his parents in order to plan a program suited to his needs? Yes No ?

....31. Is his teacher the sort of person who intellectually, emotionally, by training and experience, can plan wisely with him? Yes No ?

....32. Is his teacher given a reasonable amount of time, assistance, material, etc., to provide a good school program for him? Yes No ?

IX. $64 QUESTIONS

....33. Is he happy? Yes No ?

....34. Does his total school experience help him to grow as an individual, as a member of his group, as a citizen of a broadening social group? Yes No ?

....35. Are his total school experiences meaningful to him? Do they help him meet his day-to-day problems? Yes No ?

....36. Are his total school experiences appropriate to his maturity, his rate of growth, his capacities, interests, and needs? Yes No ?

....37. Is there desirable balance in the types of experiences available to him? Yes No ?

....38. Does his teacher feel that she has sufficient freedom (from subject matter requirements, etc.) to plan a program best suited to his needs? Yes No ?

OTHER AREAS

....39.

Yes No ?

....40.

Yes No ?

....41.

Yes No ?

....42.

Yes No ?

TIME CHART

Name _____ Week of _____

Time	Sun.	Mon.	Tues.	Wed.	Thur.	Fri.	Sat.
6–7							
7–8							
8–9							
9–10							
10–11							
11–12							
12–1							
1–2							
2–3							
3–4							
4–5							
5–6							
6–7							
7–8							
8–9							
9–10							
10–11							
11–12							
12–1							

DENVER PUBLIC SCHOOLS
DEPARTMENT OF HEALTH SERVICE

NOTICE OF HEALTH EXAMINATION

Health examinations by school physicians will be offered to the children in certain grades of .... School in the near future.

Figures from life insurance companies which offer annual health examinations show that the average length of life of their policyholders has been increased through such examinations. If such results can be gotten by examinations given after the person has reached adult age, much greater results can be gotten from annual health examinations of children. An annual health examination will enable parents to do much toward keeping a child in perfect condition. It brings to light defects which may be corrected, but which, undetected, prevent the building of a strong, healthy body.

This examination is not compulsory, but it does give parents the opportunity to find out the physical conditions of their children.

Parents are urged to be present at the examinations and to consult with the physician regarding the health of their children.

Will you kindly answer the following questions as accurately as possible, even though you may not wish to have your child examined:

Does the child drink tea or coffee? ....
Does he eat candy between meals? ....
Does he "piece" between meals? ....
Does he eat a warm breakfast practically every morning? ....
How much milk does he drink each day? ....
Does he sleep with his mouth open? ....
Does he snore? ....
At what time does he go to sleep? ....
How many hours of sleep does he get at night? ....
Does he take dancing lessons, music lessons, and other special lessons outside of school hours? ....
How much time a week is devoted to each of such lessons? ....
Does he have a cold frequently? ....
Does he have a sore throat frequently? ....
Does he have a headache frequently? ....
Does he complain of his eyes when he reads? ....
What is the total distance your child walks each day in going to and from school?
....

Which of the following diseases has your child had? It is very important for the school to have this information.

Check them:

1. Scarlet fever
2. Diphtheria
3. Whooping cough
4. Influenza
5. Pneumonia
6. Smallpox
7. Measles
8. German measles
9. Mumps
10. Chickenpox
11. Typhoid
12. Inflammatory rheumatism
13. St. Vitus's dance
14. Infantile paralysis

What year was he vaccinated against small pox?

Result ....

What year was he given toxoid for diphtheria? ....

Result ....

What year was he given whooping cough vaccine? ....

HEALTH RULES

If your child observes the following health rules, he will not be so liable to contract a communicable disease or to give one to other children:

Wash hands before each meal and after going to the toilet.

Brush teeth at least twice each day.

Cover mouth and nose with a handkerchief when coughing or sneezing.

Avoid talking directly into another person's face.

Keep fingers, books, pencils, and the like, out of the mouth.

Never exchange with others gum, candy, or food which has been in contact with one's mouth.

Breathe fresh air day and night.

Play out of doors in the sunshine at least one hour each day.

Sleep at least ten to twelve hours each night.

Drink from four to six glasses of water each day.

Have a regular bowel movement at a regular time each day, preferably just after breakfast.

IF YOU HAVE NOT ALREADY DONE SO, HAVE YOUR CHILD IMMUNIZED AGAINST SMALLPOX AND DIPHTHERIA.

Child's name ....Age........Address..............

Grade ....Section.................Home room..............

Before we can make definite appointments with the school physician, we must know how many parents desire to avail themselves of this service for their children. Will you, then, please fill out the coupon below and return to us, regardless of your decision. If you indicate that you desire the examination, you will be notified later of the time of your appointment. We should like to have one or both parents at the examination.

.......................School Nurse

...........................Principal

PLEASE FILL OUT AND RETURN

I desire the health examination for my child.   Yes......

I expect to be present at the examination.   Yes......

...........................Parent

TIME OF YOUR APPOINTMENT

(To be filled out and sent to parents if they indicate that the health examination is desired.)

Name of child ....

Health examination appointment: Day..................Hour........

.......................School Nurse

...........................Principal

DENVER PUBLIC SCHOOLS
DEPARTMENT OF HEALTH SERVICE

PARENTS' NOTIFICATION

Date.....................

School ....Room.........Age........

To Parents:

In the health examination of your child there may have been found conditions which it would be wise for your doctor to investigate more carefully. If this is true, we advise you to consult your family physician, who will have more time to make a more thorough examination, and who, being familiar with the child's history, will be able to make an accurate diagnosis and decide if treatment is necessary.

A. L. Beaghlet, M.D.
Director of Health Service

The Health examination of ....

....

indicates ....

Height .... Weight ....

The average weight of a child of this age and height is......lbs.

Underweight, under average height, or overweight may be a family characteristic. Your family physician must decide this. However, a child who is ten per cent or more underweight, or twenty per cent or more overweight, should have his health habits carefully investigated and a thorough physical examination made to be sure there are no poor health habits or physical defects interfering with his development.

Examining physician ....

Principal ....

Take this blank with you to the family physician so that he can report the findings of his examination and any treatment which may have been given.

To Family Physician: This department will appreciate it if you will give us the results of your examination and what treatment has been given to correct this defect. This is of importance for our records and to save the time of nurses in follow-up work.

1. Diagnosis ....

2. Treatments recommended or completed ....

....

Family Physician

....

Parents

IF YOU HAVE NOT ALREADY DONE SO, HAVE YOUR CHILD IMMUNIZED AGAINST SMALLPOX AND DIPHTHERIA.

To Parents: Will you kindly sign this slip and return it to the principal.

It is a wise custom to have the family physician make an annual health examination of your child. The child's birthday is a good time to have this done.

EXHIBIT: GOALS AND DEFINITIONS OF GOALS

As Developed by a Group of
Ten- and Eleven-Year-Old Children

1. TO LEARN TO PLAY WELL TOGETHER

I mean that we need to have friends to play with.
I think we should not argue about the scores.
Always play fair.
If someone is fat or skinny, we should play with them.
Play with children of different races.
Don't fight with each other.
Don't get mad if your best "Pal" doesn't choose you.
Do not be selfish when you play.
Play with other children who do not have many friends.
Don't always play with one person. Try out new friends.
Don't be a tattletale.
Play fair, have a good time.
I mean to play well together you have to learn to like each other.
Play what other people want to sometimes and not what you want to play all the time.
To have fun playing.
To learn the rules of the game.
To be a good sport.
Do not be always teasing someone.

2. TO LEARN TO WORK WELL TOGETHER

To help people in their work.
Help people clean up.
Help people be considerate of others.
I mean that in order to work well together that you have to learn to like each other and get along together.
I mean not fight while you are working.
It means that you would cooperate with other people.
To learn to do your own work.
Take turns.
Come to attention when Miss Roberts or the planning leader says "Boys and Girls."
To cooperate with people.
To take other people's ideas.

3. TO LEARN TO LIKE EACH OTHER

To like each other no matter what they look like or what color they are.
To learn not to call people names.
To not want everything your way.
Don't be a "Just Me."
Don't start fights with best friends.

Don't argue.
To learn to play together and not fight.
To be nice to each other.

4. DO NOT FIGHT UNLESS YOU NEED TO PROTECT YOURSELF. "GOTTA"

Don't start fights. Don't start to argue with other people.
You won't have to protect yourself if you don't start to argue.
You need to be friendly and not fight unless someone is going to hurt you.
Don't get mad while you are playing because you might end up in a fight.
Not to fight just to be fighting.
Don't pick fights.
If someone hits you it's okay.
If someone takes something away from you it's okay.
Not to always be fighting.
Be nice to people.

5. DON'T ARGUE

If you argued all the time you probably would fight all the time.
It takes two to make an argument. If the other person starts an argument
    don't say anything. Stay out of the argument.
I mean by not arguing you need to get along.
That means that you don't talk back to someone if you don't argue.
Agree on some things. Don't be so fussy.
Don't want everything your way.
Don't be a "Just Me."
Don't argue means that when someone says something not to argue over it.
Take other people's ideas.
Be nice to people.

6. DON'T BE SELFISH

If you were selfish people wouldn't like you.
Share your things with other people.
Do not take anything that belongs to others.
Share your toys and working things with others.
Let people play with your toys.
Share with other people.
Let other people use your things.
Come to attention and don't keep everybody waiting.
Let other people do things you like. (sharing)

7. LISTEN TO OTHER PEOPLE'S IDEAS

If you didn't listen to other people's ideas you'd be dumb.
Keep your ears open and your mouth closed and you will learn many things.
Don't laugh at other people's ideas.
Don't just use your own suggestions if the other one is better.
Don't always want to use your ideas. Give other people a chance.
When someone is talking don't "butt" in, listen to their ideas.
Don't hog the show.
Sit up and listen. Don't talk while they are talking.

8. DON'T BE RUDE

If you were rude people wouldn't like you.
Don't raise your hand when someone is talking.
Don't interrupt people when they are talking.
I mean not to be rude, to learn manners and use them.
If you are not rude in Gym, you are going out in a straight line.
Don't just push people out of seats because you want to sit there.
Don't talk out of turn.
Don't talk when other people are talking.
By not talking in other people's faces.

9. DON'T BE GREEDY

If you were greedy people wouldn't like you.
When you have a choice don't take the best thing.
Don't always do the best things. There are other people, too.
Don't be greedy means not to be selfish.
It means not to eat up your food.
If you are first don't take more than your share.
Don't grab for everything you see.
Don't be rude means not to eat like a hog slopping food all over.
Share your toys.

10. LEARN TO OBEY

If you don't obey you might do something wrong.
When the teacher tells you to do something do it.
Learn to obey means to do what you are told to do.
Obey other people. Don't just do as you please.
Don't sass.
Do things when you are told to do them, not 10 minutes later.

11. HAVE A HEALTHY BODY

You have to have a healthy body because you can't work or play if you are
    sick.
You have to have good health habits.
It means to eat the right kind of food.
Brush teeth, comb hair and take a bath. Wash hands before meals.
Don't get too tired.
To have a healthy body means to take care of yourself.

12. BE A GOOD SPORT

Don't always try to have your own way.
Don't fight in games.
It means not to cry when you don't get your way.
It means when you're playing ball don't be stuck up if you win.
Don't keep other people from playing just because things don't go your way.
If you are a good sport you stick in the game even if it is not the game you
    want to play.
It means to not cheat.
To be a good sport follow the rules.
If you have to do something you don't want to do be a good sport and do it
    anyway.

13. BE TRUTHFUL

If you did something and you know you did it yourself tell the truth about it.
To be truthful means not to tell lies.
Always tell the truth even if it isn't the easiest way out.

14. BE HONEST

Don't steal.
Don't tell lies.
If you are being honest you tell someone you did something you did do.
It means to be honest and to tell the truth no matter how bad it hurts.

15. LEARN TO RESPECT PROPERTY

Keep your desk clean and neat.
Learning to respect property means to not destroy it.
Do not break down houses.
It means not to tear down fences, houses, etc.
Treat other people's things as you would want them to treat yours.
Don't trespass on other people's property.
Don't ruin other people's property.
It means not to start fires or something like that.
Don't play ball or anything like that on anyone else's property.

16. DON'T "ACT SMART," "SHOW OFF" OR BE A "STUCK UP"

Don't go around being mad at someone.
It means not to tease and to get along with people.
Help other people to do the right thing.
Don't think you are too good for other people.
Don't think of yourself. Think of other people.
Don't think you're smart and that you're pretty.
Don't go around with your nose in the air.
Don't make silly noises or faces. Don't blow up if someone does something you don't like.

17. HELP OTHER PEOPLE

If you didn't help other people they wouldn't like you.
Help other people when they are sick.
Help people in their work.
Help people when they need it.
Help other people if they are hurt. Don't let them suffer.
It means that if someone is in trouble help them.

18. BE ABLE TO CONTROL YOUR TEMPER

If you didn't control your temper you would probably fight people.
Don't get your temper up. Don't get so mad so easy. Be calm.
Be able to control your temper means not to blow up if something goes wrong.
It means to not get mad so easy.
Don't get mad at people unless you have to.
Don't blow up if someone does something you don't like.
Don't fly off the handle so easy.
Don't go around blowing off.

19. DON'T BE A COWARD

Means not to be scared of mice.

Don't pick on little kids then be afraid to start something with someone your size and age.

Don't run away from fights.

It means not to start a fight and then run away.

Don't be afraid to do anything.

20. HAVE GOOD MANNERS

If you didn't people wouldn't eat with you.

Do what the manners book says, that's why we made it.

Having good manners means to know when to say a mannerly thing and how.

It means not to tease people.

To say "please" when you want something and "thank you" when you get it.

Don't be rude.

Have good manners. Don't be greedy. Don't be a "Just Me."

Means not to be sloppy when you eat.

Call people their right names.

Don't spill things on yourself.

21. DON'T HURT PEOPLE'S FEELINGS

Don't tease people.

Don't call people names.

Don't tell people they are fat or thin.

It means not to talk about people.

Don't call people names or tell them they are awful. They may not be awful to other people.

22. DON'T TEASE PEOPLE

Don't call people "cooties" and "fleas," it is not nice.

It means not to hurt people.

Don't call people names.

Means not to say that they are fat or too skinny.

23. BE POLITE

Don't talk when other people are talking.

Say please.

Means not to talk too much at the table.

Don't be a "Just Me." Use your manners.

Don't be rude.

24. LEARN TO CONTROL YOURSELF

If you didn't you would probably fight.

Don't go running out into the hall.

Don't be a "Me First."

I mean to control yourself and not to blow up and get mad.

It means to be able to take care of yourself.

Know where your fingers are.

Wait your turn.

Means not to get mad so easy.

Don't blow your top.

25. KNOW WHEN TO BE SERIOUS AND WHEN TO BE SILLY

Don't act smart.
It means if something bad happens you can feel sad.
Have the right actions at the right time.
Don't be silly all the time and don't be serious all the time.
It means to be silly where there is something to be silly about.
When the teacher is out don't be silly.

26. HAVE A GOOD REASON FOR EVERYTHING YOU DO

If you didn't the teacher would blame you for something you didn't do.
It means to know what you are going to do.
It means to have a reason when you get out of your seat.
Don't just do things to be doing something.
Don't do something because you want to but have a reason for what you do.
Don't just do things to get attention.

27. BE ABLE TO THINK FOR YOURSELF

Not to do things just because your best friend does.
Don't do the wrong thing.
Don't do things because someone else told you to. Have a mind of your own.
Think of your own ideas.
To be able to think for yourself means to act right.
It means to do things for yourself.
It means to decide for yourself.

28. BE ABLE TO DECIDE FOR YOURSELF

Decide things for yourself when we are voting.
It means to know when it is alright to do something.
It means to do things for yourself.
Be able to decide between right and wrong means to know when a thing is
    alright to do or not.
Know what you want to do.
Don't let other people decide things for you.
Make your own decisions.

29. BE ABLE TO DECIDE BETWEEN RIGHT AND WRONG

Know what to do.
Know who to listen to and be able to do what they tell you to do.
It means that you must realize that if you ran down the stairs you would get
    hurt and do the right thing.
Don't do things because you think it's right, be sure it's right.
Know the difference between right and wrong.

30. KNOW WHERE AUTHORITY LIES (Group leader, teacher, parent, children)

Do what your leader says.
If you choose a child to have a position of authority be sure you choose the
    right one.
It means you have to be a good boss and know who is boss.
It means that teachers, parents, etc., tell other people what to do.

TABLE 25

RELATION OF DESCRIPTIONS OF BEHAVIOR
AND SOCIAL DISTANCE SCORE

Item No.	Description of Item	Fourth and Fifth Grades High G S D	Low G S D	Eighth Grade High G S D	Low G S D	Total High G S D	Low G S D
1.	Hard to sit still	3	4	1	1	4	5
2.	Work quietly	5	1	4	1	9	2
3.	Likes to talk a lot	3	1	5	0	8	1
4.	Doesn't like to talk much	2	1	1	1	3	2
5.	Plays active games	4	3	6	0	10	3
6.	Seldom plays active games	1	0	0	1	1	1
7.	Always ready to talk	2	0	2	0	4	0
8.	Always worried or scared	0	2	0	1	0	3
9.	Knows how to suggest and start things	6	0	5	0	11	0
10.	Lacks initiative	0	1	0	0	0	1
11.	Always seems to have a good time	5	0	3	0	8	0
12.	Never seems to have a good time	0	1	0	1	0	2
13.	Always cheerful and jolly	5	0	4	0	9	0
14.	Rather sad and worried	1	1	0	0	1	1
15.	Good looking	3	0	2	0	5	0
16.	Not good looking	0	1	0	1	0	2
17.	Neat and tidy	6	1	3	0	9	1
18.	Never neat and tidy	0	1	0	2	0	3
19.	Everybody likes him	3	0	4	0	7	0
20.	Nobody likes him	0	1	0	1	0	2
21.	Girl prefers boys books	0	1	1	1	1	2
22.	Boy prefers girls books						
23.	Girl goes out with boys or vice versa	1	0	0	0	1	0
24.	Never goes out with opposite sex	0	0	0	1	0	1
25.	Enjoys joke even on self	3	0	4	0	7	0
26.	Can't enjoy joke on himself	0	1	0	0	0	1
27.	Sees joke easily	2	0	4	0	6	0
28.	Never sees point of joke						
29.	Enjoys a fight	0	1	1	1	1	2
30.	Never fights	2	0	0	0	2	0
31.	Show off	0	0	0	1	0	1
32.	Doesn't care to be center of attention	1	0	0	0	1	0
33.	Bossy	1	1	1	0	2	1
34.	Does not mind being bossed						
35.	Very friendly has lots of friends	1	0	6	0	7	0
36.	Not friendly	0	1	0	1	0	2

Guide to Topics